THE ANGLO-IRANIAN OIL DISPUTE

OF 1951-1952

THE

ANGLO-IRANIAN

OIL DISPUTE OF 1951-1952

*A Study of the Role of Law
in the Relations of States*

BY ALAN W. FORD

1954

UNIVERSITY OF CALIFORNIA PRESS

BERKELEY AND LOS ANGELES

UNIVERSITY OF CALIFORNIA PRESS, *Berkeley and Los Angeles, California*
CAMBRIDGE UNIVERSITY PRESS, *London, England*

Copyright, 1954, by
THE REGENTS OF THE UNIVERSITY OF CALIFORNIA

Library of Congress Catalog Number: 54–6470

Printed in the United States of America
BY THE UNIVERSITY OF CALIFORNIA PRINTING DEPARTMENT
Designed by Ward Ritchie

Preface

THE PURPOSE of this study is twofold. It attempts, first, to describe the progress of the Anglo-Iranian oil dispute through July,
1952, the date of the International Court of Justice's order dismissing, for lack of jurisdiction, the United Kingdom's application to submit the dispute to the Court for a judicial determination. Second, as the subtitle states, it is also a study of the role
of law in the relations of states. In recent years a remarkable
change has occurred in the concept of the part that international
law plays in those relations. The trend of the transition has been
from the extreme legalism of the nineteenth century which envisaged international law as a panacea for the world's ills to the
"political realism" of the present which denies the existence of
international law qua law and would prefer to classify it as a
branch of ethics. There is more involved in this difference than
mere semantic difficulties, though they too frequently exist. The
difference is one between a concept of international relations as
power relationships uncontrolled and unrestrained by moral and
legal principles, and a concept (now held by very few) of international relations as relations governed by ascertainable rules
of law. There is, of course, a middle ground that is occupied by
persons who think that international law can be a vital and useful
institution for building a saner world community. I, for one, have
not been able to accept the "realistic" conclusion, reached by
some of our most eminent writers about international affairs, that

"the questions which the law and the lawyer can answer are largely irrelevant to the fundamental issues upon which the peace and welfare of nations depend . . ."[1] Such conclusions are not, I think, supported by the evidence. It is obvious to the most casual observer that no nation's foreign policies are formulated solely by reference to legal considerations. The history of the Kellogg-Briand Pact demonstrates this very clearly. However, it is not obvious that legal considerations play no part whatever. On the contrary, they are scrupulously observed in the routine affairs of state. But the real problem, and the one that this study attempts to unravel, is the role played by legal considerations in the process of policy making for nonroutine situations. A similar study could be made of the various motivating forces that guide an individual's actions, but there would be a significant difference. The law governing the conduct of states is in a primitive stage of development as compared with most modern systems of private law. There are international courts, but they have neither compulsory jurisdiction nor sheriffs to enforce their orders and judgments. There is no legislature to keep the law of nations abreast of the needs of the society within which it operates, and that society lacks the cultural homogeneity and integrated political organization that characterize modern nation-states. International law is frequently violated, but the lawbreaker pays no penalty unless he consents. Further, the subjects of international law are political organizations possessed of "sovereignty" and not individuals, as are the subjects of private law systems. Despite such systemic shortcomings, a number of distinguished scholars and men of wide experience are convinced that international law has an existence and does play a real, though limited, role in the conduct of the relations of states.[2] This study of the Anglo-Iranian

---

[1] Hans Morgenthau, "Diplomacy," *Yale Law Journal*, Vol. 55 (1946), p. 1080.

[2] For example, Philip C. Jessup, "The Reality of International Law," *Foreign Affairs*, Vol. 18 (1940), pp. 244–253, and *A Modern Law of Nations* (1949), chap. i; J. L. Brierly, *The Law of Nations* (4th ed., 1949), pp. 69–77; and Covey T. Oliver, "Reflections on Two Recent Developments Affecting the Function of Law in the International Community," *Texas Law Review*, Vol. 30 (1952), pp. 815–842.

oil dispute has confirmed their a priori judgment. As will be seen, the legal norms often received something more than lip service, and their observance proved to be more than a matter of convenience or an instrument of propaganda. It is clear that the United Kingdom, with its task of defending the status quo, usually found it much easier to follow the course of action dictated by legal considerations than did Iran. Preservation of the existing order of things is the primary function of any legal system, but the conflict between stability and change in this dispute does not suffice as a complete explanation of the United Kingdom's and Iran's conformities to and lapses from the international law standard. Instead, the ultimate explanation of much of the conduct of the governments of these two nations during the oil dispute seems to be found in their general attitude toward or predilection for the use of established international procedures.

The Anglo-Iranian oil dispute of 1951–1952 is uniquely suited to a study of the role of law in the relations of states, for it involves a Great Power and a lesser power, a traditionally imperialistic power and a traditionally colonial one, a power generally identified with the status quo and a power in the evolutionary throes of militant nationalism, and a power capable of exerting great economic and military pressures against the other whose attempts at retaliation would be relatively ineffectual. A dispute between two such states as Britain and Iran is often referred to as a classic example of a situation in which international law does not work: in which it is either ignored because its methods and procedures are inconvenient for the Great Power, or is utilized by the Great Power as an instrument of oppression and coercion. Apart from the two countries themselves, the oil dispute involves elements of direct and prime importance to the rest of the world. Iran has long been one of the world's major producers of crude petroleum, and the refinery at Abadan is the world's largest. Its oil and refining capacity are of great international importance, both economically and strategically. Further, the historic rivalry between Britain and Russia for power and influence in Iran, intensified today by the East-West struggle and the current importance of oil, makes the oil dispute an object of the greatest concern to the participants in the "cold war."

A brief historical sketch is given in Part I. Part II begins with the close of World War II and the events that led directly to the Iranian nationalization laws and the subsequent dispute with Britain. The several attempts at negotiation and the various proceedings in the International Court of Justice and the United Nations Security Council are described in some detail. The final section of the text is devoted to an examination of the law governing the right of a state to "expropriate" alien-owned property situated within its borders. In this discussion, as well as in the analysis of the proceedings in the International Court and the Security Council, I have tried to state the issues and arguments in such a manner that the nonlawyer can read with understanding and form his own opinions on what the law should be—for he is the person that should ultimately make the decisions.

A word should perhaps be said about sources. This description of the dispute is based on published reports and documents, but since this study was made almost contemporaneously with the events described, the materials available have been more limited than is desirable for historical research. I have been obliged to rely on accounts of some events given months after their occurrence, by one or another of the actors in the public forum, and it has not always been possible to corroborate the account given with other sources. With the passage of time more and more facts will become known, and the picture drawn in these pages may have to be changed. There is, in particular, a dearth of historical materials about the activities of the Anglo-Iranian Oil Company in Iran, and of knowledge of the nature and operation of the Iranian political system. Iran was an autocratic state until the end of World War II, and since then the control of the Parliament over the affairs of state, and the responsiveness of the Parliament to the electorate, has not always been clear. Indeed, it has often seemed that the support of the mobs of Tehran has been, for national political purposes, the equivalent of a mandate from the electorate. These obscurities have in many cases made it difficult to discern the source of political power and the methods by which it is exercised.

My thanks are due the administrators of the Walter Perry Johnson Graduate Research Fellowship in Law at the University of California, Berkeley, for making it possible for me to do this research and writing. I am also indebted to many friends for their help and encouragement. Especially do I want to acknowledge my great debt to Professor Covey T. Oliver, who willingly shared the fruits of his wide experience in international affairs. His generosity in many matters connected directly and indirectly with this book have always exceeded what one would expect of friendship and academic association. Professors John B. Condliffe, Albert A. Ehrenzweig, Thomas C. Blaisdell, and Frank C. Newman have all been so kind in giving of their time and thought to my problems that I want to take this opportunity to express my deep appreciation for their valuable help and criticism. My thanks are also due the British Information Services for supplying many documents that would otherwise have been difficult to obtain. Mrs. Hildegarde Millar and her staff of the Bureau of International Relations Library of the University of California were always helpful in finding and assembling information and materials. I also wish to express my gratitude to Harry Cowell, Irishman and poet, for having tried for many years, with less success than he deserves, to teach me some of the beauties of the English language. My sincere thanks go to my wife for her invaluable help with the manuscript and for her seemingly inexhaustible patience and good humor.

A. W. F.

San Francisco, 1953

Contents

xii

Abbreviations

AIOC	Anglo-Iranian Oil Company, Ltd.
AJIL	*American Journal of International Law*
BIS	British Information Services
BYBIL	*The British Year Book of International Law*
Cur. Dev.	*Current Developments in United States Foreign Policy*
DSB	*The Department of State Bulletin*
IBRD	International Bank for Reconstruction and Development
ICJ	International Court of Justice
LNTS	*League of Nations Treaty Series*
NIOC	National Iranian Oil Company
PCIJ	Permanent Court of International Justice
UNCIO	United Nations Conference on International Organization
UNRIAA	United Nations. *Reports of International Arbitral Awards*

PART I: "A PAGE OF HISTORY..."

A page of history
is worth a volume of logic
—HOLMES

THE MODERN HISTORY OF IRAN has been largely a history of Great Power rivalry. The Anglo-Iranian oil dispute of 1951–1952 is but the most recent development of this century-old rivalry. The current controversy also involves certain elements that are peculiar to the mid-twentieth century—nationalism, oil, and the East-West struggle. The Great Power rivalry of the past has traditionally been a rivalry of conflicting national interests. Today the rivalry is also one between two different ideologies: the utopia of Soviet Communism, and the less dramatic appeal of democracy from the West. A third ideology, nationalism, precipitated the nationalization of oil in Iran and the subsequent controversy between Iran and Great Britain.

§ 1. The Great Power Struggle

During the past two centuries the principal contenders in the Great Power struggle have been Britain and Russia, although other powers, notably France and Germany, have appeared for brief periods.[1] During the Napoleonic period, both France and Britain sent missions to enlist the support of Persia. Meanwhile, Persia was subjected to a series of aggressive wars by Russia (1796, 1800–1813, 1826–1828) that ended disastrously for Persia. The province of Gilan was lost to Russia in the war of 1796; and by the treaties of Gulistan (1813) and Turkmanchai (1828) all the territory west of the Aras River was ceded to

3

4

Russia, Russian nationals were accorded extraterritorial privileges in Persia, and a 5 per cent preferential tariff was established in favor of Russian goods entering Persia. The Russo-Persian Treaty of Turkmanchai thereafter became a model for commercial treaties between Persia and other European powers—the preferential tariff and extraterritorial privileges were standard provisions. During the first half of the nineteenth century Russian pressure on the northeastern frontier increased, as did Anglo-Russian rivalry throughout Asia.

To the British, the Russian threat to Persia was also a threat to India, and thus a threat to the expanding commerce and wealth of the British Empire. The Napoleonic invasion of Egypt was an added threat to India and gave urgency to British efforts to neutralize Persia. The diplomatic struggle between the French and British in Persia was finally won by the British, who signed a preliminary Treaty of Alliance with the shah in 1809, and a permanent treaty in 1814. Both were aimed immediately at France, but also at the more enduring threat of Russia. The Treaty of Tehran of 1814 provided for British subsidy and military aid to Persia in case of aggression, and Persia agreed to resist the passage of any foreign troops over her territory. After the Napoleonic threat had passed, the Treaty of Turkmanchai (1828), which marked the conclusion of the Russo-Persian war of 1826–1828, effectively neutralized the influence which the British had temporarily gained during the Napoleonic Wars. British influence shrank, and Russian political and economic domination became more pronounced. This state of affairs continued until Persia, at the instigation of Russia, attacked the Afghan fort of Herat in 1856. To protect her approaches to India, Britain went to the aid of her ally Afghanistan and declared war on Persia. The British military operation was successful, and the shah sued for peace in 1858—a peace that resulted in the restoration of some semblance of a balance between Russian influence and British influence in Persia. Victory increased British prestige and frustrated Russian plans to extend a sphere of influence into Afghanistan. The unsuccessful Crimean War (1854–1856) also contributed to the decline of Russian power and influence and strengthened the dominant position of the British.

Rather than annexing territory and establishing military and naval bases, the British exploited their newly won advantage by searching for commercial opportunities. In 1872, Baron Julius de Reuter, a British subject, was granted an exclusive concession to exploit all the natural resources of Persia, except precious stones and metals, and to build railroad and telegraph systems. The Russian government immediately protested the concession, and the shah was forced to cancel it. Thereafter, a series of concessions were granted to the British to offset the loss of the Reuter concession, with a complementary series of concessions being granted to the Russians. The *Pax Britannica* provided Persia, as well as the rest of the world, with at least a half century of peace, and the Great Power struggle became primarily a commercial rather than a military rivalry. The competition for concessions in Persia was intense, and by the end of the nineteenth century the number of concessions was so great that practically all of the country's resources and technical projects were under the control of foreign interests, predominantly British and Russian.

The beginning of the twentieth century found Persian finances in a critical state.² The concessions to foreign commercial and industrial enterprises, the shah's continual borrowing from abroad, the inefficient and dishonest administration of the internal affairs of the government, and the extravagance of the court were all factors contributing to the financial crisis. Contemporaneously a movement for political reform developed, finally leading to the bloodless revolution of 1906. The shah reluctantly granted a constitution and the forms of parliamentary democracy were introduced. The British were identified with this progressive movement, and supported the democrats in resisting the efforts of the shah (backed by the tsar) to abolish the constitution and restore the old order. However, the Persian liberals shifted their friendship from Britain to Imperial Germany after they were disillusioned by the Anglo-Russian Agreement of 1907 in which Britain and Russia, to check the growing German menace in the Middle East, composed their differences and divided Persia into two spheres of influence, each party agreeing not to seek political or commercial concessions in the sphere of the other. This agreement, quite naturally, provoked indignation among the Persians, and was a prelude to further Russian intervention in Persian affairs. The agreement was of distinct advantage to the Russians,[3] as it gave them control, vis-à-vis Britain, over a great new land area (the northern half of Persia) and brought them closer to India and the Persian Gulf. Tabriz and other parts of northern Persia were occupied by Russia in 1911, and the Russian government sent a strongly worded note to the shah demanding the dismissal of Morgan Shuster, an American who had been appointed Director-General of Finance nine months previously in an effort to bring some order out of the chaos of Persian finances.[4] A coup d'état, the dissolution of the Majlis (the National Assembly), and the dismissal of Mr. Shuster followed, and Russian influence in Tehran assumed more and more the proportions of a protectorate. Russia's position of strength consistently increased until the outbreak of World War I, when Persia became a battleground for Turkish, British, and Russian forces.

World War I again provided conditions necessitating a common Anglo-Russian policy in order to prevent Turko-German penetration toward the Caucasus and southeast Asia. Persia was officially neutral, but emotionally pro-German. Although her neutrality was repeatedly violated by both warring coalitions, she emerged from World War I with her independence intact. The Bolshevik Revolution of 1917 and the British postwar demobilization enabled her to continue this existence as an independent state. Immediately after the conclusion of the war, Lord Curzon, the British Foreign Secretary, thought the time ripe to bring all of Persia within the British sphere of influence. To do so would establish a land bridge between Iraq (then a British protectorate) and India and would complete the chain of British-dominated areas adjacent to the Persian Gulf. It would also, of course, eliminate Russian influence within Persia. To carry out this scheme Lord Curzon negotiated the unfortunate and ill-fated Anglo-Persian Agreement of 1919 which provided for British advisers to the Persian government and for British officers and equipment to strengthen the Persian army—a virtual protectorate. The treaty was bitterly criticized, and the Majlis refused to ratify it. Curzon had underestimated two things: the impact of anti-imperialist propaganda from Moscow; and Persian nationalism, encouraged, as it was, by the Wilsonian doctrine of self-determination.[5]

A traditional policy of the tsars had been southward expansion in the direction of the Persian Gulf at the expense of the independence of Persia. The Bolshevik Revolution of 1917 brought about a change of tactics but not a change of aim. The first (Communist) Congress of the Peoples' Party of the East at Baku in 1920 proclaimed the primary task of the Oriental Revolution to be conquest of Persia, preferably by infiltration.[6] But the new Soviet government was occupied with internal problems, and Russian pressure in Persia relaxed for a period of several years. In 1921 the Soviet-Persian Treaty was signed, by which the Russian Soviet Federated Socialist Republic ". . . unconditionally reject[ed] . . . [the] . . . criminal policy [of the tsars] not only as violating the sovereignty of the States of Asia but also as leading to organized brutal violence of European robbers on the living body of the peoples of the East."[7] In addition the Soviet government remitted Persian debts to the tsarist government, abandoned extraterritorial privileges for Russian nationals, renounced all Russian concessions (but with the stipulation that they could not be granted to a third party), and declared all previous treaties between Persia and the tsarist government of Russia null and void. Most important, the Soviet-Persian Treaty of 1921 gave Soviet Russia the right to enter Persia with military forces if the latter were to become a base of "anti-Soviet operations." For the Russians the treaty was a signal success, for it provided a link in a series of simultaneously negotiated treaties with Persia, Turkey, and Afghanistan—the three strategically important countries on the southern periphery of Soviet Russia. The treaty also put an end to Soviet diplomatic isolation and advertised Soviet friendship toward the peoples of Asia. The Persians welcomed the treaty as a counterweight against Curzon's schemes and enjoyed a freedom from Russian pressure unattained for the past one hundred and twenty-five years. However, two phenomena prevented the development of any real Soviet-Persian friendship. The first was the Soviet occupation of Gilan during 1920, which was shortly followed by the establishment of the Soviet Republic of Gilan. The 1921 treaty provided for the return of Gilan to Persia, but the Soviets delayed the evacuation of their troops until eight months after the effective date of the treaty provision—an unpleasant reminder that the new Russia might act very like the old. The second phenomenon was the emergence of an intense Persian nationalism, which was incapable of any real community of spirit with Soviet Communism.

§ 2. *Reza Shah and Modern Persia*

Just five days after the signing of the Soviet-Persian Treaty of Friendship, the weak and ineffectual government in Tehran was overthrown. The success of the coup d'état was due primarily to Colonel Reza Kahn, who marched his Cossack Brigade into Tehran from Qazvin. The new government was headed by Seyyid Zia ed-din, a young politician and journalist and Reza Kahn's partner in the bloodless coup. Reza Kahn was immediately named commander-in-chief of the armed forces and Minister of War, in which capacities he continued, through several cabinet changes, until 1923, when he became Prime Minister. In October, 1925, the Majlis voted to depose Ahmed Shah Qajar, whose family had occupied the Persian throne since 1779 and who had left Persia in 1923, soon after Reza Kahn had become Prime Minister. In December of 1925 a Constituent Assembly[1] was convened, and it voted to entrust the throne of Persia to Reza Kahn Pahlevi and his male descendants, and the first shah of the new Pahlevi dynasty was crowned in the spring of 1926. The early years of Reza Shah's reign were occupied by efforts to bring the whole of Persia within the control of the central government, to transform the country into a unified modern national state, to end foreign intervention and influence in the affairs of Persia, and to westernize the social and economic institutions of the country. His program was remarkably similar to that of Kemal Attaturk in neighboring Turkey.

The first government of the Pahlevi dynasty, under the premiership of Seyyid Zia ed-din, lasted but three months. Although the Soviet-Persian Treaty of Friendship of 1921 was negotiated before Zia came to power, he was responsible for its formal completion. Zia was also responsible for the express repudiation of the unpopular Anglo-Persian Agreement of 1919. On the basis of these two acts many have deduced that Zia was pro-Russian and that his government was overthrown because of Reza Kahn's lack of sympathy with such sentiments.[2] Neither of these conclusions seems to fit the facts. Zia was first and last an Iranian nationalist and an honest reformer, and both Balfour and Lenczowski have concluded that his orientation was, if anything, mildly pro-British.[3] His nationalism was apparent (and perhaps a pro-British attitude) in his refusal to permit the entry of the Soviet ambassador, Rothstein, until all Bolshevik troops were withdrawn from Persian territory. At the same time he urged the British not to withdraw their troops.

The failure of Zia's government was due in part to his unpopularity in Tehran, and in part to differences between him and

Reza Kahn. The speed and vigor with which he attempted to carry out what seemed to many to be radical reforms and his imprisonment of several leaders of the old regime contributed to his unpopularity and earned him the determined opposition of Persia's influential families, from which the country's leaders had been drawn for centuries. But the chief reason for the failure of his government was probably his disagreement with Reza Kahn, for without the support of the army controlled by Reza no government could long remain in power. The clashes between Zia ed-din and Reza Kahn culminated in the overthrow of Zia's government on May 24, 1921, and his escape to Palestine.

Reza Kahn remained in sole control of the government—a position which he could maintain by his authority over the army. He slowly consolidated his power while he reorganized the army. Foreign advisers and officers were eliminated, and the previously heterogeneous forces were integrated into one centrally controlled military organization, which Reza Kahn used successfully to subdue the rebellious provincial tribes, and with which he could effectively control the entire country from Tehran. He was so successful in this plan that, by 1923, he could confidently name himself Prime Minister, and in 1926 he was crowned Shah. His regime was marked by two basic policies: westernization and nationalism.

In his program of westernization Reza Shah was not as extreme as Kemal Attaturk. The Persian script was retained, though Western dress and headgear for men were introduced and women were unveiled. The power and prestige of the Moslem (Shia) clergy were curbed gradually: secular schools replaced religious ones; licenses were required for the wearing of clerical garb; non-Moslem foreigners were permitted to visit the many and beautiful mosques of Iran; civil marriage and divorce registers were established; civil and criminal codes replaced religious law; and the vast wealth of the church was placed under the control of the government. Reza Shah also aimed at the westernization or industrialization of the Iranian economy. To achieve economic self-sufficiency, the government was named the "supreme economic organizer" and public funds were invested in industrial and commercial enterprises. The great depression so seriously affected Iran that it was felt necessary to establish a foreign trade monopoly in 1931.[5] A ministry of national economy was established to regulate the production and distribution of the products of agriculture, commerce, and industry. The government took the lead in the formation of new companies to perform the essential services in the reorganized economy. Some were wholly owned by the government; in others it had a controlling interest; and the ownership of others was divided among the government, private stockholders, and companies already in existence. By 1936 the government had monopoly control of 33 per cent of all imports and 44 per cent of all exports.[6] Profits from the monopolies were high and, combined with tax revenues, were used in part as capital for the establishment of state-owned factories and industrial plants. The construction of the Transiranian Railroad, thousands of miles of new roads, and increased imports of trucks and passenger cars greatly enlarged the transportation facilities of the country and made possible the expansion of industry. With the help of American and German advisers, Iran's finances were reorganized and a central bank (Bank-i-Melli-yi-Iran) with the power to issue bank notes was established.[7] Reza Shah's program of industrial development was successful, but the emphasis on industry and commerce resulted in a neglect of agriculture and irrigation projects. The farming population benefited little from the expansion of industry and commerce and actually suffered a decline in its standard of living.[8]

Reza Shah's nationalistic spirit demanded the building of a powerful national state free from foreign interference and influence. In addition to harboring a suspicion of Russia and Soviet Communism, he assumed a challenging attitude toward Britain.

§ 3. Persian Nationalism and the Great Powers

When Reza Kahn came to power in 1921 British "advisers" seemed to be everywhere—in the government and in the army. A prime objective in the early years of his regime was the elimination of all foreign advisers from positions of authority and influence, but especially of the British. The British economic and military missions that had been sent to Iran after the negotiation of the 1919 Anglo-Persian Agreement were forced to withdraw after Zia ed-din's express repudiation of that agreement. Reza Kahn's reorganization of the army caused the disbanding of the South Persia Rifles, a military unit that had been organized, officered, and supplied entirely by the British. Also, British troops were evacuated immediately after the Bolsheviks withdrew from Gilan in the fall of 1921. By early 1922, evidences of British interference or influence in either the government or the army were no longer apparent, and thereafter Reza intentionally avoided hiring British advisers. Some advisers were, of course, needed for the program of industrialization and reorganization of the country's finances, and these positions were distributed among Americans, Germans, Italians, and some others, with no particular nationality being given a preference. To reorganize Iran's finances, an American, Dr. Arthur C. Millspaugh, was employed. When his five-year term of office (1922–1927) had expired, he was replaced by a German. These two men continued and completed the work that had been started by a British mission acting under the 1919 agreement. Reza's policies with regard to foreign advisers was also apparent in the building of the Transiranian Railroad. In that venture, the British were treated like any other nation, and their technicians worked side by side with employees of German, Italian, and American construction companies. The prime purpose and achievement of the railroad was to unify Iran and to contribute to the expansion of her commerce and industry. This accomplishment disappointed both Britain and the Soviet Union, since it frustrated rather than facilitated economic and strategic penetration from either the north or the south.[1]

Reza Shah's defiant attitude toward Britain was again apparent in the oil dispute of 1932–1933 (see § 4, below), and in the controversy over Bahrein. The Bahrein Archipelago is a shaikhdom, predominantly inhabited by Arabs, enjoying complete internal autonomy. By agreements with Britain in 1880, 1892, and 1914 a British protectorate over Bahrein was established, and the shaikh undertook not to enter into any relationship with another government without first obtaining the consent of Britain. The right to exploit the archipelago's mineral resources was also reserved to the British.[2] The Iranian government has claimed that Bahrein has belonged to the Persian Empire throughout history and that the British protectorate was a violation of Iranian suzerainty.[3] During the years 1928–1936 the Iranian government made repeated appeals to the League of Nations to obtain recognition of its claim of suzerainty over Bahrein. The Iranian claims received their widest airing when the Iranian government circulated among all the members of the League of Nations a note protesting the official recognition of Britain's protectorate in the Anglo-Saudi Treaty of Jidda of May 20, 1927, in which Ibn Saud acknowledged and agreed not to interfere with the protectorate. The Iranians again protested to both the British and American governments in 1930 and 1934, when the shaikh of Bahrein granted oil concessions to American and British nationals. The discovery of oil in the archipelago served to intensify Iran's desire to press its claim against Britain,[4] and the claim has been urged several times since World War II. In February of 1948, the Majlis passed a bill instructing the government to restore Iranian sovereignty over Bahrein, and on August 23, 1948, the foreign minister announced that the Iranian government considered all pacts and agreements among foreign powers recognizing any arrangement in conflict with Iran's sovereignty over Bahrein to be null and void.[5] There have also been several at-

14

tempts by Iran, thus far unsuccessful, to put the controversy on the agenda of the United Nations Security Council.

Although the Bahrein controversy and the exclusion of British advisers indicate a serious decline in British influence during the early years of Reza Shah's reign, the British still retained important interests in Iran. The situation has been summarized by Lenczowski in the following terms:

> The concession exploited by the Anglo-Iranian Oil Company continued as a powerful link between the two countries. It constituted also an instrument of British influence in that region and, naturally, like any foreign held concession, it contained seeds of disagreement between the host nation and the concessionaire. It was mainly in the field of oil exploitation that the nationalist policy of Reza Shah clashed with British interests, and it may be said without contradiction that the behavior of the Iranian ruler in this field constituted the best test of his true attitude toward Great Britain.[5]

§ 4. The Anglo-Iranian Oil Dispute of 1932–1933

The oil resources of Iran are closely connected with the Great Power struggle between Britain and Russia in Iran. The competition between the two nations for concessions to exploit Iranian oil resources has continued for half a century. Russian efforts[1] have been concentrated in the north, British endeavors in the south. However, as in all competitions, either side would be very happy to have the whole of the plum.

The original Reuter concession of 1872, giving Reuter the exclusive right, among other privileges, to exploit all the natural resources of Iran, except precious stones and metals, was canceled almost at once at the insistence of the Russian government (see p. 5). As compensation for this canceled concession and as a result of official British intervention, in 1889 the shah granted Reuter a concession in which the rights were limited to the creation of a bank and the exploitation of the country's oil resources. The Imperial Bank of Iran was then founded, and it remained the basic financial institution of the Iranian economy until the establishment of the government-owned Bank Melli in 1927. The Imperial Bank was finally forced to close its doors in January, 1952. The oil-exploitation rights granted to Reuter in the 1889 concession were renounced in 1890 after prospecting failed to produce any tangible results.

Oil was first discovered by M. de Morgan in the province of Kermanshah. De Morgan's prospecting was done at the invitation of the governor of the province, and the results of his explorations, published in Paris in 1892, indicated the existence of oil deposits in the neighborhood of Qasr-i-Shirin, near the present Iranian-Iraqi (then Persian-Mesopotamian) border. As a result of this report, William Knox D'Arcy, an Australian financier, made a successful effort in 1901 to obtain a sixty-year concession giving him access to the whole of Iran except the northern provinces of Asterabad, Khorasan, Azerbaijan, Gilan, and Mazanderan—the traditional area of Russian influence. The concession gave D'Arcy the exclusive right to construct pipe lines and the right to use all state-owned noncultivated lands that were necessary for prospecting. He was also protected against inflated prices for private lands that might be necessary to the operation. In return, D'Arcy agreed to establish within two years one or more companies for oil exploitation, make an initial payment to the Crown of £20,000 sterling and £20,000 in shares of the company, pay 2,000 tommans annually in lieu of taxes, and pay 16 per cent of the annual net profits. D'Arcy formed the First Exploitation Company, which brought in its first well in 1909. As a result the Anglo-Persian Oil Company was created and the First Exploitation Company was merged into it in 1909. (The present Anglo-Iranian Oil Company [AIOC] is identical with the original Anglo-Persian Oil Company. The change in name was made in 1935 when Reza Shah changed the name of his country from "Persia" to "Iran," and throughout these pages the company is referred to by the abbreviation "AIOC" regardless of date.)

The oil deposits that the British set out to exploit were in south-western Iran, a sparsely populated region inhabited by nomadic peoples, including the warlike Bakhtiari tribe. In order to produce oil the British found it necessary to enter into negotiations with the local shaikhs and tribal leaders to secure their friendliness, for they were not under the effective control of the central government in Tehran. In addition, a small detachment of Sikhs was brought in from India, with the knowledge and consent of the Iranian government, to protect the oil installations. But by far the most important development in the early years of AIOC's existence was the decision of the British government to replace coal with oil as fuel for the British navy. In 1914 the British Admiralty, then under Winston Churchill, negotiated a long-term contract for the purchase of fuel oil from AIOC. At the same time the British government acquired a 53 per cent interest in the company which it has continued to hold.[2] With this new capital, substantial additions to plant and equipment were made: a pipe line was constructed from the oil fields to Abadan, where work on the plant that was to become the largest refinery in the world was started.

That Iranian oil was very important to the successful prosecution of World War I is attested by Lord Curzon's oft-quoted remark that the Allies "floated to victory on a sea of oil." This fact undoubtedly provided one of the basic motivations for Curzon's unsuccessful attempt in 1919 to bring all Iran within the British sphere of influence, to establish a *de facto* protectorate. The intensity of the Iranian reaction against this scheme was undoubtedly influenced by the government's then uncordial relations with the company. The D'Arcy concession had proved inadequate for the operation of the world-wide business that unexpectedly developed on the basis of the oil produced in southwestern Iran. Differences began to develop between the government and AIOC during World War I. Under the D'Arcy concession royalties were fixed at 16 per cent of annual net profits. Before 1920 the com-

pany's stated net profits were small. This may have been partly
the result of sharp bookkeeping practices, as the Iranians alleged,
and it was certainly affected by the special price paid by the
British government for oil.[3] The Iranians saw large quantities of
oil being produced with very little in royalties reaching the
Iranian Treasury. To further aggravate the situation, in 1919 the
company refused to pay the royalties due, because of property
damage by local tribes for which it held the Iranian government
responsible. The situation steadily worsened until it was finally
submitted to arbitration in 1920. A provisional agreement was
reached on December 22, 1920, but was never ratified by the
Majlis. Royalties continued to be small[4] and tended to fluctuate
rather violently because they were tied to net profits rather than
production or gross selling value.[5] Iran's difficulties increased
when Britain went off the gold standard on September 21, 1931,
and her sterling balances in London were depreciated. Relations
between the Iranian government and AIOC continued to deteriorate until November 27, 1932, when the government notified the
company that the concession was annulled. Nine reasons were
brought forth to justify its action.[6] The British reacted promptly
and vigorously, threatening to use force if necessary to protect
British lives and property. British warships appeared in the
Persian Gulf, and the two governments exchanged a series of
strongly worded notes. Great Britain brought the dispute before
the Council of the League of Nations and made efforts to submit
the case to the Permanent Court of International Justice (PCIJ)
at The Hague. When the latter procedure was begun, Iran protested, as it was again to protest in 1951, that the Court did not
have jurisdiction, since this dispute was entirely a domestic
matter between the government of Iran and the AIOC. The question of jurisdiction was not then decided, however, for neither the
Council nor the Court attempted to take immediate action and the
matter was dropped from the agenda when direct negotiations
between the AIOC and the Iranian government were begun in

February of 1933. Dr. Beneš of Czechoslovakia, who acted as a mediator, announced in December of that year that an agreement had been reached and that a new concession had been granted to the AIOC at Tehran on April 29, 1933.[7]

The new concession was much more favorable to Iran than the former one had been. It restricted the exploitable area to half its previous size until 1938, after which, the agreement stipulated, the exploitable area would be restricted to 100,000 square miles, to be selected by the company out of the territory of the concession. The concession included all the territory south of a line established in the agreement, starting at Qasr-i-Shirin on the Iranian-Iraqi border, then running north of Kermanshah, then in a southeasterly direction through points south of Yazd and Kerman, then through Saidabad and Irafshan to the border of Indian Baluchistan. The AIOC also lost its exclusive rights to construct and operate pipe lines in Iran. The financial arrangements of the new agreement provided for the payment by AIOC to Iran of 4 shillings per ton on oil sold in Iran or exported, and 20 per cent of the dividends on ordinary shares in excess of £671,250 distributed to stockholders of AIOC, the company guaranteeing that Iran's receipts under these provisions should never be less than £750,000 per year. Paragraph V of Article 10 of the agreement secured Iran against further depreciation of the pound sterling, and provided that the government of Iran would receive an amount equivalent to 20 per cent of all payments by the company from its general reserve to its shareholders, as well as an amount equivalent to 20 per cent of the accumulated general reserve at the expiration of the concession in 1993. The company was expressly made exempt from all taxes, in lieu of which it agreed to pay during the first fifteen years of the concession 9*d.* per ton on the first 6 million tons of oil sold or exported, and 6*d.* on each additional ton, subject to a minimum payment of £225,000; and during the next fifteen years these payments were to be increased to 1*s.* per ton and 9*d.* per ton respectively, subject to a minimum payment of £300,000. New arrangements for these payments in lieu of taxation were to be negotiated before 1963. Progressive reduction of the number of non-Iranian employees and their replacement by Iranians was also provided for, the company further agreeing to spend £10,000 a year in educating Iranians in Great Britain. The Iranian government commissioner was retained, and his enumerated rights and privileges included the right to attend meetings of the board of directors and stockholders of the AIOC, to have access to information available to AIOC stockholders, and to supervise the education of Iranians in Britain who were financed by the AIOC. The company also agreed to pay him an annual salary of £2,000. In addition, it was provided that the company could not transfer the concession to another party without the consent of the Iranian government; that on the expiry of the concession in 1993 all classes of the company's property in Iran would revert to the government, and during the ten-year period preceding the expiry the company could not sell such property or export it from Iran; that the Gulf of Mexico or Rumanian price, whichever was lower, was to be taken as the basic price of oil and oil products sold in Iran, and that oil was to be sold to the public from the refinery at 10 per cent less than this basic price, and to the Iranian government at 25 per cent less. Clear, precise, and detailed provisions were made for the submission to arbitration of all differences between the company and the government of Iran (Article 22).

The new concession was much more favorable to Iran than the D'Arcy concession. It was a great victory for Reza Shah's policy of emancipating Iran from British penetration and influence. By this act, more than any other, Iran asserted her independence and proved that she would no longer be the willing tool of Western imperialism. The oil dispute of 1932–1933 was the first bold and dramatic expression of the policy of resistance that has continued unwaveringly to the present time.

§ 5.[1] *Northern Oil and Soviet-Iranian Relations*

While Reza Shah was thus freeing Iran from the encroachments of British influence and control, he was also careful to avoid similar encroachments by the new Soviet regime to the north. The shah had had contact with the Soviets as an officer in the Cossack Brigade. The Soviet-encouraged revolts in the provinces adjoining Russia (Gilan, Azerbaijan, Khorasan) strained Soviet-Iranian relations and served to strengthen the shah's already antipathetic attitude toward the Communist regime. The newly centralized army enabled the shah to effectively control the provinces, and this led to a change in Soviet tactics. To gain influence and ultimate control in the northern provinces[2] the Soviets adopted a commercial policy designed to develop an economic dependence of those provinces on Russia, and also, for purposes of direct penetration, attempted to get a concession for the exploitation of northern oil. The problem of northern oil has been the focus of the major stresses in Soviet-Iranian relations since 1921.

The first concession for the exploitation of northern oil was made in 1916 to Akakiy Khoshtaria, a Russian subject. World War I prevented its immediate development, and in 1920 Khoshtaria sold the concession to AIOC for £200,000. The North Persian Oil Company was then set up as a branch of AIOC to develop an oil industry in the concession area. British penetration into northern Iran was resented by Iran, Russia, and the United States. The Iranians feared further British penetration as an extension of imperialism and were anxious not to have substantially all the natural wealth of Iran in the hands of the British. The Russians were of course opposed to British operations in areas immediately adjoining Russian territory. The United States objected in the interest of American companies desirous of obtaining concessions in the northern provinces. The pressure of the Soviets and the natural inclinations of the Iranians led to the Iranian government's refusal to recognize the validity of the concession that AIOC had obtained from Khoshtaria. The Iranians argued that the concession was invalid because it had never been ratified by the Majlis, and because the supervening Soviet-Persian Treaty of 1921 had annulled all previous concessions granted to the tsarist government or to Russian subjects. AIOC countered with an argument that Khoshtaria's title was not annulled by the treaty, because he was not a Russian subject but a citizen of the free Republic of Georgia. This argument lost its force when the Georgian government was overthrown by a Soviet coup in 1921 and Georgia was incorporated into the Soviet Union in 1922. Khoshtaria's citizenship then became prima facie Russian.

The legal argument proved inconclusive. The British continued to insist on the validity of their claim, but the Iranians considered the matter closed and began to look about for a concessionaire from some distant country that did not have immediate interests in the Middle East and thus would not be a direct threat to Iranian sovereignty. With the aid of Morgan Shuster, former financial adviser to the Iranian government, negotiations were begun with the Standard Oil Company. When the Majlis, on November 22, 1921, authorized the government to grant a fifty-year concession to the Standard Oil Company, both the British and the Soviets objected. In the diplomatic exchange that followed, the United States government asserted the Open Door principle in support of the action of the Iranian government. But, because of the AIOC's monopoly of transportation facilities within Iran, the Standard Oil Company was finally forced to agree to share the concession with AIOC on a fifty-fifty basis. This agreement brought a storm of Russian protests, and the Iranians eventually broke off negotiations with Standard.

Reza Shah's program of reform and industrialization required money, and he continued to seek ways of exploiting northern oil. Negotiations were begun with the Sinclair Consolidated Oil Company in the hope that this corporation would be acceptable to the Soviets since they had granted it a development concession for Sakhalin Island and an exclusive distributorship for exports of Soviet oil products in the world markets. In June, 1923, the Majlis authorized the government to grant a concession to Sinclair, adding that no valid prior concession existed. To avoid the necessity of sharing the concession with AIOC because of the British monopoly of oil transportation facilities, Sinclair endeavored to obtain permission from the Soviets to transport oil through the Batum-Baku pipe line. The Soviets refused to cooperate; negotiations broke down; and, as a final blow, Sinclair's previous contract for an exclusive distributorship and its concession in Sakhalin was annulled. Sinclair was forced to abandon its efforts to get the Iranian concession, and its representatives left Iran in the summer of 1924.

For the next thirteen years the problem of northern oil lay quiescent and nothing more was attempted for its development and exploitation. Then, in 1937, a concession was granted to the Amiranian Oil Company, which was owned by the Seaboard Oil Company of Delaware. The concession was limited to Khorasan, and its terms were very similar to those of the 1933 AIOC concession. By that concession AIOC lost the exclusive right that it had previously been granted to construct and operate oil transportation facilities in Iran. In 1937 Amiranian was granted a nonexclusive right, similar to that granted AIOC in its 1933 concession, to construct and operate such facilities. Reza Shah had so consolidated his power and emancipated Iran from foreign tutelage that it seemed certain that the Amiranian concession would endure, but it ended in 1938 with Amiranian's renunciation. Unlike other concessions, Amiranian's was not only renounced by the grantee rather than the grantor, but was abandoned for commercial rather than political reasons: the pipe line that Amiranian would have had to build from the northern oil fields over the Zagros Mountains to the ports of the Persian Gulf would have been an expensive undertaking and would have cut deeply into the company's comparative advantage in the world oil market. In addition, the increasingly successful production in Saudi Arabia introduced a new factor, which added weight to the company's decision that it could not withstand the competition. The unsettled political conditions in the world in 1938 were hardly encouraging. Amiranian's renunciation ended the last attempt to exploit northern oil resources during the interwar period, and the project was not revived until 1944 (see pp. 33–36).

From the Soviet point of view, the "northern oil imbroglio"[3] clearly demonstrated Iran's duplicity and basic hostility to the Soviet regime. It added evidential support to the Marxian theme of capitalist encirclement. Although the Soviets had some difficulty in concretizing their attitude toward Reza Kahn, they finally interpreted his rise to power as the product of a national liberation movement of an anti-imperialist and semibourgeois character—a concept that dictated support by the Soviet Union, especially when the nationalist movement clashed with British interests.[4] During the northern oil dispute the USSR practiced a policy of self-restraint, limiting itself to diplomatic protests and maneuvers. When Iranian nationalism expressed itself against the West, the Russians gave their active support, meanwhile attemping to avoid such an expression against Russia. To this end the most effective and reliable Soviet weapons were economic.

As in the political sphere, Soviet economic and commercial policies retained traditional tsarist objectives but used new tactics to achieve them. The tsars had aimed at preventing or limiting Western commercial penetration by gaining exclusive privileges, and by making the northern provinces as completely dependent as possible on Russia. That the tsars had enjoyed some measure of success is attested by the fact that before World War I two-thirds of Iran's foreign trade had been carried on with Russia.

Because of their strategic importance the countries on the periphery of the USSR from the Black Sea to Mongolia were exempted from the Soviet State Trading Monopoly. A special system was devised that was intended to result in a growing economic dependence of these states on the Soviet Union.[5] In its application to Iran this policy[6] passed through several stages, the variations in which reflected the economic needs and power of the Soviet Union and its adjustment to the growing independence of Iran under the rule of Reza Shah.

During the years 1921–1927 Soviet-Iranian economic relations enjoyed their greatest freedom. There was no regulating treaty in existence, and individuals and companies of both countries operated freely in the territory of the other, transacting the business of commerce.[7] During this period Iran had a favorable balance of trade with Russia, through the export of raw materials and foodstuffs that were urgently needed by the expanding Soviet economy. These exports from Iran came primarily from the northern provinces. The Soviets intentionally put very low tariffs on these raw materials and foodstuffs, with the result that the produce of the northern provinces was soon almost completely channeled into Soviet territory and geared to the Russian market. In short, the northern provinces were quickly made economically dependent on the Soviet Union. The Soviets did not hesitate to use this dependence as a bargaining weapon during the Soviet-Iranian negotiations for a commercial treaty in 1926 and 1927. They demanded diplomatic immunities for their trading corporations and low import tariffs on Russian oil.[8] When the Iranians refused these demands, the Soviets immediately placed an embargo on trade between the two countries. The pressure which this exerted on Iran through its northern provinces[9] was effective, and the treaty was completed in 1927. This treaty met the Russian demands and introduced bilateral clearing arrangements (a variation from the *Principles of Eastern Trade*) into Soviet-Iranian trade relations. Through exclusive-dealing provisions the Soviets obtained a privileged position from which they could exert a large measure of control over the Iranian economy. Their share of Iran's external trade rose from 23 per cent in the fiscal year 1926–27 to 38 per cent in 1928–29. Iranian dependence was further increased by Soviet dumping practices. The exclusive-dealing privileges enabled the Soviets to demand relatively high prices. When Iranian merchants purchased goods elsewhere, the Soviets would dump large quantities of similar goods on the Iranian market, often at below-cost prices. This practice ruined many Iranian merchants and discouraged further attempts to deal with firms from other countries. These artificially reduced Soviet prices, by posing insurmountable difficulties of competition, also had a ruinous effect on native industry.

The Russo-Persian Treaty of 1927 expired in 1929, and for the next two-year period Soviet-Iranian economic relations were unregulated by treaty. By this time Reza Shah had become convinced that private Iranian traders could not compete successfully with the state-owned Soviet trading corporations, and that, unless drastic measures were taken, Iran would become an economic colony of the Soviet Union. As a protective measure, against cyclical fluctuations in the world trading system as well as against Soviet commercial practices, a foreign trade monopoly was established in February, 1931, by the Iranian government. In October, 1931, a new four-year treaty was concluded with the USSR. This pact included a bilateral clearing arrangement with provision for fixed quantities of specific goods, and with a most-favored-nation clause. The treaty, with minor modifications, was renewed for another three years in 1935. Both treaties, though ostensibly requiring a net balance in the trade of the two countries, enabled Russia to maintain a favorable balance through a provision that exempted certain Russian exports to Iran from the net balance. In the three-year period 1935–1938, Russia's favorable balance amounted to approximately 142 million rials.

Meanwhile, to avoid Iran's dependence on the Soviet Union for manufactured products (at Russian prices that quite often were abnormally high), Reza Shah energetically set about developing native industry to process Iranian raw materials. As it developed (see pp. 10–11) Iran became more and more economically independent of the Soviet Union, whose share in Iran's foreign trade fell from 38 per cent in the fiscal year 1928–29 to 11.5 per cent in 1938–39. The Soviet-Iranian treaty that expired in 1938 was not extended, and trade between the two countries declined even further. As the Soviet share of Iran's external trade declined, Germany, preparing for war, stepped into first place (see § 6, below).

In conclusion, we may say of Soviet-Iranian economic relations in the interwar period that the Soviets were successful in their policy of preventing the exploitation of northern oil by foreign nations, though unsuccessful in securing the concession for themselves. The Soviets also strove to foster and maintain Iran's economic dependence. Russia's predominant position in Iran's external trade, secured through this economic dependence, ended only when the USSR met with the competition of a more centralized and determined Germany and with the vigorous action of Reza Kahn in reforming the Iranian economy. The foreign trade monopoly and the completion of the Transiranian Railroad in 1938, which united economically the long-separated parts of the nation, enabled Iran to free itself from economic dependence on Russia. Contrary to the hopes of the Soviet leaders, Iranian nationalism showed itself as much opposed to Soviet as to Western imperialism. The end of the interwar period marked a measure of success for Reza Shah's policy of building a strong national state free from foreign interference and influence.

§ 6. The Emergence of Germany

The end of the interwar period also saw the emergence of a revitalized Germany as a powerful rival in Middle East politics. As the result of an intensive effort, Germany's economic and political influence in the Middle East grew to such proportions that it threatened to upset the status quo, and thus the security of both Russia and Britain. After World War I, Germany too was pursuing traditional objectives by new tactics. In the broad policy objectives of Germany there was little change, under the Kaiser, the Weimar Republic, or the Nazis: all three regimes aimed at penetration through the Caucasus and the Middle East to the wealth of southeast Asia. After the conclusion of World War I, Germany set about trying to regain the political and economic advantages of Imperial Germany in the Middle East, especially in Iran. Reza Shah, having determined on a policy of emancipation from the influence of the British and Russians, sought the friendship and support of a strong third power as a counterbalance to these two rivals. Reza would have preferred this third power to have been the United States, as witnessed by his willingness to grant oil concessions to Americans and his choice of Americans as financial advisers, but American isolationism prevented the United States from playing such a role. As a result he turned to Germany, which, he probably hoped, was sufficiently remote not to be a threat to the territorial integrity of Iran.

With the shah's permission, the Germans developed regular steamship and air transportation services to Iran. In building up Iranian industry, German machines, installations, and personnel were used almost exclusively (German machines, of course, requiring German spare parts). The penetration of Germans in all branches of industry was great, and a large number of the factories and public buildings, for which Reza Shah seemed to have a great fondness, were built by Germans. By 1932–33 Germany had regained the prewar position of Imperial Germany, with 8 per cent of Iran's external trade. The Nazis' commercial policy, designed to support the growing war machine, was so skillful that by 1940–41 approximately 45 per cent of Iran's foreign trade was with Germany.

For the most part, German commercial penetration was concentrated in the north, the trade being conducted via the Trebizond-Tabriz line rather than through the Gulf. For political reasons, as an antidote to Soviet expansionism, the British saw fit to encourage this activity. German exports to Iran, like those of Soviet Russia, were comprised almost entirely of manufactured goods. They differed, however, in that Germany, to demonstrate its assumed role as friend of the Iranian people and supporter of their national aspirations, exported great quantities of machinery and capital goods to help develop native industry, whereas Soviet Russia, as we have seen, pursued a policy of discouraging Iranian industry, and her exports to Iran were mostly confined to manufactured consumers' goods. In the year 1937–38 Germany supplied 80 per cent of Iran's imports of machinery. In return, Germany's principal imports from Iran were raw wool, cotton, grain, fruit, rice, and carpets. To unite the two economies further, and to strengthen Germany's newly won predominant position, the Nazis urged the negotiation of a bilateral clearing agreement, and such an agreement was concluded in 1935 and renewed again in 1939. Bilateral clearing agreements of this type formed an integral part of Hjalmar Schacht's "New Plan" and made possible the build-up of the German war machine by conserving Germany's foreign exchange and obtaining raw materials on what amounted to a barter basis, an arrangement that always works to the advantage of the economically stronger partner. The German-Iranian bilateral clearing agreement put the trade between the two countries in a privileged position which made effective competition from other countries much more difficult.[1]

The Nazis were also relatively successful in their vigorous efforts to effect a political *rapprochement* between the two "Aryan" cultures—Germany and Iran. German propaganda efforts, the establishment of German-managed schools in Iran, the founding of scholarships for Iranian students in German universities, and the employment of German experts in technical, economic, and cultural capacities all contributed to a growing Iranian sympathy toward Germany. At the same time (in the late 1930's) growing numbers of German "tourists" began arriving in Iran, many of whom remained as semipermanent residents. These numbered approximately two thousand in 1941 and constituted a potentially effective and dangerous fifth column.[2] After the German invasion of Russia in June, 1941, this fifth column became increasingly active as the German troops advanced across Russia and the threat of German conquest became more immediate. It was the presence and activity of these Germans in Iran that led to the occupation of that country by the British and Russians in August, 1941. The first task of the occupation troops was the internment of all Germans not attached to the diplomatic legation. However, some of them escaped internment and tried with some success to revive fifth-column activity with the aid of provincial tribesmen. They were also aided, directly and indirectly, by the sympathetic attitude of many Iranians, including some high government officials and army officers, and especially by the attitude of Reza Shah himself. The principal object of the German intrigue, as well as the reason for the British and Russian occupation, was the possession of the Transiranian Railroad, the only means of transporting supplies from the Persian Gulf to Russia. Because of the vigilance of British intelligence units, the fifth column was defeated just when it was about to fulfill its task, and by 1943 it was completely eliminated.

§ 7. Iran in World War II

During the first two years of World War II[1] Iran maintained strict neutrality, although its sympathies were with the Germans. The neutrality was profitable to both Germany and Iran, since they could continue and increase their mutually beneficial trade. This situation could exist only so long as Germany and the USSR were allied and the British too weak to move against Russia from the Middle East. But the German invasion of Russia and the subsequent Russo-British alliance changed everything. The German armies destroyed large parts of Russian industry, and supplies and equipment were needed to enable Russia to continue the war.

Except for the submarine-infested waters of the Arctic, the railway in Iran was the only feasible route by which to transport these supplies. Furthermore, the Allies could not afford to have Iran occupied by the Nazis or used as a base for Nazi activities among the tribesmen or in Afghanistan and India. The British and the Soviets therefore demanded that the Iranian government dismiss its German employees and expel all Germans from the country. The shah procrastinated. An ultimatum was delivered and ignored. On August 25, 1941, the country was invaded by the British from the south and the Russians from the north. Reza ordered the army to resist, but its morale was at such a low pitch that it offered little or no resistance and quickly collapsed. The occupation was completed in a very few days.[2] The Germans were interned, and Iran severed diplomatic relations with Germany, Italy, and, later, Japan.

The British and Soviets, by direct demands and indirect propaganda, made Reza Shah's position so intolerable that he was forced to abdicate in favor of his young son, Mohammed Ali Pahlevi. The period of Reza's dictatorship was over, and it again appeared that there was a chance that the Constitution of 1906 could be made effective. But Reza's departure, the foreign invasion, and the disintegration of the army left the administration in a state of chaos. With the central army disbanded, the tribes again took up arms and defied the government in Tehran. War had already cut off much of the country's foreign trade, and the occupying powers' monopolization of transportation facilities completely disrupted the production and distribution of goods within Iran. Internal insecurity aggravated hoarding and stimulated speculation. The result was a ruinous inflation. In any inflation salaried workers suffer most, and the Iranian bureaucracy was completely demoralized. Protected by the distractions of a general anarchy, misgovernment and misappropriation of public funds grew rapidly, and paralleled the upward spiraling prices. Finally, in 1943, after the situation had become desperate, American ad-

visers were brought in by the Iranian government in an attempt
to stabilize the economy and the administration.[3]

The occupying forces established zones of occupation, with
the Russians in the northern provinces and the British in the
south. A neutral zone was maintained around Tehran. Later, after
Pearl Harbor, American troops took over from the British the
operation of the southern part of the railroad and the Persian
Gulf ports. The *de facto* occupation was confirmed by the Tripartite Treaty of Alliance signed on January 29, 1942, by Britain, Russia, and Iran.[4] Britain and Russia undertook to "respect
the territorial integrity, the sovereignty and the political independence of Iran," to withdraw their troops from Iran not later
than six months after the cessation of hostilities, and "to use their
best endeavors to safeguard the economic existence of the Iranian
people against the privations and difficulties" arising from the
war. In return, Iran was to maintain internal security, to permit
the free passage of goods and use of transportation facilities, and
to establish censorship on all communication facilities. It was
also agreed that the presence of British and Russian troops would
not constitute military occupation, and that the Allies would dis-
turb as little as possible the administration and economic life of
the country.[5]

The long-standing rivalry between Britain and Russia in Iran
was eclipsed during the first two years of the occupation by the
urgent need to direct all their energies toward a common goal, the
defeat of Germany. As the tide of battle turned in favor of the
Allies in 1944, Britain and Russia again turned their attention to
the pursuit of long-range policies and interests. The British policy
during wartime was primarily concerned with the maintenance
of internal stability and order so as to assure the smooth flow of
supplies to the USSR, and with the suppression of any radical
labor movements which might interfere, either immediately or
in the future, with the production of oil. Both of these policies
required that the British deal directly with the tribes and local

populations, since effective control from the central government in Tehran was lacking after the Anglo-Russian occupation and the deposition of Reza Kahn. In these policies the British were relatively successful. Britain's traditional policy of favoring the maintenance of an independent Iran as a buffer between the USSR and Britain's colonies and protectorates in the Middle East and southeast Asia, dictated her support of Iranian nationalism and, of course, the speedy withdrawal of *all* foreign troops after the conclusion of the war. The wisdom and at least the temporary success of this policy were clearly demonstrated in the early postwar years, which are discussed below. In the process of propaganda, however, both the British and the American efforts were much less effective than those of the Soviet Union. The British and Americans suffered from a lack of coördination and common policy in day-to-day diplomacy, quite apart from any question of technical proficiency in the art of propaganda or of the audience's receptiveness. The general passivity of American policy (except in time of crisis) and the undoubted difficulty Americans encountered in accepting or appreciating the long-range British policy, which was a product of several centuries of active and immediate interest in Iran and the Middle East, gave the more determined policies of the USSR a particular advantage.

The occupation of northern Iran provided the Soviet Union an opportunity that was not neglected. British and Americans were excluded from the Russian zone, and "interzone" travel by Iranians was virtually prohibited by the Soviet authorities. A complete monopoly of the radio and press services was established, and the Russians' control over information ensured that all news came from Soviet sources and thus greatly facilitated the intensive Communist propaganda campaign that was carried on throughout the period of the Soviet occupation. The Communists who had been jailed by the Iranian police in 1938 at the direction of Reza Kahn were released upon the entry of the Soviet troops in 1941. In January of 1942 the *Tudeh* ("masses") party was officially created. The leaders of the newly formed party came from the group of Communists released from jail by the Soviets and from a small group of expatriates who had fled to the USSR during the reign of Reza Kahn. Important among the latter group was Ja'afar Peshavari, who later (in November, 1945) became Premier of the "Azerbaijan Republic" (see pp. 42–44). Protection by the Red Army, open support by the Soviet authorities, and official Soviet propaganda that paralleled that of Tudeh enabled the party to increase its membership, perfect an efficient working organization, and place several of its members as deputies in the Majlis by the end of the war. As will be seen, it also directly supported (and greatly aided) the actions and policy of the Soviet Union in the oil crisis of 1944 and in the postwar Azerbaijan dispute.

§ 8. Northern Oil and the Soviets in Wartime

The restriction of the area covered by the AIOC concession of 1933[1] and the failure of prewar efforts of the Soviet government and American oil companies to obtain rights to exploit the oil of the northern provinces (see pp. 20–23) left most of Iran free from any grant of oil-exploitation rights,[2] with the minor exception of a concession to the Kavir-i-Khurian Company (jointly owned by Russians and Iranians) in the area of Semnan. The area thus free from concessions included not only the northern provinces, but also the provinces of southeastern Iran; the AIOC, in limiting its concession area as required by the 1933 concession, had chosen certain sections of southwestern Iran. To obtain a new concession in the southeastern area (primarily Iranian Baluchistan) a British company sent a representative to Tehran in the fall of 1943. The spring of 1944 brought a representative of the Standard Vacuum Oil Company[3] also seeking a concession. In the meantime, the Iranian government hired two American geologists to survey the oil reserves in various parts of Iran.[4] These developments caused much discussion and some criticism in

34

Tehran, in the Majlis, and in the public press. Prime Minister Mohammed Sa'ed conducted the negotiations and periodically reported to the Majlis. Late in September, 1944, Sergei Kavtaradze, Assistant Commissar for Foreign Affairs of the USSR, arrived in Tehran, purportedly to discuss Semnan oil. After several days of speculation about the real purpose of his visit,[5] the commissar suddenly changed the announced purpose of his mission and revealed that, instead of having come to discuss Semnan oil, he was in Tehran to demand an oil concession for the Soviet Union covering the five northern provinces—Azerbaijan, Khorasan, Gilan, Mazanderan, and Asterabad. This announcement evoked new rumors concerning Soviet intentions in Iran. Some thought that the intended effect of Kavtaradze's demands was to capitalize on Iranian unwillingness to grant the concession to the USSR by forcing the Iranians to refuse all requests for concessions rather than to incur Soviet displeasure by discriminating against it. It is clear that the USSR did not want a large commercial enterprise, controlled by British or Americans, operating on the border of the Soviet Union and, in addition, probably wished to prevent, so far as possible, close ties between Iran and the United States in the postwar world. Others thought that the Soviet Union really wanted the oil[6] and perhaps the profit that could be made from it. In addition, a concession would provide a means of economic penetration such as had been attempted by trading practices in the 1920's (see above, pp. 23–26). It seems probable that both of these objectives were considered by the Soviet leaders. There can be no doubt that the USSR would prefer the exclusion of all foreigners from the oil fields of Iran unless those foreigners were employees of the Soviet government. On the other hand, the willingness of the USSR to settle the Azerbaijan dispute when granted an oil concession seems to substantiate the thesis that the Soviets wanted either the oil or a means of economic penetration (see pp. 43–44).

On October 16, 1944, Prime Minister Sa'ed announced that

the Iranian government was rejecting all offers or applications for concessions. This announcement precipitated a storm of protest and criticism from the Communist press in Iran and in the Soviet Union. Criticism was directed at the Iranian government, as well as at Prime Minister Sa'ed personally, for having created an atmosphere of tension and distrust among the Allies and for having adopted a "reactionary" policy harmful to the interests of the Iranian working people.[7] On October 24 Kavtaradze invited a large number of Iranian newspapermen to the Soviet Embassy and proceeded to attack the "disloyal and unfriendly position taken up by Premier Sa'ed" and to urge the support of the Iranian people for the granting of a concession to the Soviet Union.[8] This attack by Kavtaradze on the Iranian government, to which he was accredited, was contrary to accepted diplomatic practice and must reflect on the Soviet promise in the Tripartite Treaty of Alliance to "respect ... the sovereignty and political independence of Iran" (see p. 31).

Kavtaradze's attack was followed by a press conference called by Prime Minister Sa'ed in which he asserted that his government was merely postponing all negotiations for concessions until after the conclusion of the war, when Iran should be free of foreign troops and the confused economic situation of wartime should have clarified itself. The postponement of negotiations was not, he said, directed primarily against the Soviet Union, and, in fact, the decision had been taken before the arrival of Kavtaradze in Tehran. The publication of this statement was followed by a virulent attack by the Tudeh and its affiliated organs, which accused the government of Fascism and hostility toward the Soviet Union. Sa'ed's immediate resignation was demanded. In support of these pronouncements of the Tudeh press there were mass demonstrations in Tabriz and Tehran against Sa'ed's policy. It is significant that the participants in the Tehran demonstration were transported to Parliament Square in Soviet trucks and that the Iranian police were prevented from dispersing the mob by the curiously coincidental march of Red Army units through the square just at that time.[9]

The next event of importance was the announcement by the United States government, through its ambassador, L. B. Morris, that it recognized and supported the right of the Iranian government to refuse the granting of oil concessions to all foreigners.[10] On November 4, 1944, *Izvestia* criticized the presence of American troops in Iran in the absence of a regulatory treaty between the two countries, an accusation to which the American Department of State replied quickly and caustically.[11]

The situation steadily worsened. Tudeh, through its press and by organized popular demonstrations, continued its attacks on Sa'ed. And, despite the announced policy of the Iranian government, Kavtaradze remained in Tehran. Finally, on November 8, Sa'ed resigned and was replaced by Morteza Bayat as Prime Minister. The Tudeh attack against the government continued even after the resignation of Sa'ed. Soon after Bayat's elevation, Dr. Mohammed Mossadegh introduced a bill that would make it a criminal offense for any cabinet minister to grant an oil concession without the prior approval of the Parliament. The bill was adopted by the Majlis on December 2, 1944.[12] On December 8, Kavtaradze called another press conference, in which he again breached diplomatic procedure by severely criticizing the new law and demanding that the Majlis reconsider the whole problem. He also announced that because of the deterioration of Soviet-Iranian relations he was obliged to leave Tehran. The following day he departed for Moscow, and the oil crisis of 1944 was over.

After Kavtaradze's departure the Tudeh press turned its attention to the points of irritation between the USSR and the West. The problems of the Dardanelles, of Poland, of Greece, and of Middle East oil were discussed endlessly in a manner closely paralleling that of the official Soviet press. Although the membership of Tudeh was somewhat depleted as a result of the party's open support of the Soviet Union in the recent oil crisis, the

Tudeh continued to be used as an instrument of Soviet policy. It played an important part in the events that led to the formation of the Azerbaijan "Republic" in 1945.

§ 9. The Close of World War II

The war years were a period of transition for Iran. Its blessings were mixed. The national unity which the dictatorship of Reza Kahn had established proved to be a façade only. With his departure and the distintegration of the army, political opposition and opportunism came into the open. There were evidences of democratic tendencies, but the circumstances were hardly propitious for the development of democracy. However, for the first time the Majlis emerged as a real force in the government of Iran. The end of the dictatorship saw the revival of intellectual and political activity—political parties and newspapers appeared by the score. Most of the political groups, both new and old, were poorly organized, unstable, and short-lived, the significant exception being the Tudeh party, which had become strong, well-organized, and disciplined under the protection and tutelage of the USSR. The diplomatic and military activity of the Allies constituted the main substance of the political life of Iran during the war years. In view of the almost complete control by the Allies, there was, of course, a danger that Iran would completely lose her independence, but in spite of that the Iranians developed a political consciousness that has greatly influenced domestic and world events in the postwar period and will probably continue to do so in the years to come.

During the war years, Iran experienced a very severe inflation. The cost of living multiplied almost sevenfold between March 21, 1941, and March 21, 1945.[1] After a temporary recession, prices showed a distinct upward trend in the postwar years to a peak late in 1949, which was followed by a slight recession in 1950–51 and a sharp rise again late in 1951. These wartime and postwar inflationary movements were caused primarily by the decline in the volume of imports (most of which had been consumer goods), by the rapid rise in import prices, and by Allied military expenditures,[2] as well as by government deficit spending,[3] the low level of national output for domestic consumption, and the extensive black market and profiteering which flourished despite the efforts of the government to enforce the price-control legislation.

The size of the problem which faced the Iranian government at the end of the war and occupation can only be appreciated if it is remembered, first, that the men who would be responsible for conducting the government were relatively inexperienced, since Iran had been governed throughout most of the interwar period by an absolute monarch; second, that the economy was extremely unstable, severely disorganized, and ruinously inflated; and third, that Iran was to be one of the principal objects of attention in the "cold war" that soon developed.

PART II: POLITICS, NATIONALIZATION AND CONTROVERSY

Law is the Lord of all

—PINDAR

WITH THE CLOSE OF THE WAR in Europe in May, 1945, Iran again became the testing ground in the political rivalry of the Great Powers. The Iranians' principal desire was to remain independent of the rivalry and neutral toward the rivals, and to be free to give their time and energies to the reorganization and reconstruction of their own political and economic systems, which had been completely deranged by the wartime occupation. To do this they had first to rid the country of foreign troops—to establish anew Reza Shah's first principle: that the nation should be free and independent of foreign interference and influence.

§ 1. Soviet Policy and the Azerbaijan Crisis

Emerging from World War II as one of the two most powerful nations of the world, the Soviet Union devised a new strategy to effect the age-old Russian policy of expansion toward the Persian Gulf and India.[1] As events have developed it seems that this new strategy was planned along three clearly coördinated lines. The first of these was the revival in 1944 of a demand for an oil concession in the northern provinces, discussed above (Part 1, § 8). This effort failed when the Iranian government resolved—there were still British and American troops in Iran—to grant no further oil concessions until all foreign troops were withdrawn.

The second tactic came with the evacuation of troops. On May 19, 1945, Iran first demanded of Britain and Russia that they

41

withdraw their troops.[2] Both the British and the Russians, in their replies, stated that their troops were not legally obligated to leave until the deadline set in the Tripartite Treaty of Alliance in 1942, that is, six months after the cessation of hostilities. Nevertheless the British favored the Iranian point of view, since it coincided with their own, and immediately began a gradual withdrawal of troops from many areas. A long diplomatic argument ensued between Tehran and Moscow, the Russians insisting on the letter of the treaty although the occasion for their troops' presence there had passed. By agreement Tehran was evacuated in August, 1945, but Russian troops remained in the northern provinces, which continued to be sealed off from the rest of the country and under the complete control of the occupying forces. Soviet propaganda activities were increased, and a special effort was made to capitalize on the chronic discontent of the unassimilated northern tribes, particularly the Azerbaijani and the Kurds.[3]

In November, 1945, three months before the treaty deadline for the evacuation of troops, the Soviet-sponsored "peoples' republics" were proclaimed.[4] The story of the Russian capture of Azerbaijan illustrates both the weaknesses of the Iranian wartime government and the methods used by the Soviets in their attempts to gain a foothold south of the Caucasus. The wartime occupation of the northern provinces by the Soviets enabled the Communist Tudeh party to gain strength and to elect several party members to the Majlis, in which they formed an effective opposition bloc.

The leader of the Tudeh party at this time, and subsequently "premier" of the Azerbaijan Republic, was Ja'afar Peshavari, who had come to Iran in 1936 as a political refugee, but whose political activities had led to his imprisonment and exile by Reza Shah. He returned to Iran only after the Soviets occupied the northern provinces in 1941. In addition to promoting labor agitation among the exploited industrial workers, Tudeh also played on the long-standing animosities between the central government and the provinces. The directing influence of Soviet policy can be seen in the fact that immediately after the return of a large delegation of vacationing Iranian factory workers from Baku, in Soviet Azerbaijan, the Tudeh party of Azerbaijan voted itself out of existence. A new Democratic party, headed by Peshavari and the other leaders of the defunct Tudeh party, was formed, and it engineered the coup of December, 1945, setting up the Azerbaijan People's Republic.[5] Iranian government officials were imprisoned and many persons were killed, arms were distributed to party members and peasants, an Azerbaijan militia was formed (equipped with Soviet arms and uniforms), and party meetings were protected by Soviet troops. Soviet connivance and participation,[6] despite formal declarations by the USSR that it was assuming an entirely neutral position, became very clear when the Iranian government sent troops from Tehran to quell the rebellion: the Iranian troops were turned back at the border of the Soviet zone by the Red Army.

The Iranian government appealed to the United Nations, charging that the USSR was interfering in its internal affairs and endangering its security. The debate in the Security Council was focused on the procedural question whether a complaint of a small nation against one of the Big Five was the legitimate business of the Council. Russia's arguments were countered by the United Kingdom and the United States, both of which vigorously supported Iran's right to submit the dispute to the Council. The Security Council finally decided to keep the complaint on the agenda while the two parties negotiated a settlement[7]—a significant development in the history of the United Nations and another example of Iran's dependence on the relations between the USSR and the Western powers. Although the existence of the United Nations Security Council, its action, and the strong support by Britain and the United States undoubtedly encouraged the Iranian government to persist, the main credit for extricating Iran from a dangerous situation must go to the Iranian government itself, and especially to its new prime minister, Ahmed Qavam.

Qavam succeeded in negotiating a settlement with the Russians, announced in Tehran on April 4, 1946, by which they agreed to the immediate withdrawal of all Soviet troops in return for a long-sought oil concession[8] in the northern provinces. A Russo-Iranian company was to be formed to exploit northern oil, with the Soviet government owning 51 per cent of the shares.

The Russians were outwitted. After Qavam agreed to give them an oil concession, they began to withdraw their troops, and the evacuation was completed by May 9, 1946. The Iranian army, under General (later Prime Minister) Ali Razmara, marched into Azerbaijan without opposition in December, 1946, and the Azerbaijan and Kurdistan republics promptly collapsed. Peshavari and the "Democrats" fled to the USSR. Soviet officials were apparently unconcerned with these developments, thinking they had secured a firm foothold through the oil concession. After hedging and delaying for eighteen months, the Majlis finally refused ratification of the oil agreement by a vote of 102 to 2.[9] Soviet protests were both immediate and strong. The Soviets accused Iran of lending itself to American plans for militarizing Iran and making it a strategic base, presumably for use against the USSR.[10] Tension increased between the USSR and Iran, and threats were made by the former to invoke the 1921 Treaty of Friendship and send back its troops. The Iranian government consistently denied any hostility toward the Soviet Union. Its handling of this very delicate situation was both courageous and dignified, and the waters eventually calmed without any further overt moves by the Red Army or the Soviet government.

The third tactic was carried out indirectly through the Tudeh party. Its agitations among the oil-field workers in southwestern Iran precipitated a general strike among AIOC workers in Khuzistan. The disturbances that accompanied the strike were so serious and the central government was so weak that in August, 1946, the British government felt obliged to dispatch a brigade of troops from India to Basrah to protect AIOC's installations, and thus the security of the Empire. These troops did not move beyond Basrah. Their presence at the head of the Persian Gulf seemed sufficient to restore order and stop the rioting. This movement of troops is also significant in that it was the last use of forces from an undivided India under British direction. The partition of India in 1947 and the subsequent absence of British troops has left a vacuum that must be filled if the security and stability of the Middle East is to be assured.[11]

While some Tudeh agents were organizing the strike in the oil fields, others were actively inciting the Qashqai and neighboring tribes of southwestern Iran to rebel against the central government. The revolt of these tribes in the fall of 1946, in support of their demands for the same degree of autonomy as that achieved by Azerbaijan, led to the dismissal of three Tudeh members of the cabinet. Qavam's government made appeasing overtures toward the tribes, and a settlement was finally reached.[12] However, there were elements in both the Azerbaijan and the Qashqai revolts that existed long before the Tudeh agitation and that continue to press Tehran with demands for decentralization of government, a fairer distribution of tax revenues between Tehran and the provinces, and the extension of roads, electricity, and other public utilities. In addition to political troubles, Iran also had economic difficulties in the postwar years that have cast their shadow directly on the negotiations for settlement of the oil dispute in 1951.

§ 2. *The Seven-Year Plan*

The inflationary situation that existed in Iran during the postwar period has been mentioned above (Part I, § 9). After a temporary recession from the wartime peak of the first quarter of 1945, prices showed a distinct upward tendency, and, from July, 1946, to August, 1949, the cost of living rose 36 per cent.[1] This was primarily caused by poor harvests in 1947 and 1948, and also by increases in the local expenditures of the AIOC.[2] It should be noted that during the postwar years budgetary deficits did not exceed 5 per cent of expenditures until the fiscal year 1949–50, but at the same time approximately 11 to 15 per cent of the total budget receipts were oil royalties.[3] The effects of these and other factors in increasing demand or reducing supply were only partially offset by an expansion in imports of consumer goods and by a slight increase in industrial production. Another temporary recession occurred late in 1949. Prices fell sharply, and economic activity slackened. These conditions were mainly produced by a change in the country's foreign trade balance. During the fiscal year 1949–50 the volume of imports increased more than 62 per cent over the level of the preceding year while the volume of exports remained unchanged. This large import surplus was primarily attributable to the large imports of grain that were necessary to offset the effects of the poor harvests in 1949. The government's liberalized import policy, which was designed as a deflationary measure, and the adverse movement in the exchange rate of the dollar and pound sterling also contributed to the unfavorable foreign trade balance. This recessionary trend was reversed in the winter of 1950–51, after the beginning of the Korean war had provided the occasion for an almost world-wide inflationary movement, as well as a general increase in production and trade. Iran's exports increased substantially, and the volume of imports declined as agricultural production increased. Nevertheless, Iran's balance of trade still showed a sizable deficit on current account; and the budgetary deficit of the Iranian government was gradually increasing.[4]

Although the wartime and postwar inflation in prices and the cost of living in Iran was aggravated to a certain extent by external influences transmitted through the foreign trade balance, the inflationary movement was primarily the result of domestic conditions. The basic problem was one of productivity,[5] for productivity had to be increased if a stable economy providing an adequate standard of living were to be developed. To increase productivity, an economic development project calling for the expenditure of $650 million in seven years was formulated under the direction of the Iranian government. Relying on a statement in the Tehran Declaration of December, 1943, that ". . . the Governments of the United States, the U.S.S.R., and the United Kingdom are in accord with the Government of Iran that any economic problems confronting Iran at the close of hostilities should receive full consideration, . . . by conferences or international agencies held or created to deal with international economic matters . . . ,"[6] the Iranian government in 1947 applied to the International Bank for Reconstruction and Development (IBRD) for a loan of $250 million to be used to start the Iranian development program. A series of discussions was undertaken, but the loan was not forthcoming. Instead, the Bank followed its general practice and requested detailed information on the plan and on specific projects to be undertaken. To supply this information, the Iranian government engaged an American firm, Overseas Consultants, Inc., to survey the Iranian economy and formulate specific development projects. After working six months, Overseas Consultants submitted to the Iranian government, in October, 1949, an elaborate five-volume, 1250-page report[7] blueprinting plans for an integrated development of Iran's agriculture and industry. This report became known as the Seven-Year Plan, and, like the plan originally submitted to the IBRD, it called for the expenditure of $650 million in a period of seven years.

Meanwhile, the increasing import surpluses and budgetary deficits during the fiscal years 1948–49 and 1949–50 had deteriorated Iranian finances to such an extent that, by the end of 1949, the government could not afford to proceed with the Seven-Year Plan unless it could obtain increased revenues.[8] Iran's balance of payments and financial condition indicated that the Iranian government would not be a good credit risk,[9] and the International Bank, being a bank, refused the loan. Many Iranians (and non-Iranians) consider the International Bank an

American-controlled institution because much of its working capital has been contributed by the United States; and many Iranians seemingly—and perhaps rightly (see n. 10)—interpreted the statement quoted above from the Tehran Declaration as an American promise of large-scale economic aid. As a result, the IBRD's refusal of the Iranian government's application for a loan was considered an American refusal, to the detriment of American prestige and influence in Iran. Instead of assuring the funds needed for the Seven-Year Plan, the United States government offered, in October, 1950, to negotiate a loan of $25 million (through the Export-Import Bank), primarily for the purpose of purchasing road-building and agricultural equipment. This loan was pitifully small in comparison with Iran's needs as well as in relation to the strategic importance of Iran. For a combination of reasons, prominent among which was the rise of xenophobic nationalism, the Majlis refused to ratify this loan for more than two years. It was finally accepted during the financial crisis that followed the nationalization of the oil industry (see p. 98). The fact that the United States did not provide the means, either directly or through the IBRD, for implementing the Seven-Year Plan has contributed to the political and economic instability that has been evident in Iran throughout the postwar period. This failure has thus helped to create a situation potentially dangerous to the interests of the United States, and it also provided the first step to the steady degeneration of American-Iranian friendship in recent years;[10] and from this point of view, it is immaterial whether or not the Iranians were justified in interpreting the statement in the Tehran Declaration as an American promise.

§ 3. The Supplementary Agreement

In the spring of 1949 the Iranian government demanded increased royalties from the AIOC. This demand proceeded in part from the serious state of Iranian finances, which has been discussed above. But, in addition, there had been pressures, at least since 1940, for a revision of AIOC's royalty formula, caused in part by the disparity between the royalty formulas of Latin America (especially Venezuela) and that in the 1933 concession. Negotiations between the AIOC and the government of Iran were begun early in the summer of 1949, and on July 17 a Supplementary Agreement[1] of five thousand words, elaborately cross-indexed to the 1933 concession, was signed by representatives of the government and AIOC.[2] This Supplementary Agreement had two important provisions: (1) the royalty rate was to be increased by approximately 25 to 50 per cent, depending on variations in production and profits,[3] and (2) the company's title under the 1933 concession was affirmed. Few officials read this lengthy and complicated document. Instead they talked of the fifty-fifty profit-sharing formula in effect in Venezuela. Such an arrangement had been offered by the British early in the negotiations, although the offer was not pressed, but the Iranian representatives refused it, apparently in the hope that an even more favorable arrangement could be won.

By the fall of 1949 public opinion in Iran, including that of the United States Embassy, had crystallized: the Supplementary Agreement was inadequate. The British refused to discuss any changes until the Supplementary Agreement had been expressly rejected by the Majlis, and meanwhile the agreement was awaiting consideration by that body. In the elections of 1949 Dr. Mossadegh's National Front party secured 8 seats in the Majlis, out of a total of 136. Even with such a small number of seats, his party was so well organized[4] and its attitude of militant opposition to foreign political and economic domination struck such a responsive chord that it was able to control Iranian oil policy and prevent every attempt at ratification of the Supplementary Agreement during 1949 and 1950. The failure of Prime Minister Ali Mansur either to obtain parliamentary approval of the agreement or to induce the British to discuss the fifty-fifty formula, led to the fall of his three-month-old government in June of 1950. He was succeeded by General Ali Razmara, who realized that if ratification, now both a political and a highly emotional issue, were to be obtained, it would be necessary to induce the AIOC to make additional concessions. He urged the company to reopen negotiations, but the company refused, even though Razmara was not seeking a further increase in royalties. He asked only that the number of Iranians employed and trained by AIOC be increased,[5] and that the price of oil products sold in Iran be reduced. As the tension mounted, the British officials remained both complacent and obtuse, refusing to recognize the danger inherent in the situation generally, and particularly in the National Front campaign for nationalization. The British Foreign Office, ignoring the warning of the American Embassy in Tehran, refused throughout 1950 to intercede between the company and the Iranian government. The Foreign Office insisted that the company was a commercial enterprise, and that the Iranians would ratify the Supplementary Agreement when their need of money was great enough.[6] Finally, as the situation neared its climax early in 1951, the Foreign Office decided that it was vitally concerned with the company's policies in its dealings with Iran, and it then proceeded to take an active part in the efforts that were made to save the industry from nationalization (and thus the British government from a sizable loss in revenue).

In October, 1950, Razmara was persuaded to submit the Supplementary Agreement to the Majlis for ratification. Before debate, it was referred to the Majlis Special Oil Committee for examination. Dr. Mossadegh, leader of the National Front party, was chairman of this committee, and four of its members were also leading members of the National Front. The committee finally reported, in December, 1950, that it was not in favor of the agreement, "on the ground that it [did] not satisfactorily safeguard Iranian rights and interests."[7] In consequence, the Supplementary Agreement was withdrawn from the Majlis on December 26, and on January 11, 1951, the Majlis affirmed the committee's report and requested the committee to make a report suggesting the course the government should take in the matter. It was an unfortunate coincidence that early in January news reached Tehran of the Arabian-American Oil Company's fifty-fifty profit-sharing agreement with Ibn Saud. At this late date the company urged Prime Minister Razmara to reopen negotiations for a fifty-fifty profit-sharing agreement.[8] That Razmara did not do so is undoubtedly attributable to the following events. On February 19 Dr. Mossadegh presented to the Special Oil Committee of the Majlis a formal resolution for the nationalization of the Iranian oil industry, and immediately thereafter, the National Front party conducted its public campaign for nationalization with increased vigor. Following the introduction of this resolution Prime Minister Razmara was called upon by the Special Oil Committee to report on whether or not nationalization was practicable. He referred the problem to a panel of Iranian advisers. These advisers submitted reports stating that, in their opinion, nationalization was not practicable at that time and added that they had grave doubts of the legality of the nationalization plan. The prime minister presented these reports to the Oil Committee on March 3, at which time their contents were made public. On March 7 Razmara was assassinated. Eight days later, on March 15, the Majlis passed a "Single Article" bill nationalizing the Iranian oil industry.[9] This action was confirmed by the Senate on March 20. In April a more detailed bill of nine articles[10] was prepared and passed by both the Majlis and the Senate, and the bills received the assent of the shah on May 1 and 2.

§ 4. The Anglo-Iranian Oil Dispute of 1951–1952

Immediately after the Majlis passed the "Single Article Law of March 15th," there were a series of anti-British riots and demonstrations in Tehran. Looting was widespread, and scores of persons were injured. Before order was restored, eight Iranians and three Britons were killed. At the same time, a strike of oil-field workers, protesting the company's ill-timed withdrawal of special pay allowances for employees in undeveloped areas, mushroomed into a general strike that was not settled until the third week in April, after the allowances had been restored and a bonus added for those who stayed on the job. The new prime minister, Hussein Ala, was unable to get the coöperation of the Parliament, and his government fell on April 27, only fifty-one days after the assassination of Razmara. The next day, April 28, Shah Mohammed Reza Pahlevi named Dr. Mohammed Mossadegh Prime Minister at the request of the Majlis. Mossadegh accepted only after both the Majlis and the Senate agreed to support his policy of immediate eviction of the AIOC. This policy was implemented by a law passed by the Majlis and Senate on June 13, and eviction was accomplished in fact on October 1, 1951.

Mossadegh and his supporters were convinced that the Iranian government could operate the oil industry successfully by hiring foreign technicians, and could sell almost the same quantity of oil products[1] as the "former company."[2] This attitude, even though naïve,[3] is sufficient to explain the government's refusal to attend British urgings to reopen negotiations, and also the position taken by the government, in response to British protests, that the matter was within "the exclusive domestic jurisdiction of Iran"—a claim that was to be repeated when the British government subsequently attempted to submit the dispute to the International Court of Justice. The additional factor, one that should never be lost sight of, is that nationalization of the oil industry was a product and expression of Iranian nationalism,[4] which is both anti-imperialistic and xenophobic, especially toward the British. Both aspects of this nationalism were dramatically demonstrated in the riots that followed the enactment of the nationalization law. There were demonstrations against the "Western imperialists," and rioting crowds mobbed not only the British Embassy, but the American Embassy as well. Xenophobia, which seems to be a common element in all Middle East nationalism, has continued to find expression, both popular and official,[5] throughout the oil dispute. The nationalist policies of Mossadegh's National Front party found wide popular support. The political creed of patriotic nationalism, which was character- istic of the Middle East nationalism in the 1920's, became merged with the social struggle of the masses of poverty-ridden peasants in Iran, but the peasants' support of political nationalism in 1951 was as much the product of a reaction to years (or cen- turies) of oppression by landlords and inefficient governments as it was a reaction to abuse by foreign commercial enterprises. This present-day nationalism in Iran, as well as in the Arab Middle East generally, has been succinctly and ably described by *The Economist* (London) in the following terms:

The Arab nationalism of thirty years ago, which was reared on the pap of missionary education in Syria and educated on President Wilson's fourteen points, was a mixture of xenophobia and of religion, but it was conditioned and shaped by an ancient social order. Today nationalism remains anti-foreign but with this distinction: whereas its forerunner was merely hostile to the foreigner on the spot and regarded distant powers such as the United States as genial and tolerable, the nationalism of the fifties is directed against all foreigners, westerners and Russians alike. Likewise, it is still fired by religious emotions, as is evident in the strength of the Moslem Brotherhood in Egypt and in Mullah Kashani's power in Persia; but it is also propelled by a third and new force, social discontent.[6]

This social discontent, which is so obvious throughout most of the Middle East, is the expression of the "revolution" now in prog- ress. The real "revolutionary" force in the Middle East has not been Communism, or any other ideology, but instead, the "revo- lutionary" oil industry.[7] The introduction of Western culture and technology through the oil industry, and to a lesser extent through other commercial enterprises, has created a change in the traditional patterns of thinking, and, for Middle Easterners directly employed by the oil companies, a change in the patterns of behavior. This change in the traditional habits of thought and action is the real revolution, and it has, in turn, created pressures for changes in the traditional social order. The diminution in the power of the ancient ruling families and the growing popular influence in the domestic government reflect these pressures. As has been pointed out above (see p. 37), the close of World War II saw the emergence, for the first time, of the Parliament as a real force in the government of Iran.

A few general remarks may make the negotiations which are described on the following pages more intelligible to the reader. Each of the two parties has assumed one basic position to which it has clung tenaciously throughout the dispute: the British assumed that the Iranians *had* to sell oil; the Iranians assumed that the Western world *had* to have their oil. As the example of Mexico should have shown, and as subsequent events have proved, both parties were wrong.

The negotiations which took place—first, between the AIOC and the Iranian government and, secondly, between the United Kingdom government and the Iranian government—were conducted primarily in economic terms. The Iranians wished only to discuss how much was due the British as compensation, and the British worried themselves over the formulation of the financial terms of what they hoped would appeal to the Iranians as a "workable" agreement. Yet the real problem was not economic; it was, and is, a political problem. Differently stated, the parties have not learned, and evidently could not learn in the summer of 1951, to "get along" with each other, to live and work together harmoniously. The British have not adapted themselves to the "revolution" that has occurred in Iran in the last half century. This appears in many ways, but one of the most striking and most obvious, and one that has constantly irritated the Iranians, has been the inability (or stubborn refusal) of the British government and the AIOC to use the words "Iran" and "Iranians" in place of the terms "Persia" and "Persians," except that the company did change its name when the name of the country was changed. This practice can be seen readily enough throughout the official communications that are quoted below. The British negotiators would have done better, instead of calculating how much they could afford to advance to the Iranian government pending settlement of the oil dispute, to have pondered the advice of one of their elder statesmen, Lord Bryce: "It is not occasional acts of cruelty . . . that makes foreigners hated nearly so much as coldness, hauteur, contempt, and incapacity to appreciate or sympathise with a different set of customs or ideas." On the other hand, the Iranians have not shown any conspicuous understanding or humor in their dealings with Oxford-trained British lions.

Every fair and rational solution possible demands that the parties reach an agreement, and that they both make a serious effort to work together for their mutual benefit and improvement. Yet the problem of attaining workable methods of coöperation was the one problem that was never mentioned in the negotiations. The omission is, however, probably for the better, since this problem is one that can only be solved by understanding and sympathy, and not by negotiation.

§ 5. The Negotiations, First Phase

After the passage of the supplementary Law Regulating Nationalization of the Oil Industry, on April 30, 1951,[1] but before it became effective through ratification and promulgation by the shah on May 2, the British government still refused[2] to "admit that the contractual obligations under which the company has operated and has made this great investment in Persia can be abrogated unilaterally."[3] However, the official British attitude was still friendly and generally conciliatory, as was stated by Mr. Herbert Morrison, British Foreign Secretary, in the House of Commons on May 1.

56

We are still most anxious to settle this matter by negotiation; but we cannot negotiate under duress. We do not, of course, dispute the right of a Government to acquire property in their own country, but we cannot accept that the Company's whole position in Persia should be radically altered by unilateral action, when the agreement into which the Persian Government freely entered with the Company itself provides against such action. We have no wish that this question should become an issue between ourselves and our Persian friends, and we are only anxious to sit down with them and work out a solution in a reasonable atmosphere. Our long-standing ties of friendship with them and our many mutual interests, political as well as economic, convince us that such a solution can be found.[4]

The following day Mr. Morrison sent a personal message to Prime Minister Mossadegh embodying substantially the same proposals he had made in his speech before the Commons. In his response to the request that the Iranian government refrain from unilateral action against the company, Dr. Mossadegh reaffirmed his intention of executing the nationalization laws. However, although he made no response to Mr. Morrison's suggestion that a solution be negotiated, the reply concluded "with the statement that the 'former oil company would be invited in a few days to discuss the implementation of the law.' "[5] In reply, the United Kingdom government again asked the Iranian government to agree to negotiations and "gave warning that a refusal to negotiate or any attempt to proceed by unilateral action with the implementation of the recent legislation would have the most serious consequences."[6]

At the same time AIOC formally notified the Iranian government that it requested arbitration in accordance with the provisions of Articles 22 and 26 of the 1933 concession[7] to determine whether the latter was within its legal rights in attempting to annul or terminate that agreement. The notification called attention to the Iranian pledge in Article 21 of the concession that "this Concession shall not be annulled by the Government and the terms therein contained shall not be altered either by general or special legislation in the future, or by administrative measures or any other acts whatever of the executive authorities."⁸ This pledge is made more specific by the second paragraph of Article 26: "Before the date of December 31, 1993, this Concession can only come to an end in the case that the Company should surrender the Concession (Article 25) or in the case that the Arbitration Court should declare the Concession annulled as a consequence of default of the Company in the performance of the present Agreement."⁹ The arbitration court referred to is provided for by Article 22, which reads, in part: "Any differences between the parties *of any nature whatever* and in particular any differences arising out of the interpretation of this Agreement and of the rights and obligations therein contained as well as any differences of opinion which may arise relative to questions for the settlement of which, by the terms of this Agreement, the agreement of both parties is necessary, shall be settled by arbitration."¹⁰ The following paragraphs of Article 22 detail the means of choosing the arbitrators, the umpire who is to be appointed in the event that the arbitrators cannot agree, the procedures to be followed, and the law to be applied. Paragraph D provides that if one party fails to appoint an arbitrator within sixty days after having received notification of the request for arbitration "the other party shall have the right to request the President of the Permanent Court of International Justice . . . to nominate a sole arbitrator, . . . and, in this case, the difference shall be settled by the sole arbitrator."¹¹ In accordance with Article 22, paragraph B, AIOC notified the Iranian government that Lord Radcliffe, Lord of Appeal in Ordinary, had accepted appointment as its arbitrator and requested that the Iranian government appoint its arbitrator at its earliest convenience.

On May 19, before any reply had been made to the company's request for arbitration, Sir Francis Shepherd, British Ambassador in Tehran, presented the Iranian government with an aide-memoire which set forth in rather strong language the British government's view of the legal position of the company and specifically reserved the right to take the case to the International Court of Justice if the Iranian government rejected the company's request for arbitration. The aide-memoire also reiterated the suggestion that the problem be solved by negotiation and, in addition, contained an offer to send a mission to Tehran for that purpose.[12] During the month of May the attitude of the British government seemed perceptibly to stiffen: on May 15 it was announced that a brigade of paratroopers was being held "in readiness" in the United Kingdom to protect the lives of British nationals and prevent illegal seizure of the property of AIOC. This brigade was moved to Cyprus on May 25. However, the reference to the protection of the property of AIOC from "illegal seizure" was not repeated when Mr. Morrison described this policy in a speech before the House of Commons on June 20:

> As I have repeatedly informed the House His Majesty's Government are not prepared to stand by idle if the lives of British nationals are in jeopardy. It is the responsibility of the Persian Government to see to it that law and order are maintained and that all within the frontiers of Persia are protected from violence. If, however, that responsibility were not met it would equally be the right and duty of His Majesty's Government to extend protection to their own nationals.[13]

The day after the Iranian government received Ambassador Shepherd's aide-memoire referred to above, the Iranian minister of finance wrote to the company's representative in Tehran, Mr. Seddon, that it rejected the company's request for arbitration on the grounds that the nationalization of the Iranian oil industry was not referable to arbitration and that no international authority had competence to deal with the matter, because it was entirely and solely within the purview of the Iranian government. The finance minister's letter also invited AIOC to name representatives to meet with the Majlis Special Oil Committee to "arrange the execution of the nationalization laws."[14] Mr. Seddon received another letter on May 24, which amounted to an ultimatum. It allowed the company until May 30 to send representatives to meet with the Oil Committee, failing which the Iranian government would itself proceed to execute the nationalization laws. The reasons for the refusal to arbitrate in accordance with the provisions of the 1933 concession were elaborated by Prime Minister Mossadegh in a speech to the foreign press representatives on May 28:[15]

As I have said before, nationalization of the Oil Industry has been affected [sic] by virtue of the Iranian Nation's sovereign rights. No agreement can deprive us of this right. All legal authorities agree on this point. But our antagonists represent the matter differently; instead of admitting that the Iranian Nation has the right to nationalize whatever industry it may deem to be in its interest; they allege that the Iranian Nation has annulled the former Oil Company's agreement.

Apart from the fact that the said agreement was signed under duress and consequently not valid or even null and void, the Iranian Government and people have not considered the validity of the agreement about which the Oil Company and the British Government are raising so much thunder and fury.

The Iranian Majlis has not raised any question about the agreement or acted in any way to give the Oil Company an excuse to refer this matter to arbitration. If a question had been raised regarding the validity of the agreement, the need for arbitration would arise. I repeat that neither the Majlis nor the Iranian Government has raised any point regarding the agreement; consequently the Oil Company cannot invoke the arbitration clause.

It is true that as a result of the nationalization of the oil industry, the former Oil Company will no longer be able to exploit the oil resources of the country for its own benefit. But any agreement, no matter of what type and how worded, is subject to laws which are within the sovereign rights of nations. No agreement can prejudice the application of such sovereign laws.

To sum up, when a Government takes an action in exercise of its sovereign rights which causes loss to a private corporation the only remedy for that corporation is to claim compensation from that Government. Such compensation has already been foreseen and provided for by law.[16] The agreement of 1933 is, however, not the subject of our discussion and any mention of it is out of place.[17]

In reply to the Iranian government's refusal to appoint an arbitrator as requested, the company on May 26 stated that it had at all times "expressed its willingness to discuss and seek to solve by agreement with the Imperial Government all outstanding questions,"[18] but that since the latter had refused to agree to arbitration the company was applying to the president of the International Court of Justice at The Hague to appoint a sole arbitrator in accordance with Article 22, paragraph D, of the 1933 concession.[19] In response to the invitation to send representatives to discuss the execution of the nationalization laws with the Majlis Special Oil Committee, the company said that a representative of AIOC, Mr. Seddon, would attend the meeting "as a measure of respect to the Imperial Government and the Iranian Parliament, but only . . . to listen to what is said to him and to report the substance to the Company in London."[20]

On May 27, the Iranian government was formally notified by the British Embassy in Tehran that the government of the United Kingdom had, separately from the AIOC, brought the oil dispute before the International Court of Justice (ICJ) on May 26. The United Kingdom's "Application" asked the Court to declare that the execution of the Iranian nationalization laws, so far as they purported to effect a unilateral annulment or alteration of the terms of the 1933 concession, would be a violation of international law for which the Iranian government would be internationally responsible, and that, by rejecting the AIOC's request for arbitration, the Iranian government had denied the company the exclusive legal remedy provided in the agreement and had thereby committed a denial of justice contrary to international law. The application also argued that, by thus treating a British national (AIOC) in a manner inconsistent with the norms of international law, the Iranian government had committed a wrong against the government of the United Kingdom, for which the latter asked satisfaction and indemnity. Further, the United Kingdom asked the Court to declare that the 1933 concession could not be lawfully annulled, or its terms altered, by the Iranian government otherwise than by agreement with the company, or under the provisions of Article 26 of the agreement. Although no request was made at the time, the United Kingdom also reserved the right to request the Court, in accordance with Article 41 of the Statute of the Court, to indicate, if the circumstances should require, "any provisional measures which ought to be taken to preserve the respective rights of either party."[21]

On May 28, 1951, the president of the Court indicated that, as the applications of the British government and the AIOC had certain points in common, action on the company's application to the Court for the appointment of a sole arbitrator would be deferred for the time being.[22] On the same day, the Iranian minister of foreign affairs informed the Court that the Iranian government did not recognize the competence of the ICJ to deal with the matters in dispute between the Iranian government and the AIOC.[23]

The United Kingdom did not request the ICJ to indicate interim measures (to issue a "temporary injunction," in the language of the common law) in its application of May 26, because, as Foreign Minister Morrison made clear in a statement to the House of Commons on May 29, the British government still had hope that a settlement could be reached by agreement between the Iranian government and AIOC, and it wished to do nothing that might prejudice the chances of reaching such a settlement. In addition, Mr. Morrison stated, the British government were still anxious "to see this dispute settled by negotiation, and their offer to send a special mission, if that would help, still stands."[24] Then Mr. Morrison proceeded to make the first conciliatory gesture that had been made since the dispute began.

Moreover, as His Majesty's Ambassador in Tehran has informed the Persian Government, while His Majesty's Government cannot accept the right of the Persian Government to repudiate contracts, *they are prepared to consider a settlement which would involve some form of nationalization, provided*—a consideration to which they [the United Kingdom government] attach some importance—*it were satisfactory in other respects.* Their difficulty has been, and still is, that the Persian Government has hitherto not seen fit to respond in any way to their repeated suggestions of negotiation ... His Majesty's Government earnestly hopes that wiser counsels, taking full account of the dangerous potentialities of the present situation, will prevail in Tehran and that negotiations can be initiated in an atmosphere of reason and goodwill.[25]

In response to this statement, the Iranian government announced on May 30 that, although it would agree to a discussion with the British government on the United Kingdom's requirements of oil (note: *not* AIOC's), it would never consider the British government a party to the oil dispute, which it considered solely a domestic matter between itself and a private company, AIOC.[26] On the same day, Mr. Seddon, representative of AIOC in Tehran, had an interview with Finance Minister Mohammed Ali Varasteh and was handed by him an aide-memoire in which the Iranian government expressed a desire to use the company's knowledge and experience in making arrangements for the implementation of the nationalization laws. The company was invited to submit immediate proposals, provided they were not contrary to the "principle of nationalization," and the Iranian government promised "to give careful consideration to the proposals."[27] In the hope that this might be an opening which could lead to a settlement by agreement,[28] Mr. Seddon replied to the minister of finance that the company, though fully reserving its legal rights, would send representatives from London to Tehran as soon as possible for "full and frank discussions with the Iranian Government."[29] On June 6 the headquarters of AIOC in London announced the names of four of its directors who would go to

Iran to hold the projected discussions with the Iranian government. The mission was headed by the deputy chairman of AIOC's
board of directors, Mr. Basil Jackson. The other members were
Sir Thomas Gardiner (one of the two government-appointed
members of the company's board), Mr. N. A. Gass (who negotiated the 1949 Supplementary Agreement that bears his name),[30]
and Mr. E. H. O. Elkington. The members of the mission arrived
in Tehran on June 11 and 12, and the first meeting took place on
June 14.

In advance of this meeting Sir Francis Shepherd, British Ambassador in Iran, issued a statement in the form of a letter to
the Iranian press in which he attempted to smooth the way for
the forthcoming negotiations by reaffirming the good will of the
British government towards Iran. Further, he declared that, since
the Iranian oil industry "[could not] be conducted except by
mutual coöperation" between Britain and Iran, the only "civilized" procedure was to seek a solution by discussion round a
table. He continued:

> The arrival of the oil company delegation gives an opportunity for this
> method to be begun.
>
> I wish to state categorically that the attitude of the British Government
> to this question and in its policy toward Iran is not in the faintest degree
> animated by imperialism. On the contrary, it has been the policy of the
> British Government for many years to encourage an independent, pros-
> perous and stable Iran.
>
> I wish to state categorically that the oil company is entirely a commer-
> cial concern, and does not intervene in the politics of the country. On the
> basis of these assurances, it should be possible for discussions to proceed
> in a friendly atmosphere. This is essential for British and Iranian inter-
> ests, inextricably mingled in the business of extracting, processing and
> marketing of oil.[31]

In the meantime, members of the Mixed Board that had been
established in accordance with the Law Regulating Nationalization[32] arrived at the AIOC headquarters in Khorramshahr and

informed Mr. Drake, the general manager, that by virtue of Articles 2 and 4 of the Law Regulating Nationalization[33] the entire "earnings" from the sale of oil and oil products since March 20[34] now belonged to the Iranian government. Therefore, the board requested Mr. Drake to deliver to it immediately 75 per cent of the "earnings" that remained after operational expenses were deducted, and to deposit the remaining 25 per cent in a bank to secure the claims of the "former company." On the same day, June 13, the board issued a press advertisement in Tehran advising all persons importing Iranian oil to deal only with the board in the future. Mr. Drake replied that it was impossible for him to comply with the request to deliver "75% of all cash received from the Iranian undertaking," since there were relatively no proceeds or earnings in Iran. He explained that only a very small percentage of Iranian oil was sold within Iran, and that the proceeds or earnings of AIOC were to a large extent the product of a world-wide refining and marketing organization that refined and distributed oil from Iraq, Qatar, and Kuwait,[35] as well as from Iran.

On arriving in Tehran on June 12, Mr. Basil Jackson, leader of the AIOC delegation, made a statement to the press in which he said that the company had accepted the idea of nationalization and that the purpose of the projected talks was to explore the situation, "to discover whether there is somewhere where we can find a useful and profitable place for ourselves under nationalization."[36] However, the press report indicated that the company would not be interested in any agreement stipulating that 75 per cent of its profits go to the Iranian government, "although Anglo-Iranian still stood by the offer of a 50/50 division."[37] Mr. Jackson, in the same press statement, also underlined some technical, financial, and marketing "realities." He asserted, for example, that only AIOC could provide the capital (£100 million) needed to build a pipe line from Khorramshahr to the Mediterranean; that crude-oil production at Kuwait alone could be raised above

Iranian production within one year if AIOC were dispossessed;[38] that the even more serious loss of Abadan's refining capacity could be replaced within, at most, three years; that the tanker fleet at the disposal of the company[39] could easily and profitably be employed elsewhere, which would leave Iran with the problem how to dispose of its oil, only a very small quantity of which was consumed domestically. That these were indeed "realities" has been proved beyond question by subsequent events, and the economic pressure which they exert on Iran has been relied upon almost exclusively by the British since the Abadan refinery was shut down on July 31, 1951; but when they were repeated, immediately preceding the negotiations and later during the negotiations between the AIOC mission and Iranian government, they were interpreted by the Iranians as thinly veiled threats.[40] However, it should be noted that the Iranian finance minister, Mohammed Ali Varasteh, made some statements that were not likely to encourage a conciliatory attitude on the part of the British negotiators. On June 12 he issued a statement to the press in which he announced that he would "demand at the very outset the unconditional acceptance of nationalization as an accomplished fact."[41] To the AIOC delegation this undoubtedly sounded very different from Finance Minister Varasteh's aide-memoire of May 30, in which the company was asked to submit proposals "provided they were not at variance with the *principle* of nationalization."[42] A "principle" can be a very different thing from an "accomplished fact."

When the representatives of the Iranian government and AIOC met for the first time on June 14, Finance Minister Varasteh made another announcement, this one to the effect that the talks could not proceed further unless the company agreed at once to deliver 75 per cent of the net revenues derived from the sale of Iranian oil since March 20.[43] Talks were adjourned until June 19, in order to give the company's delegation time to formulate a reply.

On June 19 the AIOC delegation handed the Iranian delegation an aide-memoire outlining a "constructive interim proposal" that, it was thought, would provide a basis for discussion from which a "workable arrangement" could be reached." Preliminarily, the delegation offered Iran £10 million as an "advance against any sum which may become due to the Government as the result of an eventual agreement between the Government and the Company, on the understanding that the Government undertakes not to interfere with the Company's operations while discussions are proceeding."⁴⁵ The AIOC delegates offered a further sum of £3 million per month, to begin in July and continue until an agreement should be reached. It seems clear that the AIOC officials were still certain that an agreement would be reached. As suggested above, the whole tenor of the company's proposals (and of its statements to the press) show that its officials relied too much on the efficacy of what they believed to be the Iranian government's urgent need to sell oil. As a "constructive interim proposal" to serve as a basis for working out "a satisfactory arrangement which would maintain the efficiency of the industry and would be consistent with the principles of nationalization," they suggested that:

The Persian assets of the Company would be vested in a Persian National Oil Company and in consideration of such vesting the National Oil Company would grant the use of these assets to a new company to be established by Anglo-Iranian Oil Company Limited. The new company would have a number of Persian Directors on its board and would operate on behalf of the Persian National Oil Company. The distribution business in Persia would be transferred to an entirely Persian owned and operated company on favorable terms as regards the transfer of existing assets. The above is an outline only of a possible framework. We put it forward as a constructive effort to suggest a basis of discussion.

We have given the fullest consideration to the points made by His Excellency, the Minister of Finance, at our meeting on June 14th. If we were correct in understanding that His Excellency's suggestion was that as from March 20th the Company should hand to the Government the total proceeds (less expenses) from the sales of Persian oil, from which 25 percent would be deposited in a mutually agreed bank against any probable claims of the Company, we are unable to accept such a suggestion. The Delegation has come out for discussions and regard it as unjustifiable that the Persian Government should put forward a demand of this kind before discussions have even started. We are, moreover, certain that when in our future talks we have been able to explain to you in more detail the machinery of our business you will come to agree with us that such a demand would be neither commercially possible nor acceptable to any oil company.[46]

It is difficult to see any particular virtue in this proposal. Indeed, it seems to suggest only a change of form and not one of substance. The surrender of the distribution business in Iran is a very small concession, for the consumption of oil products within Iran is so small in relation to the total production of AIOC as to be of no importance to the company. In fact, it may well be that the special price discounts that the 1933 concession required AIOC to give Iranian purchasers[47] made the distribution business in Iran somewhat less than profitable.

It is difficult to see what real changes the proposal to vest the Iranian assets of AIOC in the "Persian National Oil Company" would entail, since the vesting was to be accompanied by a grant of the use of these assets to an AIOC subsidiary. To be satisfactory to AIOC, such a grant would have to be embodied in an arrangement which included a long-term contract. And that is precisely the effect of the 1933 concession. Article 20 of that agreement provides:

II. At the end of the Concession [1993] ... all the property of the Company in Persia shall become the property of the Government in proper working order and free of any expenses and any encumbrances.

III. The expression "all the property" comprises all the lands, buildings and workshops, constructions, wells, jetties, roads, pipe-lines, bridges, drainage and water-supply systems, engines, installations and equipment ... of any sort, all means of transport and communication in

68

Persia . . . , any stocks and any other object in Persia which the Company
is utilising in any manner whatsoever for the objects of the Concession.[48]

The only concrete advance (from the Iranian standpoint) over
the 1933 concession was the offer to have "a number of Persian
Directors" on the board of the new company to be formed by
AIOC. Yet the British would certainly never permit the Iranian
directors to have a majority, for if the British could be outvoted
the entire point of their proposal would be lost. But this issue, of
which the Iranians have made much, is really a minor one and
would quickly disappear if a solution for the basic problems
(see pp. 51 ff.) could be found.

However little substantive merit these proposals may have had
(and they had little), they at least had the virtue of providing
Iran with a steady income, and of the company's acceptance of
the "principle" of nationalization. These two things should have
provided a sufficient basis for the parties to continue their talks
and to attempt to find a really workable solution that would satisfy the material and spiritual needs of both. Instead, the Iranian
delegation, after less than half an hour's consideration,[49] rejected
the proposals on the ground that, as Prime Minister Mossadegh
reported to the Majlis, they were "quite inconsistent with the
laws of oil nationalization. Consequently the Iranian Government
stopped the negotiations and the British Delegation left Tehran
the following day.[50] Immediately the necessary instructions were
issued to take over the oil installations and were forthwith carried
out."[51] To the charge that the proposals were inconsistent with the
nationalization laws, Mr. Jackson replied that even if they were
inconsistent with the letter of the laws (which he did not admit),
they were consistent with the *principle* of nationalization, which
was all that was asked in Finance Minister Varasteh's aide-
memoire of May 30 (see p. 62), and were compatible with a
liberal interpretation of the laws. He added "that it was apparent
that the Persian representatives were expecting complete capitu-

lation to their demands without discussion, that he noted with regret the Persian decision to break off the talks and that he was left with no alternative than to communicate that decision to London and ask for instructions." Instructions were sent, and the Jackson mission left for London on June 22.

While discussing the Iranian rejection of the AIOC proposals before the House of Commons on June 20, Foreign Secretary Morrison assured the British in Iran that they would be protected,[53] and he added: ". . . we propose to follow up the application we have already made to the Hague Court by a further application for an indication of provisional measures to preserve the rights of the United Kingdom pending a decision of the merits of the case."[54] The International Court of Justice had announced on June 6 that it accepted lodgment of the United Kingdom's case, and on June 22 a "Request for the Indication of Interim Measures of Protection" was filed with the registrar of the Court.[55]

Before the British "case" for interim measures could be argued before the International Court a number of things happened in Iran that increased the tension and ill feeling between the parties. The "necessary instructions" for taking over the Iranian oil industry, which have been referred to above,[56] were issued in the form of decrees by the Iranian Council of Ministers on June 20, to the following effect:

a) No operational instructions issued by the Anglo-Iranian Oil Company Management should be valid unless counter-signed by the Temporary Board [of the National Iranian Oil Company (NIOC)].

b) Persian officials should take over the installations of the Kermanshah Petroleum Co., Ltd. [a subsidiary of AIOC] at Kermanshah and Naft-i-Shah in West Persia.

c) Persian officials were to assume the supervision of the Anglo-Iranian Oil Company's Tehran Office and its sales organization in Persia.

d) The Anglo-Iranian Oil Company Information Departments in Persia should be closed.

e) The name of the National Iranian Oil Company should take the place of the name of the Anglo-Iranian Oil Company on all Company signboards in Iran.

f) All Anglo-Iranian Oil Company revenues received from internal sales in Iran should be deposited in Government accounts.[57]

Pursuant to these instructions the Temporary Board addressed letters personally to Mr. Drake, general manager of the AIOC in Iran, advising him, *inter alia,*

a) To refrain from granting leave to members of his staff.

b) To inform all concerned that orders issued by the Anglo-Iranian Oil Company were not valid without counter-signature by the National Iranian Oil Company Managing Board.

c) To dissolve the Anglo-Iranian Oil Company Information Department at Abadan.

d) To delete the name "Anglo-Iranian Oil Company" on all installations in South Iran.

e) To hand over the proceeds of all sales of oil in Iran to the local Government office representing the Persian Ministry of Finance.[58]

On June 21, the day Mr. Drake received these letters, AIOC's nameboard was removed by the police from the company's general office at Khorramshahr. On the same day, a crowd forcibly entered the company's principal office and one suboffice in Tehran and demolished an electric sign and signboards bearing the company's name on the outside of the building. The police also closed a suboffice in Tehran that had been used for information purposes by the company and stopped all mail to and from that office. Throughout Iran the obliteration of the company's monogram on its road tankers and distribution installations seemed to be a favorite sport of the public.

On the same day (June 21), the Iranian government presented the Majlis with a "double urgency"[59] sabotage bill, the text of which is reported as follows:

For a year from the date of approval of this law, any persons engaging treacherously or with ill-intent in activities in connection with the operation of the Persian National Oil Industry, resulting in cutting oil pipelines or rendering unserviceable refineries or facilities for transport of oil, or causing fire in oil wells or oil storage tanks or causing destruction of railway lines, railway tunnels, railway bridges or rolling-stock, *shall be condemned to penalties ranging from temporary imprisonment with hard labour to execution.* These same penalties will be applied to instigators and accomplices as to those actually committing the crime. *These offences shall be dealt with by military courts.*[60]

The extreme character of such a law, as well as its ambiguity, needs no elaboration. The possibilities of its application were made strikingly apparent within a few days after its introduction to the Majlis.

In his argument of the British case before the ICJ on June 30, Sir Frank Soskice related the following events.[61] On the night of June 21 the AIOC printing works at Abadan were "forcibly seized" on behalf of the Temporary Board of NIOC. The printers were ordered[62] to print certain forms of receipts which acknowledged that oil received on board tankers was received from the NIOC and that the consignee was responsible for payment of the purchase price to NIOC. The Temporary Board then demanded that the masters of tankers in port sign receipts in this form, with the threat that port clearance would be refused if they failed to sign. The general manager of the AIOC refused to authorize the ships' masters to sign such receipts.[63] Within twenty-four hours the general manager and the board worked out a compromise whereby the masters signed the Iranian receipts, but with the endorsement that they reserved the rights of their principals. The endorsement also denied any admission of liability for the purchase price on the part of consignees.[64] In effect, the receipt was nothing more than a certification of the amount of oil shipped. This was not what the Temporary Board wanted, and, on June 23, it demanded a receipt in the following form.

National Iranian Oil Company Receipt for Shipments of Oil

I, the undersigned captain of s.s. .... have received at Abadan, as per bill of lading No. ......, ... tons of oil for the account of .... and delivery to .... at destination port ....

Signed ....

Master[65]

Mr. Drake, general manager of AIOC, authorized the signing of this receipt form, provided an endorsement were added stating that the signature was "without prejudice to the right of the Anglo-Iranian Oil Company." Such an endorsement was refused by the Temporary Board.

On the same day, June 23, the general manager received a number of letters from the Temporary Board, one of which asserted that he had not complied with the previous requirement (to which, it was alleged, he had agreed) to collect receipts from tankers carrying oil exports. The letter stated that the tankers' captains had refused to give the required receipt, or would do so only with such reservations that the receipt was rendered invalid. Finally, "it was claimed that *'this policy can mean nothing but ill-intentions and sabotage,'* and that if any delay occurred in export operations and if tankers refused to take delivery of oil, the General Manager would be held responsible."[66]

The other letters received by Mr. Drake gave instructions directing (*a*) that two Iranians be nominated to supervise AIOC's Information Department[67] on behalf of NIOC; (*b*) that certain railway tank cars of the Iranian State Railway, normally used at the discretion of AIOC for the transport of oil in Iran, be filled with oil immediately; and (*c*) that application for oil cargoes be made by all incoming tankers to the Temporary Board of NIOC and that the NIOC form of receipt be signed without endorsement for all oil exported. On the same day the AIOC sales

manager in Tehran was instructed to hand over 75 per cent of
net revenues received from oil sales in Iran. Similar instructions
were given the following day to distribution managers at Ahwaz,
Abadan, and Masjid-i-Sulaiman.[68]

On the twenty-fifth of June a letter was received by the general
manager, informing him that no checks could be issued by AIOC
unless countersigned by persons nominated by the Temporary
Board. Another letter, received on the same day, referred to a
previous inquiry whether Mr. Drake was willing to continue service as an employee of the Temporary Board and advised him that
if he did not reply by 8:00 A.M. on June 28 he would be regarded
as having resigned. In an interview with the Temporary Board
that day Mr. Drake requested that the board withdraw its letter
intimating a charge of "sabotage" in connection with his policy
on tanker receipts. His request was refused and, in view of the
provisions of the "sabotage bill" introduced to the Majlis on June
21, he left Iran for Basra on the advice of the British ambassador
and of AIOC headquarters in London.[69]

Meanwhile, the dispute over the form of receipts to be signed
by tankers' captains had prevented all sailings since June 22. On
June 26 AIOC ordered that all tankers in port pump their cargoes
ashore and leave Abadan immediately. On the same day the Iranian customs authorities prevented the pumping of further supplies of aviation gasoline to Basra through the company's pipe
line. Iranian soldiers were stationed on the jetty at Abadan and
reportedly interfered with the movement of material and employees of AIOC.

The British reaction to these developments was stern. In a statement to the House of Commons on June 26 Foreign Secretary
Morrison announced that preparations were being made for the
protection of British subjects in Iran should the Iranian government fail to discharge its legal responsibility for their protection.
As a part of these preparations, he announced, the cruiser
Mauritius "has been ordered to proceed forthwith to the vicinity

74

of Abadan." The foreign secretary commented on the recent developments as follows:

In connection with the accusation of sabotage which the Persians have seen fit to make against Mr. Drake, the Persian Government have been repeatedly warned of the danger of the risk of accidents involving danger to life and limb which may result from interference in the working of the complex machinery of the industry. If such accidents occur it is certain that they will in no way be due to the actions of the Company's personnel, who have proved themselves thoroughly competent and have in fact been instructed to refrain from any action liable to prejudice the working of the operations. *I must therefore categorically reject in advance any suggestion that such accidents which may occur could be caused by acts of sabotage on the part of the British staff.*[70]

If the Persian Government persist in these measures they would leave the Company no alternative but to bring operations at Abadan to a stop within a matter of days.[71] Storage capacity is strictly limited, and the refinery cannot operate unless tankers are available to take oil. Clearly a most serious and difficult situation may develop in Southern Persia, for which the Persian Government would be entirely responsible.

We are still, as always, ready to discuss a settlement of the question of the future operations of the Anglo-Iranian Oil Company with the Persian Government.[72] Such a settlement remains in our opinion the only means of ensuring the continued flow of Persian oil to its natural markets. It is a matter of deep regret that the Persian Government should appear to be taking steps which cannot but involve disastrous consequences for the future prosperity of their country.[73]

On the morning of June 28 several members of the Temporary Board entered the offices of the general manager of AIOC at Khorramshahr and informed the acting general manager that they were taking over the offices. He and his staff were obliged to leave the building. The following day, Iranian Foreign Minister Kazemi replied by telegraph to the ICJ's notification of the United Kingdom's request for interim measures, and the telegraphic message was immediately transmitted to the president of the Court by the Iranian legation at The Hague. This message,

after setting forth the grievances of the Iranian government, presenting various arguments against the Court's jurisdiction, and
contesting the validity of the 1933 concession, stated: "In view
of the foregoing considerations the Iranian Government hopes
that the Court will declare that *the case is not within its jurisdiction because of the legal incompetence of the complaint and because of the fact that the exercise of sovereignty is not subject to
complaint.* Under these circumstances the request for interim
measures of protection would naturally be rejected."[74] The Iranian government chose not to be represented[75] at the hearing held
by the Court on July 30, at which Sir Frank Soskice, Attorney-
General of the United Kingdom, presented the British case.

A brief backward glance at the first phase of the negotiations
shows that the respective actions of the United Kingdom and Iran
in this period reflected noticeably different attitudes toward legal
considerations and international law obligations. The United
Kingdom relied almost exclusively on legal arguments and international legal procedures—a fact that is perhaps related to its
confidence that a solution would be worked out through negotiations, and certainly related to the fact that law seldom justifies
a violent change from the status quo. Early in May the United
Kingdom indicated that if AIOC's request for arbitration were
refused it would consider the refusal a "denial of justice" and
would submit the dispute to the International Court of Justice.
It did so on May 26. When negotiations between Iran and representatives of AIOC were subsequently broken off and AIOC's
operations were shut down by Iranian interference, the United
Kingdom further applied to the ICJ for temporary measures of
protection, instead of interfering forcibly as many feared it
would—and as it probably would have done a century earlier.

The Iranian government, however, showed little or no respect
for its international law obligations beyond recognizing that
AIOC was entitled to some compensation for its expropriated
properties, but the amount of compensation was apparently to

be determined by the Iranian Parliament rather than by the standards of international law. Contrary to its contract with AIOC, the Iranian government denied that its actions were referable to arbitration, and denied that the United Kingdom could, through the exercise of diplomatic protection, be a party to the dispute. The Iranian government also asserted that the ICJ had no jurisdiction over the dispute. That government's refusal to appear before the Court to litigate the propriety of the British request for interim measures of protection, its refusal to agree to arbitration, its forcible obstruction of AIOC's operations, and its willingness to ignore the requirements of its own constitution with reference to the effective date of national statutes when its demands on AIOC were concerned, indicate that legal considerations were of secondary importance as compared with the Iranian government's urgent desire to accomplish the expulsion of AIOC and the acquisition of the control, management, and revenues of the oil industry. The Iranian government advanced its own view of the law to justify every position it adopted, yet its respect for international law and its willingness to operate only within the limits of that law would have been more impressive if it had used legal procedures rather than unilateral pronouncements to establish its position.

§ 6. The International Court of Justice: Interim Measures of Protection

The "Request for the Indication of Interim Measures of Protection" filed in the registry of the International Court of Justice on June 22, 1951 (see p. 69), invoked Article 41 of the Statute and Article 61 of the Rules of the Court, referred to the "Application" of May 26 (see p. 60), in which the government of the United Kingdom reserved the right to request that the Court indicate such provisional measures, and requested the Court to indicate, pending a final judgment on the merits of the case, that:

a) The Imperial Government of Iran should permit the Anglo-Iranian Oil Company (Limited), its servants and agents, to search for and extract petroleum and to transport, refine or treat in any other manner and render suitable for commerce and to sell or export the petroleum obtained by it, and generally, to continue to carry on the operations which it was carrying on prior to 1st May, 1951, free from interference calculated to impede or endanger the operations of the Company, by the Imperial Government of Iran, their servants or agents, or any Board, Commission, Committee, or other body nominated by them.

b) The Imperial Government of Iran should not by any executive or legislative act or judicial process hinder or prevent or attempt to hinder or prevent the Anglo-Iranian Oil Company (Limited), its servants or agents, in or from continuing to carry on its operations as aforesaid.

c) The Imperial Government of Iran should not by any executive or legislative act or judicial process sequester or seize or attempt to sequester or seize or otherwise interfere with any property of the Anglo-Iranian Oil Company (Limited), including (but without prejudice to a decision on the merits of the case) any property which the Imperial Government of Iran have already purported to nationalize or otherwise to expropriate.

d) The Imperial Government of Iran should not by any executive or legislative act or judicial process sequester or seize or attempt to sequester or seize any moneys earned by Anglo-Iranian Oil Company (Limited), or otherwise in the possession or power of the Anglo-Iranian Oil Company (Limited), including (but without prejudice to a decision on the merits of the case) any moneys which the Imperial Government of Iran have purported to nationalize or otherwise to expropriate or any moneys earned by means of property which they have purported so to nationalize or otherwise to expropriate.

e) The Imperial Government of Iran should not by any executive or legislative act or judicial process require or attempt to require the Anglo-Iranian Oil Company (Limited) to dispose of the moneys referred to in subparagraph (*d*) above otherwise than in accordance with the terms of the Convention of 1933 or of any measure to be indicated by the Court.

f) The Imperial Government of Iran should ensure that no other steps of any kind are taken capable of prejudicing the right of the Government of the United Kingdom to have a decision of the Court in its favor on the merits of the case executed, should the Court render such a decision.

g) The Imperial Government of Iran and the Government of the United Kingdom should ensure that no step of any kind is taken capable of aggravating or extending the dispute submitted to the Court, and in particular, the Imperial Government of Iran should abstain from all propaganda calculated to inflame opinion in Iran against the Anglo-Iranian Oil Company (Limited) and the United Kingdom.[1]

In support of the United Kingdom's case, the argument of Attorney-General Soskice dealt with the three basic questions that confront every application for the indication of interim measures: (1) whether the Court can properly indicate such measures without having previously determined that it has jurisdiction to try the case on its merits; (2) whether the request at hand can be properly granted in the light of the general principles governing the indication of interim measures of protection; and (3) whether, as a matter of fact, interim measures are necessary, that is, whether irreparable damage will result, or the position of either party be prejudiced, or the dispute extended, if such measures are not indicated before the Court makes a final judgment on the merits—or, in the language of the Statute of the Court (Article 41), whether "circumstances so require."

1) *Jurisdiction.*—The substantive question of jurisdiction is discussed more fully below (see § 10), but at least a brief description of the respective positions of the Iranian and United Kingdom governments should precede the discussion of the propriety of the Court's indicating interim measures without previously determining that it has jurisdiction to decide the case on its merits. The Iranian government based its objection to the jurisdiction of the Court on the "legal incompetence of the complaint" and on "the fact that the exercise of sovereignty is not subject to complaint."[2] Thus, the Iranian government claimed that the dispute was one within the exclusive domestic jurisdiction of Iran.[3] In its application of May 26[4] the United Kingdom maintained that the Iranian government had treated a British national, AIOC, in a manner inconsistent with the requirements

of international law (that is, it had refused the company's request for arbitration under Articles 22 and 26 of the 1933 concession, and had passed laws taking the company's property in an illegal manner) and had thereby committed a wrong against the United Kingdom government. To establish the jurisdiction of the Court the application relied on the declarations[5] by which the two governments had recognized the compulsory jurisdiction of the Permanent Court of International Justice.[6] In its declaration of September 19, 1932, Iran recognized the jurisdiction of the Court only in case of disputes "with regard to situations or facts relating directly or indirectly to the application of treaties or conventions accepted by Persia."[7] To bring its case within this requirement, the United Kingdom stated in its application that there were several treaties[8] between the United Kingdom and Iran obligating the latter to accord most-favored-nation treatment to British nationals in Iran, and that there were ten treaties that Iran had concluded with other states providing for the treatment of nationals in accordance with international law. On this basis, the United Kingdom concluded (1) that Iran was bound to accord British nationals treatment in accordance with international law, (2) that Iran's failure to do so was a breach of a specific treaty obligation accepted by her, and (3) that this breach of a treaty obligation to treat British nationals in accordance with international law obliged Iran to submit to the jurisdiction of the ICJ, successor to the PCIJ, in accordance with the provisions of her 1932 declaration accepting the jurisdiction of the Court in disputes relating to the application of treaties accepted by her.

In his argument that the Court should indicate interim measures without previously determining that it had jurisdiction to decide the case on its merits, Sir Frank Soskice contended that his claim was "amply supported by the practice of the Court and other international tribunals; by opinions of publicists; and by considerations of convenience and of common sense, and of the general principles of law."[9] In regard to the jurisprudence of the

Court, the attorney-general is supported by Professor Hudson's interpretation of that jurisprudence to the effect that jurisdiction to indicate provisional measures is not dependent upon a previous determination of the Court's jurisdiction to deal with the case on the merits.[10] To support his conclusion Professor Hudson cites the *Polish Agrarian Reform* case[11] and the case of the *Administration of the Prince von Pless*.[12] In the *Polish Agrarian Reform* case the Court dismissed the German request for the indication of interim measures on the ground that the requested measures would not "have the effect of protecting the rights forming the subject matter of the dispute submitted to the Court."[13] Its decision, however, was stated to have been reached "irrespective of the question whether it may be expedient for the Court in other cases to exercise its power to act *proprio motu*,[14] and without in any way pre-judging the question of its own jurisdiction to adjudicate upon the German Government's application instituting proceedings."[15] In an order in the *von Pless* case dated May 11, 1933, the Court refused the German request for interim measures after receiving the Polish government's assurance that it would revoke previous measures considered prejudicial by the German government and would refrain from taking any other such measures until a final decision of the Court were given. The Court declared that this order "must in no way prejudge either the question of the Court's jurisdiction to adjudicate upon the German Government's Application instituting proceedings of 18th May, 1932, or that of the admissibility of that Application."[16] This order was cited by the late Judge Hammarskjöld (then Registrar of the PCIJ) as an example of an order that, under the circumstances, was the equivalent of an indication of interim measures of protection prior to a determination of jurisdiction on the merits. He commented as follows: "L'exposé des motifs de l'ordonnance explique qu'en rendant celle-ci, 'la Cour entend ne préjuger en rien la question de sa propre compétence.' Elle a donc confirmé la doctrine selon laquelle elle peut, le cas échéant, indiquer des mesures conservatoires avant d'avoir constaté que le fond de l'affaire rentre dans sa juridiction . . ."[17] In the case of the *Denunciation of the Sino-Belgian Treaty*[18] the president of the Permanent Court of International Justice indicated, by an order dated January 8, 1927, certain provisional measures designed to maintain the status quo pending either a decision by the Court that it had no jurisdiction or a judgment on the merits.[19] In a second order in the same case it was made quite clear that the order for interim measures was made independently of the question whether the Court had jurisdiction to deal with the case on the merits.[20]

The jurisprudence of the International Court on this question is supported by that of various international arbitral tribunals.[21] In addition to Professor Hudson and Judge Hammarskjöld, other publicists support, without a known dissent, the position that the Court has the right to indicate interim measures of protection in a particular case without having previously determined its right to decide the case on its merits.[22] In addition, municipal systems of law generally grant their courts a similar right.[23] That the ICJ should have such a right is supported by the practical necessity of preserving the rights of both parties and preventing irreparable damage to the interests of one party by the unilateral actions of the other, pending a decision on the merits. If the Court did not have such a right the subject matter of the dispute might be completely destroyed or so irretrievably damaged that an ultimate judgment on the merits would be incapable of execution.

While judicial decisions and opinions of publicists are only a "subsidiary means for the determination of rules of law"[24] in the ICJ, yet when combined with an almost universal recognition of a right in muncipal systems of law they indicate one of the "general principles of law recognized by civilized nations"[25] and an "international custom."[26] "International custom" is one of the primary sources of law to which the Court is referred by its Statute.[27] That the Court has the right, in its discretion, and if "circumstances so require,"[28] to indicate interim measures without having previously determined its jurisdiction seems beyond question. The exercise of this right is completely within the discretion of the Court, which can thus prevent any attempt at abuse of its process. These conclusions are amply supported by the Court's order of July 5, 1951, indicating, pending its final decision in the proceedings initiated by the United Kingdom's application of May 26, 1951, and without determining its jurisdiction to decide the dispute on the merits, "certain provisional measures which will apply on the basis of reciprocal observance."[29] In the preamble to the order the Court stated that "it cannot be accepted *a priori* that a claim based on such a complaint [see above, pp. 60–61 and 77–78] falls completely outside the scope of international jurisdiction."[30] Therefore the Court felt empowered to entertain the request for interim measures, but also felt it necessary to state that "the indication of such measures in no way prejudges the question of the jurisdiction of the Court to deal with the merits of the case and leaves unaffected the right of the Respondent [Iran] to submit arguments against such jurisdiction."[31]

In their dissenting opinion, Judges Winiarski and Badawi Pasha argued that "if there is no jurisdiction as to the merits, there can be no jurisdiction to indicate interim measures of protection,"[32] and that before it can properly indicate such measures the Court "must consider its competence reasonably probable." They further argued that because Iran "[had] not accepted the jurisdiction of the Court in the present matter"[33] there existed sufficient doubt to cause the Court to decide, provisionally, whether its competence to decide the case on its merits was "reasonably probable." Their own conclusion was that the Court did not have a "reasonable probability" of such competence and therefore should not have indicated interim measures. For the reasons stated in the preceding pages, it appears that the dissenting opinion is not in accord with the generally accepted view of the law. The dissenters' test of "reasonable probability" was

something new that had not appeared before in the jurisprudence
of the International Court. Further, if the dissenting opinion
should prevail, the Court's power under Article 41 of the Statute
would be seriously limited, contrary to the intentions of its
framers,[34] and the Court would be greatly weakened in its exercise
of a function necessary to effective adjudication.[35]

2) *General principles.*—Having once determined that the
Court does have the right to indicate interim measures without
having previously determined that it is competent to decide the
case on its merits, the next inquiry must be directed to the principles on which the Court exercises this right. For these principles
it is necessary to look to the practice of the PCIJ, since the Statute
and Rules of Court say only that the Court may indicate interim
measures "to preserve the respective rights of either party."[36] The
PCIJ considered six cases bearing on this question, but the
factual situations in two of them[37] are so different from the Anglo-
Iranian dispute that they are not strictly in point. The other four
cases illustrate several guiding principles that have been utilized
by the Court in the exercise of its right to indicate imterim
measures. In the case of the *Factory at Chorzów (Indemnities),*[38]
after the PCIJ had given a judgment dismissing Poland's preliminary objection that the Court had no jurisdiction, the German
government filed a request for interim measures. It stated that
unless payment of compensation were immediately made, irreparable damage would result, and it was therefore requested that
the Court "indicate to the respondent Government the sum to be
paid immediately, as a provisional measure and pending final
judgment . . ."[39] The Court refused the German request, on the
ground that it could not be "regarded as relating to the indication of interim measures of protection, but as designed to obtain
an interim judgment in favour of a part of the relief formulated
in the Application."[40] Thus, although a plaintiff may obtain an
interim judgment under many systems of municipal law,[41] the
PCIJ interpreted the phrase "measures which ought to be taken

to preserve the respective rights of either party" as not including the interim judgment known in the municipal systems of many civil law countries.

In the *Polish Agrarian Reform* case[42] the German government filed a request for interim measures in which it asked the Court to declare that Poland had already violated the minorities treaty, requested reparation therefor, and asked the Court to prevent the application of the Polish agrarian reform law in *all future cases* involving Polish nationals of German race. The request was refused, on the ground that it was not in conformity with Article 41 of the Statute. In its order of July 29, 1933, the Court said that "the essential condition which must necessarily be fulfilled in order to justify a request for interim measures, should circumstances require them, is that such measures should have the effect of protecting the rights forming the subject matter of the dispute submitted to the Court."[43] The Court construed the German request as asking for the indication of measures of broader scope than those necessary for the protection of the rights forming the subject matter of the dispute, and said, "the interim measures asked for . . . cannot therefore be regarded as solely designed to protect the subject of the dispute and the actual object of the principal claim, as submitted to the Court by the Application instituting proceedings."[44] That is, the Court interpreted the application as relating only to past acts, but interpreted the request for interim measures as relating to both past and future acts. The Court thus established the principle that the request for interim measures must be confined to the protection of rights asserted in the application instituting proceedings.

In the case of the *Denunciation of the Sino-Belgian Treaty*[45] the president of the PCIJ issued an order indicating provisionally certain measures to preserve the rights of Belgium and Belgian nationals in China that might be prejudiced by certain actions of the Chinese government.[46] The basis for the order was that, in the event of an infraction of these Belgian rights, "such infraction could not be made good simply by the payment of an indemnity or by compensation or restitution in some other material form."[47] A somewhat contrary view was expressed in the case of the *Electricity Company of Sofia and Bulgaria*,[48] in which the dispute concerned the rates to be charged by the company, a Belgian national. The municipality of Sofia alleged that a sum was due it from the company and threatened to institute legal proceedings in the Bulgarian courts to collect the alleged debt. After such proceedings were instituted in August, 1939, the Belgian agent filed with the PCIJ a request for interim measures on the ground that compulsory collection of the alleged debt would "seriously prejudice" the company's position and impede the restoration of its rights if the Court ultimately upheld the Belgian government's claim.[49] Thus, interim measures were requested solely to prevent the collection of a sum of money, and the request was granted by the order of December 5, 1939, in which the Court provided that "Bulgaria should ensure that no step of any kind is taken capable of prejudicing the rights claimed by the Belgian Government or of aggravating or extending the dispute submitted to the Court."[50]

Before the International Court of Justice issued its order of July 5, 1951, in the Anglo-Iranian dispute, these were the only two cases in which the International Court had indicated interim measures of protection. It was thus an open question whether such measures would be indicated only if they were necessary to prevent irreparable damage for which compensation by monetary payment would be inadequate. In its order of July 5, 1951, the ICJ made no reference to irreparable damage, although the probability that such damage would result from the enforcement of the Iranian nationalization laws had been alleged by the United Kingdom in paragraph 8 of its request for interim measures. Instead, as in the *Electricity Company* case, the Court merely indicated that both parties should ensure that no action be taken that might prejudice the rights of either party, or that might aggravate or extend the dispute, pending a final decision by the Court. The two cases are distinguishable, however, in that the *Electricity Company* case involved only a sum of money, whereas the expulsion of AIOC from Iran would have consequences for which money damages could not adequately and satisfactorily compensate.[51] Thus, the problem has yet to be resolved with finality in the jurisprudence of the Court.

When the United Kingdom request for interim measures (pp. 77–78) is considered in the light of these principles, it is clear, first, that the request did not ask for an interim judgment. Instead, the requested measures were intended to preserve the status quo, to keep AIOC operating "normally" pending a final decision by the Court. Further, the request was within the scope of the principal case, and it did confine itself to requesting protection for rights claimed in the application of May 26, 1951, instituting proceedings (see p. 60). The application asked the Court either to declare that Iran was under a duty to submit the dispute to arbitration, as provided in the 1933 concession or, alternatively, to declare that the concession could not be annulled or its terms changed, except by agreement between Iran and the company, and hence that, by refusing to arbitrate, Iran had committed a denial of justice. Thus, the application asked the Court to declare the legal validity of the 1933 concession, and the request for interim measures merely asked the Court to preserve the rights that the Company held under that concession.

3) *Factual necessity for interim protection.*—As stated above (p. 85), the United Kingdom did allege and did try to prove that enforcement of the Iranian nationalization laws would result in irreparable damage that could not "possibly be compensated by any money payment, or by any money payment which it would be within the capacity of the Iranian Government to pay."[52] On this point Sir Frank Soskice presented the following arguments: (1) If AIOC's integrated organization of skilled personnel were disrupted by the expulsion of the British technicians, either the entire industry in Iran would come to a standstill (as it did), or

its continued operation would necessarily have to be conducted under such conditions as would lead to irreparable damage to plant and machinery, as well as possible damage to the population from inexpert handling of the machinery used to control the dangerous gases released in the refining process. (2) Large numbers of Iranians (approximately 70,000) who were dependent upon AIOC for employment would be thrown out of work, and would, in addition, suffer from the stoppage of the services and supplies—domestic fuel, electricity, fresh water, and refrigeration for food preservation—that are dependent upon the continued production of petroleum and its products. (3) The disruption of the continuity in the supply of oil would be severely detrimental to the maintenance of AIOC's world-wide marketing organization and would seriously damage its good will in the markets. (4) The expulsion of AIOC from Iran would irreparably damage the company's immense undertaking and investment outside Iran in tankers, refineries, and marketing equipment and organization, all of which are based primarily upon the production of Iranian crude oil.

The Court apparently found these arguments persuasive, for, in its order of July 5, 1951, indicating interim measures of protection, it stated that it "must be concerned to preserve by such measures the rights which may be subsequently adjudged by the Court to belong either to the [United Kingdom] or [Iran]." It "indicated," pending its final decision on the merits, certain "provisional measures" that were to apply "on the basis of reciprocal observance." These were:

1. That the Iranian Government and the United Kingdom Government should each ensure that no action is taken which might prejudice the rights of the other Party in respect of the carrying out of any decision on the merits which the Court may subsequently render;

2. That the Iranian Government and the United Kingdom Government should each ensure that no action of any kind is taken which might aggravate or extend the dispute submitted to the Court;

3. That the Iranian Government and the United Kingdom Government should each ensure that no measure of any kind should be taken designed to hinder the carrying on of the industrial and commercial operations of the Anglo-Iranian Oil Company, Limited, as they were carried on prior to 1st May, 1951;

4. That the Company's operations in Iran should continue under the direction of its management as it was constituted prior to 1st May, 1951, subject to such modifications as may be brought about by agreement with the Board of Supervision referred to in paragraph 5;

5. That, in order to ensure the full effect of the preceding provisions, which in any case retain their own authority, there should be established by agreement between the Iranian Government and the United Kingdom Government a Board to be known as the Board of Supervision composed of two Members appointed by each of the said Governments and a fifth Member, who should be a national of third State and should be chosen by agreement between these Governments, or, in default of such agreement, and upon the joint request of the Parties, by the President of the Court.

The Board will have the duty of ensuring that the Company's operations are carried on in accordance with the provisions above set forth. It will, *inter alia*, have the duty of auditing the revenue and expenses and of ensuring that all revenue in excess of the sums required to be paid in the course of the normal carrying on of the operations and other normal expenses incurred by the Anglo-Iranian Oil Company, Limited, are paid into accounts at banks to be selected by the Board on the undertaking of such banks not to dispose of such funds except in accordance with the decisions of the Court or the agreement of the Parties.[53]

On July 6, 1951, the day following the issuance of this order, Foreign Secretary Morrison stated in a note to the Iranian government that the United Kingdom accepted in full the Court's decision, on the assumption that the Iranian government would similarly accept the decision in full. He added that the United Kingdom government would shortly announce its nominations to the Board of Supervision and would be happy to consult with Iran on the choice of the fifth member.[54] On July 9 the Iranian government addressed a telegram to the secretary general of the United

Nations, giving notice of that government's abrogation of its declaration of September 19, 1932,[55] recognizing the compulsory jurisdiction of the Court. This telegram was confirmed by an undated letter addressed to the secretary general and received by him on July 16.[56] The declaration had, by its terms, bound Iran to recognize the compulsory jurisdiction of the Court for a period of six years and thereafter until notice was given of its abrogation. Since the six-year period had long since elapsed, the notice given on July 9, 1951, was an effective abrogation. It could not, however, have any effect on the jurisdiction that the ICJ might have in the pending Anglo-Iranian case, because that case concerned a dispute that had arisen and been submitted to the Court before the abrogation.

The Iranian letter received by the secretary general on July 16 made a number of contentions[57] and indicated that the Iranian government regarded the ICJ's order as unenforceable, and that it would not carry out the provisional measures "indicated" by the Court. It is unfortunate that the contentions made by the Iranian government in this letter are primarily of a political rather than a legal nature, because they attempt to refute the legality of the ICJ's order by nonlegal arguments. Nevertheless the letter does suggest an important question concerning the legal obligations that flow from orders of the Court, like that of July 5, indicating interim measures of protection. The letter again[58] advanced the Iranian contention that the ICJ acted without jurisdiction, contrary to the provisions of the Statute of the Court, and in violation of the United Nations Charter.[59] The question of the Court's jurisdiction has been discussed above (see pp. 78 ff.) and is discussed in detail below (see § 10). If the conclusion is accepted that the Court may indicate interim measures without having previously determined that it had jurisdiction to decide the dispute on its merits, it follows that the Court did not have before it on July 5, 1951, any question relating to its jurisdiction. The only way the question of jurisdiction could have been raised

90

at that time was by preliminary objection,[60] and the Iranian communication of June 29 (quoted above, p. 75) did not constitute such a preliminary objection.[61] The Iranian government would have been well-advised to have filed a preliminary objection soon after it first indicated, on May 28, in commenting on the United Kingdom's application to Court of May 26, that it did not recognize the competence of the Court to render a decision on the merits of the dispute.[62] In the absence of such a preliminary objection, the Court, having satisfied itself (which it did) that the United Kingdom had presented a prima facie case, could issue the order of July 5 without in any way violating the provisions of its Statute and Rules of Court or the provisions of the United Nations Charter.

Did the Court's *indication* of interim measures create a legal obligation binding the parties before it to carry out the measures indicated?[63] This is a question of great importance for the Court as an effective institution in international affairs, as well as for the settlement of the particular dispute between Iran and the United Kingdom. This question has not been answered in the decisions of the Court, and the few publicists who have expressed an opinion on the point are divided. The "Committee of Jurists," appointed in 1920 by the Council of the League of Nations to draft the Statute of the PCIJ, borrowed the term "indicate" from the so-called "Bryan-Treaties"[64] because it possessed "a diplomatic flavor, being designed to avoid offense to 'the susceptibilities of States.' "[65] In a treatise published in 1934,[66] Professor Manley O. Hudson expressed doubt that an indication of interim measures imposed any obligation on the parties before the Court to carry out the measures indicated. Professor Hudson's doubts disappeared, however, before the publication of his more complete treatise on the International Court in 1943. As he explained in an article published in 1952: "Later, however, after a re-study of the question and in the light of the accumulating jurisprudence, the writer reached the conclusion that the term *indicate* was 'not less definite than the term *order* would have been, and it would seem to have as much effect.' The Court's own jurisprudence can hardly be said to have resolved this point with finality."[67] In his later (1943) treatise on the PCIJ, Hudson argued that if a state has joined with other states in maintaining the Court (by being a signatory to the Statute), or has accepted the general offices of the Court, or has made a declaration in conformity with Article 36 of the Statute, it admits the powers that are included in the judicial process entrusted to the Court.[68] In his opinion, it follows, when such a state is a party before the Court, that the Court's indication of interim measures creates a binding obligation for that state to carry out the measures indicated. Professor Hudson also thinks that "an indication of interim measures" is the equivalent of a judgment, and should be considered as having the same force and effect.[69]

Judge Hammarskjöld reached a different conclusion. He reasoned that because the Court could indicate interim measures without having previously determined that it had jurisdiction to deal with the case on its merits it necessarily followed that the measures indicated did not have an "obligatory character."[70]

Professor Schwarzenberger, after noting that interim measures are always expressed in an "order" as distinguished from a "judgment," states that the "essential difference between orders and judgments of the Court consists in the fact that . . . the former have neither the binding force nor the final effect of a judgment,"[71] citing a dictum of the PCIJ in an order in the *Free Zones* case to the same effect.[72] Although both the Statute and the Rules of Court include detailed provisions on the interpretation, form, legal effects, and revision of judgments,[73] and, to a lesser extent, of advisory opinions,[74] neither document includes any such provisions explaining the nature and effect of "orders." Neither Article 41 of the Statute of the ICJ nor Article 61 of its Rules of Court, both of which relate to interim measures, gives any hint of the form in which interim measures are to be indicated. However, as a matter of practice, the PCIJ always embodied an indication of interim measures in an "order," and this procedure was followed by the ICJ in the Anglo-Iranian case. Unfortunately, there are no pronouncements of the International Court (apart from the PCIJ's dictum in the *Free Zones* case) to resolve this question of the binding force of an order indicating interim measures. This uncertainty is, of course, a reflection of the fact that a request for interim measures of protection is an unusual procedure in the conduct of a case that has been submitted to the Court.[75] The lack of precedents in the jurisprudence of the PCIJ may, however, be a blessing in disguise, since the obligations of member states under the United Nations Charter are very different from those under the League of Nations Covenant.

By paragraph 1 of Article 94 of the Charter each member of the United Nations "undertakes to comply with the *decision* of the International Court of Justice in any case to which it is a party."[76] (Italics added.) Paragraph 2 of Article 94 provides that in the event that a party does not comply with a *"judgment* of the Court," the other party may have recourse to the Security Council, "which may, if it deems necessary, make recommendations or decide upon measures to be taken to give effect to the *judgment."* (Italics added.) It follows from paragraph 1 of Article 94 that a "decision" of the Court gives rise to obligations under the Charter which may be enforced by the Security Council in accordance with paragraph 2 of that article.[77] Thus the question of the binding force of an indication of interim measures depends upon whether it can be considered either a "decision" or a "judgment" within the meaning of Article 94 of the Charter. It can be argued that the requirement in Article 41, paragraph 2, of the Statute that the Court give notice to the Security Council of an indication of interim measures, implies that the Security Council has the power to "make recommendations or decide upon measures to be taken to give effect" to the interim measures indicated. If this implication is valid, it makes little difference whether the Court embodies its "indication of interim measures" in an "order" or in a "judgment" so long as the terms are considered synonymous with each other and with the term "decision." In fact, the practice of the PCIJ of using the term "order" has only confused the issue, since that practice originated long before the adoption of the United Nations Charter, Article 94 of which was drafted without any apparent thought on the problem of effectiveness created by the practice of indicating interim measures of protection in "orders" of the Court.

In regard to the implication drawn above from the provision of Article 41, paragraph 2, of the Statute, it can be observed that the basic purpose of interim measures—as Article 41 clearly indicates—is to preserve the respective rights of the parties pending the final decision of the Court. Differently stated, the purpose is to preserve the status quo in order that the final decision of the Court be not rendered incapable of execution by some act of one of the parties while the case is still *sub judice*. It is commonly accepted that a final judgment (decision) of the Court is binding on the parties and enforceable by the Security Council,[78] but a provision that the final decision (judgment) is binding becomes pointless if that decision can be negated by the actions of one party in advance of judgment. It is to prevent such an impasse that the Court is given the power to indicate interim measures "if circumstances so require," since, presumably, "circumstances" could never so require if the final judgment would be of no effect. It follows, therefore, from the binding force of final judgments, that interim measures intended to ensure the potency of those judgments are equally binding. To reach the opposite conclusion would be to limit seriously the effectiveness of the Court in its discharge of the judicial powers entrusted to it. Before the adoption of the United Nations Charter and the Statute of the ICJ, the effectiveness of the decisions of the PCIJ, whose Statute gave it the same power to indicate interim measures as the Statute of the ICJ, depended solely on the "full good faith" of the parties.[79] It was to enhance the effectiveness of the Court's decisions that Article 94 was included in the United Nations Charter.

This conclusion, that an indication of interim measures of protection creates a legally binding obligation on the parties before the Court, is supported by the rationale implicit in the ICJ's order of July 5, 1951. Apparently even dissenting Judges Winiarski and Badawi Pasha assumed that an indication of interim measures was enforceable. They argued that the Court ought not to indicate interim measures unless its competence was "reasonably probable," because interim measures are so exceptional in character that they "may easily be considered a scarcely tolerable interference in the affairs of a sovereign state."[80] An order that imposed no legal obligation could in no way interfere in the affairs of a sovereign state. Similarly, the assumption that an indication of interim measures created a legally binding obligation appears in the preamble to the Court's order. After stating that the indication of interim measures in no way prejudges the question of the jurisdiction of the Court to deal with the merits of the case, and noting the power given the Court by Article 41 of the Statute, the Court continued by saying, "it follows that the Court must be concerned to preserve by such measures the rights which may be subsequently adjudged by the Court to belong either to the Applicant or to the Respondent."[81] For these reasons, after finding that the existing state of affairs justified interim measures, the Court ordered the provisional measures which have been described above. If the Court thought that it "must be concerned to preserve the rights" of the parties pending final judgment, and issued an order indicating interim measures for this purpose, it must be concluded that the Court assumed that its order would be enforceable. It cannot be concluded that the Court believed that it was discharging its duty to preserve the rights of the parties by issuing an unenforceable order.

Although the Court's attitude seems reasonably clear, it is to be regretted that the Security Council did not act on the suggestion[82] that it request an advisory opinion from the Court on the question of the enforceability of an "order" indicating interim measures. Such an opinion would be welcome, for it is a point that has never been squarely ruled upon, and it is a question of importance for the future of the Court.

§ 7. The Negotiations, Second Phase

While the British request for interim measures was under consideration by the Court, events were occurring in Iran and elsewhere that ultimately led to the second attempt at negotiation. The stoppage of oil shipments during June (see p. 73) caused the AIOC to cut back production by approximately 45 per cent on July 1, and the output of the Abadan refinery was thereby reduced from 15 million to 8.3 million gallons per day. It was estimated that there was sufficient storage space to keep the refinery running at this reduced rate for about twenty days. Also on the first of July, the police searched the house of Mr. Seddon, AIOC representative in Tehran, and impounded all papers and documents found there. The Iranian government alleged that these documents, some of which were distributed to the press, proved that AIOC had engaged in illegal activities, including the corruption of members of the Majlis. The following day, the minister of justice announced that the state prosecutor and certain other officials would immediately begin an examination of all the documents seized from Seddon.[1]

The Iranian Embassy in London issued a statement to the press on July 2 protesting the presence of a British warship (see p. 73) off Iranian shores. Unconfirmed reports of the same date stated that additional British naval units, including an aircraft carrier, three destroyers, and several troopships, were present in the Kuwait area of the Persian Gulf.[2] The statement from the Iranian Embassy also announced that Iran had protested to Iraq "the presence of British forces in the vicinity of the frontiers of Iran and the presence of the British cruiser in Iraq waters off [the mouth of the] Shatt-al-Arab [River]," and had "demanded that the Iraq Government take necessary steps to remove this threat."³

The British staff of AIOC had notified the Temporary Board on July 2 of their refusal of an offer to work for the NIOC on an individual-contract basis. On July 4 officials of AIOC met with representatives of the Temporary Board to discuss plans for a possible shutdown of the oil industry and to consider recent Iranian action against company officials. On the same day Gach Seran, one of the principal producing areas, was shut down as a result of the cutback in refinery operations at Abadan. Refinery production was cut back another million gallons per day on July 7. Six of the ten distilling units were shut down as a result of the cutbacks. Three days later all but one of the distillation units were shut off and production was reduced to 3 million gallons per day, most of which could be used in company power plants and for distribution in Iran. AIOC officials also notified the Temporary Board, on July 7, that all members of the British staff at Gach Seran would be withdrawn, and, on July 11, the board announced that it had agreed to take over the maintenance of the Gach Seran installation. On that day the last of the British staff departed for company headquarters at Khorramshahr. Meanwhile, although no official policy had been announced regarding evacuation of British nationals from Iran, reports of a gradual evacuation persisted. These rumors ended after the ruling of the ICJ (July 5), when the company announced on July 10 that it would keep its technicians in Iran as long as possible, even if the refinery were completely shut down.⁴

On July 7 Foreign Secretary Morrison stated that the United Kingdom government would soon announce the appointment of two members to the Board of Supervisors provided for in the ICJ's order (see p. 88). On the same day, the state prosecutor in Tehran issued an indictment charging Mr. Seddon with "illegal activities," including the destruction of documents wanted by the Iranian government. Prime Minister Mossadegh transmitted this information to the Majlis several days later, and that body approved the establishment of a parliamentary committee to coöperate with the state prosecutor in examining the seized documents. Later in the month, Mr. Seddon's residence permit was revoked (on the nineteenth) and then returned (on the twenty-second), both actions being taken without any explanation.⁵ No further record is available concerning the disposition of the indictment against Seddon, and, presumably, he was evacuated with other British staff members on or before October 3.

President Truman, on July 9, replied to Prime Minister Mossadegh's letter of June 28, saying that he believed that the "complexity of the problems involved . . . require[d] a simple and practicable *modus vivendi* under which operations [could] continue" without prejudice to the interests of either party. He noted that the ICJ had suggested such a *modus vivendi* and declared: "Therefore, I earnestly commend to you a most careful consideration of its suggestion. I suggest that its utterance be thought of not as a decision which is or is not binding depending on technical legal considerations, but as a suggestion of an impartial body, dedicated to justice and equity and to a peaceful world based upon these great conceptions." President Truman then offered to send Averell Harriman, his foreign policy adviser, to Tehran to discuss "this immediate and pressing situation."⁶ Prime Minister Mossadegh, in a note approved by the Joint Parliamentary Oil Committee and by the cabinet, informed President Truman on July 11 that "the Iranian Government welcomes this gesture and hopes to take full advantage of consultations with a man of such high standing." Mossadegh also stated that the Iranian government stood ready to enter into discussions aimed at settling the oil dispute and avoiding stoppages in production, "provided, of course, that our indisputable national rights are respected in accordance with the laws concerning the nationalization of the oil industry . . ."⁷ The British reaction was at first critical, Ambassador Shepherd in Tehran saying that there was "not much point" in Harriman's going to Tehran, since the Iranian government had indicated that it did not recognize as enforceable the ICJ's interim order of July 5.[8] Ambassador Shepherd withdrew these remarks the following day, July 13, because they had given rise to misunderstanding," and said that the British government "appreciate fully President Truman's sincerity in seeking for a constructive approach, and welcome the interest the United States Government is taking in this problem."[9] The British Foreign Office in London announced in a statement to the press that there had been no suggestion that Harriman act as a negotiator or mediator in the dispute, and emphasized that the United Kingdom would maintain its position that the ICJ's interim order should be accepted as the first step toward a solution.[10] Certainly, the wording of President Truman's letter was ill-advised. He probably hoped that the words used would make acceptance of the order of July 5 easier for Iran, since nations which are concerned about their sovereign rights are unusually sensitive to "orders." But if the president of the United States considered the Court's order only a "suggestion," then it is not difficult to see why the Iranian government felt justified in ignoring it completely. The British reliance on legal procedures was apparently a wrong tack, and the optimism revealed by the British in announcing on July 10 the indefinite retention of AIOC technicians in Iran was clearly unwarranted.

Meanwhile, in Tehran, Mossadegh had asked the Parliament to authorize a public bond issue of 2 billion rials ($62.7 million) and to approve acceptance of a $25 million loan from the United States Export-Import Bank.[11] On July 16 the Finance Committee of the Majlis approved the 2 billion rial public bond issue, but postponed action on the Export-Import Bank loan. The Majlis indicated its approval of acceptance of that loan on August 9. To further ease the financial strain caused by the cessation of oil royalties, the Majlis passed a bill on July 29 authorizing the government to withdraw £14 million from its sterling balances in

London and use the money to relieve the shortage of foreign exchange by financing essential imports. The sterling balance of the Iranian government, to which the Bank of England accorded special privileges, had partially backed the Iranian currency issue.

Officials of the NIOC announced on July 14 that the Temporary Board's offer of June 13 to give established customers of AIOC priority on oil purchases from the NIOC had not been accepted by anyone, and that the NIOC therefore withdrew the offer and renounced any further obligation to such customers. The announcement continued with an open invitation to anyone to make cash purchases of Iranian oil at the Abadan docks (that is, the purchaser must supply his own tankers).

Harriman's arrival in Tehran on July 15 was the occasion for anti-British and anti-American demonstrations by the Tudeh party. Supporters of the National Front party made an unsuccessful attack on a Tudeh parade before the Parliament buildings. The Tehran police and Iranian army intervened, and before order could be restored twenty persons had been killed and approximately three hundred badly wounded. The riots provoked a government proclamation of martial law in Tehran on the following day. The police began a general arrest of the Communist demonstrators and confiscated the Communist presses. Martial law in Tehran continued until July 22, and on the day of its termination Mossadegh announced that a court-martial of the prefect of police had been ordered for his failure to control the demonstrations of July 15, and for allowing the police to fire on the demonstrators.

On his arrival in Tehran Harriman told press representatives that he had no special formula for solving the oil dispute and that he was not a mediator, but that he believed that a solution might be found through friendly negotiation. In his talks with Iranian officials, begun on July 16, he discussed the difficulties which the Iranian oil industry would face in regaining its markets if they were once lost to other sources. He also informed the Iranian officials that the United States was willing to aid Iran under the Point Four program of technical assistance, and that this assistance would not depend on a settlement of the oil dispute. It was reported that in the ensuing discussions with the Joint Parliamentary Oil Committee Harriman and his assistant, oil expert Walter J. Levy, emphasized the extreme difficulties in refining and marketing oil with which Iran would have to contend if it failed to reach an agreement with the British that would in some way make use of AIOC's technical knowledge to run the Abadan refinery, and of the AIOC's marketing organization to sell and distribute the oil and oil products. On July 21, after a series of conferences with various Iranian officials, Harriman reported to the press that the talks were proceeding "in a most cordial and friendly atmosphere" and that they had resulted in a "better mutual understanding of the basic problems which must be resolved."[12] On the same day an Iranian government spokesman said: "We are optimistic regarding the reopening of negotiations with the British, but our stand remains unchanged since the visit of the Anglo-Iranian Oil Company's delegation in June."[13]

Harriman conferred again in a session with both the Joint Parliamentary Oil Committee and the cabinet on July 23, at which time, Prime Minister Mossadegh reported, a definite formula "was drawn up and sanctioned and was submitted to Mr. Harriman as the final view of the Iranian Government." Mossadegh stated this formula in the following terms in a report to the Majlis on August 5, 1951:

1. In case the British Government on behalf of the former Anglo-Iranian Oil Company recognized the principle of nationalization of the oil industry in Iran, the Iranian Government would be prepared to enter into negotiations with representatives of the British Government on behalf of the former Company.

2. Before sending representatives to Tehran the British Government should make a formal statement of its consent to the principle of nationalization of the oil industry on behalf of the former Company.

3. By the principle of nationalization of the oil industry is meant the proposal which was approved by the Special Oil Committee of the Majlis and was confirmed by the law of Esfand 29, 1329 (March 20, 1951), the text of which proposal is quoted hereunder: . . . [The quotation omitted here is the "Single Article Law" reproduced below in Appendix IV.] In this connection for Mr. Harriman's further information a copy of the note which the representatives of the former oil company submitted to the Iranian Government on their method of accepting the principle of the nationalization of the oil industry, which [note] was not accepted is being enclosed herewith.[14]

4. The Iranian Government is prepared to negotiate the manner in which the law will be carried out in so far as it affects British interests.[15]

This "formula" was communicated to the British government by Harriman on July 24.[16] After considering the Iranian proposals in a special session, the British cabinet said that they did not appear "wholly unfavourable" but that in some respects the Iranian attitude was not entirely clear and that additional information had therefore been requested. In a statement in the House of Commons on July 25, Foreign Secretary Morrison touched on one point that almost prevented the reopening of negotiations. He said that in considering the British government's attitude toward further negotiations, the cabinet had particularly in mind "the situation as regards the Company's operations and the extent to which the Persian Government are prepared to put an end to the provocation and interference to which the Company's management and staff are being subjected."[17] On July 25 British Ambassador Shepherd conferred with Iranian Foreign Minister Kazemi in an effort to clarify certain points. A press statement from the British Embassy on the same day indicated that the United Kingdom wanted to be assured that the Iranian proposals required it to accept only the principle of nationalization as expressed in the Single Article Law of March 20, 1951, and not the specific provisions of the Law Regulating Nationalization of April 30.[18] The British also wished to ascertain whether the fact

that the Iranian government had indicated a willingness to negotiate with the British government, rather than to insist, as it had
consistently done in the past, that the issue was entirely between
itself and the AIOC, meant a change of position and attitude.
Ambassador Shepherd's efforts to clarify these points were apparently unsuccessful, and on July 27 the ambassador, Averell
Harriman, and Walter Levy flew to London to consult with the
British government on the Iranian proposals.

After the conferences in London, Harriman forwarded a note
dated July 29, 1951, from the British government to the Iranian
government which said, in part:

His Majesty's Government are desirous of availing themselves of this
invitation [to reopen negotiations] but it will be appreciated by the
Iranian Government that the negotiations, which his Majesty's Government for their part will enter into with the utmost goodwill, can be conducted in a satisfactory manner *only if the present tension which exists
in the South is relieved.* On the assurance that the Iranian Government
recognizes this fact and will enter into discussions in the same spirit, a
mission headed by a cabinet minister will immediately set out.

His Majesty's Government recognize on their own behalf, and on that
of the Company, the principle of the nationalization of the oil industry
in Iran.[19]

On the afternoon of the day on which the British note was sent
from London, Henry Grady, American Ambassador in Tehran,
suggested to Prime Minister Mossadegh that the Iranian reply
to the British note express willingness to enter into negotiation
in a spirit of good will and include a statement to the effect that
the "Iranian Government recognize[d] the desirability of easing
tension in the South . . . in the interest of the success of the negotiations."[20] Mossadegh declined this suggestion, on the ground
that the action of the Iranian government in taking over some of
the company's installations might be construed as having caused
the so-called tension and that the Iranian government would then

be under obligation to undo what it had already done. In a note prepared and dispatched that same evening (July 29) to Harriman, to be forwarded to the British government, the Iranian prime minister expressed his pleasure at being informed that the British government had recognized the principle of nationalization, and asked that the recognition be made public, and that the British government send a mission to Tehran "on behalf of the former oil company" to negotiate with the Iranian government. He said, however, that "the Iranian Government believes that no tension exists in Khuzistan" (an oil province in the south of Iran, in the AIOC concession area).²¹ On the following day (July 30), Prime Minister Mossadegh received a letter from Ambassador Grady informing him that Harriman did not wish to deliver his note of the previous day, and that Harriman considered that the language used "would not encourage the re-opening of negotiations," but felt certain a British government mission would be dispatched immediately if the Iranian note were "couched in more favorable language."²² Mossadegh replied asking Ambassador Grady to inquire of Harriman what part of his note had created the difficulty. Harriman returned to Tehran on July 31 and, presumably, made the required explanation to the prime minister. On his arrival, Harriman described the situation as "encouraging," but said that there were still several problems which he hoped to clear up in discussion with Iranian officials.²³

On July 31, a British destroyer joined the cruiser *Euryalus* in the Shatt-al-Arab River, and three more destroyers sailed up the river to Basra. Several days later an Iranian protest was filed with the British vice-consul at Abadan that Royal Air Force aircraft had violated Iranian territory while flying cover over the destroyers proceeding up the Shatt-al-Arab. On the same day, production was completely shut down at Abadan, where storage facilities had been filled to maximum capacity.²⁴ Meanwhile, in the United States, the leading oil companies had voluntarily given their support to the establishment of a Foreign Petroleum

Supply Committee under the authority of the Defense Production Act, for the purpose of studying ways of easing the expected world shortage caused by the shutdown of Abadan and the cessation of shipments from Iran. This committee, which said that it would maintain close contact with the British Oil Supply Advisory Committee, established by the three largest British companies at the request of their government, presented proposals to the administration in Washington providing for increased production by American companies in their overseas operations, for redistribution of existing supplies of petroleum and petroleum products, and for the most efficient use of transport facilities.[25] These suggestions received governmental approval on August 2. The British Tanker Company, a subsidiary of AIOC, had announced on July 18 that the tankers formerly used for carrying Iranian oil had been redeployed, and that priority on relief supplies being sent from American and British sources had been given to India, Pakistan, South Africa, and East Africa, since these countries had been most dependent on Iranian oil.

In a note of August 3, the British chargé d'affaires informed the Iranian government that his government was desirous of entering into negotiations in accordance with the Iranian "formula," but that the negotiations could not be conducted "in a satisfactory manner *unless the present atmosphere [were] relieved.*" (Italics added.) The note continued: "On the assurance that the Imperial Government recognize this fact and will enter into discussions in the same spirit, a mission headed by a Cabinet Minister will immediately set out."[26] Mr. Harriman, on his return to Tehran on July 31, must have been persuasive on the issue of "tension in the south," for the Iranian reply (August 3) to the chargé d'affaires' note said: "The Iranian Government recognizes *the essentiality,* in the interest of the success of the negotiations, of *both governments creating the best possible atmosphere,* and will enter into negotiations in the same spirit of good-will expressed by the British Government."[27] (Italics added.) Thus the delicate issue of whether there was "tension" in the oil areas of southern Iran was side-stepped by the substitution of the ambiguous word "atmosphere," used without reference to any particular part of Iran, and the way was paved for the arrival on August 4 of the British mission headed by Lord Privy Seal Richard Stokes. The notes discussed just above were published by the British government on August 4, with an explanatory statement that the "formula" referred to in the British note was paragraph 1 of the Iranian proposals (quoted by the explanatory statement) handed to Harriman on July 23 and communicated by him to the British government. It was also alleged that the Iranian government had made it clear that the basis for the acceptance of the principle of nationalization was the Single Article Law of March 20, and not the Law Regulating Nationalization of April 30, which laid down precise conditions for implementing the law of March 20. The statement also "explained" that the "Persian Government [had] confirmed to Mr. Harriman that they recognize that the reference in the exchange of messages to the necessity of relieving the present atmosphere relates particularly to the present situation in the oil areas in Southern Persia." It was also announced that Mr. Stokes would inspect the oil areas of the south on his arrival in Iran.²⁸ The confidence shown by the Foreign Office on the last two points seems somewhat ill-founded, in view of the Iranian refusal to recognize that there was any "tension" in southern Iran (see p. 103 above) and in view of the fact that the Iranians, in their note of August 3, did not speak of "relieving the atmosphere in the oilfields of southern Iran," but said that they recognized the "essentiality . . . of . . . creating the best possible atmosphere." But whether the two governments had really reached any agreement beyond the British acceptance of the principle of nationalization is immaterial, except as a somewhat rare example of beneficent results flowing from the too-often unfortunate practice of "fuzzing" in diplomatic instruments, for the exchange of notes did provide a sufficient framework for the parties to begin discussions which it was hoped would lead to a solution acceptable to all concerned.

Two days after the arrival of the Stokes mission in Tehran on August 4, the talks began. The Iranian delegation was headed by Minister of Finance Ali Varasteh, who had also led the delegation that had conferred with the representatives of the AIOC in June (see pp. 65 ff.) and included the minister of education, four members of the Joint Parliamentary Oil Committee, and Kazem Hassibi, a technical adviser and a rather extreme advocate of nationalization who had refused to participate in the earlier talks with Harriman.

The first meeting was reported to have taken place in a "friendly atmosphere." A temporary adjournment was called on August 7, to permit Stokes to visit and inspect the oil fields in southern Iran. The talks were resumed on the eighth, after Stokes returned, and at that time he reported to the press that the British staff at Abadan had given him a list of grievances and a statement setting forth the conditions under which they would be willing to continue work. The statement made it clear, Stokes said, that the staff would not work under Iranian management on the basis of individual contracts.

The Majlis passed, on August 9, a bill that had been passed by the Senate the day before, to permit the government to accept a $25 million loan from the United States Export-Import Bank (see p. 48). Also on August 9 the British and Iranian negotiators agreed to set up a subcommittee to study the troublesome question of receipts from tanker captains. It was explained that the settlement of this issue would permit the resumption of shipments from storage tanks and possibly of refinery operations at Abadan, where the staff had now been idle for more than a week.

The British delegation submitted an "Outline of Suggestions" to the Iranian delegation on August 13, to be used as a basis of discussion and a frame of reference for their future talks. Stokes explained at a press conference[29] that the British proposals were consistent with the principle of nationalization as stated in the law of March 20. He also said that the two delegations had agreed to keep the details of the proposals secret for the time being. The Iranian cabinet considered them on the fourteenth, and the two delegations met again on the fifteenth to allow the British to explain their proposals in more detail. Deputy Prime Minister Hossein Fatemi, at a press conference on August 15, complained that the British proposals were not in harmony with the formula given to Harriman (see p. 100 above), which, it had been agreed, was to be the basis of discussion. He then, despite the agreement on secrecy, proceeded to summarize the details of the British proposals. The following official text has since become available:

1. The Anglo-Iranian Oil Company will transfer to the National Iranian Oil Company the whole of its installations, machinery, plant and stores in Iran. As regards the assets in southern Iran, compensation by N.I.O.C. to A.I.O.C. would be included in the operating costs of the oil industry in the area. Compensation for the assets used in the past for distribution and marketing in Iran will be dealt with under the separate arrangements suggested in paragraph 7 below.

2. A Purchasing Organization will be formed in order to provide the assured outlet for Iranian oil which is the only basis upon which an oil industry of the magnitude of that of Iran could hope to maintain itself. This will be done by means of a long term contract, say 25 years, with N.I.O.C. for the purchase f.o.b. of very large quantities of crude oil and products from southern Iran.

3. Apart from this arrangement N.I.O.C. would be able to make additional sales of oil subject to the normal commercial provision that such sales should be effected in such a way as not to prejudice the interests of the Purchasing Organization.

4. The Purchasing Organization under the agreement will be placing at the disposal of the N.I.O.C. a world-wide transportation and marketing service, including one of the largest tanker fleets in the world, and will be entering into firm commitments with its customers for the fulfilment of which it will be relying on Iranian oil. It will, therefore, as a matter of normal commercial practice, have to assure itself that oil in the necessary

quantities and qualities will come forward at the time required. In order to secure this objective the Purchasing Organization will agree with N.I.O.C. on an Organization which, under the authority of N.I.O.C. will manage on behalf of N.I.O.C. the operations of searching for, producing, transporting, refining and loading oil within the area. The Purchasing Organization will arrange from current proceeds the finance necessary to cover operating expenses.

5. In order that the proposed Purchasing Organization can be induced to commit itself to the purchase of large quantities of Iranian oil over a long period of years, the commercial terms must be not less advantageous than the Purchasing Organization would secure elsewhere either by purchase or development. In effect this means that the Purchasing Organization would buy the oil from N.I.O.C. at commercial prices f.o.b. Iran less a price discount equal in the aggregate to the profit remaining to N.I.O.C. after allowing for the discount and for the costs of making the oil available to the Purchasing Organization.

6. In the event of the foregoing suggestions being accepted by the Iranian Government as a basis for the future operation of the oil industry in southern Iran, it is suggested that they should be expanded into the Heads of an Agreement which could later be developed into a detailed purchasing arrangement between the Iranian Government and the proposed Purchasing Organization. The Heads of Agreement would also provide for the immediate resumption of operations in southern Iran on an interim basis.

7. It is suggested that all the assets owned by the Kermanshah Petroleum Company Limited which produces and refines oil for consumption in Iran, together with the installations, machinery, plant and moveable assets of A.I.O.C. which have been used in the past for distribution and marketing of refined products within Iran, should be transferred to the Iranian Government on favourable terms.

8. There will be Iranian representation on the board of directors (or its equivalent) of the Operating Organization, which will, of course, only employ non-Iranian staff to the extent that it find it necessary to do so for the efficiency of its operations. It will also offer its full co-operation to N.I.O.C. in any program of training on which the latter may wish to embark.[30]

It is at once apparent that these proposals were only a detailed elaboration of the proposals submitted to the Iranian government by the AIOC delegation on June 19 (see pp. 66–67 above), but had the added advantage of providing a way to put the Iranian oil industry into Iranian hands within a relatively short time (see paragraph 8). These proposals were based on the British concept of a "workable" settlement as one taking account of the "realities" of the international oil business. The proposals attempted to provide, through the AIOC's international distribution network, sales organization, and transportation facilities, the long-term and large-scale outlet that is essential to an oil industry of the magnitude of that which had been developed in Iran. In order to secure a steady flow of oil and oil products in the desired quantities and qualities, the proposals also attempted to provide for a sound and integrated management capable of operating the industry in Iran efficiently. This part of the proposals would, in effect, have meant the retention of a small British staff; however, the pledge of British coöperation in an NIOC training program could, if carried out expeditiously, have made the retention of British personnel only a temporary arrangement. Paragraph 5 of the proposals incorporated provisions for a fifty-fifty profit-sharing arrangement which, considering the fact that this arrangement was becoming the standard one in other countries at that time, must be deemed fair and equitable. If the long-term purchasing contract had ever been negotiated, it would, like most concession contracts, undoubtedly have provided for periodic revision of the financial clauses. Profit-sharing provisions in concession contracts have changed radically during the last half century, and it seems likely that there will be similar changes in the years to come. The fairness of the fifty-fifty profit-sharing arrangement in the long run would, therefore, depend on the number of years it remained the controlling financial provision of the long-term purchasing contract, and on whether or not it were periodically revised to keep pace with the practice in other countries. Finally, the proposals provided for compensation for the physical assets of AIOC and its subsidiary, the Kermanshah Petroleum Company, that would be transferred to the NIOC. This provision was very favorable to Iran, in that it asked as compensation somewhat less than the law requires in cases of expropriation; and since compensation payments were to be included in operating costs,[31] the legal requirement of promptness was also disregarded.[32] Further, paragraph 7 speaks only of compensation "on favourable terms" for the physical assets of AIOC and its subsidiary; no mention is made of compensation for the good will of the business or for the profits which AIOC could normally have expected to earn in the unexpired term of the concession. Instead, AIOC would have been indirectly compensated for the good will and future profits through the fifty-fifty profit-sharing provision in the long-term purchasing contract.

However fair these proposals might seem to a Westerner, the Iranian reply of August 18 was virtually a rejection of them. Because of the tenor of this reply, Harriman reportedly urged that the reply be kept confidential, and that the Iranian government reconsider its position. In an address to the Parliament on August 22, Prime Minister Mossadegh read the unpublished Iranian reply to the British proposals. This reply[33] objected to the British proposals on the fundamental ground that they were inconsistent with the Iranian formula (see p. 100 above). First, it was said, the proposed Purchasing Organization would have a sales monopoly which would jeopardize the future of NIOC, and, since the Purchasing Organization would be merely a revival of AIOC in a new form but without change of substance, Iran would soon "be confronted with the same difficulties as it [had] experienced in the past" and from which it had gone to such lengths to extricate itself.[34] This objection seems unsound. First, nothing was said in the British proposals about a "monopoly"; rather, it was specifically provided in paragraph 3 that NIOC could make additional sales of oil, provided such sales did not impair NIOC's ability to supply to the Purchasing Organization the amount of oil called for in the contract. Although it is certain that AIOC and its subsidiaries would have supplied the tankers, sales organization, and distribution network necessary to carry out the functions of the Purchasing Organization, it is difficult to see how Iran would have been confronted with the "same difficulties it [had] experienced in the past," since the sales contract would provide, in simple terms, for the NIOC to deliver, f.o.b. some Iranian port, stated quantities of oil and oil products to the Purchasing Organization, which would in return pay to the NIOC a stated compensation.

Secondly, the Iranian reply contended that the discount provided for in paragraph 5 of the British proposals was "contrary to all existing commercial practices."[35] It was added that the British could obtain sufficient profit by adding normal profit to the cost f.o.b. Iranian ports, and presumably after adding freight and insurance charges. This undoubtedly sounds reasonable, but there is definitely no settled commercial practice in this type of situation, since the distribution of oil throughout the world is almost entirely in the hands of the companies that operate the wells. Consumers normally buy oil and oil products delivered c.i.f. their own ports, not f.o.b. the ports of the producing country. Further, as has been pointed out above, the discount, which was in effect a fifty-fifty profit-sharing arrangement, was included as a convenient means of indirectly compensating AIOC for the good will and the profits that could have been expected had its concession not been annulled. Also, it cannot be expected that AIOC, through the Purchasing Organization, would obligate itself in a long-term contract to buy large quantities of oil at a price greater than that at which it could produce oil through its own development in another country. It has in fact created such supplies by increasing production in Kuwait, where it shares a concession with the American Gulf Oil Corporation. Under the terms of the concession agreement, AIOC has these Kuwait supplies on a fifty-fifty profit-sharing basis.[36] But, despite the apparent rationality of the British proposal, it can be observed again that both parties made what have proved to be "unrealistic" assumptions, the British assuming that the Iranians had to sell their oil at any cost, and the Iranians assuming that the British had to have Iranian oil whatever the terms (see p. 54 above). That both parties failed to recognize the erroneousness of these assumptions, on the basis of which, it seems clear, the negotiations proceeded, is undoubtedly a major reason for their failure to agree upon some means of settlement.

Thirdly, the Iranian reply stated that although the Iranian government admitted the need for the assistance of foreign technicians it would not employ them as a group on the basis of a single contract. To do so, it was said, would limit the authority of the NIOC and place Iran in a situation similar to that which had existed under the 1933 concession.[37] This contention is certainly true. However, it is also true that the British had already indicated that they would not work under Iranian management on the basis of individual contracts (see p. 96 above). Thus, although Iran admitted the need for technical aid and expressed a desire to retain the British staff then in the oil fields,[38] that staff refused to work under the conditions proposed by the Iranian government, that is, under Iranian management on the basis of individual contracts. This impasse was certain to exist until either the Iranian government or the British staff (if not both) modified its position. It demonstrated again that the basic obstruction to settlement of the dispute was a political one—a failure of the two parties to appreciate and understand each other and attempt to work together for their mutual benefit.

Stokes announced on August 21 that he had withdrawn his eight-point proposal because, he said, the Iranian government "insist[ed] on reading into it intentions which are not there and which were never in my mind." He explained that Prime Minister Mossadegh had asked him (on August 20) to "eliminate . . . the operational organization and [had] suggested an alternative which, while insuring continued service of the 3,000 British of the staff of the refinery and fields, which [Mossadegh regarded] as absolutely essential, would remove the separate entity envisaged by the operational organization which itself would have acted as agent under the authority of the National Iranian Oil Company." Stokes said that he had been willing to accept the "elimination of the operational organization," for purposes of further discussion, but that Mossadegh had been unwilling to agree to any other arrangements "which either [Mr. Stokes] or Mr. Harriman, with [their] vast business experience, thought either practical or likely to keep the British staff in the service of the Iranian Government."[39]

On the day that Stokes announced withdrawal of his proposals, Harriman wrote a letter to Mossadegh, which the prime minister read to the Iranian Parliament the next day,[40] explaining that in his (Harriman's) opinion the British proposals were within the Iranian formula and were intended as an outline within which fair and practical detailed arrangements could be worked out through further negotiation in accordance with the original formula prepared by the Iranian government. Harriman emphasized that in his view an equitable solution of the dispute was possible only if recognition were given to the practical and commercial aspects of the problem. He continued:

The Iranian Government has stated in our conversation that it did not intend to confiscate the oil properties. In the view of my government, seizure by any government of foreign-owned property without paying prompt, adequate and effective compensation, or working out arrangements mutually satisfactory to the foreign owner and governments, is confiscation, rather than nationalization. Satisfactory arrangements are thus essential, and I believe these arrangements [that is, those contemplated by the British proposals] would achieve the Iranian national aspirations, including Iranian control of the oil industry within Iran, and would provide an income of [a] magnitude that would make it possible

114

promptly to carry out extensive development of the economic potential of the country.[41]

After reading to Parliament both this letter and the Iranian reply of August 18 to the British proposals (see pp. 110–112 above), Prime Minister Mossadegh explained the Iranian position further and then asked for a vote of confidence from both houses. The confidence of both the Senate and the Majlis was voted almost unanimously.[42]

The Iranian delegation submitted a further reply to the British delegation on August 22. This reply repeated many ideas that had been expressed previously, but expressed them in slightly different form and, in addition, made several new points. The following summary of this reply was given in the Security Council by Mr. Allahyar Saleh, delegate from Iran, on October 15:

i) With reference to the sale of oil, the Iranian Government is prepared to sell to the British Government the same amount of oil which it has been purchasing in previous years, say in the neighbourhood of 10 million tons per year, and to conclude a contract for a definite period of time which would be satisfactory to both parties.

ii) The price of oil shall be based on the prevailing international rates on the basis of the f.o.b. value at any Iranian port; but the Iranian Government is not ready to divide into halves the oil receipts accruing to it from its sales of oil, and is also not ready to accept any kind of partnership which is contrary to the ordinary commercial usage [See p. 111 above.]

iii) In order to manage and exploit the national oil industry of Iran on an efficient basis, the Iranian Government is prepared to employ British technicians on the basis of individual contracts with the same salaries and allowances which they have enjoyed with the former Company, and to give them sufficient freedom of action to carry on under internal regulations which would be conducive to the best management of the industry as a whole. [See p. 112 above.]

iv) With reference to the claims of the former Anglo-Iranian Oil Company regarding compensation payments, the Iranian Government is prepared to settle that question in any of the three following ways: (*a*) on the basis of the quoted value of the shares of the Company prior to the passage of the Oil Nationalization Law; (*b*) on the basis of the procedures followed by other countries where industries have been nationalized; (*c*) on any basis which would be mutually satisfactory to both parties, having due regard to the counter-claims of the Iranian Government.[43]

v) With reference to the question of oil transport, the Iranian Government is also prepared to deliver any amount of oil bought by the United Kingdom to any company which produces a receipt from the latter Government; other customers, if they desire, can make arrangements for the transportation of oil to the desired destination through that or any other establishment, provided they give the necessary order to that particular freight agency.[44]

As is indicated in the notes, most of the points raised in this reply have already been discussed. The really new point was the Iranian decision not to sell any of its oil production to AIOC, but rather to make individual contracts with AIOC's former customers and permit them, if they wished, to hire AIOC (or one of its subsidiaries) as their carrying agent. This was, of course, not acceptable to the British delegation, either on behalf of the British government or on behalf of the AIOC. One of the primary purposes of the British government's large stock ownership in AIOC has been to obtain oil products needed for its navy and air force at less than market price. If the Iranian offer quoted above had been accepted, the British government would have had to pay market price plus carrying charges—an eventuality that it would naturally avoid if possible. From the point of view of AIOC the Iranian offer held no attraction, since the most the company could benefit would be from the profits made as a freight carrier. Rather than be reduced to this position, AIOC preferred to develop other oil resources in other countries.[45]

After receiving the Iranian reply, Stokes issued the following statement, on August 22: "The Prime Minister would not accept in any suitable form any of my proposals with regard to staff security. Therefore with great regret, and in view of the negotiations that have already taken place, I have no alternative but to regard the discussions suspended and go home."⁴⁶ On the same day, the company's officials at Abadan announced that all of the AIOC British staff members had been ordered to evacuate the outlying oil fields. They also announced that on or before the end of August 16,000 Iranian employees would be dropped from the pay rolls, and that, unless oil sales from Abadan were resumed, an additional 60,000 would be dismissed in the near future.

On August 23 the British Foreign Office issued a statement on the suspension of the negotiations in which it reversed the Iranian contention and asserted that the Iranians had refused to negotiate within the terms of the Iranian formula on which the two governments had agreed. "Instead, the Persian Government were, in effect, insisting on the full implementation of the Nine Point Law [Regulating Nationalization] of May 1st, 1951."⁴⁷ The statement went on to accuse the Iranian government of failing to take steps to stop the interference with the company's personnel in southern Iran and to come to any agreement that would permit the British staff to continue to work under proper management and acceptable working conditions. The Foreign Office concluded by saying that the British government now took its stand on the ICJ's interim order of July 5, and that the United Kingdom's application to the ICJ for a definitive judgment in the dispute would be pursued. It was added, however, that the British government remained willing to resume negotiations if the Iranians demonstrated a willingness to do so in a spirit of good will and reason and in the light of the "inescapable facts" that confronted Iran.⁴⁸

Before he left Tehran on August 24, Harriman held a press conference, at which he said that the dispute could be settled if attention were paid to the practical and commercial aspects of the problem, but added that he would do nothing more unless requested. On the day of his departure from Tehran, he received a letter from Prime Minister Mossadegh stating that the Iranian replies to the British proposals had been intended as counterproposals, and that it was "the earnest desire of the Iranian Government that . . . [they] should receive careful consideration."[49] Further, he said, the Iranian government was expecting to hear the British government's opinion of these counterproposals, and desired that they should become the basis of further negotiations.

This view of the counterproposals was also expressed by the chairman of the Mixed Board on August 29, in a statement in which he too indicated that the Iranian government was expecting a reply from the British government. However, on the same day a British Foreign Office spokesman in London said that no Iranian proposals were under consideration in London at that time and added that the Iranian replies were not considered counterproposals, since the topics in them had already been covered by the British proposals.[50] Thus, this British Foreign Office statement said, in effect, that the proposals submitted to the Iranian government on August 13 were its best and final offer, beyond the principles of which it would not go.[51]

Meanwhile, the government in Tehran authorized the expenditure of the rial equivalent of $3.5 million for the rehabilitation of Iranians who had formerly been employed by AIOC and issued a list of essential imports for which foreign exchange would be made available. It also authorized the use of the £14 million recently withdrawn from its sterling reserves in London to finance purchases of these essential imports.

On August 28, the president of the ICJ announced that, at the request of the United Kingdom, he had changed the time limit for the submission of the British memorial from September 3 to October 10. Correspondingly, the time limit for the Iranian reply was postponed from December 3 to January 10.

No further development of importance occurred until September 5, when Prime Minister Mossadegh, in a speech before the Iranian Senate, said that although the Iranian government had already sent its counterproposals to the British government, a further communication would be sent to inform that government that unless negotiations were resumed promptly the residence permits of the remaining members of the British staff at Abadan would be withdrawn. He explained that this action was necessary because potential customers for Iranian oil would not take the risk of making purchases until AIOC were expelled from Iran and the oil resources were fully in the hands of the Iranian government. The Senate gave the prime minister a vote of confidence. However, when he asked for a vote of confidence in the Majlis on his proposed ultimatum, he was unable to obtain a quorum. Certain opposition deputies, who had begun to criticize Mossadegh for failure to solve the oil dispute, had decided to boycott the Majlis in order to register their opposition to the Mossadegh government.

On September 6, AIOC headquarters in London announced: "Should . . . any concerns or individuals enter into transactions with the Iranian Government in regard to the oil products concerned, they are warned that this Company will take all such action as may be necessary to protect its rights in any country." This announcement was later repeated in newspaper advertisements in leading cities throughout the world.[52] The announcement and advertisements also declared that the attempts of the Iranian government to sell oil and oil products were violations of its obligations to the AIOC and of the recent order of the ICJ. This same attitude was shown in a statement issued by the British Foreign Office on September 6, and the Foreign Office added that any attempt to expel the remaining British staff members would violate the ICJ's order. Further, Mossadegh's speech before the Senate was said to have shown conclusively that "no further negotiations with the *present* Iranian Government could produce any result," and the Foreign Office declared, "His Majesty's Government therefore now consider that the negotiations begun by the Lord Privy Seal [Stokes] are no longer in suspense but broken off."[53] This was the first indication of the British policy, later articulated, that the only remaining hope for a settlement of the oil dispute was the fall of the Mossadegh government and the accession of a new government that would be willing to negotiate on "reasonable and practical" terms. The measures that were subsequently adopted by the British government to accomplish this objective were primarily economic. The first of these was indicated on September 10, when the British Treasury announced that in view of the breakdown of the negotiations the government had decided to withdraw the exceptional privileges formerly accorded Iran for converting sterling into dollars[54] and for the automatic use of sterling for payments to and from countries in the sterling area and certain other countries. The Treasury announcement said that the "cessation of exports of oil from Persia not only removes the justification for these exceptional facilities but also makes it necessary for the United Kingdom to spend large sums of dollars on replacement oil." Therefore, it was stated, the British government had decided that it could no longer afford to supply Iran with dollars, and, further, that future payments in sterling to and from Iran would be subject to the permission of the British Treasury. The Treasury also stated that in view of the important contribution which Iranian oil had made to the economy of the United Kingdom, Iran had been given exceptional privileges to purchase certain scarce goods that were normally subject to export-license control,[55] but announced that these privileges were also being revoked and that further supply of these scarce items would be discontinued. The first action to implement this policy was taken two days later, September 12, when the British Foreign Office announced that "in conformity with the economic measures designed to protect the United Kingdom's economy . . ." the government had requisitioned 3,000 tons of railway track equipment and 2,000 tons of sugar en route to Iran and had ordered the ships carrying these cargoes to return to the United Kingdom. Responsibility for the indemnification of Iranian buyers for sums already paid was accepted by the United Kingdom government.[56] Also on September 12, Prime Minister Attlee said, in a speech at the opening of the new Fawley refinery in southern England, that through the efforts of the (British) Oil Supply Advisory Committee and the (American) Foreign Petroleum Supply Committee (see p. 103 above) Great Britain's normal consumption of oil products had been substantially guaranteed, and that the development of alternative supplies was improving rapidly.[57]

After failing to obtain a quorum in the Majlis in several successive meetings (on September 6, 9, and 10) to approve Mossadegh's proposed ultimatum to the British, Deputy Prime Minister Fatemi announced that the government would proceed on the assumption that it still had the confidence of Parliament and stated that it would accordingly send the proposed ultimatum to Harriman in Washington for transmission to London without first obtaining the approval of the Majlis. The ultimatum was delivered to Harriman in Washington on September 12, and the text was made public a week later.[58] In this communication, Prime Minister Mossadegh said that the state of suspense which had existed since negotiations were discontinued on August 23 had become "intolerable," and that, therefore, the Iranian government was offering certain proposals which were "to be regarded as a basis for starting new negotiations." The Iranian proposals which were intended as new bases of discussion were substantially identical with those contained in the Iranian reply of August 22 (quoted above, pp. 114–115). It was requested that Mr. Harriman transmit these proposals to the British government. Mossadegh's message concluded with a warning: "If in the lapse of fifteen days from the date at which this present proposal is submitted to the British Government, no satisfactory conclusion is achieved, the Imperial Iranian Government regrets to state its compulsion to cancel the residence permits held by the

British staff and experts now residing in the southern oil fields."[59]
In a personal letter to Mossadegh, delivered on September 17,
Harriman indicated his unwillingness to deliver these proposals
to the British. They were, he said, the same as those that the
Iranian government had made on August 22 and that had been
rejected by the British because "they did not conform to practical
and commercial aspects of the international oil industry." In
addition, he said, the proposals in some respects "represent a
retrogession from the positions taken during the discussions."[60]
After pointing out what he considered the defects of the Iranian
proposals (see pp. 110–112 and 114–115), he emphasized again
that the dispute could be settled only by negotiations based upon
recognition of the practical business and technical aspects of the
oil industry and conducted in a spirit of mutual good will. To
transmit the Iranian message to the British government would,
he said, only militate against a settlement of the dispute and
would further aggravate an already serious situation. For these
reasons Harriman urged Mossadegh to reconsider his proposals
and expressed the hope that a mutually acceptable basis of discussion could be developed, on which negotiations could be
resumed.[61]

Rather than reconsider, Deputy Prime Minister Fatemi said,
after a cabinet meeting, that if Harriman refused to transmit the
Iranian message to the British government, Iran would do so
herself. Accordingly, a new memorandum, without heading, date,
or signature, was prepared and handed to the British ambassador
in Tehran. Its contents were the same as those of the letter to Mr.
Harriman. The British ambassador, on instructions from his
government, informed the Iranians that the proposals were unacceptable to the British government as a basis for negotiation.[62]

Meanwhile in Tehran it had been announced that the Iranian
government had concluded a contract for the sale of $3.5 million
worth of oil to the Afghan government, to be delivered at the
border. In London an AIOC official said that the amount of oil

122

was relatively small and that no decision had yet been reached on the question whether an attempt would be made to sue the Afghan government.[63] It was also announced by AIOC that 20,000 more Iranian employees would be suspended from the pay roll as of the end of September.

In Tehran on September 14, the government-owned Bank Melli announced a prohibition on further conversion by AIOC of sterling into rials, presumably in retaliation for the British Treasury's suspension of Iran's convertibility facilities (see p. 119). However, the prohibition was rescinded on the following day in order to enable the company to meet its monthly pay roll for an estimated 40,000 Iranian employees who would otherwise have been an additional burden on the Iranian government. Another prohibition was announced by the prime minister on the eighteenth, in a memorandum in which he instructed all government departments and also the corporations and banks (except the Bank Melli) in which the government held shares to close their accounts with the British Bank of Iran and the Middle East. The privilege of buying and selling foreign exchange was also thenceforth reserved exclusively to the Bank Melli. On the same day (September 18), the resignation of the Finance Minister Ali Varasteh, leader of the Iranian delegation that had negotiated with the British in June and August, was announced. He was replaced by Mohammed Nariman.[64]

To relieve in part the strains caused by the interruption of normal trading activities, both Britain and Iran turned to countries of the "Communist bloc." Deputy Prime Minister Fatemi said on September 15 that despite the British order halting sugar cargoes bound for Iran, the country would have adequate supplies of sugar, since it produced one-half of its own consumption and expected an additional 40,000 tons annually under a barter agreement with the Soviet Union. He added that he was certain the USSR would provide even greater quantities if necessary. Ten days later a Tehran newspaper reported a new barter agreement between Iran and the Soviet Union, under which Iran would receive an additional 12,000 tons of sugar in return for Iranian wool and almonds. It was also reported that the Soviet Union was sending a representative to Tehran to discuss the expansion of trade relations between the two countries, the Soviet Union having offered to buy all the products which Iran could supply.[65] On September 19 it was reported that the British government had concluded a contract to buy 200,000 tons of fuel oil from Sovrom Petrol, a Soviet-Rumanian "trust" operating former British, French, American, and Belgian oil fields and production facilities in Rumania.[66]

The Mixed Board served notice on all the remaining British members of AIOC's staff on September 19 that they must either sign individual employment contracts with the NIOC or leave Iran. After a meeting of the board with Mossadegh the next day, the prime minister announced that because the British staff members had refused the board's offer of employment, their residence permits were rescinded and the individuals affected must leave Iranian soil within one week after September 27. Further, the offer of individual contracts was withdrawn. In Tehran the British ambassador immediately registered a protest "in the strongest possible terms," pointing out that the Iranian government must accept the consequences of its decision, which would have a grave effect on the relations of the two countries. After a cabinet meeting in London, Prime Minister Attlee dispatched an appeal to President Truman asking that the United States use its "good offices." The alternatives, he said, were capitulation, which would destroy British prestige in the Middle East, or sending in armed forces to protect the remaining three hundred and fifty Britons.[67]

At dawn on September 27, Iranian troops seized the Abadan refinery and refused admittance to all but ten key British technicians. On the same day President Truman sent a message to the British government urging it not to use armed force to prevent the expulsion of the British staff at Abadan and indicating that the United States would not support the use of force by the British. President Truman also appealed to Iran to cancel its expulsion order, saying that execution of this order would intensely aggravate the situation and make settlement much more difficult.[68]

Meanwhile units of the British army, navy, and air force grouped themselves around the eastern Mediterranean and in the Persian Gulf, ready to move if the word came from London. In Tehran the government ordered that all oil installations be blown up if any foreign forces attempted to land on Iranian soil.[69]

The British government announced on September 28 that it had requested the United Nations Security Council to intervene in the Anglo-Iranian dispute, and that it was the policy of the British government to rely on the machinery of the United Nations and the rule of law rather than on the use of force.[70] In Tehran, Prime Minister Mossadegh announced that although the Security Council was without competence to intervene in the dispute he would fly to New York to present the Iranian case to the Security Council personally. On September 29 it was announced in London that orders had been given for the evacuation of the remaining British staff at Abadan unless the Iranian government rescinded its expulsion order.[71] The evacuation was completed peacefully and without incident on October 1, three days before the deadline set in the Iranian ultimatum. The scene of events then shifted to the Security Council, which met on October 1 to consider the British application.

§ 8. The Debate in the Security Council

The British Foreign Office statement of September 28, announcing that the United Kingdom had called upon the United Nations Security Council to intervene in the Anglo-Iranian dispute, termed the Iranian expulsion order a violation of the International Court's order of July 5, an attempt to substitute the rule of force for the rule of law, and an arbitrary action contrary to elementary principles of international usage. These actions of the Iranian government had, it said,

created a situation which might well be thought to justify the use of force in order to preserve the British rights and interests involved. His Majesty's Government would, however, be reluctant to take any action which might have the effect of weakening the authority of the United Nations, on whose principles their policy is based. They have, therefore, decided that the right course in the present circumstances is to bring the situation urgently before the Security Council, which is the appropriate body to deal with matters likely to endanger the maintenance of international peace and security, and to which the provisional measures indicated by the International Court have been notified.[1]

In a letter to the president of the Security Council dated September 29 the deputy British delegate, after calling attention to the grounds of the British request for interim measures and the Court's order indicating such measures, stated that the Iranian expulsion order was clearly contrary to the Court's order. He added that the British government was "gravely concerned at the dangers inherent in this situation and at the threat to peace and security that may thereby be involved," and requested that the following item be placed on the provisional agenda of the Council: "Complaint of failure by the Iranian Government to comply with provisional measures indicated by the International Court of Justice in the Anglo-Iranian Oil Company case."[2] In view of the fact that the Iranian expulson order was scheduled to become effective on October 4, it was asked that the Council "consider this matter as one of extreme urgency" and convene on October 1 to act on the item just quoted.

Accompanying the letter of the deputy British delegate was a draft resolution which would have the Security Council recognize that Iran had refused to comply with the provisional measures ordered by the Court, and that the expulsion of the remaining British staff members was "clearly contrary to the provisional measures indicated by the Court." The draft resolution would then have the Security Council call upon the Iranian government "to act in all respects in conformity with the provisional measures indicated by the Court and in particular to permit the continued residence at Abadan of the staff affected by the recent expulsion orders . . . and to inform the Security Council of the steps taken by it to carry out the present resolution."[3]

On the same day, September 29, Deputy Prime Minister Fatemi announced in Tehran that Prime Minister Mossadegh would present the Iranian position to the Security Council. That position, he indicated, was that the Council was incompetent to consider the British complaint because Article 2, paragraph 7, of the Charter forbade the United Nations to intervene in matters essentially within the domestic jurisdiction of any member nation.[4]

When the Council met on October 1, the discussion on the item submitted by the United Kingdom was opened by the representative of the Soviet Union, who opposed inclusion of that item on the Council's agenda on the ground that a discussion of the question in the Council would "constitute interference in the domestic affairs of Iran and a gross violation of the Iranian people's sovereignty."[5] The representative of Yugoslavia also expressed an opinion that the matter was essentially within the domestic jurisdiction of Iran, adding that the fact that the Council was asked to call for compliance by Iran with the Court's order of provisional measures did not in any way affect the question of the competence of the Council.[6]

The representatives of Ecuador, Turkey, France, India, and China expressed themwselves in favor of adopting the agenda and deciding the question of the Council's competence after hearing the parties and considering the substance of the problem.[7]

The representative of the United Kingdom, Sir Gladwyn Jebb, also thought that the question of competence, if any, should be decided after the adoption of the agenda and not before. He stated that the fact that the ICJ had indicated interim measures showed very clearly that the dispute was at least prima facie justiciable, and thus not a matter solely within the domestic jurisdiction of Iran. He said that quite apart from the duty of the Security Council to enforce the judgments of the ICJ under Article 94 of the Charter (see p. 92 above), which would alone justify the Council in considering the item on the agenda, the formal basis of the British complaint was to be found in Article 35, paragraph 1, of the Charter, which gives any member of the United Nations the right to bring to the attention of the Security Council "any dispute, or any situation which might lead to international friction or give rise to a dispute, in order to determine whether the continuance of the dispute or situation is likely to endanger the maintenance of international peace and security." He submitted that there was a dispute which should now receive the Council's urgent consideration.[8]

The representative of the United States also favored the adoption of the agenda with the same reservation as expressed by the representatives of Ecuador, Turkey, France, India, and China.[9] He added that this was not only a "dispute" but a "situation," and that, since the Security Council has the primary responsibility for the maintenance of international peace and security, the Council's duty in the performance of that function required it to consider any dispute or situation that might affect the maintenance of international peace and security.[10]

The agenda was adopted by nine votes in favor and two against.[11]

Most of the remainder of the Council's meeting of October 1 was occupied by Sir Gladwyn Jebb's presentation of the British case.[12] After presenting a brief historical survey of the development of the dispute, he charged that Iran had "flouted" the decision of the International Court and had taken a series of steps which had brought the oil industry to a standstill and which had culminated in the expulsion of the remaining staff capable of operating the industry. In so doing it had, he alleged, created an inflammatory situation "which [had] engendered the maximum of international friction and which [might] constitute . . . a potential threat to peace and security."[13] It was this situation, and the international friction and threat to the peace which it engendered, he said, that provided the formal basis for the United Kingdom complaint under the provisions of Article 35 of the Charter. In addition, he argued that the Council's competence to deal with the matters on the agenda could also be based upon the functions given to it under Article 94 of the Charter, because the Court's order indicating interim measures had the same binding character as a final judgment and the Council had the power under Article 94 to decide upon measures to be taken to give effect to the "judgment" or "decision" (compare pp. 92–94). Finally, he argued that there was a political factor that the Council should not overlook; that is, that whether or not the Court's order is legally binding, nevertheless it was the expression of the opinion of the highest international judicial tribunal on what that tribunal considered necessary to preserve the rights of both parties pending a final decision on the merits. From this, he said, there arises a very strong moral obligation on all the members of the United Nations to conform to the measures indicated by the Court, and Iran's failure to do so had created a situation constituting a threat to the peace. In conclusion he urged the Council to adopt the United Kingdom's draft resolution calling upon Iran to revoke its expulsion order and to comply in all respects with the provisional measures indicated by the Court. By adopting this resolution, he said,

the Security Council will make it plain that it is determined to uphold the role of law in international affairs, to say nothing of the prevalence of reason; it will assert its authority not on behalf of the powerful against the weak but on behalf of intelligent progress as against unintelligent reaction. Finally, it will create a landmark in the vast process of peaceful adjustment between the ancient East and the industrialized West, the successful accomplishment of which is admittedly the major problem of our generation.[14]

On the conclusion of Sir Gladwyn Jebb's speech, the representative of Iran[15] asked the Council to adjourn discussion of the question for ten days in order to allow time for representatives of his government to reach New York from Tehran.[16] After having been modified by the suggestion of the representative of China to allow the president of the Council discretion to call a meeting earlier than ten days thence, the Iranian request was granted, and the next meeting of the Council was scheduled for October 11 at the latest. Subsequently, and after the last of the British staff had been evacuated from Iran on October 1, the Iranian delegate requested the president of the Council to postpone the next meeting of the Council from October 11 to October 15, in order to permit Prime Minister Mossadegh sufficient time to come to New York. The request was granted.

Before the Council reconvened on October 15, the British government filed with the International Court its memorial (October 10) requesting the Court to declare that Iran's annulment of the AIOC's concession and refusal to arbitrate as provided therein was a denial of justice, and thus a violation of international law. The memorial asked the Court for a final judgment, within the period fixed by the Court, awarding to the United Kingdom a full and complete restitution or, alternatively, adequate and effective compensation for the properties expropriated. The British government also prepared a revised draft resolution for submission to the Security Council, in the light of the fact that the last of the British staff had been evacuated since the introduction of its original resolution asking the Council to call upon Iran to permit the continued residence of the British staff at Abadan. The revised resolution called for:

1) The resumption of negotiations at the earliest practicable moment in order to make further efforts to resolve the differences between the parties in accordance with the principles of the provisional measures indicated by the International Court of Justice unless mutually agreeable arrangements are made consistent with the purposes and principles of the United Nations Charter;

2) The avoidance of any action which would have the effect of further aggravating the situation or prejudicing the rights, claims or positions of the parties concerned.[17]

On October 12, the day on which this revised draft resolution was made public, Deputy Prime Minister Fatemi made the following statement at a press conference: "The Iranian delegation is strongly opposed to any resolution which could enable the Security Council to interfere in the oil question," and he stated again, as he had in previous press conferences, that ". . . the [oil dispute] is absolutely and plainly regarded by us as a problem related to our sovereignty and independence." "Therefore," he said, "I can officially and explicitly declare that the Iranian delegation would not accept such a resolution."[18] In other words, Iran was giving advance notice that it would refuse to discharge the obligations that it had freely assumed some six years previously when it had become a member of the United Nations, if those obligations involved an admission that the Security Council could concern itself with Iran's oil nationalization. Deputy Prime Minister Fatemi was promising that Iran would consider illegal and unenforceable any affirmative action that the Security Council might take on the British draft resolution, just as it had rejected the ICJ's order of July 5. The attitude expressed by Fatemi was reinforced by Prime Minister Mossadegh's statements before the Council on the same day. If the United Kingdom once more refuses Iran's offer to negotiate outside the Security Council on the questions of compensation to AIOC and sale of oil to the United Kingdom, Mossadegh warned, "we shall have no alternative but to go home, and we think that others [other members of the Security Council] may well follow our example."[19] In concluding his plea for the Council to affirm that it had no competence to deal with the subject matter of the British draft resolution, Mossadegh ended with this warning to the Council: "Beware of taking a decision which may endanger international peace."[20]

The concept of the Security Council's powers and proper functions and of Iran's duties and obligations as a member of the United Nations revealed in these expressions of official Iranian sentiment can be contrasted with Mossadegh's emphatic asseverations to the Council on the preceding day, when he had said: "[Iran] has always shown the most devoted respect for international law and has sought scrupulously to carry out its duties as a member of this and other international organizations. We have observed, and will continue to observe, every legal limitation on our sovereignty which flows from our participation and co-operation in the affairs of the family of nations."[21] Threats to go home and to flout a decision of the Council, even if such actions involved a breach of the peace, should that decision be contrary to the wishes of the Iranian government, do not show a very "devoted respect" for international law or a very scrupulous regard for carrying out the duties of a member of the United Nations.

When the Security Council met again, on October 15, the efforts of various United States officials and Secretary General Trygve Lie having failed to persuade the parties to resume negotiations, the British representative, Sir Gladwyn Jebb, made a brief statement in explanation of his new draft resolution. There is not much point, he said, in asking the Security Council to call upon Iran to act in all respects in conformity with the interim measures indicated by the ICJ, since those measures "have, unfortunately, and to some extent been overtaken by events."[22] The fact that the revised draft resolution called for the resumption of negotiations in accordance with the principles of the interim measures indicated by the ICJ did not mean, he explained, that the British government was insisting purely and simply on a return to the status quo as it had existed prior to May 1. Instead, it meant that the British government was seeking agreement between the parties on a provisional scheme under which the flow of oil could be resumed without prejudice to the ultimate solution of the dispute. "In other words, without abandoning our struggle for the acceptance of the rule of law as opposed to the rule of force, we are trying to suggest a way by which reasonable people can, with good will, find an approach to a settlement which will enable a great industry to resume its operations. It is of course also with the object of upholding the rule of law that we have retained some reference to the International Court in the preamble."[23] He concluded by saying that the United Kingdom was anxious to resume negotiations, but desired that they be resumed in the light of a pronouncement by the Security Council indicating that the matter was not exclusively the concern of the Iranian government and that the dispute must be solved, not by ultimata, but by free negotiation in accordance with the accepted principles of international law. He then urged Dr. Mossadegh not to take an "aggressively nationalistic attitude" and not to brood on "old imagined wrongs," but to work for a constructive solution which would redound to the mutual benefit of the United Kingdom and Iran as well as to the benefit of the world as a whole.[24]

Prime Minister Mossadegh then presented a brief statement in which he reiterated the Iranian view that the Security Council had no jurisdiction to hear the United Kingdom's complaint.[25] He said that the Council could not perform its task of maintaining world peace unless it and the "great Powers" adhered to the principles which it was created to embody, and that if the Council took cognizance, "for political reasons," of a matter not within its competence it would thereby become an instrument of interference in the domestic affairs of one country by another and would in that way "lose the peoples' confidence and fail in its duty as a guardian of world peace."[26] However, in spite of his contention that the Council lacked competence to consider the United Kingdom's complaint, he urged that body "and the great Powers to help . . . [Iran] to recover its economic independence." He continued: "In order to achieve this goal, Iran expects the aid and support of the United Nations and of the peace-loving nations which are its Members. The Charter of the United Nations and the high principles contained in it require Member States to extend a helping hand to Iran today. That is the true meaning of international co-operation for the promotion of social advancement, which is the very basis of the Charter."[27] The fact that the United Kingdom did not use its vastly superior military force against Iran was, he said, evidence that the United Nations was successfully fulfilling its task of preserving world peace.[28] In his concluding remarks the prime minister stressed that Iran, in the course of the negotiations, had never ceased to manifest "the utmost good will and [had] submitted sound and constructive proposals regarding the methods of fixing compensation and the sale of oil to the United Kingdom."[29] He said that although this conciliatory attitude had proved fruitless and had aggravated Iran's economic difficulties, his government was willing to reopen negotiations on the two points just mentioned as soon as the United Kingdom showed "a real desire and intention to reach a settlement." It can be observed again that the United Kingdom did not desire to reach a settlement on those two points alone, since it was interested primarily, not in the sale of a fraction of Iran's oil to the United Kingdom, but in the sale of substantially all of Iran's oil to the AIOC. Further, so far as the available documents indicate, the negotiations never proceeded far enough for the question of methods of compensation to be discussed in any detail (see pp. 187–189 and 208–212).

Dr. Mossadegh concluded his statement by saying that he hoped the members of the Council would agree that there was no justification for the Council's "intervention" and that the Iranian government expected it to abstain from taking any action that might delay the accomplishment of Iran's task of utilizing its oil resources for the benefit of the Iranian people, "since any such delay would naturally deprive [the Iranian government] of the freedom of action which is necessary to enable [it] to continue undisturbed in [its] efforts to bring [the] present deplorable situation to an end."[30]

A more detailed statement of the position of the Iranian government was presented by a member of the Iranian delegation, Mr. Allahyar Saleh. His presentation was primarily concerned with an analysis of the legal basis of Iran's case. The basic position on which the entire Iranian case rested was stated by Mr. Saleh at the very outset:

The vital point is that the Security Council has not and cannot have competence to deal with this matter. The reason is simple. The oil resources of Iran, like its soil, its rivers and mountains, are the property of the people of Iran. They alone have the authority to decide what shall be done with it, by whom and how. They have never agreed to share that authority with anybody else or to divide their ownership of all or part of that property or what it produces with anyone. They have not submitted and will not submit their authority in that regard, or the exercise of it, to review or judgment by any persons or body outside Iran. That ownership and that authority are inalienable. They are part of the foundations on which stand our national sovereignty and our admitted equality among the other sovereign states of the community of nations and of the body in which it is organized, the United Nations.[31]

Mr. Saleh said that the provision, in the Law Regulating Nationalization, for compensation to AIOC,[32] the choice of formulae offered to AIOC (see pp. 114 and 211–212 herein), the provision that former customers of AIOC should have the right to purchase at current prices the same quantities of oil that they had previously imported from Iran,[33] and the Iranian government's offer to employ the British staff of AIOC in Iran, all showed that Iran's exercise of its sovereign rights was not "hasty, arbitrary or injurious to others . . ."[34] In regard to those rights, he said further: "It is a settled principle of international law that in matters of domestic concern, to which this question eminently relates, [the] exercise [of sovereign rights] can neither be abridged nor interfered with by any foreign sovereign or international body."[35] That principle of international law was also, he contended, the law of the United Nations by virtue of Article 1, paragraph 2, and Article 2, paragraph 7, of the Charter. It was on those articles that he relied in his subsequent argument that the Security Council was without competence to intervene in the oil dispute.

The Iranian spokesman stated that the 1933 AIOC concession was a private agreement between the AIOC and the Iranian government[36] which could in no way limit or abridge the sovereign right of Iran to dispose of its resources as it saw fit (and which gave the government of the United Kingdom no rights whatsoever), and that the United Kingdom had trespassed this sovereign right of Iran, without any legal justification whatever, in seeking to take advantage of the 1933 AIOC concession to interfere with the execution of Iranian laws. The United Kingdom government had, he said, acted in violation of international law by seeking to usurp Iran's sovereign rights in matters of domestic concern,[37] by interfering in the internal affairs of Iran, by placing its armed forces in the vicinity of Iran, and by its "abusive" use of the International Court of Justice.[38] This alleged disrespect for international law on the part of the United Kingdom he contrasted with the attitude of Iran, which has, he said, shown throughout its history "the most devoted respect for international law and has sought scrupulously to carry out its duties as a member of this and other international organizations. [Iran has] observed, and will continue to observe, every legal limitation on our sovereignty which flows from our participation and co-operation in the affairs of the family of nations."[39] Further, he expressed the view that Iran was animated by the hope that international law and international organization could be perfected so as to extend their protection to the rights of all nations, big and small, but said that this was still a vision of the future, since international law was "weak and deficient." Therefore, he said, since

the great and powerful still lord it over the world, . . . the protection of the fundamental rights of the weak requires them to be most jealous of their independence and sovereign rights . . . The limitations on sovereignty imposed by international law and international agreements are not obscure and are recognized by all governments. Outside that narrow domain, however, the sovereignty of states is unimpaired. At the heart of it is the absolute right to manage one's internal affairs without any other limitations than those contained in the principles and laws established in the country itself.[40]

From this, Mr. Saleh argued, it follows that the ICJ's order of July 5, 1951, indicating provisional measures, was invalid (as well as an attempt at unlawful interference in the internal affairs of Iran by the United Kingdom), and that, for the same reasons, the Security Council was incompetent to consider the United Kingdom's complaint.[41] This statement indicated that Iran considered the bases of jurisdiction of the International Court of Justice and the Security Council as identical in regard to the United Kingdom's applications to those two bodies for relief in the dispute over the effect of Iran's nationalization laws. This attitude communicated itself to some other Council members and created a confusion which obscured the real issues before the Security Council at the time: first, whether the Council were competent to consider the United Kingdom's complaint, based as it was on Article 35 of the Charter, and, if so, what measures should be taken or what recommendations should be made in order to adjust the situation or dispute and thereby remove the alleged threat to international peace and security. The United Kingdom's request that the Security Council call upon Iran to comply with the provisional measures indicated by the ICJ undoubtedly added to this confusion; yet, as Sir Gladwyn Jebb made clear (see pp. 127–128 above), the United Kingdom's complaint was that Iran had taken a series of steps that had brought the oil industry to a standstill and had culminated in the expulsion of the British staff operating the oil industry, and, in so doing, had created a situation "which [had] engendered the maximum of international friction and which [might] constitute . . . a potential threat to the peace."[42] Thus, if Iran would comply with the provisional measures indicated by the ICJ, the United Kingdom government believed, this compliance would reduce the friction that Iran's previous behavior had engendered and would in that way remove the potential threat to the peace. In basing its complaint to the Security Council on Article 35 (threat to the peace) the United Kingdom undoubtedly sought, in the event it proved necessary, to bring its complaint within the exception in paragraph 7 of Article 2 of the Charter. This paragraph forbids the United Nations to intervene in matters that are "essentially within the domestic jurisdiction of any state," except that this prohibition "shall not prejudice the application of enforcement measures under Chapter VII [of the Charter]," which is concerned with action by the Security Council with respect to threats to the peace, breaches of the peace, and acts of aggression. Therefore, since the United Kingdom was calling upon the Security Council to deal with a situation that was alleged to be a "potential threat to the peace," the validity or enforceability of the ICJ's order indicating provisional measures was not strictly in point, for the real question was whether or not there was a situation that constituted a threat to international peace. Nevertheless, the questions of the validity and enforceability of the ICJ's order were frequently discussed by the representatives of various member nations of the Council, several of whom, following the example of the Iranians, identified the bases of the Council's jurisdiction with those of the Court.

The Iranian representative, after reiterating the prohibition in Article 2, paragraph 7, of the Charter, began his technical argument against the Council's competence by discussing the enforceability of the ICJ's order indicating provisional measures.[43] He said that the power given the Security Council by Article 94 of the Charter to make recommendations or decide upon measures to be taken to give effect to a "judgment" of the ICJ was limited to cases in which the judgment was both final and binding. The argument in favor of enforceability, an elaboration of which has been set forth above (pp. 92–94), was said to be a statement of what the law should be rather than an exposition of existing law. The language of Article 41 of the Statute of the Court ("The Court shall have the power to indicate . . . any provisional measures which ought to be taken . . .") was, he said, exhortative and not obligatory. The provision in paragraph 2 of Article 41—that the ICJ shall notify the Security Council of measures indicated by the Court—had been designed, he said, merely to further coöperation between these two organs of the United Nations. To interpret paragraph 2 of Article 41 as giving the Security Council power to enforce the measures of which it has been notified by the Court was said to be "far-fetched" (see p. 92 above) because the Statute of the Court was said to be concerned exclusively with the rights and duties of the Court and could not, therefore, confer powers on the Security Council by implication.[44] As pointed out above, this argument is not strictly in point and, therefore, will not be discussed further.[45]

The Iranian representative next addressed himself to the task of rebutting the United Kingdom's argument that the Council was competent to consider its complaint because of the existence of a threat or potential threat to the peace. In so doing he stressed Iran's economic and military weakness, saying that it argues "a deficient sense of humour to suggest that a nation as weak as Iran can endanger world peace."[46] Whatever danger there may be to international peace and security, he said, lies in the actions of the United Kingdom and not in those of Iran. The dispatch of British land, sea, and air forces to the vicinity of Iran he saw as "ominous gestures" that might have had disastrous consequences "by lighting the flames of another world war." He then expressed the view that since the United Kingdom had publicly announced the withdrawal of its armed forces from the vicinity of Iran there was no longer any possibility of a threat to international peace and security, and that "it is not clear how the United Kingdom Government could have the hardihood to press

its complaint in the Security Council on that ground." In concluding his argument Mr. Saleh made a statement that sounds
curiously incompatible with his insistence that there was no dispute between Iran and the United Kingdom that could be a
potential threat to the peace: ". . . the political and economic independence of Iran is of the highest importance to the maintenance of international peace and security. The part of the world in
which we live is one of the sensitive areas of international life.
It is the meeting-place of the great Powers. If it is weak, the
dangers to international peace and security increase in almost
geometrical proportion to the increase in our dependence on
others."[47]

With the completion of the formal statements of the United
Kingdom and Iran, the debates in the Security Council during its
next four meetings (October 16–19) were concerned primarily
with two problems: (1) the determination whether there was a
dispute, and if so whether the dispute was a threat to international
peace and security or was essentially within the domestic jurisdiction of Iran; (2) the determination, in relation to the scope of
domestic jurisdiction, of the competence of the Security Council
and the jurisdiction of the International Court of Justice.

The members of the Security Council differed in their opinions
on the question whether there was a dispute between the United
Kingdom and Iran, and, if so, whether it was essentially within
the domestic jurisdiction of Iran, and whether it constituted a
danger to international peace and security. As indicated above
(see pp. 127–128 above), the United Kingdom representative
took the position that there was a dispute which endangered international peace and security and which was not within the
domestic jurisdiction of Iran. The Iranian representative (see pp.
134 ff.) insisted that there was no dispute between his government and the United Kingdom, and that the only dispute which
existed was between the Iranian government and a private company, AIOC, regarding a private contract to which the United

Kingdom was not a party. Therefore, he argued, this dispute was clearly within the domestic jurisdiction of Iran, and Article 2, paragraph 7, of the Charter thus precluded intervention by the Security Council (or any other organ of the United Nations). Further, he said, the dispute between the Iranian government and AIOC could not possibly involve a threat to international peace and security, and the only possibility of such a threat lay in the actions of the United Kingdom in its attempts at unlawful interference in the internal affairs of Iran.

The representative of the Soviet Union agreed with the representative of Iran and consistently maintained that the dispute was essentially within the domestic jurisdiction of Iran and that discussion of the matter in the Security Council "would constitute intervention in the domestic affairs of Iran and a gross violation of the sovereignty of the Iranian people."[48] The representative of Yugoslavia thought that there could be no doubt that there was a dispute, but that it was within the domestic jurisdiction of Iran, and therefore one with which the Council was not competent to deal. He expressed the thought, however, that an offer of the Council's good offices to the United Kingdom and Iran might help materially to provide conditions under which negotiations could be resumed and a satisfactory settlement reached.[49]

The representative of Ecuador stated that in his opinion the competence of the Security Council to deal with the United Kingdom complaint depended upon the existence of a dispute or situation between two states which involved a threat to the maintenance of international peace and security. After noting that the United Kingdom was claiming the right of diplomatic protection of its national, AIOC, he expressed the opinion that it was a "highly debatable" proposition that the mere exercise of diplomatic protection could transform a private dispute between a government and a corporation into an international dispute between two states. Before any diplomatic action is taken by a government for the protection of its nationals, he said, the existence of a denial of justice should be established, but in his opinion there had not yet been a "clear-cut" denial of justice.[50] On the question whether there was a threat to international peace and security, the representative of Ecuador had expressed the view, at the meeting of the Council on October 1, that it was "generally known" that a situation existed the consequences of which might result in an increased danger to the peace.[51] However, at a meeting of the Council on October 17, he said that, since Iran and the United Kingdom had each publicly declared that it would not attack the other, his delegation had concluded that the dispute or situation did not involve a threat to the mainte- nance of peace.[52] As a result, his delegation had also concluded that the Security Council was not competent to make recommen- dations of the kind mentioned in chapter vi of the Charter. But, like the delegate of Yugoslavia, he thought that the Council should use its "moral influence" to help the parties reach a settle- ment, and to that end he introduced a resolution that would have the Security Council "advise" the parties to reopen negotiations and settle their differences in accordance with the purposes and principles of the United Nations Charter.[53]

The representative of the United States, basing his argument entirely upon the statements of Prime Minister Mossadegh at previous meetings of the Council, asserted that the "conclusion is inescapable that a dispute exists between two governments, those of the United Kingdom and Iran, the continuance of which is likely to endanger international peace and security."[54] There- fore, he argued, there should be no doubt of the competence of the Security Council to adopt the draft resolution submitted by the United Kingdom, since it is the "high function" of the Se- curity Council to help in achieving peaceful solutions to inter- national disputes the continued existence of which would involve a threat to the peace. He indicated that, in accordance with this view, the United States would vote in favor of the adoption of the United Kingdom's draft resolution.[55] The president of the

142

Council, speaking as the representative of Brazil, indicated that his delegation would also vote in favor of the United Kingdom's draft resolution. He expressed the hope that the resumption of negotiations in accordance with the draft resolution would enable the parties to adjust all their differences and bring to an end the situation which had developed in the preceding two months and which "could hardly contribute to the maintenance of peace in the world, already so disturbed by the growing international tension."[56] The president said that technical legal arguments on the Council's competence and the definition of the concept of "domestic jurisdiction" should be avoided; that the Council was, above all, a political body, and that it could accomplish its primary task of assuring international peace and security better through the constructive work of conciliation than as a tribunal ruling on complex and intricate legal issues.[57] The United Kingdom's draft resolution as amended was, in his opinion, the best road open to the Council for the accomplishment of its task.

The representative of China considered that there was a dispute, but that it did not involve a threat to international peace and security, and therefore he proposed to delete from the United Kingdom's revised draft resolution the words concerning a threat to peace. Since he was not convinced of the competence of the Council, he thought, as did the representatives of Ecuador and Yugoslavia, that the resolution should be so framed that the Security Council could render "friendly services" to the United Kingdom and Iran by urging them to resume direct negotiations. To this end he proposed the substitution of the word "advises" for the words "calls for" in the draft resolution.[58] On the day following his offer of these amendments to the United Kingdom's draft resolution, the representative of China, still in doubt concerning the limits of domestic jurisdiction in matters of nationalization,[59] indicated that he would vote in favor of the adoption of the Ecuadorean draft resolution.[60]

These divergent views on the questions of fact—whether there was a dispute, and, if so, whether it was essentially within the domestic jurisdiction of Iran and whether it constituted a potential threat to international peace and security—were never put to the test of a vote, because of the doubts of the Council's competence. These doubts ultimately led the Council to adjourn discussion of the United Kingdom's complaint until the International Court of Justice should rule that it was or was not competent to give a final decision on the merits of the controversy submitted to the Court. However, it appears that only three of the members of the Council (the United Kingdom, the United States, and Brazil) were convinced of the existence of the fact on which the competence of the Council depended, a dispute constituting a threat to international peace and security, whereas at least four members of the Council (the Soviet Union, Yugoslavia, Ecuador, and China) thought that there was no threat to international peace and security in the situation that had developed from the nationalization of Iran's oil industry. The remaining four members of the Council (France, India, the Netherlands, and Turkey) expressed no opinion on the existence of a dispute constituting a threat to international peace and security. Their attention, as well as that of the other members of the Council, was primarily occupied with the technical bases on which the Council was competent to act.

The discussion of the Council's competence was confused not only by the difficulties of construing the phrase "domestic jurisdiction" in Article 2, paragraph 7, of the Charter, but also by the analogy (or identity) some delegates saw between the bases of the Council's jurisdiction and that of the ICJ (see pp. 136–137 above). Although this second source of confusion had been introduced by the representative of Iran (see p. 136), it was also present in the joint amendment to the United Kingdom's revised draft resolution (quoted on p. 129) offered on October 16 by the representatives of India and Yugoslavia. This amendment proposed the deletion of references to the provisional measures indicated by the ICJ, and would have made the resolution call for:

"1. The resumption of negotiations at the earliest practicable moment in order to make further efforts to resolve the differences between the parties in accordance with the purposes and principles of the United Nations Charter."

The second paragraph of the operative part of the United Kingdom's draft resolution would also have been altered, by the substitution of the word "positions" for the words "rights, claims or positions," to read:

"2. The avoidance of any action which would have the effect of further aggravating the situation or prejudicing the positions of the parties concerned."[61]

In introducing this amendment, the representative of India explained that of the five measures indicated by the ICJ in its order (quoted on pp. 87–88, three (Nos. 3, 4, and 5) had been rendered almost impossible of execution by subsequent events, and that the remaining two (Nos. 1 and 2), intended to ensure that no action be taken that might prejudice the rights of either party or aggravate the dispute, were included in paragraph 2 of the revised draft resolution. Therefore, he concluded, there was no longer any need for reference to the provisional measures indicated by the Court.[62] He mentioned, as an additional reason for omitting reference to the provisional measures, the fact that the Court itself had not finally decided the question of its jurisdiction to decide the case on the merits, and he said that it would not be "wise and proper for us to pronounce upon this question while substantially the same question is *sub judice* before the International Court of Justice."[63] The Indian-Yugoslav amendments were accepted by the United Kingdom delegation, "though with the greatest reluctance," at the next meeting of the Council.[64]

At the meeting of the Council on October 17, the delegate from Ecuador expressed the view that the central issue in the question of the Council's competence was the definition of the concept of domestic jurisdiction. This definition he viewed as a legal problem that should be decided by the International Court of Justice. He continued:

If the Court decides itself competent in the matter, it will thereby deny that the case is one for domestic jurisdiction and will give a final judgment. Then, if either Iran or the United Kingdom refuses to comply with the judgment, the other State will clearly be entitled to appeal to the Security Council in accordance with Article 94, paragraph 2, of the Charter. If on the other hand, the Court decides that it is not competent because the case falls within the domestic jurisdiction, the Security Council should not then intervene in a legal matter, as this would be, against the authority of the highest judicial organ of the United Nations.[65]

He also stated that the Security Council should not subordinate its decision on its own competence when dealing with a political problem, but that the question of the Council's competence in the matter then before it was "purely legal," and therefore that it would be inadvisable for the Council to go against the ruling of the ICJ.[66] In accordance with these views the representative of Ecuador introduced the following draft resolution:

Considering that the International Court of Justice is to express its opinion on the question whether the dispute falls exclusively within the domestic jurisdiction of Iran,

The Security Council,

Without deciding on the question of its own competence,

Advises the parties to reopen negotiations ... in accordance with the Purposes and Principles of the United Nations Charter.[67]

This resolution was never brought to a vote.

At the meeting of the Council on October 19, the representative of France moved that the Council adjourn its debate on the United Kingdom's draft resolution, as amended, until the ICJ should rule on its own competence in the matter.[68] The motion was seconded by the representative of the United Kingdom, who explained that the minority doubting the competence of the Council was large enough to prevent the adoption of the draft resolution as amended. He also expressed the belief that there could be no doubts about the Council's competence once the Court had decided its own competence and rendered a final judgment.[69]

Explaining his support of the French delegate's motion, the representative of China declared that the competence of the Court and that of the Council were not identical, and that a decision by the Court affirming or disaffirming its own competence would not automatically mean that the Council was competent or incompetent. To his delegation, he said, the French proposal meant merely that the adjournment was desirable for the sake of a settlement *inter partes*, and that the Court's explanation of its decision might throw some light on the problems confronting the Council. For those two reasons, his delegation would vote in favor of the French motion.[70]

The representative of Ecuador, although he stated that he favored the French resolution for reasons similar to those given by the representative of China, indicated that he welcomed the French proposal mainly because he considered that the Council's competence, as well as the Court's, depended on the definition of the concept of domestic jurisdiction, which he believed to be a legal issue that must be settled by the Court.[71] The representative of India expressed a view substantially the same as that of the representative of Ecuador.[72] The motion for adjournment was adopted by a vote of eight to one, with two abstentions.[73] The representative of Yugoslavia abstained because, he said, he believed the motion "implied that the question of competence of the Security Council depends, at least to a certain degree, on a decision of another United Nations body, an opinion which I do not share."[74]

Thus, proceedings in the Security Council were adjourned, for reasons which it is believed are erroneous. The representatives of China and Yugoslavia both expressed the opinion—which this

writer believes to be correct—that the competence of the Council
and that of the Court do not rest on identical foundations. Indeed,
the bases of jurisdiction of those two bodies are neither necessarily nor substantially the same. The fact that the jurisdiction of
both is limited by the provisions of Article 2, paragraph 7, of
the Charter does not mean that the competence of one depends
upon the competence of the other. It is quite clear that the Court
could be precluded from acting on a matter submitted to it because the matter was essentially within the domestic jurisdiction
of one state, whereas at the same time and with reference to the
same matter the Security Council could take enforcement measures under chapter vii of the Charter (the exception to Article 2,
paragraph 7) for the maintenance of international peace and
security.[75] Further, since both bodies can (and should) determine
their own competence,[76] and since the two bodies are essentially
different in character and functions, it is possible that each would
develop and give effect to a different conception of "matters
essentially within the domestic jurisdiction of any state."[77]

The jurisdiction of the International Court of Justice, as the
principal organ for the settlement of legal disputes, must be
determined on strictly legal grounds by examining the obligations undertaken by the parties to the Statute of the Court and,
if the compulsory jurisdiction of the Court has been accepted by
the parties in accordance with Article 36 of its Statute, by considering the effect of the declarations made under that article.
As was true in the dispute between Iran and the United Kingdom,
the relevant declarations accepting the compulsory jurisdiction
of the Court frequently incorporate by reference various treaties,
and hence these also must be construed before the Court can
finally determine its jurisdiction to deal with questions submitted
to it. On the other hand, the Security Council is a political body
the primary responsibility of which is the maintenance of international peace and security, and its competence to deal with
complaints alleging potential threats to the peace depends solely

on whether, as a matter of fact, the alleged threat to the peace exists. The fact that a situation is "essentially within the domestic jurisdiction" of one state "shall not prejudice the application of enforcement measures under Chapter VII" of the Charter; that is, enforcement measures by the Security Council are permitted in the event that there is a breach of, or threat to, the peace (Article 2, paragraph 7). The underlying causes of a situation or dispute[78] may well lie entirely within the domestic jurisdiction of one or more states, but those states are bound by Article 2, paragraph 4, of the Charter to settle the situation or dispute without the threat or use of force. This interpretation, that Article 2, paragraph 7, does not release members from their obligation under Article 2, paragraph 4, is necessary if the specific exception to Article 2, paragraph 7, is not to be rendered meaningless.[79] That exception, as stated above, permits the Security Council to intervene with enforcement measures under chapter vii of the Charter, and it would be absurd to give the Council this power and yet deny it the power to discuss and investigate matters which are alleged to constitute threats to the peace, merely because a member insists that the matter is "essentially within [its own] domestic jurisdiction." A common-sense interpretation of Article 2, paragraph 7, requires that the Council not only have the power to intervene with enforcement measures in the event that there is a threat to the peace, but that it also have the power to hold hearings and conduct investigations in order to determine whether there is such a threat, and thus a need for its intervention with enforcement measures under chapter vii. The Council is therefore not bound by the allegation of a member that the matter complained of is essentially within its domestic jurisdiction, if the Council is discussing the matter for the purpose of determining the existence of a threat to the peace.[80] Such a power of discussion and investigation is essential if the Security Council is to discharge its "primary responsibility for the maintenance of international peace and security . . ." (Article 24, paragraph 1) and if the fundamental purpose of the United Nations is not to be frustrated.

Thus, it is clear that the Security Council can intervene with enforcement measures when there is a threat to or breach of the peace, and it can hold discussions and investigations to determine whether such enforcement measures are necessary, regardless of an allegation that the matters which it is discussing and investigating are essentially within the domestic jurisdiction of a member. However, the Security Council (and all other United Nations organs) are prohibited by Article 2, paragraph 7, from intervening under chapter vi of the Charter ("Pacific Settlement of Disputes") in matters that are essentially within the domestic jurisdiction of any state. Article 2, paragraph 7, also excepts members from the obligation of submitting matters for settlement under chapter vi which are essentially within their domestic jurisdiction. Therefore, it is with reference to the Council's power to recommend procedures and methods of adjustment in matters not involving a threat to or breach of the peace that it is important to determine what matters are "essentially within the domestic jurisdiction of any state."

The basic content of Article 2, paragraph 7, was taken from Article 15, paragraph 8, of the Covenant of the League of Nations, which reads: "If the dispute between the parties is claimed by one of them, and is found by the Council to arise out of *a matter which by international law is solely within the domestic jurisdiction of that party*, the Council shall so report, and shall make no recommendation as to its settlement." (Italics added.) The fundamental idea of this section was that there are no matters which, by their very nature, are solely within the domestic jurisdiction of a state, that all matters are susceptible to being regulated by international law, and that if a matter is regulated by international law it is no longer "solely" within the domestic jurisdiction of a state. Only those matters that are not, for the time being, regulated by a rule of international law are solely within the domestic jurisdiction of a state. Differently stated, if there is no rule of international law imposing a certain obligation on states with regard to the matter in question, the state has the right, under international law, to do as it pleases.[81]

Article 2, paragraph 7, of the United Nations Charter differs primarily from Article 15, paragraph 8, of the League Covenant in that the words "by international law" have been eliminated and the word "essentially" has been substituted for the word "solely."[82] In one way this deletion of the reference to international law is regrettable, since it eliminates an objective test of the concept of domestic jurisdiction. The delegate of the United States to the San Francisco Conference on International Organization (UNCIO) explained that paragraph 7 of Article 2 of the proposed Charter was meant to deal with domestic jurisdiction as a "basic principle," and not to define it according to any "technical or legalistic formula." This change in concept, he explained, reflected the difference in character between the United Nations and the League of Nations. The powers of the United Nations were, he said, much broader than those of its predecessor, since they included functions that would enable the United Nations to eliminate the underlying causes of war as well as to deal with crises leading toward war.[83] A summary report of the drafting committee at the San Francisco Conference explained that the object of Article 2, paragraph 7, was to uphold two principles: "(1) explicit recognition of the rule that there should not be undue interference with the domestic jurisdiction of the several states; and (2) that the performance by the Security Council of its functions for the maintenance of peace and security should be assured."[84] Dr. Liang, Director of the Division of Development and Codification of International Law of the United Nations Secretariat, has expressed the view that the final form of Article 2, paragraph 7, was not intended to minimize the use of "international law" as a criterion for determining domestic jurisdiction, but rather to emphasize the "concept of international concern" and to give the political organs of the United Nations a greater discretion when confronted with a plea that a particular situation or dispute is not within the jurisdiction of any international organization because it is essentially within the domestic jurisdiction of one state.[85] However, it would seem that if the political organs of the United Nations are to have a "greater discretion" than they would normally have were they limited by the rules of international law, then the value of international law is definitely minimized as a criterion for determining domestic jurisdiction.

The substitution of "essentially" for "solely" also reflects the decline in the use of international law as a criterion, and may be interpreted as having been intended to enlarge the concept of domestic jurisdiction to include some matters formerly excluded, even though they may also be regulated by a rule of international law or may involve an obligation under an international treaty.[86] The substitution of "essentially" for "solely" has also been interpreted to mean that a state may refuse to submit a matter for settlement under the Charter or may deny the right of the United Nations to intervene if the matter is "essential" to its "sovereignty," and if the submission or intervention would be incompatible with its "sovereignty."[87] In contrast, it is equally possible to interpret Article 2, paragraph 7, as meaning that a matter is "essentially within the domestic jurisdiction" of a state only when that state is under no international (law or treaty) obligation with respect to the matter.[88] This restrictive interpretation seems more consistent with the broadened scope of the United Nations Organization as compared with that of the League of Nations. However, it is clear that the possibility of the former, more extensive, interpretation caused the doubt in the minds of the delegate members of the Security Council that led to the postponement of discussion of the United Kingdom's complaint. Had the restrictive interpretation been adopted, the Council could have applied a relatively objective criterion to determine whether

Iran was under any international (law or treaty) obligation with respect to the matters complained of by the United Kingdom. If the Council had done so, it could have rendered a constructive service to the parties and to the development of the law of the United Nations. Instead, the Security Council failed to act because the ambiguous and elusive concepts of sovereignty and domestic jurisdiction had created doubts in the minds of some of the delegates. The Council's failure to act can hardly—to quote the representative of the Netherlands—be said "to have contributed to increasing the prestige, the standing and the efficiency of the United Nations and its supreme organ, the Security Council."[89] However, it must be remembered that even if the somewhat doubtful assumption is made that a sufficient majority could have been obtained to pass the United Kingdom's draft resolution, as amended, there was a real possibility that Iran would ignore the resolution, on the same grounds as those on which it had ignored the ICJ's order of July 5.[90] If that event had occurred, any attempt at enforcement measures by the Council would almost certainly have been vetoed by the Soviet delegate, who had repeatedly expressed the opinion that it would be improper for the Council even to discuss the question. Indeed, it is probable that the Soviet delegate would have vetoed passage of the draft resolution, had it been put to a vote. The Council was, therefore, placed in the difficult position of being faced with almost certain frustration of any attempt at affirmative action, or choosing, as it did, to adjourn its discussion. The first alternative, that of forcing a Soviet veto or Iranian disobedience if either were inevitable, may have been the preferable one, since the reasons for the Council's failure to act, or the ineffectiveness of its action, would then have been made obvious to the world. The alternative chosen, adjournment, is open to the criticism that it created, for the reasons given above, an undesirable precedent on the question of the Council's competence.

It is certain that neither alternative was desirable. The fact that the Security Council was forced to choose between two such alternatives reflects the weakened position in which the Council had been placed as a result of the developing intensity of the "cold war." This tendency will certainly result, if it has not already done so, in a decline in the prestige of the Security Council and of the United Nations as a whole. Indeed, the Council has increasingly become a "sounding board," rather than, as was intended by its framers, a supreme political organ capable of prompt and effective action for the maintenance of international relations with a minimum of friction.[91]

§ 9. Further Developments

Before the Security Council adjourned its discussion, Sir Gladwyn Jebb made it clear that the United Kingdom was willing to resume negotiations on the basis of recognition of the principle of nationalization, "as that phrase is understood in the Western World," if the Iranian government was ready to examine the practical difficulties that must be faced before a settlement could be achieved.[1] This position was affirmed subsequently in statements by Prime Minister Churchill and Foreign Secretary Eden in the House of Commons, outlining the policies of the new Conservative government. A readiness to negotiate was also announced by Prime Minister Mossadegh and other Iranian officials, but the two governments were, and continued to be, far from agreement on what the basis of the negotiations would be, and, in fact, negotiations have never been resumed.[2]

At the conclusion of the Security Council's discussions, Prime Minister Mossadegh came to Washington at the invitation of President Truman. There, over a period of three weeks, the prime minister and State Department officials discussed means of settling the oil dispute. Details of these talks were not disclosed, but, after intermittent reports pointing toward success, the talks finally terminated unsuccessfully on November 13. On that day the State Department issued a statement saying, "The United

States Government has regretfully concluded that, while progress has been made, no new basis has emerged on which a practicable solution could be reached." It was added that the United States would "continue to do everything possible to assist" Iran and the United Kingdom to find a mutually acceptable basis for a satisfactory solution.[3] On the following day, Prime Minister Mossadegh announced in a speech to the National Press Club in Washington that he had appealed to the United States for a loan to prevent his country's being paralyzed from lack of funds during the ensuing twelve months. He said that, although Iran would soon have ample funds from oil revenues to repay such a loan and to embark on economic and social reforms, a substantial sum was urgently needed to tide the country over for approximately one year until the nationalized oil installations could be productively operated again. Mossadegh did not mention the size of the loan for which he applied, but it was reported to amount to $120,000,000, or $10,000,000 per month for the one-year period.[4] A State Department spokesman said that the United States would give the prime minister's request for a loan "the most careful consideration." As a stopgap, Iran withdrew $8,750,000 from its deposit with the International Monetary Fund.

On November 18, Mossadegh left Washington for Tehran. When he stopped at Cairo in the midst of the violent anti-British riots, he was received cordially by Egyptian nationalist Premier Nahas Pasha and Egyptian crowds, in a frenzy of Arab-nationalist and anti-British emotion. After several days of talks, the two statesmen signed a pact of friendship and declared that "a united Iran and Egypt will together demolish British imperialism."[5] Mossadegh then proceeded home to Tehran, where he was welcomed by wildly demonstrating crowds and a Parliament that gave him a unanimous vote of confidence. He also demanded and won approval of his plan to hold immediate elections,[6] a politically strategic move to assure the election of his supporters while the country was virtually unanimous in support of his policies and before the strain of diminishing revenues was felt too acutely.

AIOC had been the primary source of Iran's supply of foreign exchange,[7] and the lack of revenues from AIOC after nationalization finally necessitated the suspension, by the Bank Melli on December 4, of the right to open import credits abroad.[8] The following day two members of the Mixed Board, Senators Najm and Sorrori, resigned their posts, reportedly as a result of disagreements over administrative policy.[9] Several thousand Communist-led youths rioted in the streets of Tehran on December 6 protesting Mossadegh's policies. They fought with thousands of police and supporters of Mossadegh's National Front party in a battle that lasted five hours and killed five and wounded more than two hundred persons.[10] As economic collapse came nearer and social chaos spread, opposition to the National Front party grew. A number of opposition deputies took refuge in the Parliament buildings on December 8 declaring that they were being threatened by National Front extremists. The riots continued and, on December 10, extended into the Parliament buildings themselves.

On that day Prime Minister Mossadegh was explaining to the Majlis his reaction to reports that the International Bank for Reconstruction and Development (IBRD) was working on proposals for the settlement of the dispute. After promising that the persons responsible for the riots would be punished, he went on to say that he was willing to have the International Bank finance Iran's oil industry, and to have a part of the oil revenues go to the AIOC as compensation, but he declared that Iran would not accept the readmission of British technicians, even as employees of the IBRD. It was reported that the prime minister also charged that the United States Department of State was under the influence of the British government, and that the United States (because of British influence?) had never given Iran assistance of any value. He also stated that the Iranian government would shut down the oil industry before it would capitulate to the British. The session ended in a riot between the opposition deputies and Mossadegh's supporters. Crowds demonstrated outside the Parliament buildings in support of the prime minister, as they continued to do on the next several days.[11]

On December 12 the Iranian government issued an ultimatum to the former customers of AIOC giving them until December 22 to make arrangements to buy oil from the Iranian government or lose the privileges that the government had offered them. Copies of the ultimatum were sent to twenty-two legations in Tehran, including those of the Soviet Union and of the various eastern European states.[12] The British government and the AIOC again announced that they did not recognize Iran's right to sell the oil, and that such action as might prove necessary would be taken to prevent the proposed sales. The ultimatum expired on December 22 without a single acceptance of the Iranian government's offer to the former AIOC customers. However, three days later it was announced that Czechoslovakia was sending a delegation to Tehran to conclude a purchase contract.[13]

As yet, Iran's economic position had not become critical. Because of the extraordinarily high level of imports in 1950 and in the first few months of 1951, warehouses were well stocked, and, although an inflationary trend in consumer prices had begun in August, prices had not yet reached the disastrous level of 1949 (see above, pp. 37 and 45–47). Barter trade with the Germans had been restored to its prewar level (see pp. 27–28), and a new barter agreement had been concluded with the Soviets. Domestic industry, apart from the oil industry of the south, showed some improvement. But the curtailment, especially in Azerbaijan, of public works and relief programs because of financial difficulties was creating an ever larger body of unemployed. The worst unemployment was, of course, in the oil province of Khuzistan, where the unemployed oil workers were being paid out of a special fund of £14 million that had been withdrawn in July from the Iranian government's sterling balance in London for the purpose of financing essential imports. By the end of the year this sum was reduced to £3.5 million, and no new source of employment was in sight. The number of unemployed oil workers was so large that the government could not afford to employ them in its construction project on the southern railways. The majority of Iranians are small farmers, whose simple economy was much less disturbed by the growing financial strain on the government than a more complicated economic structure would have been. The fact that the basic wants of this largest section of the Iranian economy could be satisfied from domestic sources provided a real, though limited, insurance against social unrest and immediate economic disintegration.[14] To help finance public works projects to provide relief for the unemployed, Prime Minister Mossadegh appealed to his people to subscribe to a public bond issue of 2 billion rials ($40 million).[15]

The revolt of the opposition deputies who had sought refuge in the Parliament buildings continued throughout December, but without much popular approval. Their opposition did not, however, prevent the government from proceeding with the national elections, and these were begun on December 18 in the northern provinces and Tehran in a tense atmosphere that followed days of continued rioting in Tehran.[16] Early in January, 1952, it was announced that elections in the southern province of Khuzistan had been suspended because a reported plot to blow up the Abadan refinery required the maintenance of martial law. In a note to the British ambassador, Prime Minister Mossadegh charged British officials with "open interference" in the internal affairs of the Iranian government (presumably the elections?) and warned that if such conduct did not stop immediately steps would be taken by the Iranian government to end the "undesirable situation."[17] The British ambassador, on January 11, stated that he refused to accept Mossadegh's note because the mode of sending it had been contrary to "diplomatic courtesy," in that copies had been delivered to the press at the same time as to the British Embassy. As a reply, and perhaps as a strategic move to win support in the national elections, Prime Minister Mossadegh sent the British ambassador a note on January 12 ordering all British consulates in Iran closed within ten days, on the grounds that British consular officials had exceeded their proper duties and interfered in the internal affairs of Iran.[18] British protests and requests to reconsider were rejected, and the consulates were accordingly closed on January 21 amidst a mass demonstration in Tehran in support of Mossadegh's policies.[19] On the very day that the British consulates were closed, an American-Iranian agreement on Point Four aid was announced, after weeks of tedious negotiation. Soon afterward, on January 31, the American Embassy in Tehran announced that the Iranian government had ordered all foreign information and cultural centers closed immediately. The order affected primarily American, British, and Russian services in the provinces.[20]

Late in December, 1951, it had been reported that Mossadegh refused to sign an agreement with the United States for economic and military aid under the Mutual Security Act because of the provision in the act that required recipient nations to commit themselves to contribute to the "defensive strength of the free world." Mossadegh reportedly refused to make such a commitment, on the ground that Iran had already made peace commitments through its membership in the United Nations which made additional pledges of this type unnecessary, and, further, on the ground that such a pledge would violate Iran's "neutrality."[21] The Mutual Security Act gives the president of the United States the power to waive this pledge and grant economic and technical (but not military) aid if he finds that such aid would strengthen United States security and promote world peace. But, even with this waiver, Iran would still have to agree to "adopt measures mutually agreed on to eliminate the causes of international tension." An agreement (announced January 21, 1952) was finally reached on this basis, and aid totaling $23.4 million for 1952 (it had amounted to only $1.46 million in 1951) was granted for economic and technical assistance.[22] Failure to reach an agreement on military aid caused shipments of military goods from the United States to be temporarily suspended. The conclusion of the economic aid agreement for $23.4 million was undoubtedly a political victory for Mossadegh. The very size of the sum was sufficient to make the Iranian people celebrate a victory, but it also showed that the United States was not in complete agreement with the British on their policy of doing everything possible to bring about the fall of Mossadegh's government. On the contrary, the American aid granted during the Iranian national elections greatly strengthened Mossadegh's position. That it should do so demonstrates again the rather extreme nature of Iranian politics. None of the $23.4 million would go directly into the Iranian exchequer, a fact which few of the Iranian public realized.[23] Instead, much of it would go for the training of Iranian technicians in Iran and in the United States. The remainder would be used for development programs (primarily rural); these depended, however, on Iranian acceptance of the advice of an American technical adviser and on the expenditure of Iranian money and effort in carrying out that advice. Great difficulties had been incurred in meeting these two conditions in the past.[24]

Late in December, 1951, a mission from the IBRD arrived in Tehran to study the problem of formulating proposals for the settlement of the oil dispute through the mediation of the Bank. On January 3, 1952, a letter from IBRD Vice-President Garner was sent to Mossadegh, outlining the basic principles under which it was considered that oil production could be resumed with the Bank acting as an interim agent. On the following day, the Iranian government sources released the substance of these proposals and Mossadegh's reply, which rejected them in part and asked for further elaboration of other points.[25] According to these sources, the Bank had proposed that for a period of two years Iran's oil industry be put under the management of a "neutral top executive," whose personnel would be chosen by and be responsible to the Bank. Under the authority of the Bank, production would be resumed and a bulk-purchase contract covering the two-year term would be concluded for the sale of oil through established distribution channels. The proceeds of such sales would be divided three ways, the recipients to be: the bulk buyer (distributor); the Iranian government; and the Bank, which would retain one-third as security for its services and any capital that it might provide, and as a compensation fund for AIOC. The prime minister's letter asked IBRD Vice-President Garner to explain who would be considered "neutrals" and whether the bulk-purchase contract would be made with the Iranian government or with other governments. Mossadegh indicated that he would flatly reject any proposal for sharing the proceeds with a bulk buyer[26] (presumably AIOC, since it was the only large oil company with adequate and available world-wide distribution facilities), and suggested that, as an alternative to the Bank's proposed retention of one-third of the proceeds, the Bank name a flat fee for its services that would be paid by the Iranian government from the total, unshared sales proceeds. In asking whether the Bank proposed that its temporary authority be limited to technical matters or whether this authority would extend to questions of "economic policy," Prime Minister Mossadegh added that the Bank must always remember that the conduct of his country's oil industry would only be a mission temporarily entrusted to the Bank, and that the latter "must always perform its services under Iranian Government instructions."[27] The British Foreign Office announced on January 5 that it had received similar proposals from the Bank which were being studied, and that, although the principles worked out by the Bank were fair and generally acceptable to the British government, they would need some elaboration. This attitude toward the Bank's proposals was also expressed by Foreign Secretary Eden in an address at Columbia University on January 11.[28]

The IBRD mission left Iran late in January after receiving the prime minister's reply. Before the second mission was sent early in February, the Iranian government filed its memorial with the International Court of Justice at The Hague on February 4. The memorial contested the jurisdiction of the Court to hear the British complaint and presented a preliminary objection that had the effect of suspending proceedings until the Court should determine its competence to decide the case on its merits.[29]

The second mission from the IBRD arrived in Tehran on February 11 and immediately began discussions with Prime Minister Mossadegh. The riots that had plagued Iran for so long had continued to break out intermittently through most of January and February. After the arrival of the second Bank mission, there were several riots in which the demonstrators threatened the lives of its five members should any agreement be concluded between the Bank and the Iranian government. The five men had to be quartered at the Iranian Officers' Club and were constantly accompanied by armed officers wherever they went.[30]

Despite this atmosphere the discussions continued. The Bank's proposals were still substantially the same as those it had submitted to the Iranian government in January. The principal unresolved issues were centered on Mossadegh's refusal to consider any scheme whereby the Iranian government would not retain "full authority" or which provided for a discount to the wholesale distributor.[31] Mossadegh also objected to the Bank's proposal to retain a percentage of the profits as a fund for compensation to AIOC, to be paid when the problem of compensation was finally settled by the ICJ or in some other way.[32] Mossadegh announced on February 16 that agreement on the Bank's proposals was not possible; but, at the urging of the Iranian Senate, another attempt at negotiation was made, this time with the assistance of a special five-member parliamentary committee. These further talks proved no more productive than the preceding ones. The Bank mission, without formally breaking off the talks, proceeded to London to discuss the matter with British officials, and thence to New York, where it arrived on February 28.[33] A representative of the Bank returned to Tehran on March 4 and renewed the discussions, which continued until the sixteenth. On that day Mossadegh announced that no agreement had been reached on any major point. The parliamentary committee announced that the talks had been suspended and said that Iran could not agree to the use of British technicians in the Iranian oil fields. The Bank mission, it seems, had taken the position that it could not discriminate against technicians of any particular nationality. The parliamentary committee's statement also indicated that the Iranian government would not accept the IBRD proposal that the Bank operate the oil industry independently, and it was stated that agreement could not be reached on the price of oil, that is, on whether the bulk buyer (distributor) would get a wholesale price or be required to buy at the world price. Before leaving Tehran on March 23 the Bank's representative said that it was difficult to reach any agreement because "the oil problem [in Iran] is mainly a political problem."[34] A spokesman for the Bank announced in New York on April 3 that there was no apparent prospect of going forward with its proposals in the immediate future.[35]

In view of Prime Minister Mossadegh's insistence on "full authority" it is not surprising that the Bank's efforts came to nothing. It was the Bank's lack of confidence in the soundness of Iranian government management and in the ability of Iranians to put forth an efficient productive effort that had caused it to refuse repeated applications for loans since 1948 (see pp. 47–48 above). At the same time the Bank's efforts undoubtedly had the effect of confirming Mossadegh and his government in their belief that Iranian oil is vital to the Western world. If he negotiated with the Bank on the basis of this assumption, as it seems he did, the negotiations were conducted at cross-purposes, since the Bank's primary concern was to save Iran from bankruptcy and to avert a chaos that would please no one but the Soviet Union. Actually the world's production of crude oil had been at an all-time high in 1951, in spite of the Iranian shutdown,[36] and, by the end of that year, production and distribution had been sufficiently readjusted to ameliorate almost completely the temporary strain caused by the Iranian shutdown. By July of 1952, both the non-Soviet world in general and AIOC in particular had developed adequate non-Iranian supplies, and the total world production in 1952 exceeded that of 1951. Thus, Iranian oil was not at all *vital*—which is not to say not important—to either the Western world or the Anglo-Iranian Oil Company (see pp. 216–218).

Two days after the failure of the Bank's efforts were announced in Tehran, Prime Minister Mossadegh announced that he had received a communication from President Truman stating that Iran's request for a loan could not be justified before the United States Senate at a time "when Iran has the opportunity of receiving adequate revenues from its oil industry without prejudice to its national aspirations." President Truman assured the prime minister that the United States did not seek to establish Iranian acceptance of any particular proposals for a settlement of the oil dispute as a condition precedent to an American loan, and said that the United States had consistently maintained that a practical settlement consistent with the legitimate interests of both the United Kingdom and Iran was possible. He urged the Iranian prime minister to seek such a solution.[37]

It was announced on March 20 that the United States military mission that had been in Iran since World War II (see Part I, § 7, n. 3) would remain temporarily after the expiration of the formal military agreement on March 20. As has been mentioned above (see p. 159), this agreement had not been renewed, because of Mossadegh's objection to the pledges required by the

164

United States Mutual Security Act. On April 24 it was announced that, as a result of an exchange of notes between United States Ambassador Loy Henderson and Prime Minister Mossadegh, the Iranian government had agreed to accept continued American military assistance. Shipments of military goods, which had been suspended since January, 1952, were resumed. In the exchange of notes, the Iranian prime minister had stated, "Iran supports and defends the principles of the United Nations to the extent that its resources and general conditions permit . . ." The United States government had decided to accept this assurance in lieu of the formula prescribed by the Mutual Security Act.[88]

The Iranian government requested the ICJ on April 6, 1952, to grant a one-month postponement of the hearings, scheduled to begin May 6, on Iran's preliminary objection. The Iranian government sought this postponement in order to permit Prime Minister Mossadegh (who planned to appear before the Court himself) to make a report to the Majlis on his oil policies as soon as the national elections had been completed. The Court granted the Iranian request on April 9, and the hearings were postponed until June 9.

After the unsuccessful conclusion of the Bank's efforts at mediation, both the United Kingdom and Iran seemed to await the proceedings in the International Court as a next step and to avoid any further effort toward a negotiated settlement in the interim.

§ 10. Preliminary Objection to the Jurisdiction of the International Court of Justice

The United Kingdom's "Application" of May 26, 1951, requested the International Court of Justice to declare that Iran was under a duty to arbitrate with AIOC in accordance with the provisions of Articles 22 and 26 of the 1933 concession or, alternatively, to declare that unilateral alteration or cancelation of the 1933 concession by the Iranian government would be a denial of justice, and thus a violation of international law, for which the Iranian government would have to give satisfaction and indemnity. In its alternative prayer, the United Kingdom asked the Court to adjudge Iran's liability and to determine "the manner of such satisfaction and indemnity."[1] The British memorial in support of this application was filed on October 10, 1951 (see above, p. 129). Within the time limit fixed for the presentation of its countermemorial, the Iranian government submitted to the Court on February 4, 1952, a document entitled "Preliminary Observations: Refusal of the Imperial Government to Recognize the Jurisdiction of the Court." This document was treated as a preliminary objection and therefore had the effect of suspending the proceedings on the merits.[2] Oral pleadings on the preliminary objection were begun at The Hague on June 9, 1952, and the Court announced its judgment sustaining the objection on July 22, 1952.[3]

The jurisdiction of the Court depended upon the declarations made by the United Kingdom and Iran under Article 36 of the Statute of the Court, on condition of reciprocity. However, since the parties were agreed that the Iranian declaration was more restrictive than that of the United Kingdom, the decision turned on the Court's interpretation of the Iranian declaration of September 19, 1932, which reads, in part, as follows:[4]

Le Gouvernement impérial de Perse déclare reconnaître comme obligatoire, de plein droit et sans convention spéciale, vis-à-vis de tout autre État acceptant la même obligation, c'est-à-dire sous condition de réciprocité, la juridiction de la Cour permanente de Justice internationale, conformément à l'article 36, paragraphe 2, du Statut de la Cour, sur tous les différends qui s'élèveraient après la ratification de la présente déclaration, au sujet de situations ou de faits ayant directement ou indirectement trait à l'application des traités ou conventions acceptés par la Perse et postérieurs à la ratification de cette déclaration, exception faite pour: . . .

166

Translation by the Secretariat of the League of Nations:

The Imperial Government of Persia recognizes as compulsory *ipso facto* and without special agreement in relation to any other state accepting the same obligation, that is to say, on condition of reciprocity, the jurisdiction of the Permanent Court of International Justice, in accordance with Article 36, paragraph 2, of the Statute of the Court, in any disputes arising after the ratification of the present declaration with regard to situations or facts relating directly or indirectly to the application of treaties or conventions accepted by Persia and subsequent to the ratification of this declaration, with the exception of: . . .

The United Kingdom and Iran were agreed that this declaration confers jurisdiction on the Court only in the case of a dispute relating to the application of a treaty or convention accepted by Iran. But they disagreed on the question whether the Court's jurisdiction was limited to the application of treaties or conventions accepted by Iran after the ratification of this declaration (September 19, 1932), or whether it extended to the application of treaties and conventions accepted by Iran at any time. The Iranian government argued for the restrictive interpretation, pointing out that the phrase "et postérieurs à la ratification de cette déclaration" followed immediately after the reference to "traités ou conventions acceptés par la Perse." The United Kingdom argued that the phrase "et postérieurs à la ratification de cette déclaration" modified the expression "au sujet de situations ou de faits," and that, therefore, the jurisdiction of the Court extended to the application of treaties or conventions accepted by Iran at any time.[5]

The Court, agreeing with the Iranian argument, thought that the linking of the phrase "et postérieurs à la ratification de cette déclaration" to the expression that immediately precedes it, "traités ou conventions acceptés par la Perse," was a "natural and reasonable way of reading the text."[6] The Court substantiated its conclusion on this point by other findings, which are discussed below, but before proceeding to them it may be well to explore the question whether this is a "natural and reasonable way of reading the text." The Court's conclusion is more credible if only the English translation is consulted, since the comma which follows the phrase "après la ratification de la présent déclaration" has been omitted by the translator. When the official French text is read with attention to the placing of the commas, the phrase included within them, "au sujet de situations ou de faits ayant directement ou indirectement trait à l'application des traités ou conventions acceptés par la Perse et postérieurs à la ratification de cette déclaration," is a double-dependent clause qualifying the principal phrase of the paragraph, beginning "sur tous les différends . . ." Thus, if the declaration is read with attention to the punctuation, it would seem that the "natural and reasonable" way of reading it is to consider the phrase "et postérieurs à la ratification de cette déclaration" as merely reinforcing the qualification to the principal statement that the disputes must arise after ratification of the declaration by requiring that the situations or facts that form the basis of the disputes must also arise after the ratification of the declaration. The Court's construction of a single dependent clause requires the reader to ignore and delete the word "et" before "postérieurs." If the phrase "postérieurs à la ratification de cette déclaration" really referred, as the Court said, to "traités ou conventions acceptés par la Perse," the conjunction "et" would be completely unnecessary. In a carefully drafted document, as this declaration obviously was, it seems incomprehensible that an unnecessary "et" would be inserted in such a manner that the text could be read meaningfully (from the point of view of the Iranian government's argument and the Court's "natural and reasonable" reading) *only* if this word is disregarded. At best the Court's conclusion was only the choice between two equally good alternatives.[7] The alternative chosen has done little to encourage a belief in the Court's ability to deal effectively and fairly with a type of dispute which has thus far remained outside the regulating influence of international law and international procedures.[8]

The United Kingdom presented the argument that the construction ultimately adopted by the Court necessarily implied that the declaration contained some superfluous word or words, although the particular word or words were not cited in the judgment. The British argument was based on the rule of construction that requires a legal text to be interpreted "in such a way that a reason and a meaning can be attributed to every word in the text."[9] The Court agreed that this should be the rule of interpretation for the text of a treaty, but added that the Iranian declaration was "not a treaty text resulting from negotiations between two or more States," but rather, was the "result of unilateral drafting . . . [with] a particular degree of caution" for "special reasons."[10] The Court said, "[Iran] appears to have inserted, *ex abundanti cautela,* words which, strictly speaking, may seem to have been superfluous."[11] This is rather weak reasoning with which to justify an interpretation that results in one too many "et's." It is, at best, rather difficult to see in this argument a "natural and reasonable way of reading the text."

The "special reasons" to which the Court referred, and the principal support for the conclusions it reached in construing the text of Iran's declaration, were Iran's denunciation and repudiation, on May 10, 1927, of all treaties relating to the regime of capitulations, and its desire to except the capitulatory treaties from its declaration of acceptance of the compulsory jurisdiction of the Court. Because of these considerations the Court found it to have been the "manifest intention" of Iran to except disputes relating to treaties "accepted" prior to the "ratification" of the declaration.[12] It should be noted that the words "accepted" and "ratification" used by the Court in the paragraph just referred to were also the words used by the government of Iran in the first paragraph of its declaration. Iran accepted as compulsory the jurisdiction of the Court in disputes relating to the application of treaties *"accepted"* by it "and subsequent to the *ratification* of this declaration." (Italics added.) The point of quoting this again is to indicate that the drafter of the Iranian declaration apparently ascribed some difference of meaning to the italicized words. In neither English nor French do these words have the same meaning. In both languages the verb "accept" implies a measure of mental consent, of affirmative approval; whereas "ratification" refers to formal legal consent by a properly constituted body. Therefore, it would seem that if the government of Iran had intended its declaration to have the meaning attributed to it by the Court it would have specified that its acceptance of the compulsory jurisdiction of the Court applied only to disputes relating to the application of treaties *ratified* by it after the ratification of the declaration. However, in the declaration as finally deposited at Geneva, the draftsman could reasonably have thought that by the use of the word *"acceptés"* rather than *"ratifiés"* the declaration applied only to those treaties to which the government of Iran gave its affirmative assent and approval, that is, it did not apply to those capitulatory treaties that the Iranian government had publicly repudiated several years before the ratification of its declaration. This construction would give meaning to the *"et"* that so troubled the Court and would, at the same time, except the capitulatory treaties that provided the foundation for the only argument with any real substance that the Court put forward to sustain its interpretation of the Iranian declaration. Such a construction would give "a reason and a meaning to every word in the text" and would avoid the tenuousities involved in the argument *ex abundanti cautela.*

The Court found "decisive confirmation" of Iran's "manifest intention" to exclude treaties "accepted" by Iran prior to the ratification of its declaration in a statute passed by the Iranian Parliament on June 14, 1931, approving the declaration which had been deposited with the Court on October 2, 1930, although it was not ratified until September 19, 1932. The 1931 statute paraphrased the conditions of the declaration without quoting them textually. One of these conditions was stated thus: "In respect of all disputes arising out of situations or facts relating, directly or indirectly, to the execution of treaties and conventions which the Government will have accepted after the ratification of the Declaration." This statute was a domestic instrument. Its text was not communicated to other states, but it was published in the Corpus of Iranian Laws. The Court, though stating that such a law could not constitute a basis for its jurisdiction, nevertheless accepted the law in evidence as "*decisive* confirmation of the intention of the Government of Iran at the time when it accepted the compulsory jurisdiction of the Court"[13] (italics added)—and thus, it would seem, affirmed that such a law could at least be relied upon as a basis for denying the jurisdiction of the Court. Concluding its interpretation, the Court held that the Iranian declaration was limited "to disputes relating to the application of treaties or conventions accepted by Iran after the ratification of the Declaration."[14] Sir Arnold McNair, President of the Court, in his separate concurring opinion, indicated that he would have preferred to exclude the Iranian statute from being received in evidence, that its admissibility was "open to question" and its "evidentiary value" was slight.[15] Judge Hackworth, in his dissenting opinion, accepted the Court's conclusion that the Iranian declaration was limited to the application of treaties or conventions accepted by Iran after the ratification of the declaration, but argued that admission of the Iranian statute in evidence was unnecessary and improper. The Court, he said,

must look to the public declarations by States made for international purposes, and cannot resort to municipal legislative enactments to explain ambiguities in international acts. . . . When a State deposits with an international organ a document [such as the Iranian declaration] . . . upon which other States are expected to rely, those States are entitled to accept the document at face value; they are not required to go back to the municipal law of that State for explanations of the meaning or significance of the international instrument.[16]

Although Judge Hackworth's statement is a correct exposition of
the legal efficacy of the Iranian statute, such a law may, nevertheless, have some probative value as evidence of the intention of
the government of Iran at the time when its declaration was prepared. But the statute should have been admitted in evidence only
if a finding on the Iranian government's intention was necessary
to explain an irreconcilable ambiguity in the text of the declaration. From the analysis on the preceding pages it should be clear
that there was not such an irreconcilable ambiguity as to justify
the admission of the Iranian statute in evidence, and the propriety of its admission seems especially questionable when it was
used as the sole support of an argument as contrived and tenuous
as the Court's appears to be. From another point of view, the
variations in wording between the Iranian statute and the declaration, the deletion of "and" and putting the verb "accept" in the
future rather than past tense, suggests that the declaration may
have been deliberately "fuzzed" and made ambiguous (and thus
misleading) for purposes of international prestige. To the lay
reader, the declaration would appear to be a much broader undertaking than the statute indicates. If this be true, then the Iranian
government should have been held responsible for an interpretation of the text at face value and in such a manner that a reason
and a meaning could be given to every word. The text was not so
interpreted by the Court, and the use of the Iranian statute to
sustain a construction in which at least one word must be regarded
as superfluous is open to serious question. It may also be suggested at this point that if the Iranian government had been
especially concerned to exclude the treaties relating to the regime
of capitulations from the terms of its declaration it could have
done so very simply by making their exclusion the subject of a
specific exception. This would appear to have been the obvious
way of handling the problem, especially in light of the fact that
a public repudiation of those treaties had already been made. It
can be added that such a course of action would not have had any

adverse effect on Iran's international prestige beyond that (if any) which the government had already incurred by its repudiation of the capitulatory treaties.

The agent of the United Kingdom argued that even if the Court did construe the Iranian declaration as pertaining only to disputes that related to the application of treaties accepted by Iran after the date of the ratification of the declaration (September 19, 1932), it still had jurisdiction to consider the United Kingdom's application of May 26, 1951. In this argument it was stated that Iran had violated its obligation to treat British subjects in accordance with the requirements of international law, which obligation Iran had undertaken in treaties or conventions with Switzerland, Denmark, and Turkey, all concluded after the date of the ratification of the declaration, and the treaties of 1857 and 1903 which Iran had concluded with the United Kingdom and which pledged that the treatment of British subjects and their trade should "in every respect, be placed on the footing of the treatment of the subjects and commerce of the most-favoured nation [in Iran]."[17] Article IV of the commercial treaty of February 20, 1934, between Iran and Denmark, contained a pledge by Iran to treat Danish nationals, "as regards their persons and property, in accordance with the principles and practice of ordinary international law."[18] The agent of the United Kingdom argued that through the operation of the most-favored-nation clause in the Anglo-Iranian treaties of 1857 and 1903 Iran became bound to treat British nationals in accordance with the principles of international law. He also argued that the conduct of the Iranian government toward AIOC was not in accord with the requirements of international law,[19] and that, therefore, the dispute between the United Kingdom and Iran concerned situations or facts relating directly or indirectly to the application of a treaty—the Danish-Iranian Treaty of 1934—accepted by Iran after the date of ratification of its declaration. The Court rejected this argument, stating that the United Kingdom was not in a position to invoke the Danish-Iranian Treaty to establish the jurisdiction of the Court. The treaty containing the most-favored-nation clause was the "basic treaty" on which the United Kingdom must rely, the Court declared, and a treaty concluded by Iran with a third state, to which the United Kingdom was not a party, could not form a basis for the establishment of the jurisdiction of the Court. It was not, the Court said, the application of the Danish treaty of 1934 that was in dispute, but the application of the British treaties of 1857 and 1903, both of which were concluded before the ratification of the declaration and were, therefore, excluded by its terms.[20]

Relying on the word "indirectement" in the phrase "au sujet de situations ou de faits ayant directement ou indirectement trait à l'application des traités ou conventions," the agent of the United Kingdom argued that the dispute did involve the Danish treaty through the operation of the most-favored-nation clause. The Court rejected this argument also, saying that the phrase "directement ou indirectement" referred only to the manner in which the situations or facts forming the subject matter of a dispute relate to the treaty, and that the treaty to which they relate must be the "basic treaty" to which both Iran and the United Kingdom are parties. The fact that the situations or facts forming the subject matter of the dispute between Iran and the United Kingdom may be indirectly related to the Danish-Persian Treaty of 1934, said the Court, is of no help to the United Kingdom in its effort to establish the jurisdiction of the Court, since the United Kingdom was not a party to that treaty. The Court held that a treaty concluded by Iran with a third party could not be relied on by the United Kingdom as forming a basis, through the operation of the most-favored-nation clause, for the establishment of the jurisdiction of the Court.[21] Sir Arnold McNair expressed a similar view of this problem in his separate concurring opinion.[22]

Judge Hackworth, in his dissenting opinion, said that the Court placed the emphasis on the wrong treaty when it called the treaty containing the most-favored-nation clause the "basic treaty." In his opinion, the treaties that Iran had concluded with Denmark, Switzerland, and Turkey after the ratification of its declaration were the basic treaties. They were the treaties that determined the rights of British nationals in Iran to be accorded treatment in accordance with international law. The most-favored-nation clause with nothing more, he maintained, confers no rights; it is operative only when a later treaty with some third nation grants certain rights, for these rights are then accorded to the nationals of the most favored nation. Prior to the conclusion of the Danish-Iranian Treaty, Judge Hackworth argued, the most-favored-nation clauses in the British-Iranian treaties were merely promises of inchoate rights to claim something in the future. But when Iran conferred on Danish nationals the right to claim treatment in accordance with the requirements of international law, that right immediately became available to British nationals. He concluded, therefore, that the new treaty, the Danish-Iranian Treaty of 1934, was "in law and in fact, the fountainhead of the newly-acquired rights." He considered it a much too restrictive interpretation of the Iranian declaration to conclude that the United Kingdom could not rely in part on the Danish-Iranian Treaty as a basis for the jurisdiction of the Court. Judge Hackworth was convinced that the dispute between the United Kingdom and Iran did relate indirectly to the application of a treaty accepted by Iran after the date of the ratification of its declaration.[23] A similar view was expressed by Judge Levi Carneiro in his dissenting opinion.[24] Judge Read reached the same conclusion. In his argument he stressed the deliberate use by the Iranian government of the disjunctive "or" in the phrase "directly or indirectly" at a time when that government must have been aware of the continued existence of its treaties with the United Kingdom which contained the most-favored-nation clauses. The Iranian government had, in fact, affirmed its adherence to those treaties in an exchange of notes in 1920 and again in 1928.[25] Judge Read was of the opinion that the draftsman of the Iranian declaration was trying to ensure, by this phrase, that the declaration would be sufficiently broad in scope to include within its terms disputes having an indirect relation to the treaties in question.[26]

The agent for the United Kingdom also argued that the 1933 concession granted by the Iranian government to AIOC should be regarded as a "treaty or convention" within the meaning of the Iranian declaration. After reciting the history of the 1933 concession and stating that it had been negotiated under the auspices of a mediator (Eduard Beneš of Czechoslovakia) appointed by the Council of the League of Nations (see pp. 17–18 above), he concluded his argument with the assertion that the concession had a double character, being both a concessionary contract between the Iranian government and AIOC and a treaty or convention between Iran and the United Kingdom. He argued, therefore, that it came within the term "traités ou conventions" in the Iranian declaration and that the jurisdiction of the Court could be predicated upon it.

The Court rejected this argument, primarily because the United Kingdom was not a party to the 1933 concession. It refused to attribute any importance to the fact that the concession was negotiated under the auspices of a mediator appointed by the Council of the League of Nations. In referring the dispute that developed in 1932 over Iran's cancelation of the D'Arcy concession to the Council of the League, the Court said, the United Kingdom was only exercising a right of diplomatic protection. The intergovernmental dispute, and the exercise of diplomatic protection, ended with the negotiation of the new concession. At no point in the proceedings before the Council, nor during the negotiations, nor in the 1933 concession, did Iran undertake any obligation toward the United Kingdom. For these reasons, the Court concluded that no treaty or convention between the two countries resulted from these proceedings.[27] Judges McNair, Hackworth, and Levi Carneiro all reached the same conclusion on this point.[28] Judge Read presented an interesting argument to the effect that the Court was not competent in preliminary proceedings to decide whether or not an international agreement had arisen between Iran and the United Kingdom as a result of the proceedings in 1932 and 1933, because such a decision related to the merits of the dispute. The only question, in his opinion, that the Court was competent to decide in the preliminary proceedings was whether the alleged international agreement was a treaty or convention within the meaning of the Iranian declaration.[29]

The remaining argument presented to the Court by the agent of the United Kingdom was that the Iranian government had, by submitting to the Court for decision several questions that related to the merits of the dispute and not to the question of jurisdiction, conferred jurisdiction on the Court on the basis of the principle of *forum prorogatum,* that is, the Iranians impliedly consented to the jurisdiction of the ICJ by pleading questions related to the merits of the dispute. The Court rejected this argument, stating that Iran had consistently denied the jurisdiction of the Court and had done nothing that would indicate consent to its jurisdiction. The Iranian arguments on the merits, said the Court, were "clearly designed as measures of defense which it would be necessary to examine only if Iran's Objection to the jurisdiction were rejected. No element of consent can be deduced from such conduct . . ." Accordingly, the Court held (July 22, 1952) that it had no jurisdiction to consider the application of the United Kingdom of May 26, 1951, and indicated that its order of July 5, 1951, indicating interim measures of protection, consequently ceased to be operative.[30]

The Court's decision to dismiss the United Kingdom's application on the ground of lack of jurisdiction is, it is submitted, regrettable. If the foregoing analysis of this decision is correct, the important conclusion to be drawn is that the Court was faced with a question to which there was more than one answer con-

sistent with law and logic,[31] and that in making its choice it rejected an equally sound solution to the problem of jurisdiction.
In so choosing it did nothing to encourage a belief in its ability
to settle a type of dispute, usually (as in this case) fraught with
political problems and tensions, that has thus far remained
beyond the regulating influence of international law and international judicial procedures. Of all the major nationalizations
that readily come to mind—in Mexico, the Soviet Union, and
eastern Europe, for example—none have been settled according
to the requirements of the international norm, nor have they been
settled through the employment of impartial international judicial tribunals. But settlement of such disputes is primarily a legal
problem, and the question can therefore rightly be asked: Does
international law, or do the tribunals that administer it, have a
solution to offer that is capable of reconciling the nationalistic
aspirations and feelings of the expropriating states and the
legitimate interests of the alien property owner and his government? At present, it would seem, it does not, and the ICJ sacrificed a great opportunity, by denying jurisdiction in the *Anglo-
Iranian Oil Company* case, to make a valuable contribution to
international law and to demonstrate its ability to deal effectively
and fairly with this type of dispute. In light of the fact that there
was a legally sound alternative available to the Court, there
seems to be no justification for its failure to address itself to this
urgent and pressing problem.

The Court's failure to do so has been interpreted by one influential journal of the business world as suggesting that "all agreements reached between local governments and foreign companies
are none of the Court's business," and that the decision will "have
a deplorable effect on the mind of the large-scale investor overseas . . . to the detriment of all countries which seek to increase
their industrial potential by encouraging foreign investment."[32]
In view of the fact that study after study is issued by the United
Nations Economic and Social Council affirming the need for

large-scale capital investment for economic development, and the
repeated asseverations by government after government of their
particular needs, the Court's decision would seem to hinder the
aim expressed in the preamble to the United Nations Charter of
promoting social progress and higher standards of living. Great
masses of people need many more of the basic essentials of
civilized life, and these can be had only through increased productivity. Increased productivity requires, in almost all cases,
the application of capital to existing resources—and one source
of capital is the large-scale international business, typified today
by the oil industry. So long as corporations of the size and power
of AIOC can be expelled from a country without having recourse
through international legal channels, other investors will be
hesitant to send their capital abroad where it could serve in the
attainment of the basic objectives of human welfare.

It will be suggested that the Court should not make an unenforceable order, or one that will obviously be disobeyed. The
conduct of the Iranian government may or may not have indicated that it would refuse to obey a final judgment on the merits
of the dispute if one were rendered by the Court. However, even
assuming that the final judgment on the merits would have gone
against Iran, and that the Iranian government would have refused
to obey the judgment, it would seem a preferable course of action
for the Court, rather than denying jurisdiction to avoid such a
situation, to have assumed jurisdiction and rendered a judgment.
Rather than damaging the Court's prestige, it seems more probable that it would make the world dramatically aware of the
forces that resulted in the failure of international legal institutions to resolve a serious dispute. As it now stands, the Court's
decision to deny jurisdiction is interpreted by much of the lay
public as either a victory on the merits for Iran or as an admission
of weakness by the Court. Neither is a salutary result. Both
obscure what should be the obvious fact that nationalism of
Mossadegh's type is incompatible with a society in which respect

for the obligations of international law can be maintained. If this one issue could be made clear to the general public everywhere, the Court would render an invaluable service to peace through international coöperation. It would sharpen the issue, the alternatives could be more easily ascertained, and the choice between an international anarchy and a world community (cf. p. 221) could be presented in such a way that an intelligent decision could be made.

It should also be clear that no institution will advance itself very far in the long run by doing nothing. It will only demonstrate its uselessness. It has often been recognized that one of the greatest contributions made by the PCIJ was the development of international law through its decisions in contentious cases.[33] The paucity of the ICJ's decisions in contentious cases has resulted in little or no contribution in this vital area. This has been partly due to the lack of opportunities, but it has also been the result of the Court's refusal to act on the opportunities that have been presented.

The Court's dismissal, on July 22, 1952, of the United Kingdom's complaint because of lack of jurisdiction is a convenient point in the chronology of events at which to end this study. The oil dispute itself is not ended, and, although a resolution of the controversy would be a welcome development, it is not essential for the purposes of our study of the role of law in the relations of states involved in the dispute. Such a study could begin or end with any given date, and since the Court's decision was the last major event at the time of writing, it provides a fitting breakoff point. Before the study is concluded, however, two of the fundamental legal problems involved in the Anglo-Iranian oil dispute remain to be discussed. These problems, treated in the following section, are the propriety of Britain's attempt to exercise diplomatic protection, and the international law governing the expropriation of the private property of aliens.

§ 11. Some Legal Issues on the Merits of the Dispute

There are two basic questions to be discussed in this section. The two questions are closely interrelated. Both concern the legal validity of the Iranian nationalization laws and of the actions taken in the course of their execution, as well as the international responsibility for such actions. The first question concerns the propriety and implications of the United Kingdom's exercise of diplomatic protection. The second question, to be discussed below, concerns the international law governing the right of a state to expropriate the private property of aliens located within its borders.

It has already been mentioned that the British-Iranian treaties of 1857 and 1903 obligate Iran to accord most-favored-nation treatment to British nationals and their property in Iran.[1] In other treaties Iran has undertaken to treat the nationals of other states (parties to those treaties) "in accordance with the principles and practice of ordinary international law."[2] The most-favored-nation clause requires Iran to treat British nationals in the same manner, and, in fact, the pledge to accord to British nationals and their property treatment according to the principles of international law was directly given in an exchange of notes between the United Kingdom and Iran on May 10, 1928.[3] With this obligation established, the principal inquiry to show the existence of a denial of justice, and thus the prerequisite for diplomatic intervention by the United Kingdom, then becomes a question whether Iran has committed a violation of international law in the course of action it has pursued against AIOC. In this inquiry, it is important to distinguish between acts that constitute internationally illegal conduct on the part of Iran, and acts that tend to show a failure on the part of Iran to afford adequate means of redress to AIOC for the consequences of such illegal conduct. The former would establish the international responsibility of Iran; the latter would justify the diplomatic interposition of the United Kingdom.

It is an elementary principle of international law that a state has the right to protect its nationals when they have been injured by the internationally illegal conduct of another state. If the state takes up the case of its injured national, through diplomatic channels or by instituting international judicial proceedings, the fact that the dispute originated in an injury to a private person or interest is irrelevant, since the state is asserting its own right. The injury to the national is an injury to the state, and, internationally, the state is the sole claimant.[4] It is equally well settled that a state can interpose on behalf of a corporation incorporated under its own laws, the nationality of the corporation being derived from the place of incorporation. In the present case, it is clear that AIOC is a British national on whose behalf the British government would be entitled to interpose if it is established that AIOC suffered injury as a result of the illegal conduct of another state. AIOC was formed and registered as a British company in London on April 14, 1909,[5] and its shares are almost entirely held by the British government or British nationals. The fact that the British government owns a majority of the shares of AIOC's capital stock has no effect on the corporate personality, which has been preserved and respected by the British government. It would serve no purpose to "pierce the corporate veil" and find the ownership of the British government, since that would only put the Iranian government in the unenviable position of having expropriated the property of another sovereign in violation of the 1933 concession, which must then be considered a treaty or convention.[6] Moreover, the British government has never maintained that it was acting in reliance on its interests as a shareholder in AIOC, but only as a sovereign on behalf of one of its subjects. With these basic propositions established, there remain only the difficult questions of determining whether Iran did act illegally and whether it failed to afford adequate means of redress to AIOC. If these questions are answered in the affirmative, it must be concluded that the diplomatic interposition of the United Kingdom was proper.

To determine whether Iran has committed an internationally illegal act, it is necessary to look first to the purposes and effects of the Iranian nationalization laws.[7] The Single Article Law of March 20, 1951, had the purpose and effect (at least from the point of view of domestic Iranian law) of canceling and nullifying the 1933 AIOC concession, which had granted to AIOC "the exclusive right, within the area of the Concession, to search for and extract petroleum as well as to refine or treat in any other manner and render suitable for commerce the petroleum obtained by it."[8] The law of March 20 "nationalized" the oil industry throughout Iran and expressly stated that "all operations of exploration, extraction and exploitation shall be carried out by the Government." This law and the Law Regulating Nationalization of the Oil Industry[9] also had the purpose of appropriating[10] the physical installations of AIOC in Iran, and this purpose was completely carried into effect with the dispossession of AIOC and the expulsion of its non-Iranian staff from Iran, in September and October, 1951. The Iranian government took complete possession of the entire industry that was formerly operated by AIOC in Iran. Thus the purposes and effects of the Iranian nationalization laws have been twofold: (1) to cancel the AIOC concession of 1933; and (2) to appropriate all the property of AIOC in Iran and vest it ultimately in the public corporation, NIOC. The cancelation of the 1933 concession was a mere breach of contract, and as such would not ordinarily be regarded as a violation of international law. But the concession involved not only simple contractual obligations, but also property rights, since it provided the framework within which, and in reliance on which, large expenditures of labor and capital had been made to build an oil industry of immense value. Therefore, the cancelation of the 1933 AIOC concession was both a breach of contract and a tortious delict, because it infringed and destroyed both contractual and property rights.

The legal validity of Iran's appropriation of the property of

AIOC in Iran is the central legal issue of the merits of the dispute, but it also has relevance for the problem of the existence of a denial of justice, on which the propriety of Britain's exercise of diplomatic protection rests. In order to constitute legal expropriation the compulsory taking of the private property of aliens by a sovereign must be for reasons of public utility,[11] in the cases and in the manner prescribed by law, and balanced by prompt, adequate, and effective compensation.[12] Correlatively, it is a well-settled rule of international law that the duty not to confiscate (that is, illegally appropriate) the private property of aliens is binding upon states apart from the obligations of treaties and municipal law.[13] Similarly, states cannot avoid responsibility for the delict of confiscation by pointing to contrary norms of their own municipal law.[14] Thus international law requires states, as members of the international community, to assure one another's nationals a determinate minimum of legal protection of property rights and interests.[15] The legal validity of expropriations of the private property of aliens is recognized, and confiscation is forbidden. However, it must be emphasized that the conditions precedent to legal validity are that the appropriation must be (1) for reasons of public utility; (2) carried out by a legal procedure not arbitrary in nature, and (3) accompanied by prompt, adequate, and effective compensation.[16] The state has an uncontestable legal right to initiate social and economic reforms for the general welfare of its people, but international law requires that in so doing the state shall not confiscate the private property of aliens. This obligation is one of the substantive standards of international justice the violation of which is called a "denial of justice."[17] An exact definition of this term is neither possible[18] nor necessary for the purposes of this discussion. It is clear, however, that the confiscation of the private property of aliens comes within the scope of the term "denial of justice."

It must be admitted without argument that the appropriation

of the property of AIOC by Iran was for purposes of public utility and in the manner prescribed by the Iranian municipal law. It is on the question of compensation that the issue of denial of justice turns. If the Iranian government appropriated the property of AIOC without standing ready to pay prompt, adequate, and effective compensation, that appropriation must be termed a confiscation and, therefore, an internationally illegal act. If, however, Iran was willing and able to compensate AIOC, the appropriation was a legal expropriation. It was provided in the Law Regulating Nationalization that the Mixed Board appointed thereunder should dispossess AIOC and "investigate the lawful and rightful claims of the Government as well as those of the Company," and should give effect to its views on these claims after receiving the assent of the Parliament.[19] The Mixed Board was also authorized to set aside ". . . up to 25% of the current income, less cost of production . . . ," to secure the claim of AIOC to compensation. In addition, the Iranian government offered on many occasions to negotiate with both AIOC and the United Kingdom government on the question of compensation. As has been said above, the failure of Iran to afford adequate means of redress through domestic procedures for internationally illegal acts is a prerequisite to the right of diplomatic interposition by the United Kingdom government. In other words, international law gives every state a plenary power over the international consequences of illegal acts committed within its territory to the detriment of aliens. By adequately redressing the injuries inflicted on the persons and property of foreigners it avoids responsibility to other states for its violations of international law. This plenary power is expressed in the norm of international law that requires that an alien who has suffered injury at the hands of a state exhaust the local remedies available to him before the state of which he is a national is justified in intervening diplomatically or by instituting international judicial proceedings. Correlatively, every state is required by international law to maintain adequate judicial protection for the rights of aliens. The close relationship between these two rules frequently produces confusion, because of the failure to distinguish between the substantive denial of justice produced by the initially illegal act, for redress of which the alien is required to exhaust local remedies, and the procedural denial of justice that may be incurred by the failure of domestic tribunals to administer justice according to reasonable standards of civilized law and procedure.[20] The proof of a procedural denial of justice is not a prerequisite to the pursuit on the international level of a claim based on a substantive denial of justice. There is sufficient cause for transposing the claim from the domestic to the international level if the alien has exhausted the remedies provided by the delinquent state *without receiving adequate or effective redress*. A procedural denial of justice may add a new claim to that of the initial violation of international law, but the incurrence of the procedural denial of justice is not a condition precedent to the pursuit of the original violation of international law on the international level—through diplomatic channels or in international judicial proceedings. The only condition precedent is the exhaustion of local remedies without receiving adequate or effective redress,[21] but the local remedies need not be exhausted when they are nonexistent or plainly inadequate, when there is no possibility of obtaining adequate redress under the laws of the delinquent state.[22] However, these are matters that must ultimately be determined by an international tribunal as jurisdictional questions.

In the Anglo-Iranian oil dispute, it is obvious that Iran has not afforded adequate or effective redress to AIOC for the appropriation of its property. Therefore, the appropriation is prima facie an illegal confiscation for which Iran is internationally responsible. However, before the United Kingdom has the right to intervene diplomatically to obtain the Court's declaration of that responsibility it must be shown that AIOC has exhausted its local remedies. The writer is unaware of any Iranian law giving an alien the right to sue the Iranian government in its domestic courts for breach of contract or tortious delict. The refusal of the Iranian government to arbitrate in accordance with the terms of Article 22 of the AIOC concession cannot in itself be regarded as a denial of justice. It is nothing more than a breach of contract and, like any other violation of international law, can be discharged by the Iranian government's affording AIOC adequate redress for the injury suffered thereby. The only local remedy that has been provided by the Iranian law (offers to negotiate cannot be considered as a "remedy" in the legal sense) has been described above (p. 184). In effect, the remedy provided is a determination of AIOC's claims for compensation by a board composed of members of the Iranian Parliament.[23] This determination is then subject to ratification by the Parliament as a whole. Such a procedure is not a judicial remedy. AIOC is not given the legal right to present evidence and have that evidence heard by an impartial tribunal. The right to do so is the essence of the judicial protection that international law requires every state to afford aliens lawfully within its borders. The remedies afforded by a system of judicial protection are those that the local remedy rule requires aliens to exhaust before the state of which they are nationals is justified in interposing diplomatically. But even if it is assumed that the remedy provided by the Law Regulating Nationalization is a "remedy" within the meaning of the local remedy rule, can it also be assumed that it would provide adequate redress? Is it clear that the remedy so provided would be plainly inadequate or unsatisfactory—that there is no possibility of obtaining adequate and effective redress under the provisions of the Law Regulating Nationalization? The answers to these questions will determine the propriety of the United Kingdom's intervention. The remedy provided is to be administered, not by a court, but by members of the Iranian Parliament, without the participation of the claimant. Members of parliament, in Iran as elsewhere, are generally politicians, and it cannot be assumed that they are trained in the judge's art of weighing evidence. It is certain that they are not experts in the petroleum industry, and yet the primary problem with which they would be concerned would be the evaluation of the property that the Iranian government had appropriated. This property in the aggregate is an oil industry. It includes some of the most complicated construction and machinery to be found in any industry anywhere in the world. Its value is astronomical. The problem of its evaluation is unbelievably complex. Most judges would quickly refer such a problem of evaluation to a master with an expert knowledge of the oil industry. The Iranian law makes no provision for such a reference. Instead, it delegates the job to a group of members of Parliament, many of whom may never have seen a refinery, much less have any conception of its operation. On this ground alone, it would seem that the remedy is plainly inadequate and need not be exhausted. Indeed, how could the remedy be exhausted by AIOC? The legal right to take an affirmative action to obtain a remedy is implicit in the duty to exhaust it. But under the Iranian law, AIOC is not even given the right to participate in the investigation to be conducted by the Mixed Board, and it certainly is given no right to initiate such an investigation. The remedy afforded by the Iranian law appears, therefore, to be plainly inadequate. If this conclusion is correct, then it follows that the United Kingdom was justified in intervening diplomatically.[24]

A further argument can be made for the plain inadequacy of the "remedy" provided in the Iranian nationalization laws. It is obvious that Iran is unable to pay compensation, despite its frequently expressed willingness to do so. Should AIOC be forced to "exhaust" the only remedy available when there is not a shadow of hope for prompt, adequate, and effective redress? The latest available official figures (June, 1950) indicate that the total gold and foreign exchange in the Iranian exchequer amounted to $239 million.[25] Although receipts from AIOC were greater in the fiscal year 1950–51 than in 1949–50,[26] it is unlikely that the total holdings of gold and foreign exchange increased, if at all, to any marked degree, since imports also increased considerably during 1950–51. Moreover, even if it be assumed that holdings of gold and foreign exchange remained approximately the same until the nationalization and ouster of AIOC in 1951, and thus the loss of the principal source of supply of gold and foreign exchange, it is certain that those holdings have decreased markedly since the nationalization and loss of revenues from AIOC. Even the exchequer holdings as of June, 1950, were probably somewhat less than the value of the Abadan refinery alone, without considering the refinery at Kermanshah or any of the other property belonging to AIOC in Iran. Although the value of the Abadan refinery is unknown, some idea of its value can be ascertained by comparing the cost of refineries being constructed in England. The Shell-Mex Company and Burmah Petroleum Company have just completed a £100 million program of refinery construction. These refineries include four catalytic cracking units of the type used for the production of high-octane gasoline. AIOC had ten catalytic cracking units of a similar type at Abadan.[27] By simple deduction it would seem that the value of the Abadan refinery at the time of nationalization was approximately £250 million or $700 million, which is roughly three times the total gold and foreign exchange holdings of the Iranian exchequer as of June, 1950, a total that was greatly decreased by the summer of 1952.[28] Thus, the ability of the Iranian government to pay prompt, adequate, and effective compensation depends upon its ability to produce and sell oil, and no one with even a slight acquaintance with the international oil industry would be willing to assume that the Iranian government has that ability. In addition, the Iranian law provided only for compensation from current income of the oil industry. During the time (since October, 1951) that the Iranian government has had possession of the oil industry there have not only been no profits, but the government itself has been brought to the edge of bankruptcy.[29] This lack of income makes the provision, in the Law Regulating Nationalization, for setting aside 25 per cent of net profits completely ineffectual as a guarantee of compensation to AIOC. It can also be observed that even if it is unrealistically assumed that Iran could make the same annual net profit as that made by AIOC in 1950 from its entire world-wide operation,[30] the compensation by way of 25 per cent of net profits would not be prompt as required by international law, and there is a serious question whether it could be "effective." AIOC's net profits in 1950, before United Kingdom taxes, were approximately £84 million, 25 per cent of which would be £21 million. On the basis of the rough estimate made above—that the Abadan refinery is worth approximately £250 million—it would require about twelve years to compensate AIOC for the Abadan refinery alone. There is no information available on the value of the other property of AIOC that has been appropriated by the Iranian government, but that property is probably at least equal in value to the Abadan refinery. If so, it would require twenty-four years, more or less, to pay compensation on the basis of the 25 per cent of current net profits formula, and on the assumption that the Iranian government could earn profits equal to those earned by AIOC in 1950. Such compensation can hardly be described as prompt. Also, since Iran would very likely have great difficulties in selling much of its oil for currencies readily convertible to sterling (at least in the foreseeable future), the compensation afforded by the 25 per cent of current net profits formula might easily be considered ineffective as well as lacking in promptness (see the discussion below, pp. 190–208).

It follows from this analysis that the United Kingdom was justified in exercising a right of diplomatic protection. There was a denial of justice to a British national, AIOC, whose property was taken by a government that failed to provide a local remedy and that was incapable of paying prompt, adequate, and effective compensation as required by international law. This conclusion indicates that from a legal point of view, as well as a political and economic one, the dispute was not purely a domestic one between the Iranian government and a private corporation, as Prime Minister Mossadegh and the Iranian government had consistently contended (see pp. 59–60, and 134–135).

❖   ❖   ❖

The following paragraphs are concerned with an examination of the norm of international law that requires prompt, adequate, and effective compensation for expropriations of the private property of aliens.

The principal issue on the merits of the Anglo-Iranian oil dispute involves a problem that received a great deal of attention in the years between the two world wars in both legal and nonlegal literature. The issue relates to the right of a state in pursuit of social and economic reforms for the general welfare of its people to nationalize, or generally to appropriate, the private property of aliens, the duty of the appropriating state to make compensation, and the kind of compensation that must be made.

Although the formulation of a coherent theory of expropriation has received but scant attention in the literature of international law,[31] there was during the nineteenth century and the years preceding World War I a fully established and universally recognized body of rules governing the expropriation of the private property of foreigners.[32] Expropriation was a legal institution recognized by both muncipal and international law. As has been mentioned above, legal expropriation, as distinguished from illegal confiscation, was described as the compulsory taking of private property for reasons of public utility, in the cases and in the manner prescribed by law, and balanced by prompt, adequate, and effective compensation. Correlatively, it was universally recognized that the duty not to confiscate the private property of aliens was a rule of general international law, binding upon states apart from the obligations of treaties and municipal law, and that a state could not avoid international responsibility by pointing to contrary norms of its municipal law or by averring that it had treated aliens equally with, and in the same manner as, nationals.[33] Thus the rule required that nations, members of the international community, were under a mutual obligation to assure one another's nationals a determinate *minimum* of legal protection. It followed, also as a universally recognized rule of general international law, that the state of which the alien was a national had the legal right to protect him abroad.[34] These rules of general international law recognizing the legal validity of expropriations accompanied by prompt, adequate, and effective compensation, and forbidding the confiscation of the private property of aliens, were unanimously upheld by the writers,[35] the decisions of international arbitral tribunals, and the practice of states.[36]

The expression of a changing philosophical concept of private property and of its social function was evident in social developments occurring in many parts of the world in the years immediately preceding and following World War I.[37] These changes were not universal, but they were of sufficient magnitude to destroy the universality that had characterized the conception of private property and of its social function during the era of the *Pax Britannica.*[38] They were also of sufficient magnitude to destroy the unanimity of agreement that characterized the pre-1914 era, on the law regarding the private property of aliens. Dissenters from what may be called the pre-1914 rule have made themselves heard, and several new theories of expropriation have made their appearance in the literature of international law and in diplomatic correspondence.

The pre-1914 rule was based on an individualistic concept of property inherited by western European civilizations from the Roman law.[39] It is a concept that was proclaimed as one of the

sacred basic rights of man in the French Revolution[40] and recorded in the Code Napoléon,[41] as well as in other civil law
codes.[42] Similar conceptions are firmly grounded in English and
American common law.[43] Although individualist ideals have
maintained supremacy in the age-old controversy between individualism and collectivism during most of the modern era, the
last half century has seen changes in the social order that reflect
a more socially oriented form of thinking. There has been a
philosophic reaction to the extreme individualism of the nineteenth century, accompanied as it was by economic imperialism.[44]
The new legal theories which have expressed this reaction have
taken many forms: the unmitigated glorification of the state and
community by the neo-Hegelians;[45] Radbruch's moderate relativ-
istic socialist legal philosophy;[46] the institutional theory of the
neo-Thomists;[47] the conception of private property as a *fonction
sociale* in Léon Duguit's sociological doctrine;[48] Erhlich's and
Pound's sociological jurisprudence;[49] and the Communist theories put into practice in the Soviet Union.[50] Although these
theories differ greatly, they have one thing in common, to a
greater or lesser degree: a reaction to the idea that the autonomy
of the individual will over the uses of property is desirable. Many
of the social upheavals that have plagued the twentieth century
have resulted directly from attempts to translate these and similar theories into practice.[51] However, these theories are by no
means directed toward the abolition of private property. Instead,
they attempt to satisfy the claims of the community to social and
economic services by barring private ownership from certain
areas of the economic system, or merely by regulating it without
complete or partial abolition.[52] Although the institution of private
property still exists throughout the world,[53] the changes in the
philosophical conception of it have presented a challenge to the
pre-1914 rule of international law forbidding the confiscation
of the private property of aliens.

The laws and constitutions adopted in many countries in the

periods following the two world wars evidenced a trend toward collectivism and, after World War I, provided for the first time the possibility of "legal" expropriations of private property without prompt and adequate compensation.[54] Many of the constitutions adopted since World War I have provided that property should not be expropriated except in the public interest and according to law, and that expropriation should be accompanied by just compensation *unless otherwise provided by national law*.[55] The states that have adopted such provisions in their fundamental law have, of course, under international law, the right to treat their own nationals as they choose,[56] but the adoption of such provisions cannot *ipso facto* change the rule of international law forbidding confiscation of the private property of aliens. The rights of aliens are derived from international law, and the fact that states can expropriate the property of their own nationals without compensation cannot excuse their similar treatment of aliens.[57] The international rule can only be changed by international procedures, and so long as it continues to be accepted by the overwhelming majority of states it continues to be the rule of law.[58]

It should be emphasized that the provisions of most of the constitutions mentioned above envisage the possibility of expropriation without adequate compensation only in cases of agrarian reform. In this regard, there has definitely been a challenge to the international norm and a new theory has been developed. This new theory has not, however, been accepted by the majority of states as a rule of international law. The agrarian reforms of the interwar period, in which land was expropriated from both nationals and aliens without any or without adequate compensation, were a part of general reforms for high social purposes and applied to national and alien without discrimination. The laws enacted by these states ultimately came before national courts,[59] mixed arbitral tribunals,[60] and, by way of appeal, before the Permanent Court of International Justice.[61] The most widely publicized of the international disputes engendered by appropriations of land belonging to aliens, for the purpose of agrarian reform, were the Hungarian-Rumanian optants' dispute and the Mexican-American dispute. In these two cases the arguments of the appropriating states, Rumania and Mexico, denying the binding force of the pre-1914 rule forbidding appropriation without compensation to alien owners of private property, were much the same: the controversial character of the international norm;[62] equality in treatment of nationals and aliens;[63] sovereignty, including the right to enact impersonal laws for purposes of social justice; and the financial impossibility of paying full compensation.[64] These arguments, with the exception of the equality doctrine, which is not relevant, were also the same arguments that Iran did make or could have made in the Anglo-Iranian oil dispute. A discussion of them is, therefore, thought expedient.

A small group of publicists attempted to provide a theoretical basis for the agrarian reform legislation and to defend the measures taken by Mexico and Rumania. As counsel for Rumania in the optants' dispute some leading publicists developed the theory that expropriations for the purpose of a general agrarian reform constitute an exception to the pre-1914 rule and a separate category in international law.[65] A similar argument was made in defense of appropriations (nationalizations) of industrial properties for social purposes. Other writers, not directly involved in the disputes, defended the right of a state to institute agrarian reforms and appropriate industrial properties for social purposes without paying any or adequate compensation by contending that the rule of international law as known before 1914 no longer existed. It was argued that the prohibition against confiscation might rest on treaties that were binding on particular states, but that a *general* customary rule of international law binding on all states did not exist and that the most an alien could ask was equality with nationals.[66] Sir John Fischer-Williams defended the same idea, adding as a caveat that a distinction must be made between isolated and sporadic appropriations directed against the alien as such, and general impersonal expropriations, for the purpose of social reform, affecting national and alien alike.[67] Professor Brierly, stating that the precedents are indecisive, concludes that ". . . there is not, nor is it desirable that there should be, any absolute rule forbidding the taking of an alien's property by a state without compensation."[68]

The challenge presented by the agrarian reforms of the interwar period ended rather indecisively with the pre-1914 rule still firmly established. No international tribunal had given its assent to the "agrarian reform doctrine," and no state, other than those few which had themselves instituted agrarian reforms, had lent its assent. The overwhelming majority of states were firm in their support of the pre-1914 rule, as were the great majority of writers.[69] A League of Nations Conference on the Codification of International Law (1929–1930)[70] failed, however, to reach any definite conclusion,[71] because a small number of states vigorously urged the acceptance of the "agrarian reform" and "equality" doctrines and the majority participating in the conference refused to modify their opposition. These two doctrines were, of course, the central issues in the challenge that emanated from the agrarian reform programs.

As has been stated above, the "equality" doctrine is not relevant to the Anglo-Iranian dispute and will not be discussed here. The agrarian reform doctrine, however, inasmuch as it denies the existence of a legal duty of the appropriating state to pay prompt, adequate, and effective compensation for the private property of aliens that has been appropriated, has also been urged in relation to the appropriation (nationalization) of industrial properties for social purposes. It is therefore directly apposite to the Anglo-Iranian dispute. The substance of this issue is well illustrated by the dispute between the United States and Mexico over the rights of American nationals to compensation for properties appropriated by the Mexican government in pursuit of its agrarian reform program. This dispute ended indecisively with the conclusion of a diplomatic agreement[72] that provided a welcome[73] practical solution but, like many diplomatic agreements, left the legal problems unresolved.[74]

The diplomatic correspondence between the United States and the Republic of Mexico before the conclusion of the agreement[75] reveals that the two governments were in agreement on the right of a sovereign to expropriate the property of aliens within its borders, and that the expropriations must be for reasons of public utility. The two governments were further agreed that the Mexican land appropriations were in fact made for reasons of public utility;[76] that title to land is to be determined by the law of the place where it is located; and that expropriations must be carried out in the manner and in the cases prescribed by municipal law. Further, they were agreed that a violation of an alien's property rights in contravention of municipal law would also be a denial of justice and thus a violation of international law.[77] Consequently, the real controversy centered on that part of the international norm requiring prompt, adequate, and effective compensation. The United States insisted "that the applicable precedents and recognized authorities on international law support its declaration that, under every rule of law and equity, no government is entitled to expropriate private property [of aliens] without provision for prompt, adequate, and effective payment therefor."[78] Further: "The taking of property without compensation is not expropriation. It is confiscation."[79] The right to expropriate was thus conditioned on ability and willingness to pay compensation.[80] No other conclusion would be consistent with the pre-1914 rule. In reply to the American position, the notes of the Mexican minister of foreign affairs used many words discussing Mexico's claim of a sovereign right to "organize herself autonomously," the exalted social purpose of the agrarian reforms,[81] and (as in Rumania) the "impossibility of paying *immediately* the value of the properties" taken for the agrarian reforms. Such discussions both camouflaged and confused the real and very basic issue. It cannot be supposed that Mexico or any other government would formally contend that a plea of financial embarrassment is sufficient to relieve a government (or a person) of its legal obligations, or that binding norms of international law can be changed by the contradictory legislation of one state. Such a contention, carried to its logical conclusion, would be a denial of the very existence of international law, an argument that the Mexican government has never advanced.[82] Instead, that government has for more than a century and a half, and especially since the 1910 revolution, consistently affirmed the existence of international law in its relations with other states.[83] In its dispute with the United States over the agrarian appropriations it relied almost exclusively on legal arguments. The stress placed by the Mexican minister on sovereignty, social purpose, and financial impossibility must be read against the background of his government's denial of the applicability of the particular rules of international law urged by the United States.[84] The Mexican government contended "that there is in international law no rule *universally* accepted in theory nor carried out in practice, which makes obligatory the payment of immediate compensation, *nor even of deferred compensation, for expropriations of a general and impersonal character* like those which Mexico has carried out for the purpose of redistribution of the land."[85] Thus Mexico, while admitting the *general* rule that expropriations must be accompanied by prompt, adequate, and effective compensation, contended that it was not applicable to *all* expropriations. There is an *exception* to the general rule, it was said, when the expropriations are of a general and impersonal character for purposes of social reform, in which instance there is no universally accepted[86] international norm that imposes a binding obligation on the expropriating state to pay any compensation to alien property owners affected by the expropriations.[87] Mexico would thus establish a particular category of expropriations as exempt from the operation of the pre-1914 rule. This argument was emphatically denied by the United States[88] and, in a note of July 21, 1938, the secretary of state proposed that there be submitted to arbitration the question whether "there has been compliance by the Government of Mexico with the rule of compensation as prescribed by international law in the case of the American citizens whose farm and agrarian properties have been expropriated by the Mexican Government . . ."[89] The offer was declined, and the basic question raised by the dispute has yet to be determined authoritatively by an international judicial tribunal, although the weight of doctrinal opinion and state practice have consistently denied the validity of the Mexican argument. It is to be regretted that Mexico did not accept the American proposal to arbitrate. An arbitral decision would have clarified the situation and would have dispelled any doubts that may have been raised by the contentions of the Mexican and Rumanian governments and the few publicists who supported their position. The Mexican government has never abandoned its assertion of the agrarian reform doctrine. At least in theory, Mexico regarded the agreement that it finally concluded with the United States, obligating it to pay compensation, as being based on the idea that compensation was required by the municipal law of Mexico and not by international law.[90]

Nothwithstanding the challenge presented by those who urged the agrarian reform doctrine, the pre-1914 rule survived the interwar period unchanged and unimpaired. It should be emphasized that the general validity of the pre-1914 rule was never attacked by any state. Certain states, notably Rumania and Mexico, did try to establish an exception to the pre-1914 rule for general and impersonal appropriations for social purposes (mostly agrarian reforms) that affected citizen and alien alike. In such cases, and only in such cases, it was contended, the pre-1914 rule did not apply. The arguments of these states failed to win the concurrence of the majority of other states. Instead, the

pre-1914 rule was affirmed by the overwhelming majority of
states,[91] international tribunals,[92] and writers.[93] During the years
following World War II,[94] the trend toward collectivism continued and many countries throughout the world undertook programs of agrarian reform and nationalization of key industries.
Many of these programs involved the appropriation of sizable
alien investments, but in these recent postwar years, as compared
with the interwar period, the international legal effects of such
appropriations have received little attention in the current literature, and little of the diplomatic correspondence relative to the
international reclamations has been made public. The correspondence that has been made public indicates that there has
been very little discussion on the diplomatic level of the applicable legal principles—as there was, for example, in the American-Mexican dispute of 1938. This is in part a reflection of the
fact that the appropriating states (including Iran) know what
the legal norm requires—prompt, adequate, and effective compensation—but are unable, in most cases, to fulfill the requirement. Failure to fulfill the requirements of the norm, for whatever reason, logically implies that the act of appropriation is a
nullity. If a state lacks the capacity to fulfill the requirements of
the norm by paying prompt, adequate, and effective compensation, it has no international right to appropriate the property of
an alien within its borders, since the right to expropriate is conditioned on prompt, adequate, and effective compensation to the
alien whose property has been expropriated.[95] Despite the prima
facie internationally illegal character of their acts, many governments appropriated the property of aliens on a large scale in the
period immediately after World War II,[96] and most of them have
been unable to pay compensation and have made no effort to do
so. The obvious legal alternative is restitution, but the political
atmosphere of the postwar world has precluded any attempt, national or international, to enforce restitution. The argument that
a state has a "sovereign right" to appropriate property situated

within its borders, without any limitations whatever, has no theoretical validity, but states have done just that and their actions must be regarded as *faits accomplis*. It must be remembered that the pre-1914 rule was developed in the nineteenth century, in the era of free trade and laissez faire economics, when state ownership was practically nonexistent and appropriations of private property were rare and usually of small amount and for purposes of public utility (for example, rights of way for water mains and highways). The political relationships of the nineteenth century that made possible the efficient and effective functioning of the international norm no longer exist, and the political and economic system which has replaced that of the nineteenth century does not permit the efficient and effective functioning of the international norm, for a number of reasons.

The development of the international norm was closely related to the history of "imperialism."[97] That "imperialism" no longer exists, and, although it has been replaced by another imperialism of a more subtle type, states (especially those formerly in the "exploited" class) now jealously insist on political and economic autonomy. The political and economic nationalism of the mid-twentieth century has completely reshaped the traditional (that is, nineteenth-century) patterns of international trade and investment, and it has rebuffed all serious efforts at extension of international control into areas that the proponents of nationalism regard as exclusively within their domestic domain. This is especially true in economic affairs. The efforts to establish a world government were concentrated upon international control of the use of force, and emphasis was placed on the retention of economic autonomy.[98] The International Monetary Fund was established to provide international machinery for the adjustment of the multilateral payments system (formerly provided by the gold standard), but it was doomed to failure by the large measure of control that individual states could exercise through domestic fiscal policies. The powers given to the Fund were so weak that it was unable to control or counteract the disruptive effects of the domestic fiscal policies of individual nations.[99] Similarly, almost the whole sphere of international economic relations has consistently remained outside the domain of international law and within the "domestic" jurisdiction of the several states that make up the international community. In the absence of the regulating influence of an effective legal system there can be no assurance that individual states will formulate their economic policies so as to protect only the reasonable interests of their own nation without infringing the reasonable interests of other states.[100] The law of the responsibility of states for the appropriation of the property of aliens, with which we are concerned here, is, therefore, not a part of an integrated system of law controlling the whole field of international economic relations. Rather, it is an isolated phenomenon—a fact that makes its enforcement and its effectiveness more difficult. International law does not assert its regulating influence through the rules of state responsibility until after laws have been passed and actions have been taken by national authorities. The difficulty of undoing such actions and enforcing restitution in the present-day world is as formidable as the proverbial problem of reassembling Humpty Dumpty.

Many of the nationalization and agrarian reform programs of the period since World War II have been carried out in a manner inconsistent with the requirements of the international norm. The property of aliens has been appropriated in many countries without prompt, adequate, and effective compensation. The difficulty, or rather, the impossibility of enforcing restitution has been mentioned above. There are several reasons for failure to pay compensation. When the appropriation for which compensation is required is sufficiently extensive, the problem of compensation becomes a mixed problem of law and economics. There is no question about what the law requires,[101] but there have been frequent allegations of economic and financial incapacity to meet the requirements of the international norm. Lack of capacity on the part of many nationalizing countries to pay prompt, adequate, and effective compensation stems from a number of factors. The ravages of war destroyed much of the wealth of many eastern European countries.[102] In addition, many of the nationalizing countries were poor and unindustrialized, and even had there been no war damage it is unlikely that prompt, adequate, and effective compensation could have been paid to all alien property owners when the appropriations extended, as they did in many eastern European countries, to the entire industry of a particular country.[103] Foreign exchange was necessary if the compensation to alien property owners was to be "effective"—and its shortage in eastern Europe was not a new phenomenon suddenly produced by World War II. Those countries have never had foreign exchange in the quantities that would be necessary to compensate foreign property holders for the properties appropriated in the postwar years in pursuit of nationalization and agrarian reform programs. Apart from the problem of adequacy, the shortage of foreign exchange made it difficult for the eastern European countries to make "effective" compensation to their principal creditors, who were primarily Belgian, French, British, and American.[104] This difficulty was accentuated by two other factors: (1) xenophobia, especially towards investors from western Europe and the United States, that was as much a part of the political and economic nationalism as the nationalization programs themselves;[105] and (2) the frequently found laws that prohibited reinvestment by foreign investors even if they were willing to accept compensation in local currency.[106] Finally, it can be observed that, in all the cases in which there have been international reclamations problems because of the incapacity of the appropriating state to pay prompt, adequate, and effective compensation to foreign property owners (including the cases of Mexico, the Soviet Union, Rumania, Poland, Czechoslovakia, Bulgaria, Yugoslavia, Albania, Bolivia, and, it can be added, Iran), the appropriating states have been of the sort that are today loosely termed "underdeveloped" countries and that have been traditionally "debtor" countries.[107] They have been poor, unindustrialized nations that have hoped by the process of nationalization and state planning to bridge the gap between a semifeudal and a modern industrialized economy in the space of a few short years. Similar economic development in Britain, the United States, and western continental Europe has taken a century, more or less. Apart from the problem of building new industries, many of these countries have an insufficient number of trained native technicians to operate the industries that they have nationalized. Xenophobia prevents them from utilizing the foreign capital and technical skill that might otherwise be available to them, both for the operation of established industries and for the establishment of new ones.

Since neither restitution nor prompt, adequate, and effective compensation has been a practicable solution to international reclamations problems in the postwar period, the creditor nations have been faced with the choice of fruitlessly insisting on compensation for the property of their nationals according to the international norm, or of looking for an extralegal method of settlement that would provide a workable solution without at the same time impairing the validity of the pre-1914 rule. That such methods of settlement were needed and have been found clearly indicates that the compensation requirements of the pre-1914 rule no longer provide a practicable solution to the problems of state responsibility that are involved in appropriations of large amounts of alien-owned property in pursuit of agrarian reform or nationalization policies. The development of extralegal solutions when the established but unchanging international norm fails to provide them is a reflection of one of the most serious shortcomings of the present international legal system: the rudimentary character of the institutions for the making of the law. There is no international legislature to keep the law abreast of the changing needs of international society. The scope within which "judicial reason" can elaborate sufficiently detailed rules from general principles to provide for the constantly increasing variety of factual situations is limited, yet in the absence of a legislature these established general principles must be applied, with but a narrow margin of adjustment, to situations that could not have been imagined at the time the general principles were formulated. A customary system of law cannot be adequate for any but a primitive society. International society is far from primitive in a material sense, and as it becomes more and more interdependent economically, the need for a system of law capable of regulating the clashes implicit in the growing interdependence becomes greater. But such a system of law is impossible unless the development of a world community keeps pace with the growing material interdependence. As Professor Brierly has stated it, "Some sentiment of shared responsibility for the conduct of a common life is a necessary element in any society, and the necessary force behind any system of law; and the strength of any legal system is proportionate to the strength of such a sentiment. . . . [So long as the spiritual cohesion of international society is weak, it] will inevitably be reflected in a weak and primitive system of law."[108] Such a system of law will necessarily find (as in the agrarian reform and nationalization cases) great difficulty in providing adequate solutions for the problems posed by the rapid technological advancement in modern economic practice.

To fill the gap left by the inadequacies of the pre-1914 rule many governments turned to what may be called the "lump-sum settlement." It was first tried, but without success, as a means of settling American claims for the appropriations of the new Soviet government.[109] It was used with limited success in the settlement of the Mexican expropriations.[110] Since the end of World War II it has been used a number of times as a means of settling compensation claims arising from the nationalization and agrarian reform programs of the eastern European countries.[111] The "lump-sum settlement" is, roughly speaking, a bilateral agreement fixing, as its name implies, an aggregate figure in satisfaction of certain claims of one state against the other. Since financial incapacity has been the usual reason for by-passing the normal legal method of settlement, the success of the lump-sum settlement has depended on the fortuitous coincidence of various economic factors. Two of the settlements made since World War II, the British-Czech and the American-Yugoslav, will illustrate this.

In both the British-Czech and the American-Yugoslav agreements, the creditor country had an inducement to offer the debtor, and the inducement proved to be the means of payment.[112] The British-Czech agreement[113] provided that Czechoslovakia should pay the United Kingdom the lump sum of £8 million in satisfaction of all claims arising from Czechoslovakia's nationalization of British-owned property. A contemporaneous "Trade and Financial Agreement"[114] provided that Britain should permit the importation from Czechoslovakia of manufactured goods to the value of £8.75 million annually, in addition to "essential goods," which were separately scheduled. The Czechs thereby secured an outlet for increased production from their nationalized industries, a means of earning sterling with which to strengthen their foreign exchange holdings and to pay compensation to the United Kingdom for the British-owned property that was appropriated by the Czech government. Thus, the Czechs pay as they earn. No figures have been published to indicate how closely the £8 million figure approximates the aggregate value of the properties that were appropriated. Other compensation agreements between European countries have utilized the trade-agreement method, of which the British-Czech settlement is a good example.

The American-Yugoslav settlement was made possible by the presence of a deposit in the Federal Reserve Bank of New York of $46.8 million in Yugoslav gold. The gold had been there before the outbreak of World War II and was impounded by the United States to prevent it from getting into the hands of the Germans. At the end of the war the United States refused to release the gold at the request of the Yugoslav government, and that government was unable to get possession of the gold until it agreed to discuss American pecuniary claims against Yugoslavia together with the gold issue. The result of these discussions was a settlement[115] by which the United States agreed to release the Yugoslav gold and Yugoslavia in turn agreed to pay to the United States the sum of $17 million in settlement of the American claims. Thus the inducement was again, as in the British-Czech case, the means of payment.[116] However, it may well prove that $17 million is inadequate to satisfy all the legitimate claims of American property owners. The United States Treasury's wartime census indicated that Americans owned property in Yugoslavia totaling $50.6 million in value,[117] and, because of Yugoslav controls, little or none of this was removed after the war. Of course, the figure must be somewhat depreciated to account for war damage, but it must also be appreciated to account for inflation.

The lump-sum settlement has been necessary because the normal legal method of redress has been either nonexistent or inadequate. But the lump-sum settlement also has several serious limitations as a method of redress. The willingness of a creditor nation to accept, as the United States did in the American-Mexican and American-Yugoslav settlements,[118] a lump-sum settlement in an amount that is somewhat less than the value of the appropriated property—on the basis that some compensation is better than none—is both a fault and a virtue. Furthermore, lump-sum settlements may often be impossible because the creditor nations will encounter difficulty in finding ways to offer the debtor nations sufficiently attractive inducements that will also provide the means of payment. The circumstances that made possible the American-Yugoslav settlement were rather unusual and are not likely to be found often in the future. The trade-agreement method of the British-Czech settlement requires as a condition precedent that the economies of the two nations involved are complementary and that the balance of trade either is or can be swung in favor of the debtor nation without undue difficulty. It also requires that the creditor nation exercise rigid control over its exports and imports through quotas, state purchasing monopolies, or other methods of control. These would, of course, conflict with the philosophy of the General Agreement on Tariffs and Trade and other efforts that have been made toward the liberalization of international trade. To establish these preconditions is not always possible, and it would be especially difficult in a situation involving an economy as relatively self-sufficient as, for example, that of the United States, which is also committed to the "free trade" principle.

On the other hand, the lump-sum settlement as a method of redress does have some solid advantages. It offers a means of obtaining some compensation for appropriated properties when otherwise none might be forthcoming. It also has the effect of giving the individual property owner a claim against his own government rather than a claim against the appropriating government in its own courts. In these days of international tension, when national passions and prejudices are frequently at a fever pitch, this substitution is a welcome one from the point of view of the foreign investor. Finally, the administration of the lump-sum settlements through domestic commissions or national courts of the creditor countries may provide the necessary precedents for the needed reformulation of the international norm. If the administration of the claims agreements is conducted in accordance with the principles of international law, as the United States International Claims Commission is directed to do,[119] it will certainly add to the growing body of international jurisprudence on the problem of international reclamations. As our knowledge of the difficulties and problems grows, we may be able to reformulate the international norm in such a way that it will again be capable of providing a solution to the problems that are raised by the appropriations of foreign-owned property. If international law is to provide the solution, it must operate by international procedures rather than through bilateral agreements negotiated at arm's length. But the effectiveness of international procedures depends in large measure on the spiritual cohesion of international society, on the existence of some sentiment of shared responsibility for the conduct of a common life, which at the time of writing seems to be at one of the lowest points in modern history (see n. 108). As a way out of this dilemma, an instructive precedent may be found in the League of Nations loans made to Hungary, Bulgaria, Greece, Estonia, and Danzig in order to protect them from the practice of forcing excessive loans on borrowers. The international norm could perhaps be reformulated to require, as a prerequisite to the appropriation of foreign-owned property, that countries obtain sufficient funds from the IBRD to pay compensation (and to finance their domestic program) in those cases in which the appropriating country is incapable of paying prompt, adequate, and effective compensation for the property that it plans to appropriate. To be efficient, such a solution would require that the IBRD have some degree of control over the conduct of the nationalized industry until its loan is paid. If the nationalizing country failed to obtain financial help from the IBRD and failed to pay prompt, adequate, and effective compensation, then the United Nations Security Council should become a sort of international sheriff and enforce restitution. There are obviously many difficult technical problems in such a solution, but the major problems are political, and if they could be solved the others would cause little real difficulty.

It is clear that the Iranian government is incapable[120] of paying prompt, adequate, and effective compensation to AIOC for the oil industry that it has nationalized, notwithstanding the oft-repeated asseverations of the Iranian prime minister of his government's willingness to pay.[121] Indeed, Iran has been on the verge of bankruptcy since early in 1952. It follows that it is impossible for the Anglo-Iranian dispute to be resolved in accordance with the international norm unless restitution can be enforced through some international procedure, and this is extremely unlikely in view of the inclination of both the Security Council and the ICJ to treat the problem as one within the domestic jurisdiction of Iran. The lump-sum settlement is a feasible method of solution only if the Iranian government and AIOC are willing to coöperate to a greater extent than they have been thus far. In effect, the British proposals of August 13, 1951 (see above, pp. 107–108), were proposals for a lump-sum settlement. These proposals offered the Iranian government a means of selling its oil and thus of earning sterling and dollars with which to pay compensation to AIOC, and to pay for the imports that are necessary for the maintenance of a reasonable standard of living. The British asked, it is thought reasonably, for at least temporary British management, in order to assure themselves of a steady supply of oil from Iranian wells and refineries. The readjustment of AIOC's patterns of supply and distribution, after supplies of Iranian oil were cut off with the closure of Abadan in July, 1951, cost that company many thousands of pounds. Had the Iranian government accepted the British proposals of August 13, a similar readjustment back to the pre-July patterns of supply and distribution would have been required at a similar cost. It is unreasonable to believe that AIOC would be willing to make such a readjustment if the Iranian oil industry were being operated by a management that AIOC considered unstable or incompetent, and one that made a steady supply of oil and oil products appear uncertain. The problem is further complicated by the fact that only AIOC had the transportation and world-wide distribution facilities on the scale necessary for the profitable disposal of the oil products that Iran is capable of producing. No other oil company of any nationality had enough tankers and a distribution network of sufficient size available to absorb a substantial portion of Iran's production. Therefore, if Iran is to sell great quantities of oil in the near future—and she must do this if the industry is to produce the wealth urgently needed to raise the living standards of the Iranian people, or if AIOC is to be compensated—then it would seem that the Iranian government must make use of the facilities that AIOC has and that it has offered to the Iranians. It is, however, questionable, in view of the success of AIOC's efforts to replace the lost Iranian sources and facilities, whether AIOC would now be willing to make an offer similar to that contained in the proposals of August 13. The proposals made by the IBRD (see pp. 160–161) faced the same difficulties. Of necessity the Bank had to insist on foreign management (probably British or American) and to plan on making use of AIOC's transportation and distribution facilities. The Iranian government rejected the Bank's proposals for the same reasons that it had given for rejecting the British proposals (see pp. 110–112).

If it be assumed that Iran is capable of paying prompt, adequate, and effective compensation, the problem of the measure of damages remains. There is a great body of international arbitral and judicial jurisprudence on this problem,[122] and the legal principles are well established. Computation of damages according to these principles is primarily an accounting problem. Just compensation implies a complete restitution of the status quo ante, including both the damages suffered (*damnum emergens*) and the profits lost (*lucrum cessans*).[123] The profits lost must be the direct fruit of the breached contract and must be neither remote nor speculative.[124] The damages directly suffered are always recoverable, usually on the basis of "fair market value," but if (as in the Anglo-Iranian dispute) there is no real *market* value the courts and arbitral tribunals tend to look to "fair value" of the property, which is roughly equated with replacement value. The problem of evaluating the damages suffered by AIOC as a result of the Iranian nationalization are many, but they can be settled without undue difficulty by a court or an arbitrator, or by a master appointed by one of them. The legal principles are well established and need not be discussed in any detail here.

The bases on which the Iranians have offered to pay compensation to AIOC do, however, require some comment. On August 22, 1951, the Iranian government informed Mr. Stokes, head of the British government's mission, that it was prepared to settle the question of compensation to AIOC in any of three ways: "(*a*) on the basis of the quoted value of the shares of the Company prior to the passage of the Oil Nationalization Law; (*b*) on the basis of the procedures followed by other countries where industries have been nationalized; (c) on any basis which would be mutually satisfactory to both parties, having due regard to the counter-claims of the Iranian Government."[125] The meaning of the phrase "quoted value of the shares of the Company" is not entirely clear. Does it mean "par value" of the shares, that is, stated capital, or does it mean the price at which the shares were sold on the London or New York stock exchanges? If it means stated capital, the Iranian government offered to pay AIOC £32,843,752 ($91,962,505) as compensation for an industry that was undoubtedly worth at least $1 billion.[126] If the phrase "quoted value of the shares of the Company" is taken to mean the value quoted on the London or New York stock exchanges, there is some difficulty in deciding the period within which such quotations are to be considered. If the highest quotation during the first three months of 1951, £6⅜,[127] is taken as the basis of computation, Iran offered to pay AIOC £209,378,919 as compensation. This is still approximately £150,000 less than $1 billion, which is probably less than the real value of the nationalized industry. Therefore, this Iranian formula (if its intended meaning has been discovered) is open to the criticism that it does not approach the "adequacy" required by the legal norm.

Compensation "on the basis of procedures followed by other countries where industries have been nationalized" also does not approximate the requirements of the international norm, as has been pointed out above at some length. The nationalizations in the interwar period and in the period since World War II have resulted either in no compensation at all (as in the case of the Soviet Union) or in payment of inadequate and dilatory compensation (as in the case of the Mexican oil nationalization). In addition to the examples of property appropriation in the Soviet Union,[128] Mexico,[129] Czechoslovakia,[130] and Yugoslavia,[131] which have been mentioned above, the Bolivian oil expropriations of 1937 can also be mentioned. A settlement was not arranged until 1942, and the amount paid as compensation was only 10 per cent of the 1937 valuation of the expropriated company (Standard Oil Company of New Jersey) as given on its own balance sheet.[137] Obviously, compensation at a rate comparable to the rates in the Bolivian and Mexican oil nationalizations (10 per cent and 25 per cent respectively) would be as unacceptable to AIOC as it is incompatible with the international norm. The Iranian proposal states, however, that compensation shall be made "on the basis of *procedures* followed in other countries." What is meant by "procedures"? Does it mean the mode of reaching a settlement? If so, its meaning is substantially the same as that of the third alternative mentioned in the Iranian communication of August 22, that is, a settlement on a basis "mutually satisfactory to both parties," since compensation claims arising in all modern nationalizations have been settled, if at all, by means of negotiated agreements that were, presumably, "mutually satisfactory to both parties." Does it mean the method adopted in the settlement agreement? If so, it could mean either payment of an agreed aggregate figure, as in the Mexican and Bolivian cases, which would be unacceptable to AIOC for the reasons given above, or it could mean a trade agreement of the British-Czech type (see pp. 204–205). As has been stated (p. 209), the British, in their negotiations with the Iranian government in the summer of 1951, were urging a solution similar to that of the trade agreement. Such a solution was impossible then, and it will continue to be impossible until the Iranian government is willing to agree to conditions that will ensure a steady flow of oil and oil products from its wells and refineries.

§ 12. Envoy

One of the purposes of this study has been to record the role of law as a determinant in the relations of the states involved in the Anglo-Iranian dispute. It was hoped at the time this study was begun that this description would include the role of law in the settlement of that dispute. Unfortunately, however, almost three years have passed since the enactment of the Iranian nationalization laws, and the possibility of settling the dispute on a mutually satisfactory basis still seems remote. Although a resolution of the controversy would be a welcome development, it is not essential to this study, which has been concluded with the decision of the International Court of Justice on July 22, 1952, that it did not have jurisdiction to consider the United Kingdom's complaint.

July of 1952 found Iran on the verge of bankruptcy and chaos. A new Majlis reëlected Dr. Mossadegh as Prime Minister on July 6, but less than two weeks later he was forced to resign when the shah refused his request for unlimited power to rule by personal decree for a period of six months. His successor was Ahmed Qavam, a wealthy, moderate businessman who, as Prime Minister in 1946, had succeeded in securing the removal of Soviet troops from the northern provinces (see above, pp. 43–44). Qavam immediately announced that he would reverse Mossadegh's oil policy, which, he said, had changed what was "essentially a legal question into enmity between nations," and would seek a settlement to the oil dispute with Britain on such terms that the "moral and material interests of Iran will be secured." This announcement was followed by continuous violent and bloody rioting in Tehran, led by a strange coalition of nationalist and Communist extremists, protesting any settlement with Britain. Qavam was forced to resign after only four days in office. When Mossadegh was reinstated as Prime Minister, rioting mobs roamed Tehran in search of Qavam for the purpose of lynching him as a traitor. Several days later the abdication of King Farouk of Egypt touched off further riots, which, like the anti-Qavam riots, were led by nationalist and Communist extremists demanding that the shah be deposed and his office abolished. The rioters were finally quieted through the influence of the powerful religious leader and unofficial head of Fadayan Islam, Mullah Ayatullah Kashani, who emerged from the chaos as the second most powerful man in Iran. Subsequently he was elected Speaker of the Majlis. The Communist Tudeh party also emerged in a new position of strength and power, although its uneasy nationalist partners in the riots quickly abandoned the temporary coalition. The Tudeh had become so active and powerful that, early in August, 1952, special cabinet meetings were held in London and Washington to discuss the danger of a Communist coup d'état in Tehran. The reaffirmed spirit of Iranian nationalism, which ousted Qavam and reinstated Mossadegh and Kashani, also displayed its xenophobic character. An anti-British spirit figured prominently in the riots that deposed Qavam. Late in July, frequent demands were heard on the floors of both houses of Parliament for the expulsion of American military and Point Four aid missions.

Early in August, Mossadegh's request of July 13 was granted by the almost unanimous voice of both houses of Parliament and he was given absolute power to rule by personal decree, a power that it seemed he would have to share with the Mullah Kashani. There were, however, good reasons for doubting that the partnership of these two men would prove very durable, for the only thing they had in common was a dislike of foreigners in general, and of the British in particular. Indeed, by the end of 1952, the two men were actively opposing each other, and Kashani suffered a major defeat in January, 1953, when the Majlis ignored his pleas and extended Mossadegh's power to rule by decree for another six-month period. Kashani was decisively defeated in an upheaval that occurred during the first days of March, 1953. Three days of rioting in Tehran left Mossadegh firmly in control with only the growing power of the Tudeh to worry him.

In addition to these political developments, there were other factors that made a settlement of the oil dispute difficult. Settlement of the dispute meant, in effect, an agreement on the amount and method of compensation to AIOC, since there appeared to be not the slightest possibility of restitution, at least so long as Mossadegh's government, or one of similar temper, remained in power. Payment of compensation by Iran will remain impossible until the oil industry, the major source of wealth and foreign exchange, is again operating at a profit. It has been demonstrated that the Iranian government is incapable of operating the oil industry without the help of non-Iranian technicians, if not management, and the Iranian government has been unable or unwilling to secure foreign technicians to fill this need. It has also been unwilling to allow AIOC to operate the industry under any arrangement yet suggested, and the ouster of AIOC seems to have become such a matter of national pride that it is unlikely that any Iranian government could safely invite AIOC back on any terms. But, so long as the oil industry remains idle it will be impossible to train Iranian technicians and administrators, and the day when they will be capable of operating the industry alone is thus still further postponed. Even if the Iranian government could find the technicians and management to produce oil and oil products without the coöperation of AIOC, it would still have to face the difficulty of finding the transportation and marketing facilities that are necessary to deliver the oil to the consumers. To make the immense profits that Iran urgently needs, the nationalized industry must produce and sell great quantities of oil, but transportation and marketing facilities capable of handling such quantities are available only with the coöperation of the world's six or seven largest oil companies, and especially that of AIOC, which has by far the largest world-wide marketing organization. The Iranian government has had little success in disposing of its oil by bartering with the Soviet Union and various eastern European governments, partly because of the difficulties involved in producing the oil, and partly because of the scarcity of tankers that the Soviet and eastern European governments have had available. Construction of a pipe line across the Zagros and Elbruz Mountains, from the oil fields in southwestern Iran to the Soviet Union, would be a major engineering triumph and would require great quantities of time and capital. The capital would have to be secured from non-Iranian sources, and it is extremely doubtful that the Iranian government would be willing to accept the investment from the Soviet Union. The construction itself, if undertaken, would necessitate the presence of many foreigners (probably Russian, if the investment were Russian), and it is unlikely that they would be welcome.

The problem is further complicated by the fact that Iranian oil is not, as the Iranian government has assumed, "vital" to the West. After the shutdown of Abadan in July, 1951, production in oil fields and refineries in other countries was increased, with the result that world production for the year 1951 was the greatest in history. Similarly, AIOC managed to obtain sufficiently increased supplies of crude oil from its interests in Kuwait, Iraq, and Qatar to offset the discontinuance of supplies from Iran. AIOC's construction of new refineries in the United Kingdom, France, Italy, Germany, Belgium, and Australia, and the increased capacity of existing refineries, also had the effect of replacing the lost capacity of the Abadan and Kermanshah refineries. During 1951 AIOC secured its position more firmly by negotiating new concession contracts with Iraq and Kuwait. These developments and the additional investment that would be required to readjust patterns of supply and distribution and to resume production in Iran, suggest that AIOC would not be overanxious to return or to conclude a bulk-purchase contract with the Iranian government unless arrangements could be worked out that AIOC considered "realistic," that is, arrangements that would assure stable management and a steady flow of oil and oil products. However, the Iranian government gave no indication of its willingness to agree to such "realistic" arrangements; on the contrary, it indicated its unwillingness in unequivocal terms.

Until the dispute is settled and AIOC admits or a judicial tribunal adjudicates that the title to Iranian oil (produced within the AIOC concession area) has passed from AIOC to the Iranian government, AIOC's threat to take legal action against any concern or individual attempting to buy oil from Iran will probably continue to deter tanker owners from countries west of the Iron Curtain from taking advantage of the low prices offered by the Iranian government in an attempt to find buyers.[1] Even if this threat be discounted, the small number of tankers not under control of the world's major oil companies could not possibly carry oil from Iran in substantial quantities. In addition, whatever the reasons, the major oil companies would not be likely to risk a dispute with AIOC by buying oil from the Iranian government. Even if adequate transportation facilities could be found to carry Iranian oil to the world's markets, the fact remains that Iranian oil has at this time lost its place in these markets, which are now divided among seven or eight large corporations that number among the most modern and efficient in the world in any industry. These large corporations can produce oil at a cost lower than that at which the Iranian government has yet offered to sell it. Further, the glut of supplies on the world oil market that developed in 1953 made it unlikely that any of the leading oil companies would be interested in purchasing Iranian oil in the immediate future. Thus, to reëstablish the position formerly held by the Iranian oil industry in the world market will require a competitive advantage that can only be provided by a production, refining, transportation, and distribution organization equal in competence with those already in the business. The cost of producing oil in Iran has been low as compared with the cost of production in the Western Hemisphere, and, although Iranian oil can be sold profitably at a cost that is relatively low, its cost is no lower than that of other oil produced in the Persian Gulf littoral. The Iranian oil industry must still be prepared to meet the competition.

The picture is not an attractive one. There is no apparent possibility that Iran will make sizable profits, if any, from its oil industry in the near future unless it makes a settlement with AIOC and invites foreign technicians and management personnel to operate the oil industry, and there is little hope that such a solution will occur in the foreseeable future. By the expulsion of AIOC Iran lost its principal source of foreign exchange, with which it regularly paid for imports of a value far in excess of its exports other than oil. In addition to the revenues that it derived directly from the AIOC concession contract, Iran received millions of pounds sterling annually (see Appendix II, table 4) from AIOC's domestic expenditures. In fact, the conversion of sterling into rials for domestic expenditures usually yielded more foreign exchange than total concession revenues. In addition, the Iranian government lost the special privileges, formerly granted it by the British Treasury, of converting large amounts of sterling into dollars which it used to pay for its imports from the dollar area. These imports, in 1948, amounted to 42 per cent of the total imports of Iran. As a result of this loss of foreign exchange, practically all of Iran's nonbarter imports were stopped,[2] and some of the disastrous effects of this stoppage on the Iranian economy were already apparent by the end of 1952. The readjustment that would be required, in the light of the loss of imports and foreign exchange, to restore stability to the Iranian economy would be extremely difficult and would result in even lower living standards than existed before nationalization. Prime Minister Mossadegh promised such a readjustment in his request for the power to rule by decree. In this he failed, and the then desperate economic situation has continued to deteriorate (see § 11, n. 120). There is always a danger of violent revolution in such a situation. As living standards fall and unemployment increases, hope for relief disappears and the danger of such a revolution becomes more and more real.[3] This possibility was suggested by the special cabinet meetings that were held in Washington and London to discuss the "alarming reports" from Iran, and by the urgent dispatch of several British naval groups toward the vicinity of the Persian Gulf in the first week of August, 1952. In view of past warnings by American State Department officials[4] that a Communist coup d'état in Iran would precipitate a third world war, it is greatly to be desired that some action be taken to remove even the possibility. The reluctance of the United States to grant Mossadegh's request for a loan in November, 1951, is understandable in light of the situation then existing (see above, pp. 154 and 163). However, the internal developments in Iran during July and August, 1952, and the gradually increasing strength of the Tudeh party since that time, should suggest that the reasons for that reluctance be reëxamined. If a loan from the United States could help avert a Communist coup in Iran, the prevention of a third world war should take precedence over a policy designed to exert economic pressure for a settlement of the oil dispute.

◇   ◇   ◇

The conduct of the parties in the Anglo-Iranian oil dispute is striking in that, despite the intensity of the feelings aroused and the violence of the language that was frequently used, both parties constantly appealed to legal arguments to justify their actions. Usually the British did this with more facility than the Iranians, a fact that may be ascribed primarily to the nature of the dispute, since the British argued for the preservation of the status quo from violent change, whereas the Iranian arguments attempted to legally justify a sudden change in the established order. Every legal system, international or domestic, is the custodian of the established order from which its authority derives, and any but a gradual change in the society within which the legal system operates will destroy the very foundations of the system. For this reason, if for no other, the British found the established legal principles much more congenial to their position than did the Iranians.

The central legal issue of the dispute is the right of a state to appropriate or nationalize property within its borders. The international norm requires that appropriations of the property of aliens be accompanied by prompt, adequate, and effective compensation. It must, therefore, be concluded that Iran did commit an internationally illegal act in appropriating the property of the Anglo-Iranian Oil Company when the government was patently incapable of paying prompt, adequate, and effective compensation. However, for the reasons given above, it must appear that the international norm is antiquated. The function of every legal norm is to strike a balance between what are seen as opposing interests. In respect to the international norm requiring prompt, adequate, and effective compensation for appropriations of alien-owned property, the design was to strike a balance between the interest of society in the preservation of property rights (there is some correlation between the stability of such rights and the stability of society) and the interest of states in controlling property within their borders. The international norm did this efficiently and effectively in the era in which it was formulated, an era in which appropriations of foreign-owned property were as rare as they were small in extent, and in which private ownership was almost universal. This situation no longer exists; today in many parts of the world state ownership of property is extensive, and in some places it is virtually complete. The interest of society in preserving the stability of property rights remains the same, since it is an interest closely related to the society's very existence, but the interest of states in controlling property within their borders is now conceived by many to be considerably broader than it formerly was. Therefore, in the eyes of those holding such conceptions, the international norm no longer strikes a proper balance. The nonintegrated character of international society has permitted states to give effect to those conceptions; that is, some states have violated the international norm by appropriating the property of aliens within their borders when there was no possibility of paying prompt, adequate, and effective compensation, and international society has failed to provide an effective means of redress for the patently illegal act. This situation exists today, and, indeed, the Anglo-Iranian case is but another example of a type of conduct that has occurred often in the past. The fact that it has occurred many times in the past, and that there is no evidence that it will not recur in the future, indicates that the control of property is passing beyond the regulating influence of international law and the dominion of international society. International society and its legal system are, therefore, faced with the choice of accepting a constantly growing anarchy that threatens their very existence, or of reformulating the international norm in such a manner that it will provide workable solutions to the international problems that are created by nationalizations. Only by accepting the second alternative is there hope for the reassertion of the regulating influence of international law and the preservation of the dominion of international society over property rights and economic relations in the international sphere. It is unfortunate that the International Court of Justice declined the opportunity given it to make such a reformulation of the norm.

Such a reformulation is also to be desired by the private investor whose property has been (or may be) appropriated by a state of which he is not a national. If the control of property rights can once more be brought under the aegis of international institutions it is probable that the foreign investor will be more satisfactorily compensated for his loss than he will be under the somewhat anarchical situation that exists today. Redress for his loss today often depends on the fortuitous coincidence of various factors over which he has no control whatever. This is shown clearly by the British-Czech and American-Yugoslav settlements described above (§ 11).

Apart from the fundamental issue of the right to nationalize, the records of the United Kingdom and Iran for reliance on international law and international procedures during the dispute are very different. The United Kingdom's "Application" of May 26 is the first instance of a nationalization being referred to the International Court of Justice. Britain's request for interim measures to preserve the status quo pending settlement of the dispute and its complaint to the Security Council for the same purpose should be landmarks in the history of international law and organization. It is hardly open to question that one hundred years ago Britain would not have hesitated to use force to preserve and protect what it considered the rights and interests of its nationals.[5] The Charter of the United Nations has made illegal the use of force (Article 2, paragraph 4), except in self-defense (Article 51), by states in their relations with one another. Britain's forbearance to use force while Iran expelled British nationals and, at least in the eyes of the British, confiscated British property, was entirely consistent with the Charter and the only legal course of conduct open to it. Of course, the "political realists" will explain that the British government chose not to use force because of its fear that the Soviets would interpret armed intervention as a threat to themselves and would invoke the 1921 Soviet-Persian Treaty of Friendship, invade Iran, and start a third world war. There are many possible rationalizations for every human action, and the real reasons for the British forbearance are known only to the men who made the decision not to use force, if, indeed, even to them. It is within the realm of reason that this decision did not derive entirely from an abstract belief in the virtues and efficacy of law, though it would be difficult to find a nation in which that belief is more firmly cherished than in Britain. However many the reasons that contributed to the decision not to use force, the fact remains that the decision was made and that the conduct of the British government in every way complied with the letter *and the spirit* of the law. It is difficult to accept the "realistic" explanation that it was solely, or even primarily, the fear that the Soviet Union would use Britain's forceful intervention in Iran as an excuse for initiating a new war that caused the British government to refrain. As the British government knew, the Soviet Union has had ample opportunities to find excuses for war, and it is a stretch of the imagination to think that if the Soviet Union wants war, and is ready and willing to wage it, it would delay initiating a war indefinitely until a sufficiently attractive excuse presented itself, especially an excuse as transparent as Britain's intervention in southern Iran would have been.[6]

The Iranian government's reliance on the rule of law is less impressive than Britain's. In much of its conduct, the Iranian government seems to have acted first and looked for legal justifications second. Had it really wished to fit its conduct to the rules of law, rather than the rules of law to its conduct, it would have obeyed the International Court's order of July 5 indicating interim measures. Its failure to do so can only be interpreted as a legal delinquency and as revealing a lack of faith in the ability of the Court to protect Iran's rights and interests pending either a decision that it had no jurisdiction or a judgment on the merits. The fact that the Court has subsequently decided that it has no jurisdiction to decide the case on the merits cannot ameliorate the delinquency, for jurisdiction on the merits was not an issue before the Court at the time it indicated the interim measures, and a finding that the Court had jurisdiction to decide on the merits was not a prerequisite to its right to issue interim measures. It is true that the obligatory character of an order indicating interim measures has never been affirmed (or denied) by the PCIJ or the ICJ, nor is it explicitly stated in the Statute or the Rules of Court. However, as has been indicated above (pp. 90–94), there are persuasive reasons for believing that such orders are enforceable and binding on the parties before the Court. But even if the reasons presented are not regarded as persuasive, orders indicating interim measures cannot be regarded as patently unenforceable and not binding, and if the Iranian government was concerned to demonstrate its faith in the rule of law it should have obeyed the order of July 5 and relied on the Court to protect its rights and interests. However, since Dr. Mossadegh's government was formed on the precondition that the Parliament would agree to his policy of immediate expulsion of AIOC from Iran, to have obeyed the Court's order of July 5 would probably have led to the fall of that government. This possibility can, of course, have no effect on Iran's international obligations, although it does make the Mossadegh government's refusal to obey the Court's order easier for the observer to understand. This refusal, especially when coupled with the statements by Prime Minister Mossadegh and those by Deputy Prime Minister Fatemi to the effect that Iran would refuse to obey any affirmative resolution that might be adopted by the Security Council,[7] does suggest, however, that Mossadegh's assertion in the Security Council that Iran has always shown "the most devoted respect for international law and has sought scrupulously to carry out its duties as a member of this and other international organizations"[8] must be taken *cum grano salis*. Indeed, the tenor of the remarks of Mossadegh and Fatemi, predicting Iran's refusal to comply with any affirmative action by the Security Council, seems to be indicative of the attitude of the Iranian government throughout the entire progress of the dispute. That government's initial position (see above, pp. 59 and 135) that the nationalization was entirely a domestic affair and that the dispute, if any, was entirely a private one between it and a private company, was equivalent to saying that the nationalization program could not have any international ramifications that should be the concern of established international institutions or create any problems the solution of which should be the subject of international procedures. Implementation of this point of view meant that Iran would, as it did, consistently refuse to make any attempt to settle the dispute by reference to international law or international procedures. Even

Iran's participation in the efforts at negotiation, all three of which were undertaken at the instigation and insistence of others (AIOC, the United Kingdom, and the IBRD), cannot fairly be described as an endeavor to exchange ideas for the purpose of finding a common basis of agreement. Instead, the Iranian government stubbornly insisted (with a zeal that seemed to become more extreme as time progressed) on its original position that AIOC be expelled from Iran and that the British company thereafter should have no contact whatever (except possibly as a freight agent for an oil buyer) with the Iranian oil industry. Expulsion of AIOC was certainly the overriding aim of the Iranian government during the first six months after passage of the nationalization laws by the Iranian Parliament, and at times it seemed to be the only objective. Implicit in this singleness of purpose was a persistent refusal to recognize the real nature of the international oil business and the complexity of the problems involved in the successful operation of Iran's newly nationalized oil industry—at least to the extent of making any allowance for these considerations in official policy formulations. So long as such an attitude of willful ignorance persisted, a negotiated settlement of the dispute was impossible.

One other occurrence should be mentioned in connection with the conduct of the Iranian government during the oil dispute. Almost nine months elapsed from the time when the British application was filed with the International Court before the Iranian government filed its preliminary objection to the Court's jurisdiction. The Iranian government had meanwhile twice requested, and been granted, postponements of the time fixed by the Court for submission of its written memorial. It was, of course, within its legal rights in waiting as long as it did to file the preliminary objection, since the Rules of Court (Article 62) require only that preliminary objections be filed before the time limit fixed for the delivery of the first pleading. However, the Iranian government had from the very beginning contended that the Court did not have jurisdiction, and, if that government had been concerned, as it professed to be, to obtain an expeditious termination of the dispute according to the rules of international law, its preliminary objection could have been filed months sooner. As it is, the repeated delays have the appearance of mere procastination.

The Security Council and the International Court of Justice are also open to criticism for their conduct in the Anglo-Iranian oil dispute. The Court's decision that it did not have jurisdiction to rule on the merits of the United Kingdom's application has been criticized in some detail above. The point in making such a detailed criticism was to indicate that the questions confronting the Court were not clear-cut, that there was not one inevitable and unavoidable answer consistent with law and logic. Instead, as has been shown, there were at least two possible courses of action open to the Court. It can be questioned whether, by declining jurisdiction, the Court was really willing to follow the precedent of its predecessor, the PCIJ, and feel at liberty "to adopt the principle . . . best calculated to ensure the administration of justice."[9] Instead, the Court's denial of jurisdiction appears to affirm the contention that the administration of justice (through the Court) is not concerned with the position of the investor who operates under contractual arrangements with foreign governments. It has been so interpreted by influential chronicles of the business world,[10] and the inevitable result of such an interpretation must be to discourage investors from placing their funds in foreign countries, to the detriment of the many areas in the world that desperately need investment capital to provide the basic services of civilized society and for economic development in general.

By denying its jurisdiction, the Court failed to take advantage of the opportunity presented it. It could have made an invaluable contribution to international law and could have demonstrated its ability to settle, fairly and effectively, a type of dispute that has thus far remained beyond the regulating influence of international law and international procedures. Such a demonstration would have contributed, in turn, to the stability of international society, on which a steady flow of investment capital depends, and would perhaps have avoided the difficult situation that exists in Iran today. Bold and enlightened action on the part of the Court to provide a just and realistic solution to the Anglo-Iranian dispute would have done much to dispel the antipathies that have arisen between the British and Iranian governments and would have demonstrated to all nations the desirability of settling their disputes in a friendly fashion before an impartial international judicial tribunal.

The failure of the Security Council to attempt effective action on the United Kingdom's complaint was but another step in the decline of the Council's prestige in international affairs. Constitutional limitations and the political rift between East and West have contributed to this decline, and perhaps made it impossible for the Council to act effectively on the United Kingdom's complaint in the Anglo-Iranian dispute. However, the Council's adjournment because of doubts on its competence may have the unfortunate result of making a bad situation worse by creating an undesirable precedent further limiting the area in which the Council is competent to act. The delegates' uncertainty about the Council's competence was perhaps a convenient reason to avoid a difficult political problem, but it might have been a preferable course of action to have put the United Kingdom's complaint to a vote and thereby to have placed on public record the positions of the various member nations (see above, pp. 152–153). Such a procedure would at least have had the virtue of making the situation clear to world public opinion, whereas the course of action chosen, adjournment, has had the effect of bemuddling the public. Few will take the time and trouble to read the Council's debates in an effort to determine why it acted as it did. As the supreme political organ of the United Nations, the Security Council can never afford to disregard the political pressures that are capable of being generated by world public opinion, upon the support of which, in the last analysis, the authority of the Security Council rests.

The Anglo-Iranian oil dispute of 1951–1952 will give little comfort to the "political realists." The existence of international law has been affirmed, not only by the conduct of the United Kingdom, but also by the behavior of those individuals, nations, and corporations that have been deterred from buying Iranian oil because of doubts on the legal ownership of the oil. They were deterred solely by AIOC's threat of legal action, and not by that of the British government.[11] In addition, it can be observed that neither the United Kingdom nor Iran acted according to its "national interest," as this term is usually defined in the literature of "political realism." The United Kingdom had alternative courses of action available. With the aid of hindsight, it can be seen that the course chosen, that of legal procedures, was not as effective in advancing the cause of the British "national interest" as one of the other possible courses might have been. As for Iran, stubborn insistence on what it conceived to be its legal rights brought the Iranian nation to the brink of ruin, which is hardly in the "national interest."

The Anglo-Iranian oil dispute has not been settled, and neither Britain nor Iran has emerged victorious. Instead, both nations incurred heavy losses. The dispute was, as Ahmed Qavam said, essentially a legal problem. The existence of the international norm prohibiting the use of force, supported by the public opinion that is essential to the existence of all law, effectively prevented the introduction of organized violence into the dispute. But neither the techniques of diplomacy, attempts at negotiation, nor pursuit of the "national interest" succeeded in solving the basic problem. Moreover, settlement of the dispute was not prevented by a "lack" of law or of available legal procedures. Instead, it was prevented by a lack of faith in and willingness to submit to those procedures on the part of Iran, and a failure to take bold and enlightened action on the part of the international institutions involved, and especially of the Court, an institution that should not be affected by the political competition that makes the veto a powerful brake on the Security Council. In a customary system of law the tribunals that apply the law are the primary agencies responsible for its development, shy though they may be of admitting their legislative function. If the rules of law applicable in the Anglo-Iranian dispute were antiquated, or failed to provide principles decisive of the particular case, the Court could have and should have boldly carved a new path. By declining the opportunity to do so, the Court failed to demonstrate to the nations of the world the ability of international law and its institutions to provide solutions for their problems. If nations like Iran are to gain confidence in the efficacy of the international legal system, the Court itself must first demonstrate confidence in its own capabilities and in the law that it administers. Faith in the Court and in international law by the community of nations would do much to increase the stability and concord of their relations, but until the nations of the world acquire such faith we shall have to change Pindar's famous dictum from the present tense into the subjunctive, to read:

"Law *should be* the Lord of all."

Postscript

Just as this book is going to press, the government of Dr. Mohammed Mossadegh, in office since April, 1951, has been overthrown in an army coup led by General Fazollah Zahedi. On August 13, 1953, Shah Mohammed Reza Pahlevi signed a decree naming General Zahedi Prime Minister. Dr. Mossadegh refused to be dismissed, and, after an aborative attempt by the shah's Imperial Guard to arrest Mossadegh and his ministers, the shah fled the country on August 16. Three days later the army, apparently with popular approval, triumphed in a violent battle in Tehran, and General Zahedi was established in office. Mossadegh was imprisoned to await trial on charges of treason, and the shah returned to this throne. These developments do not, however, seriously affect the conclusions reached in the preceding pages. During his last year in office, Mossadegh allowed the Communist Tudeh party to become strong and powerful. Since Tudeh actively supported Mossadegh in this latest fight with the shah and the army, Mossadegh's defeat was also a defeat for Tudeh. But the party is still strong, and one of the most difficult problems facing Zahedi's government is to bring the Tudeh party, as well as some of the more extreme of Mossadegh's supporters, under control. Mossadegh's government has also left Iran in a state of financial and economic chaos, a situation that cannot be solved, even temporarily, without financial help from external sources. But General Zahedi and his supporters are, like Mossa-

231

degh, Iranian nationalists, and they are not likely to bind themselves too closely to a foreign government. The overthrow of Mossadegh's government does not mean that the Iranian dislike of foreigners has been eradicated. Indeed, it would seem that the continued existence of Zahedi's government will depend in part on its ability to avoid being identified in the minds of the people with any particular foreign government. It is improbable that the nationalization will be revoked, and the Anglo-Iranian Oil Company be invited to return to Iran. Nevertheless, any permanent solution of Iran's problems will depend on a resuscitation of the Iranian oil industry, and that will be impossible until a compromise can be reached between the demands of Iranian nationalism and that country's dependence (at least, in the foreseeable future) on foreign capital, technological skills, and marketing organizations for economic well-being. How such a compromise can be reached remains the unanswered question.

The problems facing Zahedi's government are, therefore, much the same as those that had plagued Mossadegh for the previous two years. It is hoped that General Zahedi will prove more capable of solving them than his predecessor was, and will be willing to accept the burden of making a positive approach toward their solution. Meantime, the need for temporary solutions is urgent, and there are indications that the British and American governments will try to extend a helping hand as quickly and tactfully as possible.

Appendix I

Agreement Between the Imperial Government of Persia and the Anglo-Persian Oil Company, Limited, Made at Teheran on April 29th, 1933

Preamble

For the purpose of establishing a new Concession to replace that which was granted in 1901 to William Knox D'Arcy, the present Concession is granted by the Persian Government and accepted by the Anglo-Persian Oil Company Limited.

This Concession shall regulate in the future the relations between the two parties above mentioned.

Definitions.

The following definitions of certain terms used in the present Agreement are applicable for the purposes hereof, without regard to any different meaning which may or might be attributed to those terms for other purposes:

"The Government" means the Imperial Government of Persia;

"The Company" means the Anglo-Persian Oil Company Limited and all its subordinate companies;

"The Anglo-Persian Oil Company Limited" means the Anglo-Persian Oil Company Limited or any other body corporate to which, with the consent of the Government (Article 26), this Concession might be transferred;

"Subordinate Company" means any company for which the Company has the right to nominate directly or indirectly more than one-half of the

234

directors, or in which the Company holds, directly or indirectly, a number of shares sufficient to assure it more than 50 per cent of all voting rights at the general meetings of such a company.

"Petroleum" means crude oil, natural gases, asphalt, ozokerite, as well as all products obtained either from these substances or by mixing these substances with other substances.

"Operations of the Company in Persia" means all industrial, commercial, and technical operations carried on by the Company exclusively for the purposes of this Concession.

Article 1.

The Government grants to the Company, on the terms of this Concession, the exclusive right, within the territory of the Concession, to search for and extract petroleum as well as to refine or treat in any other manner and render suitable for commerce the petroleum obtained by it.

The Government also grants to the Company, throughout Persia, the non-exclusive right to transport petroleum, to refine or treat it in any other manner and to render it suitable for commerce, as well as to sell it in Persia and to export it.

Article 2.

A. The territory of the Concession, until December 31st, 1938, shall be the territory to the south of the violet line drawn on the map signed by both parties and annexed to the present Agreement.

B. The Company is bound, at latest by December 31st, 1938, to select on the territory above-mentioned one or several areas of such shape and such size and so situated as the Company may deem suitable. The total area of the area or areas selected must not exceed one hundred thousand English square miles (100,000 square miles), each linear mile being equivalent to 1,609 metres.

The Company shall notify to the Government in writing on December 31st, 1938, or before that date, the area or areas which it shall have selected as above provided. The maps and data necessary to identify and define the area or areas which the Company shall have selected shall be attached to each notification.

C. After December 31st, 1938, the Company shall no longer have the right to search for and extract petroleum except on the area or areas selected by it under paragraph B above, and the territory of the Concession, after that date, shall mean only the area or areas so selected and the selection of which have been notified to the Government as above provided.

Article 3.

The Company shall have the non-exclusive right to construct and to own pipe-lines. The Company may determine the position of its pipe-lines and operate them.

Article 4.

A. Any unutilised lands belonging to the Government, which the Company shall deem necessary for its operations in Persia and which the Government shall not require for purposes of public utility, shall be handed over gratuitously to the Company.

The manner of acquiring such lands shall be the following: Whenever any land becomes necessary to the Company, it is bound to send to the Ministry of Finance a map or maps on which the land the Company needs shall be shown in colour. The Government undertakes, if it has no objection to make, to give its approval within a period of three months after receipt of the Company's request.

B. Lands belonging to the Government, of which use is being made and which the Company shall need, shall be requested of the Government in the manner prescribed in the preceding paragraph, and the Government, in case it should not itself need these lands and should have no objection to make, shall give, within a period of three months, its approval to the sale asked for by the Company.

The price of these lands shall be paid by the Company; such price must be reasonable and not exceed the current price of lands of the same kind and utilised in the same manner in the district.

C. In the absence of a reply from the Government to requests under paragraphs A and B above, after the expiry of two months from the date of receipt of the said requests, a reminder shall be sent by the Company to the Government; should the Government fail to reply to such reminder within a period of one month, its silence shall be regarded as approval.

D. Lands which do not belong to the Government and which are necessary to the Company shall be acquired by the Company, by agreement with the parties interested, and through the medium of the Government.

In case agreement should not be reached as to the prices, the Government shall not allow the owners of such lands to demand a price higher than the prices commonly current for neighbouring lands of the same nature. In valuing such lands, no regard shall be paid to the use to which the Company may wish to put them.

E. Holy places and historical monuments, as well as all places and sites of historical interest, are excluded from the foregoing provisions, as well as their immediate surroundings for a distance of at least 200 metres.

F. The Company has the non-exclusive right to take within the territory of the Concession, but not elsewhere, on any unutilised land belonging to the State, and to utilise gratuitously for all the operations of the Company, any kinds of soil, sand, lime, gypsum, stone and other building materials. It is understood that if the utilisation of the said materials were prejudicial to any rights whatever of third parties, the Company should indemnify those whose rights were infringed.

Article 5.

The operations of the Company in Persia shall be restricted in the following manner:

1) The construction of any new railway line and of any new port shall be subject to a previous agreement between the Government and the Company;

2) If the Company wishes to increase its existing service of telephones, telegraphs, wireless and aviation in Persia, it shall only be able to do so with the previous consent of the Government.

If the Government requires to utilise the means of transport and communication of the Company for national defence or in other critical circumstances, it undertakes to impede as little as possible the operations of the Company, and to pay it fair compensation for all damages caused by the utilisation above mentioned.

Article 6.

A. The Company is authorised to effect, without special licence, all imports necessary for the exclusive needs of its employees on payment of the Custom duties and other duties and taxes in force at the time of importation.

The Company shall take the necessary measures to prevent the sale or the handing over of products imported to persons not employed by the Company.

B. The Company shall have the right to import, without special licence, the equipment, material, medical and surgical instruments and pharmaceutical products, necessary for its dispensaries and hospitals in Persia, and shall be exempt in respect thereof from any Custom duties and other duties and taxes in force at the time of importation, or payments of any nature whatever to the Persian State or to local authorities.

C. The Company shall have the right to import, without any licence and exempt from any Custom duties and from any taxes or payments of any nature whatever to the Persian State or to local authorities, anything necessary exclusively for the operations of the Company in Persia.

D. The exports of petroleum shall enjoy Customs immunity and shall be exempt from any taxes or payments of any nature whatever to the Persian State or to local authorities.

Article 7.

A. The Company and its employees shall enjoy the legal protection of the Government.

B. The Government shall give, within the limits of the laws and regulations of the country, all possible facilities for the operations of the Company in Persia.

C. If the Government grants concessions to third parties for the purpose of exploiting other mines within the territory of the Concession, it must cause the necessary precautions to be taken in order that these exploitations do not cause any damage to the installations and works of the Company.

D. The Company shall be responsible for the determination of dangerous zones for the construction of habitations, shops and other buildings, in order that the Government may prevent the inhabitants from settling there.

Article 8.

The Company shall not be bound to convert into Persian currency any part whatsoever of its funds, in particular any proceeds of the sale of its exports from Persia.

Article 9.

The Company shall immediately make its arrangements to proceed with its operations in the province of Kermanshah through a subsidiary company with a view of producing and refining petroleum there.

Article 10.

I. The sums to be paid to the Government by the Company in accordance with this Agreement (besides those provided in other articles) are fixed as follows:

a) An annual royalty, beginning on January 1st, 1933, of four shillings per ton of petroleum sold for consumption in Persia or exported from Persia;

b) Payment of a sum equal to twenty per cent (20%) of the distribution to the ordinary stockholders of the Anglo-Persian Oil Company Limited, in excess of the sum of six hundred and seventy-one thousand two hundred and fifty pounds sterling (£671,250), whether that distribution be made as dividends for any one year or whether it relates to the reserves of that company, exceeding the reserves which, according to its books, existed on December 31st, 1932;

c) The total amount to be paid by the Company for each calendar (Christian) year under sub-clauses (*a*) and (*b*) shall never be less than seven hundred and fifty thousand pounds sterling (£750,000).

II. Payments by the Company under this Article shall be made as follows:

a) On March 31st, June 30th, September 30th and December 31st of each year, on each occasion one hundred and eighty-seven thousand five hundred pounds sterling (£187,500) (the payment relating to March 31st, 1933, shall be made immediately after the ratification of the present Agreement);

b) On February 28th, 1934, and thereafter on the same date in each year, the amount of the tonnage royalty for the previous year provided for in sub-clause I (*a*) less the sum of seven hundred and fifty thousand pounds sterling (£750,000), already paid under sub-clause II (*a*);

c) Any sums due to the Government under sub-clause I (*b*) of this article shall be paid simultaneously with any distribution to the ordinary stockholders.

III. On the expiration of this Concession, as well as in the case of surrender by the Company under Article 25, the Company shall pay to the Government a sum equal to twenty per cent (20%) of:

a) The surplus difference between the amount of the reserves (General Reserve) of the Anglo-Persian Oil Company Limited, at the date of the expiration of the Concession or of its surrender, and the amount of the same reserves at December 31st, 1932;

b) The surplus difference between the balance carried forward by the Anglo-Persian Oil Company Limited at the date of the expiration of the Concession or of its surrender and the balance carried forward by that Company at December 31st, 1932. Any payment due to the Government under this clause shall be made within a period of one month from the date of the general meeting of the Company following the expiration or the surrender of the Concession.

IV. The Government shall have the right to check the returns relating to sub-clause I (*a*) which shall be made to it at latest on February 28th for the preceding year.

V. To secure the Government against any loss which might result from fluctuations in the value of English currency, the parties have agreed as follows:

a) If, at any time, the price of gold in London exceeds six pounds sterling per ounce (ounce troy), the payment to be made by the Company in accordance with the present Agreement (with the exception of sums due to the Government under sub-clause I (*b*) and clause III (*a*) and (*b*) of this article and sub-clause I (*a*) of Article 23) shall be increased by one thousand four hundred and fortieth part $\dfrac{1}{1440}$ for each penny of increase of the price of gold above six pounds sterling (£6) per ounce (ounce troy) on the due date of the payments;

b) If, at any time, the Government considers that gold has ceased to be the general basis of values and that the payments above mentioned no longer give it the security which is intended by the parties, the parties shall come to an agreement as to the modification of the nature of the security above mentioned, or in default of such an arrangement, shall submit the question to the Arbitration Court (Article 22) which shall decide whether the security provided in sub-clause (*a*) above ought to be altered and if so, shall settle the provisions to be substituted therefor and shall fix the period to which such provisions shall apply.

VI. In case of a delay, beyond the dates fixed in the present Agreement, which might be made by the Company in the payment of sums due by it to the Government, interest at five per cent (5%) per annum shall be paid for the period of delay.

Article 11.

I. The Company shall be completely exempt, for its operations in Persia, for the first thirty years, from any taxation present or future of the State and of local authorities; in consideration therefor the following payments shall be made to the Government:

a) During the first fifteen years of this Concession, on February 28th of each year and, for the first time, on February 28th, 1934, nine pence for each of the first six million (6,000,000) tons of petroleum on which the royalty provided for in Article 10, I (*a*), is payable for the preceding calendar (Christian) year, and six pence for each ton in excess of the figure of six million (6,000,000) tons above defined;

b) The Company guarantees that the amount paid under the preceding sub-clause shall never be less than two hundred and twenty-five thousand pounds sterling (£225,000) ;

c) During the fifteen years following, one shilling for each of the first six million (6,000,000) tons of petroleum, on which the royalty provided for in Article 10, I (*a*), is payable for the preceding calendar year, and nine pence for each ton in excess of the figure of 6,000,000 tons above defined.

d) The Company guarantees that the amount paid under the preceding sub-clause (*c*) shall never be less than three hundred thousand pounds sterling (£300,000).

II. Before the year 1963, the parties shall come to an agreement as to the amounts of the annual payments to be made in consideration of the complete exemption of the Company for its operations in Persia from any taxation of the State and of local authorities, during the second period of thirty years extending until December 31st, 1993.

Article 12.

A. The Company, for its operations in Persia in accordance with the present Agreement, shall enjoy all means customary and proper to ensure economy in and good returns from its operations, to preserve the deposits of petroleum and to exploit its Concession by methods in accordance with the latest scientific progress.

B. If, within the territory of the Concession, there exist other mineral substances than petroleum or woods and forests belonging to the Government, the Company may not exploit them in accordance with the present Concession, nor object to their exploitation by other persons (subject to the due compliance with the terms of clause C of Article 7) ; but the Company shall have the right to utilise the said substances or the woods and forests above mentioned if they are necessary for the exploration or the extraction of petroleum.

C. All boreholes which, not having resulted in the discovery of petroleum, produce water or precious substances, shall be reserved for the Government which shall be immediately informed of these discoveries by the Company, and the Government shall inform the Company as soon as possible if it wishes to take possession of them. If it wishes to take possession, it shall watch that the operations of the Company be not impeded.

Article 13.

The Company undertakes to send, at its own expense and within a reasonable time, to the Ministry of Finance, whenever the representative of the Government shall request it, accurate copies of all plans, maps, sections and any other data whether topographical, geological or of drilling relating to the territory of the Concession, which are in its possession.

Furthermore, the Company shall communicate to the Government throughout the duration of the Concession all important scientific and technical data resulting from its work in Persia.

All these documents shall be considered by the Government as confidential.

Article 14.

A. The Government shall have the right to cause to be inspected at its wish, at any reasonable time, the technical activity of the Company in Persia, and to nominate for this purpose technical specialist experts.

B. The Company shall place at the disposal of the specialist experts nominated to this end by the Government, the whole of its records relative to scientific and technical data, as well as all measuring apparatus and means of measurement, and these specialist experts shall, further, have the right to ask for any information in all the offices of the Company and on all the territories in Persia.

Article 15.

The Government shall have the right to appoint a representative who shall be designated "Delegate of the Imperial Government." This representative shall have the right:

1) To obtain from the Company all the information to which the stockholders of the Company are entitled;

2) To be present at all the meetings of the Board of Directors, of its committees and at all the meetings of stockholders, which have been convened to consider any question arising out of the relations between the Government and the Company;

3) To preside ex officio, with a casting vote, over the Committee to be set up by the Company for the purpose of distributing the grant for and supervising the professional education in Great Britain of Persian nationals referred to in Article 16.

4) To request that special meetings of the Board of Directors be convened at any time, to consider any proposal that the Government shall submit to it. (These meetings shall be convened within fifteen days from

242

the date of the receipt by the Secretary of the Company of a request in writing to that end.)

The Company shall pay to the Government to cover the expenses to be borne by it in respect of the salary and expenses of the above-mentioned delegate a year by sum of two thousand pounds sterling (£2,000). The Government shall notify the Company in writing of the appointment of this delegate and of any changes in such appointment.

Article 16.

I. Both parties recognise and accept as the principle governing the performance of this Agreement the supreme necessity, in their mutual interest, of maintaining the highest degree of efficiency and of economy in the administration and the operations of the Company in Persia.

II. It is, however, understood that the Company shall recruit its artisans as well as its technical and commercial staff from among Persian nationals to the extent that it shall find in Persia persons who possess the requisite competence and experience. It is likewise understood that the unskilled staff shall be composed exclusively of Persian nationals.

III. The parties declare themselves in agreement to study and prepare a general plan of yearly and progressive reduction of the non-Persian employees with a view to replacing them in the shortest possible time and progressively by Persian nationals.

IV. The Company shall make a yearly grant of ten thousand pounds sterling in order to give in Great Britain, to Persian nationals, the professional education necessary for the oil industry.

The said grant shall be expended by a Committee which shall be constituted as provided in Article 15.

Article 17.

The Company shall be responsible for organising and shall pay the cost of the provision, control and upkeep of sanitary and public health services, according to the requirements of the most modern hygiene practised in Persia, on all the lands of the Company and in all buildings and dwellings, destined by the Company for the use of its employees, including the workmen employed within the territory of the Concession.

Article 18.

Whenever the Company shall make issues of shares to the public, the subscription lists shall be opened at Teheran at the same time as elsewhere.

Article 19.

The Company shall sell for internal consumption in Persia, including the needs of the Government, motor spirit, kerosene and fuel oil produced from Persian petroleum, on the following basis:

a) On the first of June in each year, the Company shall ascertain the average Roumanian f.o.b. prices for motor spirit, kerosene and fuel oil and the average Gulf of Mexico f.o.b. prices for each of these products during the preceding period of twelve months ending on April 30th. The lowest of these average prices shall be selected. Such prices shall be the "basic prices" for a period of one year, beginning on June 1st. The "basic prices" shall be regarded as being the prices at the refinery.

b) The Company shall sell (1) to the Government for its own needs, and not for resale, motor spirit, kerosene and fuel oil at the basic prices, provided in sub-clause (*a*) above, with a deduction of twenty-five per cent (25%); (2) to other consumers at the basic prices with a deduction of ten per cent (10%).

c) The Company shall be entitled to add to the basic prices mentioned in sub-clause (*a*), all actual costs of transport and of distribution and of sale, as well as any imposts and taxes on the said products.

d) The Government shall forbid the export of the petroleum products sold by the Company under the provisions of this article.

Article 20.

I. (*a*) During the last ten years of the Concession, or during the two years from the notice preceding the surrender of the Concession provided in Article 25, the Company shall not sell or otherwise alienate except to subordinate companies, any of its immovable properties in Persia. During the same period, the Company shall not alienate or export any of its movable property whatever except such as has become unutilisable.

b) During the whole of the period preceding the last ten years of the Concession, the Company shall not alienate any land obtained by it gratuitously from the Government; it shall not export from Persia any movable property, except in the case when such property shall have become unutilisable or shall be no longer necessary for the operations of the Company in Persia.

II. At the end of the Concession, whether by expiration of time or otherwise, all the property of the Company in Persia shall become the property of the Government in proper working order and free of any expenses and of any encumbrances.

III. The expression "all the property" comprises all the lands, buildings and workshops, constructions, wells, jetties, roads, pipe-lines, bridges, drainage and water-supply systems, engines, installations and equipment (including tools) of any sort, all means of transport and communication in Persia (including, for example, automobiles, carriages, aeroplanes), any stocks and any other object in Persia which the Company is utilising in any manner whatsoever for the objects of the Concession.

Article 21.

The contracting parties declare that they base the performance of the present Agreement on principles of mutual goodwill and good faith as well as on a reasonable interpretation of this Agreement.

The Company formally undertakes to have regard at all times and in all places to the rights, privileges and interest of the Government and shall abstain from any action or omission which might be prejudicial to them.

This Concession shall not be annulled by the Government and the terms therein contained shall not be altered either by general or special legislation in the future, or by administrative measures or any other acts whatever of the executive authorities.

Article 22.

A. Any differences between the parties of any nature whatever and in particular any differences arising out of the interpretation of this Agreement and of the rights and obligations therein contained as well as any differences of opinion which may arise relative to questions for the settlement of which, by the terms of this Agreement, the agreement of both parties is necessary, shall be settled by arbitration.

B. The party which requests arbitration shall so notify the other party in writing. Each of the parties shall appoint an arbitrator, and the two arbitrators, before proceeding to arbitration, shall appoint an umpire. If the two arbitrators cannot, within two months, agree on the person of the umpire, the latter shall be nominated, at the request of either of the parties, by the President of the Permanent Court of International Justice. If the President of the Permanent Court of International Justice belongs to a nationality or a country which, in accordance with clause C, is not qualified to furnish the umpire, the nomination shall be made by the Vice-President of the said Court.

C. The umpire shall be of a nationality other than Persian or British; furthermore, he shall not be closely connected with Persia or with Great

Britain as belonging to a dominion, a protectorate, a colony, a mandated country or other country administered or occupied by one of the two countries above mentioned or as being or having been in the service of one of these countries.

D. If one of the parties does not appoint its arbitrator or does not advise the other party of its appointment, within sixty days of having received notification of the request for arbitration, the other party shall have the right to request the President of the Permanent Court of International Justice (or the Vice-President in the case provided at the end of clause B) to nominate a sole arbitrator, to be chosen from among persons qualified as above mentioned, and, in this case, the difference shall be settled by this sole arbitrator.

E. The procedure of arbitration shall be that followed, at the time of arbitration, by the Permanent Court of International Justice. The place and time of arbitration shall be fixed by the umpire or by the sole arbitrator provided for in clause D, as the case may be.

F. The award shall be based on the juridical principles contained in Article 38 of the Statutes of the Permanent Court of International Justice. There shall be no appeal against the award.

G. The expenses of arbitration shall be borne in the manner determined by the award.

Article 23.

I. In full settlement of all the claims of the Government of any nature in respect of the past until the date of coming into force of this Agreement (except in regard to Persian taxation), the Company: (a) shall pay within a period of thirty days from the said date the sum of one million pounds sterling (£1,000,000) and, besides, (b) shall settle the payments due to the Government for the financial years 1931 and 1932 on the basis of Article 10 of this Agreement and not on that of the former D'Arcy Concession, after deduction of two hundred thousand pounds sterling (£200,000) paid in 1932 to the Government as an advance against the royalties and £113,403 3s 10d. placed on deposit at the disposal of the Government.

II. Within the same period, the Company shall pay to the Government in full settlement of all its claims in respect of taxation for the period from March 21st, 1930, to December 31st, 1932, a sum calculated on the basis of sub-clause (a) of clause I of Article 11, but without the guarantee provided in sub-clause (b) of the same clause.

Article 24.

If, by reason of the annulment of the D'Arcy Concession, litigation should arise between the Company and private persons on the subject of the duration of leases made in Persia before December 1st, 1932, within the limits allowed by the D'Arcy Concession, the litigation shall be decided according to the rules of interpretation following:

a) If the lease is to determine, according to its terms, at the end of the D'Arcy Concession, it shall retain its validity until May 28th, 1961, notwithstanding the annulment of the said Concession;

b) If it has been provided in the lease that it shall be valid for the duration of the D'Arcy Concession and, in the event of its renewal, for the duration of the renewed Concession, the lease shall retain its validity until December 31st, 1993.

Article 25.

The Company shall have the right to surrender this Concession at the end of any Christian calendar year, on giving to the Government notice in writing two years previously.

On the expiry of the period above provided, the whole of the property of the Company in Persia (defined in Article 20, III) shall become free of cost and without encumbrances the property of the Government in proper working order and the Company shall be released from any engagement for the future. In case there should be disputes between the parties concerning their engagements before the expiry of the period above provided, the differences shall be settled by artitration as provided in Article 22.

Article 26.

This Concession is granted to the Company for the period beginning on the date of its coming into force and ending on December 31st, 1993.

Before the date of December 31st, 1993, this Concession can only come to an end in the case that the Company should surrender the Concession (Article 25) or in the case that the Arbitration Court should declare the Concession annulled as a consequence of default of the Company in the performance of the present Agreement.

The following cases only shall be regarded as default in that sense:

a) If any sum awarded to Persia by the Arbitration Court has not been paid within one month of the date of the award;

b) If the voluntary or compulsory liquidation of the Company be decided upon.

In any other cases of breach of the present Agreement by one party or the other, the Arbitration Court shall establish the responsibilities and determine their consequences.

Any transfer of the Concession shall be subject to confirmation by the Government.

Article 27.

This Agreement shall come into force after ratification by the Majlis and promulgation by Decree of His Imperial Majesty the Shah. The Government undertakes to submit this Agreement, as soon as possible, for ratification by the Majlis.

Made at Teheran the twenty-ninth April one thousand nine hundred and thirty-three.

For the Imperial Government of Persia:
(Signed) S. H. TAQIZADEH

For and on behalf of the Anglo-Persian Oil Company Limited:
(Signed) JOHN CADMAN, Chairman
W. FRASER, Deputy Chairman

(This Agreement came into force on May 29th, 1933, following its ratification by the Majlis on May 28th, 1933, and the Royal Assent, given on May 29th, 1933.)

Source: League of Nations Official Journal, 14th Year, No. 12, 77th Session (December, 1933), pp. 1653–1660. Annex 1467. (Translation.)

Appendix II

Tables—Financial and Personnel Statistics

TABLE 1

Increase of Money in Circulation, and Indexes of Wholesale Prices, Import Prices, and Cost of Living

Fiscal year beginning March 21	Money in circulation[a] outstanding at end of year	Index of money in circulation, yearly avg.	Index of wholesale prices,[b] yearly avg.	Index of cost of living,[c] yearly avg.	Index of import prices, yearly avg.
1937–38....	0.8	100	100	100	100
1938–39....	0.8	100	105	114	101
1939–40....	1.0	125	116	121	116
1940–41....	1.2	150	131	134	142
1941–42....	1.7	212	166	184	184
1942–43....	3.7	462	292	326	353
1943–44....	6.0	750	535	787	726
1944–45....	6.7	840	580	916	805
1945–46....	6.8	850	544	779	684
1946–47....	7.0	870	525	698	549
1947–48....	7.0	870	562	707	593
1948–49....	6.6	825	610	775	585
1949–50....	6.3	790	571	845	563
1950–51....	5.8	725	481	692	517

[a] In billion rials. Excluding notes in the Banking Department of the Bank-Melli-yi-Iran.
[b] Geometric average of sixty-five items quoted in Tehran.
[c] The higher rate of cost of living is due to greater increase of rent, and retail prices of basic food and clothes.
Source: U. N. Secretariat, Department of Economic Affairs, *Public Finance Information Papers: Iran* (1951), ST/ECA/SER. A/4, p. 17.

TABLE 2
Employees Engaged in the Oil Industry in the Middle East

Country and date	I Total number of employees	II Number of local employees	III Population in thousands	IV Col. II as percentage of Col. III	V Col. II as percentage of Col. I
Iran, Jan., 1949..........	72,380	67,903	18,387	0.37	93.8
Bahrein, 1948	6,078	4,650	110	4.23	76.5
Iraq, Dec., 1948..........	14,241	13,463	4,800	0.28	94.5
Kuwait, Mar., 1950.......	10,050	4,500 [a]	170	2.65	44.8
Saudi Arabia, Dec., 1949..	16,084 [b]	10,026 [b]	6,000	0.17	62.3
Egypt, July, 1947	(3,113)	......	(20,045)	...	...
Total [c]	118,833	100,542	29,467	0.34 [d]	84.6 [d]

[a] Estimate.
[b] Excluding the number of workers employed by contractors, amounting to 4,000 at the end of 1948.
[c] Excluding Egypt.
[d] For comparison, the percentages in Venezuela in 1948 were 1.23 and 93.0 respectively; the number of local employees was estimated at 53,940 of a total of 58,000 in the industry.
Source: U. N. Secretariat, Department of Economic Affairs, *Review of Economic Conditions in the Middle East* (1951), p. 63.

TABLE 3
Total Anglo-Iranian Oil Company Personnel in Iran as of March, 1951

Classification	Iranian	Non-Iranian [a]	Total
Staff:			
Senior	30	89	119
Other	5,492	3,534	9,026
Labor:			
Top grade	17,550	896	18,446
Middle grade...................	12,225	1	12,226
Lower grade	4,411	....	4,411
Unskilled	13,925	....	13,925
Apprentices and trainees...........	3,392	....	3,392
Contractors' employees	13,603	....	13,603
Total	70,628	4,520	75,148

[a] Non-Iranian includes British, Indian, and Pakistani.
Source: Anglo-Iranian Oil Company, *The Anglo-Iranian Oil Company and Iran* (July, 1951), p. 14.

TABLE 4

Actual Oil Revenue of the Government and the Sterling Conversion of the Anglo-Iranian Oil Company. (In million pounds sterling)

Fiscal year ending March 20	Total oil revenue	Royalties	Taxes	Share in dividends	Annual conversion[b] of pounds into rials
1941–42......	4.03	2.63	0.57	0.83	0.36
1942–43......	4.05	2.68	0.45	0.92	0.38
1943–44......	4.05	2.52	0.61	0.92	2.61
1944–45......	4.52	3.28	0.51	0.73	3.58
1945–46......	5.68	4.30	0.65	0.73	4.47
1946–47......	7.19	5.29	0.77	1.13	10.30
1947–48......	7.15	5.26	0.76	1.13	12.43
1948–49......	9.17[a]	6.58	0.95	1.64	16.16
1949–50......	13.50[a]	...	...	...	18.86
1950–51......	16.00[a]	...	...	...	21.50

[a] Unsettled.
[b] Conversions for domestic expenditures of the Anglo-Iranian Oil Company.
Source: U. N. Secretariat, Department of Economic Affairs, *Public Finance Information Papers: Iran* (1951), ST/ECA/SER. A/4, p. 51; British Information Services, *Anglo-Iranian Oil Negotiations,* ID 1062 (New York, June, 1951).

TABLE 5

Gold and Foreign Assets Held by Bank Melli and Iranian Treasury, Government Receipts and Expenditures

	1938	1943	1946	1947	1948	1949	1950 (June)
	In millions of United States dollars						
Gold	26	111	149	142	140	140	140
Foreign exchange........	12	110	90	104	134	103	100
Total	38	221	239	246	273	243	239
	In millions of Iranian rials						
Expenditures[a]	1,375	4,093	6,095	8,121	7,154	11,117	10,060
Receipts[a]	1,376	1,891	5,464	5,559	7,154	7,785	10,060
Surplus, or deficit....	1	–2,202	–631	–2,562	....	–3,332	....

[a] Budget estimates.
Source: U. N. Secretariat, Department of Economic Affairs, *Review of Economic Conditions in the Middle East* (1951), pp. 76, 78.

Appendix III

Extract from Chapter X, Entitled "Conclusions," of Labour Conditions in the Oil Industry in Iran *(Geneva, 1950), the Official Report of the Special Mission of the International Labor Organization*

In the foregoing chapters the Mission has contented itself with describing the conditions which it found in Iran. It now remains to sum up its impressions and formulate its conclusions.

The first observation to be made is that the oil industry in Iran, with its large-scale activities and its modern techniques, is not operating in an industrial area, alongside other industries, but in a remote and almost barren region, in a country in which industry is of very recent growth. The same is true, of course, of the oil industry in a number of other countries, but the point needs to be borne in mind.

Regarding the oil areas in Iran, it is necessary to remember also their situation, climate and general characteristics—the desert surroundings of Abadan, the wild and rocky hills in which the oil is found, the low rainfall and the tropical heat. The great extent of the oilfields is another factor: each large field stretches for many miles, and the fields are separated from one another by several hours of driving over mountain roads. Even by aeroplane the journey from Abadan to Masjid-i-Sulaiman or from Masjid-i-Sulaiman to Agha Jari takes an hour. Abadan, though a single area, is nevertheless of the size of a very large town. Its concentration of tens of thousands of workers, nearly all dependent upon the one great refinery, is one of the most important factors to be taken into account in any attempt to understand the industry's problems. Hardly less important is the fact that the growth of this population has during certain periods been extremely rapid.

251

Added to these circumstances are the virtual isolation of Abadan and Fields [the oil fields], which are far removed from the other important industrial areas of the country, and the inadequacy of communications of all kinds or of local public services.

Concerning the oil workers, there is a striking difference between the qualifications which the local labour possesses and the qualities which the industry needs. The petroleum industry calls for men with every degree of skill to undertake a considerable variety of jobs, whereas the workers available in Iran were at first illiterate, untrained and completely devoid of any industrial background or traditions. Even now, after 40 years of activity, almost every worker taken on by the Company has to be educated, trained and initiated into the ways of industry.

In dealing with this labour force account must be taken of their particular form of family life, their tribal loyalties, their attachment to nomadic habits and the influence of their ancient traditions. While mutual help is practised within the family and the tribe, there is still a need for greater co-operation over wider areas. This is one of the obstacles to be overcome in developing a sense of common interest among workers in the same grades and categories who work under the same conditions and have to face the same problems.

Workers bred in such an atmosphere expect to be cared for by persons in authority; they are willing to follow a leader and to be told what they should do; they do not look for responsibility and they regard their difficulties as personal grievances which should be brought to the notice of people with influence. Their system of society for many centuries was autocratic. Their minds have been formed in what used to be called the unchanging East, but profound changes have occurred and are still occurring, sometimes with disconcerting effects. The development of modern industry in Iran implies that people whose minds are firmly set in traditional ways are exposed to powerful influences from a different world of thought and action. The fact that the old ways are so deeply rooted constitutes one of the big problems of the industry; but an even greater problem arises from the fact that the new ideas are producing profound and rapid changes in people's lives and thoughts.

Clearly, therefore, the labour and social problems of the petroleum industry in Iran—and presumably in the other countries of the Middle East—are very different from those encountered in highly industrialised countries, particularly in the West.

RECRUITMENT

The arrangements made by the Anglo-Iranian Oil Company for the recruitment of its workers seem to correspond closely to the needs and conditions of the country. The arrangements appear to be well organised and complete. Full employment records are kept in respect of each worker, and it is therefore possible for every man's position to be considered at any time in full knowledge of the facts.

There is no apparent over-all shortage of recruits for the industry, though the number of men presenting themselves for employment tends to vary considerably with the seasons. There is, however, a definite shortage of workers with the required skills. The problem of recruitment, and many of the other personnel problems, is complicated by the high rate of turnover in some at least of the grades. It may be anticipated that as long as the general shortage of skilled labour in Iran persists, many trained workers will leave the Company's service every year in order to take jobs in more attractive areas or in their native towns and villages. Accordingly, the Company will presumably continue to enrol and train many more workers than would normally be needed for its own operations.

On the other hand, it will be difficult to increase the rate at which Iranian nationals are recruited for employment in the higher categories of wage earners and as members of the supervisory staff. There is no reluctance on the part of the Company to recruit and promote Iranians for those categories. On the contrary, the Mission understands that the positions are open to all who acquire the necessary qualifications and experience. In any case, the proportion of Iranians in the Company's employment is large, even in the higher categories, and it is increasing.

TRAINING

The Mission was impressed by the extent of the Company's training scheme and the efficient way in which it is organised. Training is provided by the Company for every kind of job, industrial and commercial, and for every category and grade. Theoretical and practical instruction are successfully combined, and it is obvious that the courses have been carefully planned and that considerable thought has been given to the teaching methods to be employed. The Technical Institute in Abadan, which is the apex of the Company's training system, is considered to be one of the foremost educational institutions in the country. The Mission was struck not only by the arrangements for training but also by the serious and concentrated manner in which the trainees apply themselves to their tasks, whether in the Technical Institute or in the adult training centres or in the apprentice workshops. Another notable feature of the scheme is that it provides opportunities for further training for those who fail to pass their tests. The whole scheme offers an inducement to workers to improve their education and skill and thus to qualify for increments in wages and for promotion. On the whole, the Mission formed the view that the Company's training scheme is adequate and will in time provide all the trained Iranian personnel required to fill any post in the Company's service.

WAGES AND PRICES

The Company's wage structure includes definite rates for every grade and category, with provision for increments after periods of satisfactory service and promotion from grade to grade. As a result, the overwhelming majority of the workers receive more than the statutory minimum wage. Such complaints as the Mission heard related not so much to the wage scales as to the relation between wages and prices. As far as the Mission was able to judge, the Company scrupulously observes the provisions of the law concerning the minimum wage; the Mission feels, however, that a bigger effort might be made by the authorities to control the prices of essential commodities on the free market and to ensure that greater quantities of these commodities are made available.

Some of the trade union representatives complained that the authorities have fixed the minimum wage on the basis of a combination of free market prices and of the prices of goods obtainable in the Company's shops, whereas they felt that it should have been fixed on the basis of the free market prices only. If this idea were adopted, however, it would seem (a) that there would no longer be any reason for the Company to continue its present policy of importing and distributing essential goods at controlled prices; (b) that an immediate and substantial increase in wages would be necessary; and (c) that, as a result of inflationary pressure and the discontinuance of Company imports, the prices on the free market would increase in even greater proportion than wages. The consequences of such developments would be disastrous for all the parties concerned. In the Mission's view the real problem—and it is a serious one which needs the full co-operation of the Company, of the workers and of the authorities— is to maintain the purchasing power of wages. For this reason it would seem to be essential to retain the Company's food distribution scheme for the time being and to support it by effective measures of price and rent control. It would also be desirable to encourage every effort made to increase the production of food and other necessities in the Company's areas and to promote the import of such commodities.

HOURS OF WORK

No specific complaints were submitted to the Mission with regard to hours of work, and it would indeed seem that the hours will bear comparison with those of other industries in Iran and with those worked in the petroleum industry in other countries. Such grievances as exist can be dealt with through the existing machinery of consultation.

WORKING CONDITIONS

Generally speaking, the working conditions appear to be acceptable to the workers and the unions, though there are naturally a number of grievances, some slight, some transitory and others more serious. The smaller grievances can, of course, be adjusted without much difficulty, but there are a few which are not so easily disposed of, especially those which arise out of the nature of some of the industrial processes.

Requests for a more generous distribution of ice to men employed in parts of the refinery where the work is particularly oppressive, or for more frequent rest periods in hot weather for the women employed in the laundry, are examples of problems which need not present any great difficulty. On the other hand, it is clear that difficulties of a more serious nature are likely to arise in connection with processes which are by their nature disagreeable and perhaps even dangerous. The workers drew the attention of the Mission in particular to the discomforts of the men who work in dust while handling sulphur and to the anxiety of those employed in the SO_2 plant who fear that their lungs may be affected by the fumes. Work of this kind has to be done, but the reactions of the men are only to be expected. Similarly, with regard to the wearing of protective clothing by men in contact with acids, although the men know that the clothing is needed for their own protection, they feel aggrieved at having to wear it, especially in the heat of the Persian Gulf. Problems of this kind are not easy to remove entirely and they should be given continuing attention through the machinery which already exists.

SOCIAL INSURANCE

Social insurance provisions in operation in Iran provide (a) benefits to wage earners who suffer accidents and illness as a result of employment, and (b) benefits in case of marriage, pregnancy, large families, childbirth, burial and legal aid. The Labour Law also provides for assistance to workers and members of their families in case of accident or illness not caused by employment and for old-age and disablement benefit, but the regulations for the application of these provisions have not yet been issued and the provisions of the Law are not in force. This gap is partly filled by the various benefits provided voluntarily by the Company for its workers. The situation would, however, be eased for all concerned if these regulations could be issued and the intentions of the Law put into operation.

SAFETY

The Company is giving serious attention to the safety of the workers, both by attempting to make their jobs as safe as possible and by providing safety devices and protective clothing when the risks cannot be removed entirely. Although safety questions are already discussed to a certain extent by the joint departmental committees, it would be an advantage if special safety committees could be established for the various parts of the Company's operations. This would encourage safety consciousness and at the same time promote the broad idea of joint consultation between the Company and the workers. Consideration might also be given to the possibility of extending job safety training among the supervisory staff.

CONTRACT LABOUR

The problem of contract labour is a serious one in the oil industry of Iran by reason of the conditions of the country and of the large number of contract workers involved—over 7,000 in Abadan and over 8,000 in Fields [the oil fields]. There is, of course, a case for letting out certain jobs to contractors, but it should not be overlooked that the workers employed by the contractors are carrying on activities which are essential for the industry. In every country in which this industry exists some work is normally done by contractors. In the industrial countries, however, the contractors' men enjoy the same protection from the law and from collective agreements as other workers, and they have their own homes. Where a contract has to be carried out in a remote district of one of these countries it is usual for temporary accommodation to be provided. In Iran, however, the workers employed by contractors are not so well protected as the Company's employees, principally because the legal provisions are not so strictly applied. The purchasing power of their wages is less, since they do not receive the same advantages as the men employed by the Company in regard to the provision of food and medical aid. The jobs of the contractors' men are also more precarious because the contractors depend almost exclusively on the Company for their business and do not as a rule have alternative sources of employment. In these circumstances the welfare of the contract labour is a matter of far greater concern to the Company than it would be in an industrial country. The Company has recognised its position in this matter by the insertion of a special clause in contracts, but it is doubtful whether this clause completely fulfils its purpose. The Mission formed the impression that more energetic action needs to be taken by the public authorities to safeguard the position of contract labour. Much could be done, for example, by the organisation of an efficient system of labour inspection to ensure the observance of the minimum statutory standards for conditions of employment and by the control of rents and prices which was suggested in an earlier paragraph.

The position would be greatly eased if the Company could reduce the amount of work done by contract labour and employ more of these workers directly. This would give a large number of workers greater protection and the right to participate in the benefits which the Company provides for its own employees. It would appear, however, that the amount if not the proportion of contract labour has recently tended to increase, in part, no doubt, in response to a desire on the part of the Iranians themselves that greater opportunities be given by the Company to local contractors. The employment of more direct labour would, of course, aggravate the Company's problems in regard to housing, food supplies, health services, etc. In the long run the remedy would seem to lie in the development of local enterprises and the assumption of greater responsibility by the public authorities for the welfare of their citizens.

HOUSING

Housing is the most serious problem in the Company's areas and the one which gives most cause for concern. The problem of providing houses for the oil workers is a gigantic one, especially in Abadan, because of the large numbers to be housed, the fact that there have been periods of extremely rapid increase in the population, the almost complete absence of building materials and housing components, and the shortage of qualified building labour. These factors increase the difficulty of providing houses in sufficient numbers and render the cost of building extremely high. The provision of homes for such a large population would be a major problem even in a well-organised country where there were no shortages and where all the resources of municipal and private enterprise could be mobilised. It must be recognised therefore that the Company has had a colossal task to face in coping with this situation. The difficulties were further increased by the fact that during a part of the war period the building of houses was practically brought to a standstill, though the labour force was being rapidly extended.

258

When all this is said, however, the conclusion can hardly be avoided that a large and rapid increase in the construction of houses is both necessary and possible. The shortage of housing accommodation is one of the most serious causes of discontent in the Company's areas. In spite of the tremendous effort that has been made, the end of the programme of construction is not yet in sight. Although thousands of houses have been built and hundreds are still under construction, very large numbers of workers see no hope of securing a house for years to come. In this connection a question arises concerning the relation between the standard of accommodation and the rate at which it can be provided. It has been suggested that if houses of a lower standard were designed, they could be built more rapidly and could accommodate larger numbers of workers. So far, however, the Company has set its face against the building of houses which are not of substantial construction and provided with water-borne sanitation, individual drinking water supplies and other necessary services. It may nevertheless be possible, without depressing the standard of accommodation below a decent level, to construct a larger number of less costly houses which fulfil all reasonable requirements. The problem is so big and so acute that only an urgent effort on a large scale can meet it.

Complaints were heard by the Mission regarding the points system under which the houses are allocated. The system has hitherto worked well, but it would seem that the time has now come for it to be adjusted in order to give more weight to length of service. In present circumstances wage earners in the lower wage groups with many years of service may have to wait a long time before acquiring the necessary number of points. It would seem to be desirable to give such men an opportunity of qualifying for a house more quickly. A readjustment of the points system to permit of this would not, of course, solve the problem of shortage of accommodation. Only a much greater building effort could do that.

In addition to whatever measures the Company itself might take, it would seem to be indispensable for the Government and the local authorities to encourage the greatest possible amount of private building and to insist upon adequate rent controls until a sufficient number of houses has been built.

DISTRIBUTION OF COMMODITIES

One of the Company's most remarkable achievements has been the organisation of its scheme for the distribution of food, clothing and other essential commodities. This has involved the purchase of articles in short supply and arrangements for importing, storing and distributing them in an orderly manner among large numbers of people. As part of this scheme it has been necessary to work out a rationing and price system, to build stores and shops, to organise transport, to open canteens and restaurants and to undertake agricultural development projects. There can be no doubt that this scheme has resulted in the provision of vast quantities of commodities which would not otherwise have been available and has contributed towards holding down prices and supporting the purchasing power of wages. In the circumstances which at present exist in the area, the continuance of the scheme would seem to be an absolute necessity. If the scheme were abandoned there would soon be an acute shortage of articles of prime necessity, and prices in the local markets would soar. It is difficult to see what other arrangements could be made to supply the needs of the population of Abadan and Fields, unless the public authorities were to organise the supply and distribution of commodities on an adequate scale. One step in the right direction, however, would be the organisation of co-operative societies among the oil workers. Plans for this are already on foot and it is to be hoped that the initial difficulties will soon be overcome.

HEALTH SERVICES

No one who visits the Company's areas can fail to recognise the efforts which the Company has made in organising its health and medical services. In addition to the usual safety, hygiene and first-aid arrangements inside the plant, there are health services for the prevention of disease and medical services for the various forms of treatment. The preventive services include drainage, sewerage, the provision of pure drinking water, anti-malarial campaigns, inoculation and vaccination and the destruction of pests; while facilities for treatment include hospitals, dispensaries and various kinds of clinics. The hospital at Abadan is claimed to be the finest in the Middle East. These arrangements are all the more important because the health services of the municipality were quite rudimentary until recently, there is no other hospital in the area, and the number of doctors and dentists other than those employed by the Company is very small indeed.

A great strain is thrown upon the Company's medical services by the fact that although they were designed primarily for the Company's own employees, they are in fact used extensively by the workers' families and even by people who have no connection with the Company. It is desirable that the Company's medical facilities should be extended, and the Company is taking steps towards this end, but it is also evident that more vigorous action should be taken by the public authorities to provide for the health needs of the local population. It is therefore to be hoped that the Company's programme for the extension of the main hospital in Abadan and for additional clinics in the oilfield areas, as well as the plans for the erection of a municipal hospital in Abadan, may soon be carried out. The Mission fully appreciates the difficulties, financial and otherwise, in the way of a large-scale development of the medical services of these areas, but the needs of the local population are pressing and the facilities are still far from adequate.

EDUCATION

It will have been noticed that in addition to organising training schemes the Company has participated in the arrangements for the education of children and in the organisation of night classes for adults. The shortage of schools and teachers in Iran is so great that it will be many years before it will be possible to provide every child with an elementary education and to develop satisfactory arrangements for secondary and higher education. Remarkable progress is, however, being made in some areas and among these Abadan and Fields take a high place, thanks to the combined efforts of the authorities and the Company. The future industrial and social development of Iran will be influenced in a high degree by the progress which is made in the sphere of education, and the efforts put forward in the Company's areas to provide increased educational facilities will produce their reward not only for the Company but for the country generally. Continued close co-operation between the Company and the authorities in these matters is therefore to be recommended. Among the practical measures which are urgently needed are the provision of more primary and secondary schools and the training and settlement of a greater number of school teachers in these areas.

TRADE UNIONS

It is important to bear in mind that trade unionism in Iran is of very recent growth, and that the trade union movement is not united. It will be recalled that the main division inside the trade union movement is between the E.S.K.I. and E.M.K.A. organisations. In addition to this, however, the oil workers' unions are virtually separate, though links are now being forged between them and the organisations in other industries. Trade unions are legally recognised in Iran and are given certain important functions under the Labour Law, but it is obvious that their members still stand in fear of arbitrary administrative action and of dismissal or other forms of victimisation for their trade union activities. From statements made to the Mission it appears that the fear is genuine, though to what extent it is justified it is difficult to say.

It is unfortunate that the oil workers are not united among themselves. There seems to be no compelling reason why the split in the organisation in Abadan should continue or why there should be separate unions for Abadan and Fields. It would be an advantage if there could be a single union or federation for the oil workers in Abadan and if the organisations in Fields could be associated with it. There are difficulties in the way of maintaining contact between the oil workers in Abadan and those in Fields, and even between the workers in the different parts of the Fields area, but these could be overcome if there were a real desire for united organisation and action.

Closer organisation and more effective action will presumably come as the organised oil workers develop a greater measure of genuine trade union activity. To do this, however, they will need to recognise that the personal grievances of an individual are the problems of whole groups of workers and that such problems should be decided according to common rules or principles to be applied to all who are concerned. The oil workers' unions—like other unions in Iran—also need more experience in organising, in the conduct of union business and in the formulation of policy, but such experience is not likely to be acquired quickly.

Other factors which would encourage the growth of sound and responsible trade unionism among the oil workers are a development in the processes of collective bargaining (in which the joint departmental committees could play an important educative role among representatives both of the workers and of the management) and improvements in the handling of differences and disputes. Here it is not so much a matter of devising new machinery—since the existing machinery has not yet been fully tested—as of encouraging the joint examination and discussion of questions at all levels and thereby preventing differences from developing into open disputes.

Much could be done to assist the oil workers in improving their organisation and acquiring greater responsibility if closer contacts could be developed between them and the trade unions of other countries. They would benefit, in particular, from a closer knowledge of the aims, purposes and methods of trade unionism as understood in other countries, the successes, failures and lessons of trade unionism, and the methods and procedures employed for the organisation and financing of unions, the holding of union elections, the conduct of meetings and the formulation and application of union policies.

One matter which seems to have caused deep feeling among the oil workers' unions is their failure to secure a seat on the High Labour

262

Council [of Iran] at the conference held in December 1949 for the purpose of electing the workers' representatives to this body. As the voting at the Congress was on the basis of one vote per union the oil workers were at a disadvantage and their candidate could only have been elected with the help of a number of votes from other organisations. These were not forthcoming. It is nevertheless desirable for the oil workers to be represented on the High Labour Council, since they are the largest single body of workers in the country and constitute a high proportion of the total labour force. Such representation could be secured if the other unions were willing to give due weight to the claims of the oil workers. Alternatively it might be possible either to alter the basis of voting at the Congress or to amend the regulations concerning the High Labour Council so as to reserve a seat for a representative of the oil workers.

LABOUR-MANAGEMENT RELATIONS

The provisions of the Labour Law concerning labour-management relations are of great importance, since they embody the tripartite principle of discussion and decision in councils and committees containing representatives of the Government, the employers and the workers. The Law itself has only been in existence since 1946, and it is still too early to express a confident opinion regarding its provisions, especially as a number of changes are only now being put into effect. It is, however, clear that bodies such as the factory councils, the boards for the settlement of disputes and the High Labour Council are needed at their respective levels, though there may be room for differences of opinion regarding their composition and their achievements.

In general it may be said that the setting up of these bodies was calculated to improve labour-management relations by making provision for the regular discussion of labour problems at the plant and national levels and by providing procedures for the settlement of disputes. The factory councils give opportunities for discussing problems that arise at the plant level; they appear to deal mainly with welfare problems, grievances and minor disputes, though they are entitled to exercise certain other functions, e.g., in regard to problems of production. The Mission feels that the factory councils, whether in their present form or on a more widely representative basis, should be encouraged, both because they help to give the workers' representatives greater experience and responsibility and because they provide a channel through which the managements can give and receive information and opinions. The boards for the settlement of disputes seem to be concerned mainly with complaints regarding dismissals and with the fixing of minimum wages. The Mission was not able to form a very clear opinion as to the suitability of their composition and procedure, but it is obvious that some bodies of the kind are needed at this level. Regarding the High Labour Council, the Mission can be more definite. This body has apparently given most of its attention to the preparation of draft laws and regulations, the fixing of minimum wages, the application of labour legislation and the supervision of funds. The establishment of the High Labour Council was an important development in such a country as Iran. The Council has great responsibilities and considerable power, and its membership therefore needs to comprise men of experience and ability who truly represent their respective interests. It is to be hoped that the departments and organisations concerned will continue to participate fully in its work.

Good results may also be expected from the joint departmental committees set up on the initiative of the Anglo-Iranian Oil Company. These bodies bring the process of consultation right down to earth, so to speak, since they deal with problems affecting the workers in each of the various departments of the plant and comprise representatives who are workers themselves. They may therefore be of great value in dealing with problems which the workers understand and by which they are directly affected. The joint departmental committees are not yet fully appreciated by the workers, however, and there is still some reluctance to accept them. This is due in part to a natural slowness in understanding the aims and methods of such bodies and in part, perhaps, to a certain suspicion of them among the leaders of the unions. Nevertheless the confidence of the general body of workers in the joint departmental committees seems to be increasing, even if only slowly. At present the workers' representatives tend to use the meetings of the committees too largely for the ventilation of complaints and too little for putting forward constructive suggestions, while the management places more emphasis upon the explanation of regulations and questions of discipline than upon the discussion of some of the more fundamental problems which it would be desirable for the workers to understand. Further experience of the working of the committees, however, will no doubt help to make them more effective.

Generally speaking the Mission formed the impression that relations between the Company and the workers, though not completely harmonious, are developing on the right lines. Some of the suspicion which grew up in the past has not yet been entirely dissipated. Relations are for the most part friendly on the job and there is a marked mutual respect among the workers and their immediate supervisors. It is not surprising that difficulties arise in view of the numerous opportunities for friction, and it is interesting to note that the complaints made against the Company as an employer are fewer than those which relate to its housing facilities, food and clothing schemes and health services. The Company appears to be genuinely anxious to promote good industrial relations, and in this respect its policy seems to have advanced considerably in recent years. Difficulties must still arise when such large numbers of workers are concerned, and when so many problems present themselves. The Mission is confident that if political complications could be avoided the relations between management and workers would continue to improve.

GENERAL OBSERVATIONS

It is necessary to emphasise once again that the petroleum industry in Iran is a unique feature of the country's economic life. It should also be made clear that it is an industry regarding which a great deal of misinformation and misunderstanding prevails. The general population knows little of the industry or of the conditions of its workers, and is unable to compare its conditions with those in other industries. Having regard to the great distances and to the difficulties of communication, it is not surprising that relatively few people from other areas visit Abadan and Fields to see things for themselves, but this does not suffice to explain the extent of the misapprehensions. In view of the importance of the industry to the country it would be a public service if the authorities and the press would take steps to provide the population with more information regarding the true state of affairs in the petroleum areas. The publication of factual material regarding conditions in the petroleum industry in other countries would also be helpful.

At the risk of repetition the Mission feels it desirable to refer once more to the general conditions of the country—its great size, its comparative isolation, its natural resources which are so difficult to exploit, its extremes of climate and its retarded industrial and agricultural development—all of which must be taken into account when the conditions of the petroleum industry are being considered. The Mission would also recall the widespread poverty, malnutrition and disease, the low standards of housing, the inadequate educational facilities, the need for improved health and medical services and the failure to develop many of the public services, such as water supplies, sewage disposal and local transportation. Against this background the working and living conditions of the oil workers appear as an encouraging example of what can be done. Notable improvements have also taken place, of course, in some of the other industries and these developments have been greatly stimulated by the example of the factories set up by the Government.

The existence of unsatisfactory conditions in other industries and in other parts of the country does not imply that the oil workers have no cause for complaint. But the fact that such conditions are still so widespread emphasises the great effort which the oil industry has already made. It is true that the Anglo-Iranian Oil Company may be better equipped than some of the other employers to deal with industrial relations and with the social problems of its workers, and it is also true that the Company has various conditions to fulfil under the terms of its Concession, as well as moral obligations towards the country and its people. But in a sound national economy it is necessary for progress to be general and not to be confined to favoured industries or areas; improvements in working and living conditions should therefore be accelerated for all workers throughout the country. It is gratifying to note that efforts are being made to bring about some of the much needed improvements, e.g., through the machinery of the seven-year plan and the services of the [Iranian] Ministry of Labour.

It seems to the Mission that there is a clear need for improvements in the Labour Law and for a stricter enforcement of its provisions throughout the country. The regulations for carrying out the intentions of the Law are not yet adequate and there is a strong case for a more effective system of labour inspection, which implies, among other things, better facilities for the training of inspectors. The [Iranian] Ministry of Labour, which is still in its infancy, needs to be given greater support, and its services, both at the centre and in the localities, require considerable reinforcement.

Alongside the efforts to promote improvements in industry generally there should be more adequate arrangements for contact and co-operation between the Anglo-Iranian Oil Company and the authorities. The Mission was struck by the large number of problems which are handled by the Company, not only as an employer of labour but as a provider of public services, and it felt that there was an urgent need for more representatives of the national and municipal authorities to be co-operating in the solution of these problems with officials of the Company at the various levels. It seemed to the Mission that there was a good deal of misunderstanding regarding the nature and extent of the problems and the efforts made to overcome them, and that this should be dissipated in the interests of all concerned.

In this connection the Mission would point out that the Government of Iran is strongly critical of the Company's policy and activities in regard to some of the problems mentioned in the preceding paragraphs. The Mission has attempted to describe the situation objectively and to give an honest opinion on every point. It has not hesitated to express approval when it was favourably impressed or to draw attention to matters in regard to which more energetic action might be taken or a different policy pursued. It realises, however, that the Government might not be disposed to endorse all the favourable comments made by the Mission and that in regard to some of the subjects it would go much further than the Mission in criticising the Company's policy and actions. Furthermore, the Mission is aware that on certain questions the Government takes a different line from the Company with regard to the division of responsibility between the Company and the authorities. For these reasons it would emphasise the view expressed in the preceding paragraph regarding the need for dissipating misunderstandings.

Among the subjects on which divergent views exist are wages, housing, food supplies, health services and education. The Company feels that it is fulfilling its obligations in regard to these matters and that in some cases it is doing more than can reasonably be expected of it, though it admits that there are still problems which have not yet been satisfactorily solved. It claims, moreover, that in some instances the responsibility for action lies with the country's authorities, though it is willing to co-operate in such action where possible and appropriate. On the other hand, the Government feels that the problems of the petroleum areas have been created by the operations of the Company, that the Government has already incurred heavy expenditure in these areas, and that it cannot be expected to expend more money and effort on what it considers to be a vast factory called into being by the Company. The Government maintains that the Company should pay more attention to the problems of housing, health, food supplies and education in the petroleum areas and that the Company has the main responsibility for supplying the needs of the workers and the general population. In view of the important issues involved, the Mission expresses the hope that these and other unresolved questions will be further discussed between the Company and the authorities at all levels, and that all their aspects will be kept constantly under review.

Suggestions were made to the Mission by Government officials in Iran to the effect that a comparative study of some of the economic problems of the petroleum industry and of certain aspects of the industry in the producing countries, such as the problem of wages and that of royalties payable to the Governments of the countries concerned, would be of considerable importance and it would seem that consideration might well be given to the possibility of undertaking studies of this kind.

Finally, the Mission is aware that many of the problems dealt with in these pages exist in other oil-producing countries as well. It feels that the possession of more information about the conditions in these countries would be helpful to all who are interested in the welfare of this important industry. Studies of these problems would help to establish the facts, to clear away misunderstandings, and to encourage further progress. The Mission hopes that it will be possible for such studies to be undertaken.

Appendix IV

Texts of the Laws Nationalizing the Oil Industry of Iran, 1951

The Single Article Law of March 20, 1951

For the Happiness and Prosperity of the Iranian Nation and for the purpose of securing world peace, it is hereby resolved that the oil industry throughout all parts of the country, without exception, be nationalized; that is to say, all operations of exploration, extraction and exploitation shall be carried out by the Government.

Passed by the Majlis on March 15, 1951, and by the Senate on March 20, 1951. Signed and promulgated by the Shah May 1, 1951.

Source of text: Iranian Embassy, Washington, D.C., *Some Documents on the Nationalization of the Oil Industry in Iran* (n.d. [1951], p. 2.

Law Regulating Nationalization of the Oil Industry

1) For the purpose of regulating the execution of the Law of 20th March which nationalizes the Oil Industry throughout the country, a Mixed Board shall be formed. This Board shall consist of five members of the Senate and five Deputies of the Majlis to be elected by each of these two bodies, the Minister of Finance in office or his deputy, and one other person to be selected by the Government.

2) Under the supervision of the Mixed Board the Government is charged to remove forthwith the former Anglo-Iranian Oil Company from control of the Oil Industry of the country; should the Company make its claim for compensation an excuse to forestall prompt delivery, the Government may deposit up to 25% of the current income, less cost of production, in the Bank Melli or any Bank acceptable to both parties to secure the claim.

268

3) Under the supervision of the Mixed Board the Government is charged to investigate the lawful and rightful claims of the Government as well as those of the Company, to report its views thereon to the two Houses of Parliament and upon ratification to give effect thereto.

4) From Esfand 20th 1329 [March 20, 1951] when the Bill for the nationalization of the Oil Industry received the ratification of the Senate, the Iranian nation being lawfully and unquestionably entitled to the entire earnings derived from Oil and Oil Products, the Government, under the supervision of the Mixed Board, is charged to investigate and check the accounts of the Company; similarly, the Mixed Board must meticulously supervise the exploitation of the Oil Resources from the date this Law went into effect until the appointment of a Board of Management.

5) As soon as possible, the Mixed Board shall prepare the Charter of the National Oil Company including therein provision for the appointment of a Board of Management and a Board of Technical Experts; such Charter shall be submitted to the Houses for their ratification.

6) For the purpose of gradually replacing foreign technicians, the Mixed Board is charged to draw up regulations for the annual selection through competitive examinations of students to be sent abroad for education, training and experience in the various branches of the Oil Industry; these regulations after being ratified by the two Houses shall be put into effect by the Ministry of Education. The cost of education of these students shall be paid out of the oil earnings.

7) Purchasers of the products of the oil fields from which the former Anglo-Iranian Oil Company has been removed can hereafter purchase annually at the current world market prices the same quantities purchased by them during the period commencing from the beginning of 1948 up to 29th Esfand 1329 [March 20, 1951]; for any additional quantities they shall also enjoy priority, other conditions being equal.

8) All proposals of the Mixed Board shall be delivered to the Majlis and if approved by the Oil Commission the latter shall submit a report thereon to the Majlis for ratification.

9) The Mixed Board must complete its work within three months of the ratification of the Law and submit a report of its action to the Majlis in accordance with Article 8. Should the Board need a longer period of time it may ask for an extension giving adequate reasons therefor.

Passed by the Majlis on April 30, 1951 and by the Senate on May 1, 1951. Signed and promulgated by the Shah on May 2, 1951.

Source of text: Iranian Embassy, Washington, D.C., *Some Documents on the Nationalization of the Oil Industry in Iran* (n.d. [1951]), pp. 3–4.

Appendix V

Iranian Declaration Accepting as Compulsory the Jurisdiction of the Permanent Court of International Justice

Le Gouvernement impérial de Perse déclare reconnaître comme obligatoire de plain droit et sans convention spéciale, vis-à-vis de tout autre État acceptant la même obligation, c'est-à-dire sous condition de réciprocité, la juridiction de la Cour Permanente de Justice Internationale, conformément à l'article 36, paragraphe 2, du Statut de la Cour, sur tout les différends qui s'élèveraient après la ratification de la présente déclaration, au sujet de situations ou de faits ayant directement ou indirectement trait à l'application des traités ou conventions acceptés par la Perse et postérieurs à la ratification de cette déclaration, exception faite pour:

a) les différends ayant trait au statut territorial de la Perse, y compris ceux relatifs à ses droits de souveraineté sur ses îles et ports;

b) les différends au sujet desquels les Parties auraient convenu ou conviendraient d'avoir recours à un autre mode de règlement pacifique;

c) les différends relatifs à des questions qui, d'après le droit international, relèveraient exclusivement de la juridiction de la Perse.

Toutefois, le Gouvernement impérial de Perse se réserve le droit de demander la suspension de la procédure devant la Cour pour tout différend soumis au Conseil de la Société des Nations.

La présente déclaration est faite pour une durée de six ans; à l'expiration de ce délai, elle continuera à avoir ses pleins effets jusqu'à ce que notification soit donnée de son abrogation.

Genève, 2 Octobre 1930
(signé) Hussein Ala

(Translation by the Secretariat of the League of Nations)

The Imperial Government of Persia recognizes as compulsory *ipso facto* and without special agreement in relation to any other state accepting the same obligation, that is to say on the condition of reciprocity, the jurisdiction of the Permanent Court of International Justice, in accordance with Article 36, paragraph 2, of the Statute of the Court, in any dispute arising after the ratification of the present declaration with regard to situations or facts relating directly or indirectly to the application of treaties or conventions accepted by Persia and subsequent to the ratification of this declaration, with the exception of:

a) disputes relating to the territorial status of Persia, including those concerning the rights of sovereignty of Persia over its islands and ports;

b) disputes in regard to which the parties have agreed or shall agree to have recourse to some other method of peaceful settlement;

c) disputes with regard to questions which, by international law, fall exclusively within the jurisdiction of Persia.

However, the Imperial Government of Persia reserves the right to require that the proceedings in the Court shall be suspended in respect of any dispute which has been submitted to the Council of the League of Nations.

The present declaration is made for a period of six years. At the expiration of that period, it shall continue to bear its full effects until notification is given of its abrogation.

> Geneva, October 2nd, 1930
> (signed) HUSSEIN ALA

Source of texts: PCIJ, Ser.D.6.53 (French), Ser.E.7.465 (English translation).

Date of ratification: September 19, 1932.

Date of abrogation: July 19, 1951 (U. N. Document, Press Release PM/2219).

A Time Table of Events in the Anglo-Iranian Oil Dispute

1949

July   Supplementary Agreement to 1933 concession signed.

1950

Jan.   Prime Minister Ali Mansur's government falls; succeeded by that of General Ali Razmara.

Oct.   Razmara submits Supplementary Agreement to Majlis. Referred to Special Oil Committee, chairman: Mohammed Mossadegh.

Dec.   Special Oil Committee reports unfavorably on Supplementary Agreement.

1951

Jan.   Majlis affirms committee's report, and directs committee to make a further report on the course of action the government should take.

                AIOC urges Razmara to reopen negotiations on the Supplementary Agreement, and offers to conclude a fifty-fifty profit-sharing agreement with the Iranian government.

Feb. 19   Mossadegh presents to the Special Oil Committee a resolution calling for nationalization of the oil industry.

                National Front party's campaign for nationalization continues with increased vigor.

Mar. 3   Razmara reports to the Special Oil Committee that his panel of advisers has informed him that nationalization is not then practicable and that they have doubts of its legality.

Mar. 7	Razmara assassinated. Hussein Ala named Prime Minister.
Mar. 14	British government notifies Iran that it considers the proposed nationalization illegal.
Mar. 15	Majlis passes Single Article Law nationalizing the oil industry.
	There is widespread anti-British rioting in Tehran, and a strike in the southern oil fields.
Mar. 20	The Single Article Law is passed by the Senate.
Apr.	Strike in the southern oil fields settled.
Apr. 27	Hussein Ala's government falls. British protest the nationalization law.
Apr. 28	Mossadegh accepts prime ministership after Senate and Majlis agree to his program of immediate eviction of AIOC.
Apr. 30	Law Regulating Nationalization of the Oil Industry passed by the Majlis.
May 1	Law Regulating Nationalization passed by the Senate.
	Single Article Law signed and promulgated by the shah.
May 2	Law Regulating Nationalization signed and promulgated by the shah.
	British Foreign Secretary Morrison sends Mossadegh a personal message asking the Iranian government to refrain from unilateral action against AIOC, and suggesting that the problem be settled by friendly negotiation. Mossadegh, in reply, reaffirms his intention of fully executing the nationalization laws, and ignores the proposal to negotiate.
	AIOC notifies the Iranian government that it requests arbitration in accordance with Articles 22 and 26 of its 1933 concession, and announces the appointment of Lord Radcliffe as its arbitrator.
May 15	A brigade of paratroopers is held "in readiness" in the United Kingdom to protect British lives and property in Iran if necessary.
May 19	British ambassador in Tehran presents Iranian government with an aide-memoire stating his government's view of the legal position of AIOC, and reserving his government's right to take the case to the ICJ if Iran refuses AIOC's request for arbitration. Negotiation is again suggested as the means of finding a solution.

274

May 20	Iranian Minister of Finance Varasteh notifies AIOC that Iran rejects the request for arbitration, and invites AIOC representatives to meet with the Majlis Special Oil Committee to "arrange execution of the nationalization laws."
May 24	AIOC is given a maximum of six days to send representatives to meet with the Majlis Special Oil Committee.
May 25	The brigade of paratroopers is moved from the United Kingdom to Cyprus.
May 26	AIOC notifies the Iranian government that it is appealing to the president of the ICJ to appoint a sole arbitrator in accordance with Article 22 (D) of the 1933 concession.
	The government of the United Kingdom files an "Application" to submit the dispute to the ICJ.
May 28	Mossadegh, in a speech to foreign press representatives, outlines his view of the legal position of AIOC.
	Iranian minister of foreign affairs notifies ICJ that his government does not recognize the competence of the Court to consider the United Kingdom's application.
May 29	Morrison again expresses a desire for negotiation and offers to send a mission from London for that purpose. He suggests that a settlement could be reached involving "some form of nationalization."
May 30	Iranian government announces that it is willing to discuss the United Kingdom's requirements of oil but does not consider the United Kingdom a party to the dispute between it and AIOC.
	Varasteh asks AIOC to submit proposals not contrary to the "principle of nationalization" expressed in the Single Article Law of March 20.
	AIOC announces that it will send a mission from London for discussions with the Iranian government.
June 11–12	AIOC mission, headed by Basil Jackson, arrives in Tehran.
June 12	Jackson, in press conference, states that AIOC has accepted nationalization in principle, and that it is still ready to discuss a fifty-fifty profit-sharing arrangement.
	Varasteh promises that in the projected talks with Jackson's mission he will demand at the outset "unconditional acceptance of nationalization as an accomplished fact."

June 13	Iranian Mixed Parliamentary Board demands that AIOC deliver 75 per cent of all "earnings" directly to the Iranian government, and deposit the other 25 per cent in a bank to secure compensation claims. Drake, AIOC's general manager in Iran, refuses.

June 13   Iranian Mixed Parliamentary Board demands that AIOC deliver 75 per cent of all "earnings" directly to the Iranian government, and deposit the other 25 per cent in a bank to secure compensation claims. Drake, AIOC's general manager in Iran, refuses.

NIOC offers "former" AIOC customers priority in oil purchases, and warns all importers of Iranian oil to deal only with it in the future.

June 14   Representatives of the Iranian government and AIOC meet for the first time. Varasteh states that the talks cannot continue unless AIOC agrees immediately to hand over all proceeds from sales of Iranian oil, less operating expenses and 25 per cent to cover compensation claims. The talks are adjourned until June 19.

June 19   The Jackson mission submits its proposals to the Iranian government. Offers £3 million per month until a settlement is reached, plus £10 million as an advance on future royalties. Refuses to turn over 75 per cent of its proceeds, as demanded by Varasteh.

Jackson proposals are rejected by Iranian government on the ground that they are inconsistent with the nationalization laws. Negotiations halted.

Jackson states that the proposals are consistent with the "principle of nationalization" as requested in Varasteh's aide-memoire of May 30.

June 20   Morrison assures Britons in Iran that they will be protected, and announces that the United Kingdom will ask the ICJ for "interim measures of protection" pending a final decision on the merits of the dispute.

Iranian Council of Ministers issues instruction for taking over the oil industry from AIOC.

June 21   Crowds obliterate AIOC signs and monograms in Tehran and the provinces.

Government introduces a "sabotage bill" in the Majlis.

AIOC printing works at Abadan seized.

June 21–22   Drake and Temporary Board of NIOC have dispute over tanker receipts and reach temporary agreement.

June 22   Jackson mission returns to London.

276

June 22 *(Cont.)*	United Kingdom files with the ICJ a "Request for the Indication of Interim Measures of Protection." Dispute over tanker receipts is renewed and prevents all sailings.
June 23	Temporary Board of NIOC demands new form of tanker receipts. Drake refuses to authorize tanker captains to sign it without a special endorsement. Temporary Board rejects special endorsement. Temporary Board accuses General Manager Drake of "sabotage" for refusing to permit the tanker captains to sign re-receipts as demanded by NIOC. Temporary Board advises AIOC sales manager in Tehran to turn over all receipts to NIOC. Similar instructions sent to sales managers in Ahwaz, Abadan, and Masjid-i-Sulaiman the following day.
June 25	Drake is advised by Temporary Board that he must issue no checks unless countersigned by members of the Temporary Board. Drake requests the Temporary Board to withdraw the charge of sabotage. They refuse. Drake leaves Iran for Basra on the advice of the British ambassador.
June 26	AIOC orders that all tankers in port at Abadan pump cargoes ashore and leave Abadan. Iranian customs officials close pipe line from Abadan to Iraq. Morrison repeats his announcement that British subjects in Iran will be protected, and adds that the cruiser *Mauritius* has been ordered to the vicinity of Abadan.
June 28	Temporary Board takes over the main offices of AIOC at Khorramshahr. The British staff is expelled.
June 29	Iranian foreign minister telegraphs ICJ that in the view of his government the Court has no jurisdiction to indicate interim measures. Mossadegh tells United States Ambassador Grady that the "sabotage bill" will be withdrawn from the Majlis.
June 30	ICJ holds a hearing on the British "Request for the Indication of Interim Measures." Sir Frank Soskice presents the British case. Iran is not represented.

July 1   AIOC cuts back production by 45 per cent because of the stoppage in tanker shipments.

Police search the house of Seddon, AIOC representative in Tehran, and impound all papers and documents found there.

July 2   Iranian state prosecutor begins examination of documents found in Seddon's house.

Iran protests the appearance of a British warship off Iranian shores, and complains to Iraq of the presence of British forces in Iraq near the Iranian border.

British personnel of AIOC announce their refusal to work for NIOC on the basis of individual contracts.

July 5   ICJ orders interim measures to preserve the rights of both parties pending final disposition of the British "Application" (May 26) to submit the dispute to the ICJ for decision.

July 6   Morrison announces that the British government accepts the Court's order and is anxious to coöperate with Iran in carrying it out.

July 7   State prosecutor of Iran issues an indictment charging Seddon with "illegal activities."

July 9   Iran notifies the secretary general of the United Nations that it abrogates its "Declaration" of September 19, 1932, recognizing as compulsory the jurisdiction of the Court.

Truman, in a letter to Mossadegh, urges consideration of the ICJ's "suggestion" of July 5, and offers to send Averell Harriman to Tehran to discuss the situation.

July 10   All but one distillation unit at Abadan is shut off, and production is cut to 3 million gallons per day. However, AIOC announces that it will retain its British personnel in Iran indefinitely.

July 16   Secretary general of the United Nations receives a letter from the Iranian foreign minister stating that Iran does not recognize as valid and enforceable the Court's order of July 5.

Mossadegh accepts Truman's offer to send Harriman to Tehran.

Harriman's arrival is the occasion for Communist-led anti-British and anti-American demonstrations in Tehran. Twenty

July 16 (Cont.)	persons are killed, three hundred injured. Martial law is declared in Tehran.
	A bond issue for 2 billion rials requested by Mossadegh is approved by the Majlis.
July 19	Seddon's residence permit is seized.
July 22	Seddon's residence permit is returned to him without explanation.
	Martial law in Tehran is suspended.
July 23	Iranian government submits to Harriman its "final view" on the subject of negotiations with the British government.
July 24	Harriman communicates the Iranian statement to the British.
July 25	British government requests further elaboration of some points of the Iranian proposals.
July 27	Harriman flies to London to consult with British officials.
July 29	Britain informs Iran that it recognizes the principle of nationalization but that it is unwilling to enter into negotiations unless the tension in southern Iran is relieved.
	Mossadegh answers the same day, expressing his pleasure at hearing that the British government is going to send a mission "on behalf of the former oil company," but stating that no tension exists in the south of Iran.
July 30	Harriman refuses to deliver Mossadegh's answer to the British.
July 31	Harriman returns to Tehran.
	More British warships appear in the Shatt-al-Arab River.
Aug. 2	Iran protests to Britain that Royal Air Force aircraft have violated Iranian territory.
	Production is completely shut down at Abadan.
	Major British and American oil companies announce proposals to coöperate in solving the problems created by the shutdown of Abadan.
Aug. 3	Iran agrees to coöperate with Britain in "creating the best possible atmosphere" for negotiations. "Tension in the south" is not mentioned.
Aug. 4	British mission headed by Lord Privy Seal Stokes arrives in Tehran.

Aug. 6	Talks between Stokes mission and Iranian delegation headed by Finance Minister Varasteh begin.
Aug. 7	Temporary adjournment of talks to permit Stokes to visit the southern oil fields.
Aug. 8	Talks resumed after Stokes's return. Stokes announces that the British staff of AIOC would not work for NIOC on the basis of individual contracts.
Aug. 9	Majlis gives the Iranian government permission to accept a $25 million loan from the United States Export-Import Bank.
	Negotiators establish a subcommittee to study the problem of tanker receipts.
Aug. 13	Stokes mission submits "Outline of Suggestions" to Iranian delegation to be used as a basis of further discussion.
Aug. 14	Iranian cabinet considers the "Outline of Suggestions."
Aug. 15	The two delegations meet to allow the British to explain their proposals.
Aug. 18	Iranian delegation rejects the Stokes proposals as inconsistent with the principle of nationalization and contrary to commercial practices.
Aug. 21	Stokes withdraws his proposals because, he says, the Iranians insist on misreading them.
Aug. 22	Mossadegh, after reporting the rejection of the Stokes proposals to the Iranian Parliament, gets a unanimous vote of confidence from both houses.
	Iranian delegation makes a further reply and "counterproposals" to Stokes.
	Stokes announces that he will return to London. Does not mention the "counterproposals."
Aug. 23	British Foreign Office statement accuses the Iranian government of not being willing to negotiate on the agreed basis, and announces that the British government takes its stand on the ICJ's order of July 5 and that it will pursue a definitive judgment in the ICJ. First hint of the British policy favoring the fall of Mossadegh's government as a prerequisite of a settlement of the oil dispute.
Aug. 24	Harriman leaves Tehran for Washington.

Aug. 24 *(Cont.)*	Mossadegh announces that his government is awaiting a reply to its "counterproposals."
	British Foreign Office announces that no Iranian proposals are under consideration.
Sept. 5	Mossadegh says that if negotiations are not resumed promptly all residence permits of the remaining British staff will be withdrawn.
Sept. 6	AIOC makes public announcement that it will take legal action against anyone purchasing oil from the Iranian government.
	British Foreign Office announces that negotiations begun by Stokes are not suspended but are broken off.
Sept. 6, 9, 10	Because of the efforts of some opposition deputies, Mossadegh is unable to get a quorum in the Majlis to approve his ultimatum to the British to reopen negotiations.
Sept. 10	British Treasury cancels Iran's extraordinary convertibility privileges.
Sept. 12	Mossadegh's ultimatum is delivered to Harriman in Washington for transmission to the British government. Deadline is set at fifteen days after its delivery to the British.
Sept. 14	Bank Melli bans further convertibility of sterling into rials, but revokes the order so that AIOC can meet its Iranian pay roll.
Sept. 15	Iran announces a new barter agreement with the USSR.
Sept. 17	Harriman informs Mossadegh that he is unwilling to deliver the ultimatum, and urges him to reconsider.
Sept. 18	Ultimatum delivered to the British ambassador in Tehran, who replies that the Iranian "counterproposals" are unsatisfactory as a basis on which to reopen negotiations.
	All Iranian government departments are instructed to close their accounts with the British-owned Bank of Iran and the Middle East. The privilege of buying and selling foreign exchange is reserved exclusively to the Bank Melli.
	Finance Minister Varasteh resigns.
Sept. 20	Mossadegh announces that all British staff members in southern oil fields must leave Iran within one week after September 27.

The British ambassador in Tehran protests, and Prime Minister Attlee appeals to the United States to use its "good offices."

Sept. 27 Iranian troops seize Abadan refinery.

Truman appeals to Iran to cancel its expulsion order.

Units of British army, navy, and air force group themselves round the head of the Persian Gulf and eastern Mediterranean.

Iranian government orders its army to blow up the Abadan installations if foreign troops attempt to land.

Sept. 28 Britain requests the United Nations Security Council to intervene.

Mossadegh announces that he will fly to New York to appear before the Security Council. He states that the Council is without competence to intervene in the Anglo-Iranian dispute.

Sept. 29 London announces that remaining British staff have been ordered evacuated.

Oct. 1 Evacuation of British staff is completed without incident, three days before the deadline.

Security Council votes to put the United Kingdom's complaint on its agenda. Sir Gladwyn Jebb argues the British case. Council adjourns for ten days to allow Mossadegh time to get to New York.

Oct. 10 Britain files with the ICJ a memorial in support of the British position in the case submitted (May 26) to the Court.

Oct. 12 Deputy Prime Minister Fatemi says in press conference that Iran will not accept the Security Council's decision if it adopts the United Kingdom's resolution.

Oct. 15–19 Debate in the Security Council.

Security Council adjourns its debate until the ICJ rules on its jurisdiction to deal with the British "Application" of May 26.

Oct. 20– Mossadegh talks with United States officials in Washington,
Nov. 13 but the talks are terminated without success. It is announced that Mossadegh's request for a loan from the United States government is being given the "most careful consideration."

282

Nov. 18	Mossadegh leaves Washington to go to Tehran via Cairo.
Nov. 26	Mossadegh gets parliamentary approval of his plan to hold elections immediately.
Dec. 4	Bank Melli imposes restrictions upon the right to open import credits abroad.
Dec. 6	Communist-led anti-Mossadegh demonstrations in Tehran clash with National Front supporters: five killed, more than two hundred injured.
	Opposition deputies take refuge in Parliament buildings because of threats from supporters of the National Front party.
Dec. 10	Riots still continuing.
Dec. 12	Iran sends ultimatum to former AIOC customers to make arrangements within ten days to buy oil or lose the privileges offered by the Iranian government. Offer expires without any acceptances.
Dec. 18	Elections begin in northern provinces and Tehran after weeks of bloody rioting.
Dec. 23	IBRD survey mission arrives in Iran.

1952

Jan. 3	IBRD sends its proposals to Mossadegh, who rejects them in part and asks for further elaboration of some points.
Jan. 11	Mossadegh, in a note to the British ambassador in Tehran, charges British officials with "open interference" in the internal affairs of Iran.
Jan. 12	Mossadegh orders all British consulates in Iran closed within ten days.
Jan. 20	After much argument, agreement is finally concluded for $23.4 million in economic and technical aid from the United States to Iran.
Jan. 21	The British government's protests are ineffective and its consulates are closed.
Jan. 31	Iranian government orders all foreign informational and cultural centers in Iran closed immediately.
Feb. 4	Iran files a preliminary objection to the jurisdiction of the ICJ.
Feb. 11	A second IBRD mission arrives in Tehran.

Feb. 16	Mossadegh announces that agreement with the IBRD is impossible. At the insistence of the Iranian Senate he agrees to make another attempt at negotiation.
Feb. 28	IBRD mission returns to New York, and then goes back to Iran on March 4. Discussions are continued until March 16, when Mossadegh announces that there has been no agreement on any major point.
Mar. 23	IBRD mission abandons its effort and returns to New York.
Mar. 25	Truman informs Mossadegh that the United States could not justify a loan to Iran at this time. He urges Mossadegh to seek a negotiated settlement of the oil dispute.
Apr. 9	At Iran's request, the ICJ postpones hearings on the preliminary objection from May 6 to June 9.
Apr. 24	After great difficulty, Iran agrees to accept continued military aid from the United States. Shipments of military goods, suspended since January, are resumed.
June 9–23	ICJ holds hearings on Iran's preliminary objection to its jurisdiction. Mossadegh, Navab, and Henri Rolin appear for the Iranian government; Sir Lionel Heald and Sir Eric Beckett represent the United Kingdom.
July 6	A new Majlis reëlects Mossadegh Prime Minister.
July 16	Mossadegh resigns when the shah refuses his request for power to rule by decree.
July 17	Ahmed Qavam named Prime Minister.
July 21	Qavam forced to resign after four days of continuous rioting led by a coalition of Communists and supporters of National Front party under the direction of Ayatullah Kashani.
July 22	ICJ gives judgment affirming its lack of jurisdiction to consider the United Kingdom's application of May 26, 1951.
July 23	Mossadegh is reinstated as Prime Minister. Riots are finally quelled by Mullah Kashani, who emerges as Speaker of the Majlis and second most powerful man in Iran.
Aug. 3	Both houses of Parliament vote overwhelmingly in favor of granting Mossadegh power to rule by decree for a period of one year. The shah consents.

Notes

PART I: "A PAGE OF HISTORY..."

§ 1. THE GREAT POWER STRUGGLE

[1] On the history of Persia and the Great Power struggle during the nineteenth century and thus far in the twentieth, see George Lenczowski, *Russia and the West in Iran, 1918–1948* (1949); Sir Reader Bullard, *Britain and the Middle East from the Earliest Times to 1950* (1951); Elgin Groseclose, *Introduction to Iran* (1947); *The Middle East, a Political and Economic Survey* (1950), published by the Royal Institute of International Affairs, pp. 199–236; L. V. Thomas and R. N. Frye, *The United States and Turkey and Iran* (1951); Sir Percy M. Sykes, *A History of Persia* (3d ed., 1930), 2 vols.; L. P. Ellwell-Sutton, *Modern Iran* (1941); and W. S. Haas, *Iran* (1946).

[2] In general, see *The Middle East...*, pp. 219–235; Morgan Shuster, *The Strangling of Persia* (1912), chap. ii; and Lenczowski, *op. cit.*, p. 5.

[3] It was regarded by many as a diplomatic defeat for Britain. For example, see *The Middle East...*, pp. 206–207; the Earl of Ronaldshay, *The Life of Lord Curzon*, Vol. III (1928), pp. 5, 43–44, 219; and Violet Conolly, *Soviet Economic Policy in the East* (1933), pp. 58–59.

[4] This period is described in Mr. Shuster's book *The Strangling of Persia*, chaps. iv–viii.

[5] For the point of view of Curzon, who thought that the Majlis did Persia a great disservice by rejecting the treaty, see Ronaldshay, *op. cit.*, Vol. III, pp. 208–233, esp. 221–223. Also see Lenczowski, *op. cit.*, p. 47; and Émile Lesueur, *Les Anglais en Perse* (1922), Part I, chaps. ii and iii.

[6] Lenczowski, *op. cit.*, pp. 6–11.

[7] Quoted in Lenczowski, *op. cit.*, p. 51. The text of the treaty can be found in *British and Foreign State Papers*, Vol. 114 (1921), p. 901.

§ 2. REZA SHAH AND MODERN PERSIA

[1] Changes in the Constitution of Persia can be made only by a Constituent Assembly, the composition of which is somewhat different from that of the Majlis.

[2] Émile Lesueur, *Les Anglais en Perse* (1922), Part III, chap. iv.

[3] See George Lenczowski, *Russia and the West in Iran, 1918–1948* (1949), pp. 70–71.

[4] Reza Kahn restored the ancient name "Iran"; as of 1935 foreign governments were

284

requested to use "Iran" as the official designation of the country that had formerly been called Persia.

[5] Soviet trading practices were also an important factor. See § 5, pp. 23–26.

[6] Donald N. Wilbur, *Iran, Past and Present* (1948), p. 130. This work gives a partial record of the development of Iranian industry and commerce on pp. 129–130. See also R. N. Gupta, *Iran, an Economic Study* (1947).

[7] Simultaneously, the power to issue bank notes was taken away from the British-controlled Imperial Bank of Iran, which had been organized under an 1889 concession to Baron Julius de Reuter. This concession, replacing the 1872 concession to which the Russian government had violently objected, also granted the right to exploit the oil deposits of the country. See p. 14.

[8] Wilbur, *op. cit.*, p. 100.

§ 3. PERSIAN NATIONALISM AND THE GREAT POWERS

[1] See L. V. Thomas and R. N. Frye, *The United States and Turkey and Iran* (1951), p. 226.

[2] *The Middle East, a Political and Economic Survey* (1950), p. 118.

[3] See the excellent article by Majid Khadduri, "Iran's Claim to the Sovereignty of Bahrayn," *American Journal of International Law* (periodical hereafter abbreviated as *AJIL*), Vol. 45 (1951), pp. 631–647; and a book by Mostafa Mesbah Zadeh, *La Politique de l'Iran dans la Société des Nations. La Conception iranienne de l'organisation de la paix* (1936), pp. 120–131.

[4] Strangely enough, Bahrein's oil is being exploited by the American-owned (Standard of California and the Texas Company) Bahrein Oil Company. British capital was not available to develop the oil resources and the concession was relinquished in favor of Gulf Oil Company, from which it passed into the hands of Standard of California. At latest estimate, it is producing approximately 30,200 barrels per day, and the Bahrein Petroleum Company's 160,000 barrel a day refinery processes some of the crude oil pumped on the mainland of Saudi Arabia. See "Middle East," *The Lamp* (periodical published in New York by the Standard Oil Company of New Jersey), Vol. 33, No. 2 (June, 1951), pp. 1, 22–23.

[5] *The Middle East, a Political and Economic Survey*, p. 118.

[6] George Lenczowski, *Russia and the West in Iran, 1918–1948* (1949), p. 76.

§ 4. THE ANGLO-IRANIAN OIL DISPUTE OF 1932–1933

[1] For Russian attempts to acquire oil concessions in Iran, see § 5, pp. 20–23. (For the sake of convenience, the term Iran is used from this point on, in relation to events before its official adoption in 1935.)

[2] Today the British government owns 52 per cent of the shares of the first privilege and 55 per cent of the ordinary shares. The capital of the AIOC is stated to be £32,843,752. The Admiralty, one of AIOC's biggest customers, controls the government's shares but in practice does not interfere in the conduct of the company's business, except in matters involving "important policy decisions." See B. Cheng, "The Anglo-Iranian Dispute," *World Affairs*, Vol. 5 (1951), pp. 387–388; and British Information Services (hereafter abbreviated BIS), *Anglo-Iranian Oil Company, Some Background Notes*, ID 1059, New York, May, 1951, pp. 1–3.

[3] The actual price has never been made public, but the British have never denied that it is lower than the market price.

⁴ The Iranians calculated that royalties paid to their government during the years 1901–1932 amounted to £11 million, and that normal taxes, from which the company was exempt, would have amounted to £22 million.

⁵ The royalties, profits, and gross sales figures are reported and discussed in "Persian Oil," *The Economist*, Vol. 115 (December 3, 1932), pp. 1019–1020.

⁶ "Britain and Persia," *The Economist*, Vol. 115 (December 17, 1932), pp. 1125–1126. These reasons were again reviewed in a report presented by the National Iranian Oil Company (successor to AIOC after the nationalization in March, 1951) to Averell Harriman, Special Envoy of the President of the United States, in Tehran, August 1, 1951. The principal contentions of the Iranians were that AIOC never permitted the government to inspect and audit its books, which were alleged to be fictitiously prepared so as to conceal real profits and thus reduce the amount of royalties due; that royalties on the profits of AIOC were never paid and that such payments were due, even though the profits were made on operations outside Iran; that the company wrongfully withheld a part of the royalties for property damage for which the government was not responsible; and that the acquisition of stock by the British government in 1914 amounted to a transfer of the concession and was contrary to provisions of the concession and without the consent and against the wishes of the Iranian government, to which it caused "tremendous political and economic harm." Economic pressure, internal agitation, and interference in the internal affairs of Iran were also alleged. See *Some Documents on the Nationalization of the Oil Industry in Iran* (1951), pamphlet distributed by the Iranian Embassy in Washington, pp. 5–8. See also Mostafa Mesbah Zadeh, *La Politique de l'Iran dans la Société des Nations. La Conception iranienne de l'organisation de la paix* (1936), pp. 63–87.

⁷ Reproduced as Appendix I herein. Official confirmation, in the form of ratification by the Majlis and approval by the shah, was completed May 29, 1933. In a speech before the United Nations Security Council on October 15, 1951, Dr. Mossadegh asserted that "Iran was coerced into concluding the 1933 Agreement," but he did not make it clear whether the alleged coercion stemmed from British threats to use force or from Iran's ruler, Reza Shah. U. N. Security Council, *Official Records*, 560th Meeting (October 15, 1951), pp. 17–18. Contrary to Dr. Mossadegh's attitude in 1951, the new concession was generally regarded as a great diplomatic victory for Reza Shah. Lenczowski, *op. cit.*, pp. 80–81. It was so regarded by Dr. Mossadegh in 1944: see the quotation by Sir Gladwyn Jebb from a speech made by Mossadegh in the Majlis on October 29, 1944, in which Mossadegh also opposed unilateral cancelation of the concession, U. N. Security Council, *Official Records*, 561st Meeting (October 16, 1951), p. 9.

§ 5. NORTHERN OIL AND SOVIET-IRANIAN RELATIONS

¹ This section is substantially based on materials found in George Lenczowski's *Russia and the West in Iran, 1918–1948* (1949), pp. 81–167.

² That is, the provinces of Azerbaijan, Khorasan, Gilan, Mazanderan, and Asterabad.

³ The term is Lenczowski's; see his *Russia and the West in Iran . . .*, p. 81.

⁴ Lenczowski, *op. cit.*, pp. 86–91.

⁵ See Violet Conolly, *Soviet Economic Policy in the East* (1933), pp. 53–76.

⁶ Soviet policy was codified in the official publication of the Union of Soviet

Socialist Republics, *Principles of Eastern Trade* (1923), printed as Appendix I to Violet Conolly's book, *Soviet Economic Policy...*, pp. 140–142. There were five basic principles: (i) Soviet manufactured goods were to be exchanged for raw materials; (ii) the USSR would not insist on a favorable balance of trade with the Eastern countries; (iii) Soviet industrial goods were to be sold at lower prices in the East than in the West as direct encouragement of trade with the Eastern countries; (iv) Eastern merchants were to be permitted to sell their goods individually in Russia; and (v) mixed Soviet-Eastern companies were to be promoted.

[7] This was the period of the "New Economic Policy" in the Soviet Union.

[8] The bulk of the oil products consumed in Iran came from the Batum-Baku area in Soviet Russia. Because of transportation difficulties these could be obtained cheaper than could Iranian oil from the refinery at Abadan.

[9] The greater part of Iran's population, its agriculture, and its industry (excluding oil), is concentrated in the northern provinces, where the plains adjoining the Caspian Sea receive sufficient rainfall to make farming profitable.

§ 6. THE EMERGENCE OF GERMANY

[1] Donald B. Marsh, *World Trade and Investment* (New York, Harcourt Brace, 1951), pp. 367–372; P. T. Ellsworth, *The International Economy* (New York, Macmillan, 1950), pp. 622–625; Howard S. Ellis, *Exchange Control in Central Europe* (Cambridge, Mass., Harvard University Press, 1941), pp. 201–222; and John B. Condliffe, *The Commerce of Nations* (1950), pp. 741–746.

[2] George Lenczowski, *Russia and the West in Iran, 1918–1948* (1949), pp. 162–166.

§ 7. IRAN IN WORLD WAR II

[1] The events of the war period are recorded in great detail by George Lenczowski in his *Russia and the West in Iran, 1918–1948* (1949), pp. 167–284; and by Arthur C. Millspaugh in his *Americans in Persia* (1946). See also Sir Reader Bullard, *Britain and the Middle East from the Earliest Times to 1950* (1951), pp. 132–146; and L. V. Thomas and R. N. Frye, *The United States and Turkey and Iran* (1951), pp. 229–235.

[2] Winston Churchill, *The Grand Alliance* (1950), pp. 476–486.

[3] The details of the unofficial Millspaugh financial mission and the details of the Iranian wartime economy are recorded by Dr. Millspaugh in his book, cited above in this section, *Americans in Persia*. American advisers were appointed not only to Dr. Millspaugh's mission, but also to the Iranian ministries of health, food, war, and the interior. The gendarmerie was under the supervision of the ministry of the interior and had the difficult task of restoring and maintaining order. See Millspaugh, *op. cit.*, pp. 44–45.

[4] The text of the treaty is given in Millspaugh, *op. cit.*, p. 276; and also in W. S. Haas, *Iran* (1946), p. 252.

[5] Since the United States was not a party to the treaty, American troops went into Iran as "British forces" and were confined to the British zone. Although American troops were in Iran for the sole purpose of operating transportation facilities to get supplies through to the Soviet Union, the latter found it convenient to criticize this arrangement during the oil crisis of 1944, when the United States government supported the Iranian nationalist policy of refusing to grant any oil concession to foreigners. See p. 36.

§ 8. NORTHERN OIL AND THE SOVIETS IN WARTIME

[1] After 1938 it was restricted to 100,000 square miles. See § 4, pp. 18–19; and see, in Appendix I, Article 2 of the 1933 concession contract.

[2] Iran being comprised of approximately 628,000 square miles, roughly five-sixths of its territory was free of concessions in 1944. The area of the Kavir-Jihurian Company's concession was negligible.

[3] The Standard Vacuum Oil Company is jointly owned by the Standard Oil Company of New Jersey and the Socony-Vacuum Oil Company. See *The International Petroleum Cartel*, U. S. Senate Select Committee on Small Business, 82d Cong., 2d sess. (1952), chart 14.

[4] George Lenczowski, *Russia and the West in Iran, 1918–1948* (1949), p. 216.

[5] Reported by Lenczowski, *op. cit.*, pp. 216–217.

[6] Whether the Soviet Union needed the oil is problematical, in view of the available statistics. Compare the figures reported by Lenczowski, *op. cit.*, p. 218. And see below, Part II, § 1, n. 8.

[7] Lenczowski, *op. cit.*, p. 218. The attitude of the Tudeh party toward foreign concessions at this time should be compared with its attitude after the nationalization in 1951. See Part II, p. 213, of the present study.

[8] *Tass* dispatch in *New York Times*, October 25, 1944, p. 5.

[9] Reported by Lenczowski, *op. cit.*, p. 220.

[10] *Ibid.*, p. 221.

[11] *New York Times*, November 5, 1944, p. 6.

[12] It was this law which enabled the Iranian government under Qavam Sultaneh to turn the Azerbaijan crisis into a diplomatic victory. See Part II, § 1.

§ 9. THE CLOSE OF WORLD WAR II

[1] Indexes of money in circulation, wholesale prices, cost of living, and import prices are given in Appendix II, table 1.

[2] Although actual figures for Allied military expenditure are not available, their magnitude can be deduced from the fact that the Iranian government's holdings of gold and foreign exchange (primarily sterling and dollars) increased from $44 million in 1940 to a total of $244 million in 1944. International Monetary Fund, *International Financial Statistics*, April, 1940, pp. 84–85; U. N. Secretariat, Department of Economic Affairs, *Public Finance Information Papers: Iran* (1951), ST/ECA/SER. A/4, p. 12.

[3] The Public Finance Information Paper on Iran referred to in the preceding note points out, at pages 13–14, that because of the unavailability of detailed statistics, it is impossible to measure the inflationary impact of Iran's wartime deficit spending. The deficits were financed through borrowing from the Bank Melli (either outright advances or note issues guaranteed by the government). This practice would appear highly inflationary, but, as the document referred to points out, may not have been, since government financial operations during this period were of lesser importance to the Iranian domestic economy than they would have been in most countries, and, in addition, many of the expenditures financed by the deficit spending were not inflationary in character.

PART II: POLITICS, NATIONALIZATION, AND CONTROVERSY

§ 1. SOVIET POLICY AND THE AZERBAIJAN CRISIS

[1] This policy was most clearly formulated in Nazi-Soviet negotiations during the brief alliance of Russia and the Reich in the early years of World War II. In a report dated November 26, 1940, Count von Schulenberg, German Ambassador to Moscow, stated that, subject to certain conditions, Molotov was prepared to enlarge the Nazi-Soviet agreement into a Four Power Pact with all the Axis nations. One of the conditions was that "the area south of Batum and Baku in the general area of the Persian Gulf be recognized as the center of the aspirations of the Soviet Government." *Nazi-Soviet Relations*, U. S. Department of State Publication 3023 (1948), pp. 258–259.

[2] American troops began to leave immediately after V-E Day and were quickly evacuated.

[3] It can be noted that in Iran, as well as in other Asian countries, Soviet strategy has seemed to prefer the suborning of discontented minorities rather than the more orthodox Marxian reliance on the class struggle.

[4] The establishment of the Kurdish People's Republic was the result of the insistence, by the Kurdish tribes, on a separate, autonomous state in the general area of the Iranian-Iraqi-Turkish border, to be composed of territory parts of which were then situated in each of those three countries. See G. G. Stevens, "Reform and Power Politics in Iran," *Foreign Policy Reports*, Vol. 26 (February 15, 1951), pp. 216–217. See also L. V. Thomas and R. N. Frye, *The United States and Turkey and Iran* (1951), pp. 236–242.

[5] Stevens, *op. cit.*, pp. 216–217.

[6] The timing of the Azerbaijan revolt, in Soviet policy, was undoubtedly influenced by factors other than the approaching evacuation date set in the Tripartite Treaty. At this time the question of revision of the Turkish Straits Convention was at issue between Russia and the Western powers. Negotiations were at an impasse when the rebellions in Azerbaijan and Kurdistan erupted. The significance of the proximity of the two "peoples' republics" was probably not lost on Turkey.

[7] U. N. Security Council, *Official Records*, 40th Meeting (May 8, 1946), p. 1.

[8] In addition to the long history of Russian efforts to obtain an oil concession in the northern provinces, Stalin announced in February, 1946, at the height of the Azerbaijan crisis, that the Soviet Union urgently needed to double its oil production capacity. Estimates of sources within the Soviet Union indicate that this goal would be impossible to attain if reliance were placed solely on domestic resources. See Olaf Caroe, *Wells of Power. The Oilfields of South-Western Asia* (1951), pp. 75–76.

[9] *Ibid.*, p. 74. It should be noted that Mossadegh was responsible for the law which required ratification by the Majlis of all oil concessions. See Part I, § 8, p. 36, herein.

[10] American support in the Azerbaijan crisis was followed by a *rapprochement* between the United States and Iran. In 1947 the United States military and gendarmerie missions were extended and, in general, closer relations were cultivated by both governments. This should be compared with the effect of the American position during the oil dispute of 1951–1952 on American-Iranian relations. See Part II, § 9.

[11] See Caroe, *op. cit.*, Part I, chap. v.

[12] See *ibid.*; George Lenczowski, *Russia and the West in Iran, 1918–1948* (1949), pp. 303–306; Thomas and Frye, *op. cit.*, p. 240; Donald Wilbur, *Iran, Past and Present* (1948), pp. 105–106; and Sir Reader Bullard, *Britain and the Middle East from the Earliest Times to 1950* (1951), pp. 163–165.

§ 2. THE SEVEN-YEAR PLAN

[1] See Appendix II, table 1.

[2] Local expenditures by AIOC in 1948 and 1949 actually exceeded the direct payments to the Iranian government. In 1948 and 1949 local expenditures totaled 2,068 and 2,240 million rials respectively, whereas direct payments to the government totaled 1,174 and 1,284 million rials respectively. U. N. Secretariat, Department of Economic Affairs, *Review of Economic Conditions in the Middle East* (1951), p. 63. See also Appendix II, table 4, herein.

[3] U. N. Secretariat, Department of Economic Affairs, *Public Finance Information Papers: Iran* (1951), ST/ECA/SER. A/4, pp. 33–34.

[4] *Ibid.*, pp. 15–18.

[5] See the discussion at pp. 33–36 and the tables at pages 45–47 in U. N. Secretariat, Department of Economic Affairs, *Review of Economic Conditions in the Middle East*.

[6] *In Quest of Peace and Security. Selected Documents on American Foreign Policy, 1941–1951*, U. S. Department of State Publication 4245 (1951), pp. 11–12.

[7] Overseas Consultants, Inc., *Report on the Seven Year Development Plan for the Plan Organization of the Imperial Government of Iran* (1949), 5 vols.

[8] U. N. Secretariat, Department of Economic Affairs, *Review of Economic Conditions in the Middle East*, pp. 70, 72, 74, 76, 78.

[9] *Ibid.*, pp. 74, 76.

[10] In the words of Henry Grady, United States Ambassador to Iran during 1950 and 1951: "Our Government never formally promised the large amounts of aid which the Iranians expected—$250,000,000 was the favorite figure. Technically, from a standpoint of war damage due to the occupation of our forces, Iran had no claim on our Treasury beyond that settled on and paid right after the war ended. But from the standpoint of our own interests and as a critical spot in the effort to contain Russian aggression, there was every reason why we should have given active assistance. This is particularly true since countries not nearly so strategic—in fact, not strategic at all—have received great monetary support from the American Government. I repeat, I find it impossible to understand American policy toward Iran. . . . The weakness of our effort was on the side of adequate financial assistance. If we had come in quickly and with adequate amounts, the whole situation in Iran might very well be different today." Henry Grady, "What Went Wrong in Iran?" *Saturday Evening Post*, January 5, 1952, pp. 56–57.

§ 3. THE SUPPLEMENTARY AGREEMENT

[1] "The Supplementary Agreement" is a popular name, the official title being "The Gass-Golshaian Agreement."

[2] The experience which the British had with this complicated and lengthy document may have inspired this statement by Assistant Secretary of State George McGhee in outlining United States oil policy: "4. The relationships between the oil companies and governments should be embodied in simple straight-forward contracts

understandable by the peoples of the countries. They must not only be fair, they must be demonstrably fair." George McGhee, "The Oil Problem in the Middle East," *Department of State Bulletin* (periodical hereafter abbreviated as *DSB*), Vol. 25 (October 15, 1951), p. 614.

[3] Although the formula of the Supplementary Agreement was quite complicated, the main provisions can be summarized as follows:

1) The royalty was increased from 4 to 6 shillings per ton, subject to the fluctuations in the price of gold as provided in the 1933 concession.

2) The payment in lieu of income tax was to be 1 shilling per ton.

3) There was to be an immediate tax-free payment of 20 per cent of the company's general reserve, and annual payments of 20 per cent of the sums paid into the general reserve during the year.

4) The provision requiring payment of 20 per cent of the amount of dividends in excess of £671,250 remained unchanged.

5) AIOC guaranteed payment of a minimum of £4 million per year for payments on account of dividends and allocations to the general reserve.

6) Oil sold in Iran for the use of Iranians would be sold at 25 per cent (instead of at 10 per cent as stipulated in the 1933 concession) below the Mexican Gulf or Rumanian price (whichever was lower).

7) The Supplementary Agreement would be retroactive to January 1, 1948.

The 25–50 per cent evaluation in the text is only a rough estimate based on the increase during the years 1948–1950. Under the Supplementary Agreement Iran would have received approximately £18.7 million in 1948 (as against £9.2 million under the 1933 concession), £22.9 million in 1949 (as against £13.5 million under the 1933 concession), and £25.0 million in 1950 (as against £16.0 million under the 1933 concession).

In considering these figures and comparing the terms of the Supplementary Agreement with the fifty-fifty profit-sharing principle, it is well to remember that in the lean years there are little or no profits to share. In such years the guarantees provided in both the 1933 concession and the 1949 Supplementary Agreement would ensure a greater income to Iran. This was stated by Sir William Fraser, chairman of the AIOC board of directors, in a statement to the stockholders, in December, 1951: "If there had been no interruption in the Company's operations, it is estimated that the payment to the Government from a 50-50 sharing of 1951 profits from Iran operations would ... have been of the order of £50 million. This is a greater sum than Iran would have received from the Supplemental Agreement. In comparing the two systems, the basic fact is that although the 50-50 system would be more profitable to Iran in years of high profit margins, the Supplemental Agreement system would be better when profit margins are low. But the weight of evidence is that over a term of years there is little to choose between them." Sir William Fraser, "Report to the Stockholders" [of AIOC], *The Economist*, Vol. 161 (December 1, 1951), pp. 1363–1364. Such an argument, even if demonstrably valid, does not have the psychological appeal of the fifty-fifty profit-sharing formula.

[4] With the exception of the Communist Tudeh party, political parties in Iran were not parties in the American or British sense. Party discipline was almost unknown, and party membership and platforms were extremely flexible. For these reasons a small and determined group could exercise a degree of political power completely disproportionate to their numbers. The success of the National Front party and Dr. Mossadegh can be partly explained by such organization. In addition, the National

Front party had at this time the support of the mullahs (religious leaders), who were anxious for a return to power after having been barred from politics by Reza Shah in the 1920's.

⁵ This issue has been vigorously argued by the Iranians in all oil discussions, at least since 1949. It was also an issue in the 1932 dipute. It was repeated by Mossadegh in the United Nations Security Council on October 15, 1951: "Instead of adopting an effective plan to reduce the number of foreign employees and experts and to replace them by Iranian nationals, the Company has not only avoided reducing the number of foreign employees but has increased them from 1,800 in 1933 to 4,200 in 1948. No technical Iranian staff has been trained; eighteen years after the date of the Concession, the directors of the former Company look with satisfaction at the results of their policy of sabotage of the principle of Iranian technical development." U. N. Security Council, *Official Records*, 560th Meeting (October 15, 1951), p. 19. The next day, Sir Gladwyn Jebb, speaking on behalf of the United Kingdom, added that during the same period the number of Iranian employees increased from 14,000 to approximately 70,000, and, simultaneously, the production of oil rose from 7 million to nearly 27 million tons annually. Security Council, *Official Records*, 561st Meeting (October 16, 1951), p. 11. Some of the relevant statistics are given herein, in Appendix II, tables 2 and 3. More detailed information is contained in the International Labor Organization's report entitled *Labour Conditions in the Oil Industry in Iran* (1950), a part of the final chapter of which is attached hereto as Appendix III.

⁶ Henry Grady, "What Went Wrong in Iran?" *Saturday Evening Post*, January 5, 1952, p. 58.

⁷ Fraser, *op. cit.*, pp. 1364–1365.

⁸ In his "Report to the Stockholders," referred to in the preceding note, Sir William Fraser states that the company deferred to "Iranian susceptibilities" and took no steps to explain the Supplementary Agreement to the people of Iran, since the Iranian government regarded it as its responsibility to inform the public on a matter of such importance. Whether or not the government requested the company to refrain is not stated. In any even, only sporadic and ineffectual attempts were made by the government of Iràn to explain the complicated agreement to the public. Later, and at the request of the government, the company did make full information available to the press and radio in Tehran, but "by that time the National Front propaganda had gained a firm foothold and there were few who were ready to be receptive to a factual appraisal of the Agreement." *Ibid.*, p. 1364. On whether or not it could have been popularly explained, compare above, nn. 2 and 3. See also the company document seized by the Iranian government and quoted by its representative, in U. N. Security Council, *Official Records*, 563d Meeting (October 17, 1951), pp. 24–26.

⁹ The text of the Single Article Law, passed by the Majlis on March 15 and by the Senate on March 20, 1951, is reproduced in Appendix IV. It did not become effective until signed and promulgated by the shah on May 1, 1951.

¹⁰ The text of the Law Regulating Nationalization of the Oil Industry is reproduced in Appendix IV.

§ 4. THE ANGLO-IRANIAN OIL DISPUTE OF 1951–1952

¹ Henry Grady, "What Went Wrong in Iran?" *Saturday Evening Post*, January 5, 1952, p. 58.

[2] Since the enactment of the nationalization laws in March and April, official documents of the Iranian government have refrained from reference to AIOC by name. Instead, all references are to the "former Company." "NIOC" (National Iranian Oil Company) was substituted for "AIOC" on all public signs in Iran.

[3] The attitude is naïve, for even if Iran could obtain foreign technicians (she certainly does not have enough of them herself) a competent and efficient management would have to be found to run the industry. In addition, she would have to find a tanker fleet to transport the oil to the world's markets, if, indeed, in the highly competitive market for oil products, she could find many buyers. All these problems, though not insoluble, are extremely difficult ones which must be solved if Iran is to earn badly needed revenue and if the British are to be compensated for the nationalized property. See § 9, n. 2, and also, in the text, pp. 100, 109–113, and 215–217.

[4] See George Lenczowski, "Iran: Nationalism Erupts," *Current History*, Vol. 21 (July, 1951), pp. 12–18.

[5] It is recorded in such official actions as the Iranian refusal of United States Point Four aid, because the agreement required that the Iranian government pledge itself to contribute to the "defense of the free world," a standard clause the meaning of which is so vague that the United States could not hold the Iranians to any specific duty or action on the basis of it. The Iranian government finally agreed to accept the aid after the wording was changed. Another example can be found in the closing of the foreign cultural and information centers in January, 1952. However, this could also be interpreted as a measure to effect internal security, to prevent foreign infiltration and propaganda. In addition, the whole course of the negotiations with the various British missions, and with Averell Harriman, demonstrates this element, as does the original negative reaction to the efforts of the International Bank for Reconstruction and Development. The Iranian government's use of the phrase "former Company" in its references to AIOC can also be noted. See also the statements of Prime Minister Mossadegh and M. Saleh before the United Nations Security Council on the fifteenth and seventeenth of October. See § 9, pp. 132–133, 134–137.

[6] "Mobs Without Masters," *The Economist*, Vol. 161 (December 15, 1951), pp. 1443–1444.

[7] On this point it is interesting to remember that the rise of the Standard Oil Company almost precipitated a social disturbance in the United States. See Ida Tarbell, *The History of the Standard Oil Company* (1904), 2 vols.

§ 5. THE NEGOTIATIONS, FIRST PHASE

[1] See Appendix IV.

[2] As it had previously in notes dated March 14 and April 27, 1951.

[3] BIS, *Anglo-Iranian Oil Company, Some Background Notes*, ID 1059, New York, May, 1951, p. 9.

[4] *Ibid.*

[5] From the statement by Sir Gladwyn Jebb before the U. N. Security Council, *Official Records*, 559th Meeting (October 1, 1951), p. 16.

[6] *Ibid.*

[7] See Appendix I of the present work.

[8] *Ibid.*, Article 21.

[9] *Ibid.*, Article 26. "Default" is defined in the following paragraph as (a) failure

to pay a sum awarded to Iran by the arbitration court, and (b) a voluntary or compulsory liquidation of the company.

[10] *Ibid.*, Article 22, paragraph A. Emphasis added.

[11] *Ibid.*, paragraph D.

[12] Described by Mr. Morrison in a speech before the House of Commons on May 29, 1951. BIS, *Legal Aspects of the Anglo-Iranian Oil Question*, ID 1063, New York, June, 1951, p. 6.

[13] Text distributed by BIS, as *Persian Oil*, T. 34, Washington, D.C., June 21, 1951, p. 3.

[14] Quoted by Mr. Morrison. BIS, *Legal Aspects of the Anglo-Iranian Oil Question*, ID 1063, p. 6.

[15] See *Text of Speech of Dr. Mohammad Mossadegh, Prime Minister of Iran, to the Foreign Press Representatives on May 28th, 1951*, distributed by the Iranian Embassy, Washington, D.C., in June, 1951.

[16] This is a reference to Articles 2 and 3 of the Law Regulating Nationalization of the Oil Industry. See Appendix IV in the present work.

[17] The validity of these arguments is considered in § 6, § 10, and § 11, of this Part.

[18] Quoted in BIS, *Anglo-Iranian Oil Negotiations*, ID 1062, New York, June, 1951, p. 5.

[19] See Appendix I in the present work.

[20] BIS, *Anglo-Iranian Oil Negotiations*, ID 1062, p. 5.

[21] The text of the United Kingdom's "Application" is quoted by the International Court of Justice in its judgment of July 22, 1952. *Anglo-Iranian Oil Company Case (Preliminary Objection)*, 1952 ICJ Reports 95–96.

The application is also described by Manley O. Hudson, in "The Thirtieth Year of the World Court," *AJIL*, Vol. 46 (1952), pp. 15–16. For the grounds on which the application relied to establish the jurisdiction of the Court, see pp. 78–79 and 310 of the present work.

[22] *ICJ Yearbook, 1950–1951*, p. 48. Cited in Hudson, *op. cit.*, p. 16. Also reported by Sir William Fraser, chairman of the board of directors of AIOC, in his "Report to the Stockholders," *The Economist*, Vol. 161 (December 1, 1951), p. 1365; and see the *Wall Street Journal*, November 30, 1951, p. 8.

[23] See p. 75 in the text.

[24] In the House of Commons on May 29, 1951. Quoted from BIS, *Anglo-Iranian Oil Negotiations*, ID 1062, p. 6.

[25] *Ibid.* (emphasis added) ; BIS, *Legal Aspects of the Anglo-Iranian Oil Question*, ID 1063, pp. 6–7.

[26] Iran has adhered to this position consistently since May, 1951. See Dr. Mossadegh's statement quoted on pp. 59–60. And see also, pp. 75–76 and 134–137.

[27] So stated in a letter from Dr. Mossadegh to President Truman in reply to a letter from President Truman urging Iran to negotiate with the British. *The Nationalization of the Oil Industry in Iran* (distributed by the Iranian Embassy in Washington, D.C. [June, 1951]), pp. 3–8. President Truman sent a similar letter to Prime Minister Attlee at the same time, June 1.

[28] In the words of Sir William Fraser, "the company took advantage of this opening to emphasize its continued readiness to solve all difficulties and differences by negotiation." Fraser, *op. cit.*, p. 1365.

[29] *Ibid.*

[30] "The Gass-Golshaian Agreement"; see § 3, n. 1, above.

[31] BIS, *Anglo-Iranian Oil Negotiations*, ID 1062, pp. 6–7. This is quite obviously somewhat overstated, but the intention is clear. It is interesting to compare with this the statement made by Mr. Morrison before the House of Commons on June 4: "His Majesty's Ambassador at Tehran, on my instructions, has again made it clear to the Persian Prime Minister that we cannot accept his contention that the dispute is solely between the Persian Government and the Company, but on the contrary, as has been repeatedly made clear, His Majesty's Government have every right to intervene in defense of this great British interest in the matter by reason of their majority holding in the Company." (BIS, *Legal Aspects of the Anglo-Iranian Oil Question*, ID 1063, p. 7.) Rightly or wrongly, this smacks of imperialism to the Iranians.

[32] See Appendix IV in the present work.

[33] *Ibid.*

[34] It should be noted that the nationalization laws are considered retroactive to March 20 (the date of the Senate's assent to the Single Article bill—see Appendix IV) by the Iranian government, although they did not become effective until signature and promulgation by the shah on May 1 and 2.

[35] BIS, *Anglo-Iranian Oil Negotiations*, ID 1062, pp. 7–8; Sir Frank Soskice, *Attorney-General's Speech at International Court of Justice, The Hague, June 30, 1951* (verbatim report), pp. 17–19.

[36] Reported by the London *Times*, June 12, 1951, p. 4.

[37] *Ibid.* If the company had "stood by" an offer of a fifty-fifty division in 1949 and 1950, when the Iranians had asked for it, it is within the realm of possibility that nationalization, and the troubles which have attended it, could have been avoided in large measure. Instead, AIOC did not start "standing by" its fifty-fifty offer until February, 1951, by which time Dr. Mossadegh's nationalization "snowball" had gained considerable momentum. See the discussion comprising § 3 of this Part.

[38] Of course, he did not add that since the Kuwait Oil Company is half owned by Gulf Exploration Corporation (an American company), the other half being owned by AIOC, the utilization of more than half of any increased production would necessitate payment in dollars to the Gulf Company. AIOC did, in fact, turn primarily to increased production in Kuwait after the Abadan refinery was shut down on July 31, 1951, and it has been estimated that the dollar drain on the already seriously depleted sterling area reserves amounted to approximately $350 million in the last five months of 1951 and the first two months of 1952. If this estimate is correct, the "sterling crisis" in the first quarter of 1952 cannot be laid solely to economic difficulties.

[39] At the end of 1951 the British Tanker Company, a wholly owned AIOC subsidiary, owned 1,854,000 d.w. tons in its tanker fleet and had an additional twenty-one ships on order. AIOC had a further 2 million d.w. tons under charter and had made arrangements to extend this tonnage as soon as its charterer could build more tankers. Fraser, *op. cit.*, p. 1366; B. Cheng, "The Anglo-Iranian Dispute," *World Affairs*, Vol. 5 (1951), p. 387.

[40] See *Some Documents on the Nationalization of the Oil Industry in Iran* (1951), pamphlet distributed by the Iranian Embassy in Washington, pp. 39–46.

[41] "Developments of the Quarter," *Middle East Journal*, Vol. 5 (Summer, 1951), p. 342. (Later references to this news department of the *Middle East Journal* do not include the departmental heading.)

[42] See n. 27 above; and see BIS, *Persian Oil: The Company's Aide-Memoire*, T. 35, Washington, D.C., June 22, 1951.

[43] See BIS, *Persian Oil: The Company's Aide-Memoire,* T. 35; and see pp. 64 and 70 in the present work.

[44] The text of the company's "aide-memoire" was distributed by the British Information Services on June 22; BIS, *Persian Oil: The Company's Aide-Memoire,* T. 35.

[45] *Ibid.* The reasons for this proviso, from the company's point of view, were stated by Sir William Fraser in his annual report to the AIOC stockholders: "While these meetings were in progress, the campaign of abuse and misrepresentation against the Company continued unabated in Iran, and early in June the Iranian Government appointed a temporary board of the specially formed National Iranian Oil Company to take over the installations of the 'former' Anglo-Iranian Oil Company. The temporary board proceeded to the oilfield areas and thereupon began interfering with the Company's management there; this interference steadily increased in intensity and aggressiveness." Fraser, *op. cit.,* p. 1365.

[46] BIS, *Persian Oil: The Company's Aide-Memoire,* T. 35, pp. 1–2.

[47] See, in the present work, Appendix I, Article 19.

[48] *Ibid.,* Article 20.

[49] Reported by Sir William Fraser, in Fraser, *op. cit.,* p. 1365; and by Foreign Secretary Morrison in the House of Commons on June 20, BIS, *Persian Oil,* T. 34.

[50] They did not leave until three days later, that is, on June 22.

[51] These instructions were not completely carried out until October 1, when the remaining British technicians were evacuated. The quotation is from Prime Minister Mossadegh's report to the Majlis, August 5, 1951. See *Some Documents on the Nationalization of the Oil Industry in Iran,* p. 27.

[52] BIS, *Persian Oil,* T. 34, p. 2.

[53] *Ibid.,* p. 3; quoted in the present work on p. 58.

[54] BIS, *Persian Oil,* T. 34, p. 2.

[55] For the substance of the "Request" and the Court's action, see § 6 of this Part.

[56] See p. 68.

[57] From Sir Frank Soskice's speech before the ICJ on June 30, 1951, in a verbatim report distributed by the British Foreign Office: Soskice, *op. cit.,* p. 5.

[58] *Ibid.*

[59] A "double urgency" bill is one that can be debated and passed at one sitting of the Majlis. The ordinary bill must have three readings on three separate days.

[60] As quoted by Sir Frank Soskice before the Court: Soskice, *op. cit.,* p. 5. Emphasis added.

[61] *Ibid.,* pp. 5 ff. The accuracy of this account is confirmed for the most part, though some details are missing, by the following factual reports of developments: "Breakdown in Persia," *The Economist,* Vol. 160 (June 23, 1951), pp. 1487–1488; "A Cruiser for Abadan," *The Economist,* Vol. 160 (June 30, 1951), pp. 1547–1548, and also, in the same issue, "Can Persia Refine?" pp. 1567–1568.

[62] Sir Frank Soskice uses the phrase "compelled by threats" instead of "ordered." See Soskice, *op. cit.,* p. 6.

[63] The general manager's authority derived from the fact of ownership of the tankers by the British Tanker Company, an AIOC subsidiary. See n. 39 above.

[64] The consignee was, in most cases, AIOC or one of its subsidiaries. To have acceded to the Iranian receipt would have been to admit a duty to turn over the proceeds of sales of oil, which the company had previously denied when the demand was presented more directly. See, in the present work, pp. 64–65, 67, and 70.

[65] Soskice, *op. cit.*, p. 6.

[66] *Ibid.* (emphasis added). See also Sir Frank's quotation from the "double urgency" sabotage bill, given on p. 70 of the present work.

[67] Described by the Temporary Board of NIOC as the "former propaganda Department"; Soskice, *op. cit.*, p. 6.

[68] *Ibid.*, pp. 6–7.

[69] Henry Grady, "What Went Wrong in Iran?" *Saturday Evening Post*, January 5, 1952, pp. 30, 58; and see BIS, *Persian Oil* [statement made in the House of Commons by Foreign Secretary Morrison on June 26], T. 37, Washington, D.C., June 26, 1951.

[70] Mr. Henry Grady, United States Ambassador to Iran, had protested the sabotage law to Prime Minister Mossadegh on June 26, the day of Mr. Morrison's speech here quoted in the text. Three days later, on June 29, the Iranian prime minister informed the United States ambassador that the bill would be withdrawn from the Majlis unconditionally. Apparently it was, for no further mention of it is made by either the British or the Iranians. See Grady, *op. cit.*, p. 58; and see *Middle East Journal*, Vol. 5 (Autumn, 1951), p. 487.

[71] It was shut down on July 31; see the narration of the events of that day on p. 103 of the present work.

[72] On further negotiations, see § 7 of this Part.

[73] BIS, *Persian Oil*, T. 37, pp. 1–2. Emphasis added.

[74] Quoted by the Court in its order of July 5. See ICJ, *Anglo-Iranian Oil Company Case: Request for the Indication of Interim Measures of Protection. Order, 5th July, 1951*, 1951 ICJ Reports 91. See also Hudson, *op. cit.*, pp. 15–16. Emphasis added.

[75] Hudson, *op. cit.*, p. 15.

§ 6. THE INTERNATIONAL COURT OF JUSTICE:
INTERIM MEASURES OF PROTECTION

[1] Quoted by the Court in its order of July 5. See ICJ, *Anglo-Iranian Oil Company Case: Request for the Indication of Interim Measures of Protection. Order, 5th July, 1951*, 1951 ICJ Reports 90.

[2] *Ibid.*, p. 92.

[3] See reservation *c* of the Iranian declaration of September 19, 1932, recognizing the compulsory jurisdiction of the Permanent Court of International Justice. Reproduced in Appendix V.

[4] See § 5, pp. 60–61 of the present work. See also Manley O. Hudson, "The Thirtieth Year of the World Court," *AJIL*, Vol. 46 (1952), p. 16.

[5] The Iranian declaration is reproduced in Appendix V herein. The United Kingdom's declaration of February 13, 1946 (not subject to ratification), can be found in *ICJ Yearbook 1946–1947*, p. 217. The British declaration was renewed February 12, 1951. See *ICJ Yearbook 1950–1951*, p. 205.

[6] These declarations *ipso facto* recognize the compulsory jurisdiction of the International Court of Justice by force of Article 93, paragraph 1, of the United Nations Charter and Article 36, paragraph 5, of the Statute of the Court.

[7] See the first paragraph of the Iranian declaration, in Appendix V.

[8] "Commercial Convention Between Great Britain and Persia, Signed at Tehran, February 9th, 1903," *British Foreign and State Papers*, Vol. 96 (1903), pp. 51–84; "Agreement Between the United Kingdom and Persia, Modifying the Commercial

Convention of February 9, 1903. Tehran, March 21, 1920," *League of Nations Treaty Series* (series hereafter abbreviated *LNTS*), Vol. 4 (1921), pp. 48–92, Reg. No. 102.

[9] Sir Frank Soskice, *Attorney-General's Speech at International Court of Justice, The Hague, June 30, 1951* (verbatim report), p. 11.

[10] Manley O. Hudson, *The Permanent Court of International Justice, 1920–1942* (1943), p. 425, n. 12.

[11] Ser. A/B.58.

[12] Ser. A/B.54.

[13] Ser. A/B.58.177.

[14] Rules of Court, Article 61, paragraph 6. It should be noted that the pertinent parts of Article 41 of the Statute and Article 61 of the Rules of Court of the ICJ are the same as the similarly numbered articles of the Statute and Rules of Court of the PCIJ. See Georg Schwarzenberger, *International Law as Applied by International Courts and Tribunals* (2d ed., 1949), pp. 583, 610.

[15] Ser. A/B.58.179.

[16] Ser. A/B.54.153.

[17] Åke Hammarskjöld, "Quelques questions des mesures conservatoires," *Zeitschrift für ausländisches öffentliches Recht und Völkerrecht*, Vol. 5 (1935), p. 19; reprinted in his *Juridiction internationale* (1938), p. 313. For the interesting remainder of this passage see n. 71 below.

[18] Ser. A.8.

[19] Ser. A.8.6. It should be noted that Article 57 of the Rules of Court of 1922 and 1926 delegated to the president of the Court power to indicate provisional measures. This provision was deleted in 1931. But cf. Article 61, paragraph 3, of the 1936 and 1946 Rules.

[20] Ser. A.8.10.

[21] Analyzed and discussed by Edward Dumbauld, *Interim Measures of Protection* (1932), see esp. p. 144. Accord: *Trail Smelter Arbitration* (U. S. / Canada), in United Nations, *Reports of International Arbitral Awards*, Vol. III (1948), see esp. pp. 1934–1938, 1941. (This four-volume United Nations compilation of arbitration cases is cited hereafter as *UNRIAA*; and, since the pagination is continuous throughout the four volumes, the volume number is not given in subsequent references.)

[22] E.g., Schwarzenberger, *op. cit.*, p. 430; Dumbauld, *op. cit.*, p. 186; Étienne Kertesz, "Le Droit international et l'affaire des mitrailleuses de Szent Gotthard," *Revue générale de droit international public*, Vol. 35 (1928), pp. 481–482; Hudson, "The Thirtieth Year of the World Court," p. 22.

[23] Dumbauld, *op. cit.*, p. 186.

[24] Statute of ICJ, Article 38, paragraph *d*.

[25] *Ibid.*, Article 38, paragraph *c*.

[26] *Ibid.*, Article 38, paragraph *b*.

[27] *Ibid.*, Article 38.

[28] *Ibid.*, Article 41, paragraph 1.

[29] ICJ, *op. cit.* (in n. 1 above), p. 93.

[30] *Ibid.*

[31] *Ibid.*

[32] *Ibid.*, pp. 96–98.

[33] The dissenting opinion made no mention of the prima facie effect of the Iranian declaration of 1932 accepting the compulsory jurisdiction of the Court. See Appendix V herein.

[34] See PCIJ, Ser. D.2 (2d add.), pp. 253–254; Hudson, *The Permanent Court of International Justice, 1920–1942*, p. 198.

[35] Hudson, "The Thirtieth Year of the World Court," p. 22.

[36] Article 41 of the Statute; Article 61 of the Rules of Court.

[37] The *Southeastern Greenland Case*, Ser. A/B.48, order dismissing the request for interim measures, Ser. C.69.15; *Administration of the Prince von Pless*, Ser. A/B.54.

[38] Ser. A.12.

[39] Ser. A.12.6.

[40] Ser. A.12.10.

[41] E.g., that of France, Italy, the Netherlands, Spain, and some of the Latin-American countries.

[42] Ser. A/B.58.

[43] Ser. A/B.58.177.

[44] Ser. A/B.58.178.

[45] Ser. A.8.

[46] Ser. A.8.6.

[47] Ser. A.8.7.

[48] Ser. A/B.79.

[49] Ser. A/B.79.196.

[50] Ser. A/B.79.199.

[51] For example, how could any amount of money buy exploitation rights to deposits of oil comparable to those AIOC enjoyed in Iran if such deposits are unknown or do not exist? Such rights are irreplaceable. Further, how could damages be estimated for the disruption which the expulsion of AIOC from Iran caused to the company's world-wide marketing system? Or how could damages be estimated for the dollar drain on sterling area reserves caused by AIOC purchases from American companies after shipments from Iran were stopped, which purchases were necessary to fulfill AIOC's long-term marketing contracts?

[52] Sir Frank Soskice, *op. cit.*, p. 15.

[53] ICJ, *op. cit.* (in n. 1 above), pp. 94–95. As has been noted in the text (p. 82), Judges Winiarski and Badawi Pasha filed a dissenting opinion on the ground that the Court acted without jurisdiction.

[54] Statement in the House of Commons, July 9, 1951, text in BIS, *Developments in Persia*, P. 107/1, Washington, D.C., distributed by the British Embassy, July 10, 1951. Secretary Morrison also indicated that a "mission" had been appointed to investigate means of implementing the ICJ's order of July 5, and to make proposals to the Iranian cabinet.

[55] The Brookings Institution reports that Secretary Makki of the Temporary Board announced on July 6 that Iran would "reject" or "ignore" the ruling of the Court, *Current Developments in United States Foreign Policy*, Vol. 5 (July–August, 1951) p. 37. (This news periodical, published by the Brookings Institution, is cited hereafter as *Cur. Dev.*)

[56] U. N. Document C.N.89.1951; U. N. Document Press Release, PM/2219.

[57] Much of the text of the letter is reproduced by Hudson in "The Thirtieth Year of the World Court," pp. 20–21.

[58] As it had on May 28 and June 29, 1951. See pp. 61 and 75 of the present work.

[59] Quoting Article 2, paragraphs 1 and 7. Compare Article 36, paragraph 6, of the Statute of ICJ and PCIJ, the opinion of the PCIJ in the *Interpretation of the Greco-Turkish Agreement of 1926*, Ser. B.16.20, and the opinion of the ICJ in the *Corfu Channel (Preliminary Objection)* case, 1947–1948 ICJ Reports 28.

[60] Under Article 62 of the Rules of Court (1946).

[61] See Schwarzenberger, *op. cit.*, pp. 431, 433; Hudson, "The Thirtieth Year of the World Court," p. 22; and the opinion of the PCIJ in *Minority Schools in Upper Silesia (Judgment, 1928)*, Ser. A.15.22.

[62] It could also have filed a preliminary objection after the order of July 5 had been issued. If one were filed and the Court then decided that it had no jurisdiction on the merits, the order of July 5 would have been automatically revoked. Hudson, *The Permanent Court of International Justice, 1920–1942*, p. 426. The fact that seven months had elapsed after the issuance of the order of July 5 before the Iranian government did file a preliminary objection, although it had continued to proclaim a lack of jurisdiction in the Court (in press releases, before the Security Council, etc.), may indicate that the Iranian government was not particularly anxious to have an expeditious determination of the Court's jurisdiction or a judicial settlement of the dispute. See § 10 of the text.

[63] It should be noted that both Iran and the United Kingdom are parties to the Statute of the ICJ, and that both had accepted the compulsory jurisdiction of the Court under the provisions of Article 36 of the Statute. See nn. 5 and 6 above.

[64] See, in *Treaties, Conventions, International Acts, Protocols, and Agreements, Between the United States of America and Other Powers*, Vol. III (1923), "Treaty Between the United States and France, September 15, 1914," p. 2589 (38 Stat. 1887); "Treaty Between the United States and China, September 15, 1914," p. 2514 (39 Stat. 1642); and "Treaty Between the United States and Sweden, October 13, 1914," p. 2854 (38 Stat. 1872).

[65] Hudson, *The Permanent Court of International Justice, 1920–1942*, p. 425.

[66] Manley O. Hudson, *The Permanent Court of International Justice* (1934), p. 415.

[67] Hudson, "The Thirtieth Year of the World Court," pp. 22–23, quoting his *Permanent Court of International Justice, 1920–1942*, p. 425, where he also points out that "little significance should be attached to the phrase 'measures suggested' in paragraph 2 of Article 41, no equivalent of which appears in the French version."

[68] Hudson, *The Permanent Court of International Justice, 1920–1942*, p. 426.

[69] *Ibid.*

[70] The order of May 11, 1933, in the *Administration of the Prince von Pless*, Ser. A/B.54.153, ". . . a donc confirmé la doctrine selon laquelle elle peut, le cas échéant, indiquer des mesures conservatoires avant d'avoir constaté que le fond de l'affaire rentre dans sa juridiction, *ce qui présuppose*—on l'a vu—*que les mesures n'ont pas un caractère obligatoire*." Hammarskjöld, "Quelques questions de mesures conservatoires," p. 19, reprinted in his *Juridiction internationale*, p. 313. Emphasis added.

[71] Schwarzenberger, *op. cit.* (2d ed.), p. 434.

[72] Ser. A.22.13.

[73] Articles 56–61 of the Statute of the ICJ, and Articles 74–81 of the Rules of Court (1946).

[74] Articles 65–68 of the Statute of the ICJ, and Articles 82–85 of the Rules of Court (1946).

[75] Only six such requests were made of the PCIJ during its entire existence. Hudson, *The Permanent Court of International Justice, 1920–1942*, p. 424.

[76] On the question when is a state a party, see Article 36, paragraph 6, of the Statute of the Court: "In the event of a dispute as to whether the Court has jurisdiction, the matter shall be settled by the decision of the Court." See also Article 35.

[77] As appears in the text, Article 94, paragraph 2, of the Charter uses the word

"judgment," yet it is not clear that any real distinction can be drawn from the use of the word "decision" in paragraph 1. The plain meaning of the article is that both paragraphs refer to the same thing. A similar use of "decision" and "judgment" appears in Articles 59 and 60 of the Statute.

[78] See Articles 59 and 60 of the Statute of the Court, and Article 94 of the United Nations Charter.

[79] Article 13, paragraph 4, of the Covenant of the League of Nations.

[80] ICJ, *op. cit.* (in n. 1 above), pp. 96–98.

[81] *Ibid.*, p. 93.

[82] U. N. Security Council, *Official Records*, 562d Meeting (October 17, 1951), p. 8.

§ 7. THE NEGOTIATIONS, SECOND PHASE

[1] *Cur. Dev.*, Vol. 5 (July–August, 1951), p. 36.

[2] *Ibid.*

[3] *Ibid.*

[4] *Ibid.*, pp. 36, 37, 38.

[5] *Ibid.*, pp. 39–40.

[6] Text of President Truman's letter in "Consultations with Iran on Anglo-Iranian Dispute," *DSB*, Vol. 25 (July 23, 1951), p. 129.

[7] Text of Prime Minister Mossadegh's reply, *ibid.*, p. 130.

[8] It should be noted that President Truman's offer to send Harriman to Tehran was made on the same day that Iran communicated its "rejection" of the ICJ's interim order and, therefore, presumably without knowledge of that "rejection."

[9] *Cur. Dev.*, Vol. 5 (July–August, 1951), p. 38.

[10] *Ibid.*

[11] The loan was negotiated in October, 1950, for the purchase of road-building and agricultural equipment, but was never accepted by the Iranian government. See p. 48 in the text.

[12] *Cur. Dev.*, Vol. 5 (July–August, 1951), p. 39.

[13] *Ibid.*

[14] The substance of the note referred to has been quoted in the text, § 5, pp. 66–67.

[15] From *Some Documents on the Nationalization of the Oil Industry in Iran* (1951), pp. 27–28.

[16] The Iranian "formula" was not made public until some days later.

[17] Quoted from *Cur. Dev.*, Vol. 5 (July–August, 1951), p. 40.

[18] Both laws are reproduced in Appendix IV.

[19] As quoted by Prime Minister Mossadegh in his report to the Majlis on August 5, 1951. *Some Documents on the Nationalization . . . in Iran*, p. 30. Emphasis added.

[20] *Ibid.*

[21] *Ibid.*, p. 31.

[22] *Ibid.*, pp. 31–32.

[23] *Cur. Dev.*, Vol. 5 (July–August, 1951), p. 40.

[24] *Ibid.*, pp. 40–41.

[25] *Middle East Journal*, Vol. 5 (1951), p. 487.

[26] Quoted by Prime Minister Mossadegh in his report to the Majlis on August 5, 1951. *Some Documents on the Nationalization . . . in Iran*, p. 33.

[27] *Ibid.*

[28] The explanatory statement and the notes of August 3 were quoted in the BIS

release, *Persia: Negotiations to Open,* 108/1, Washington, D.C., British Embassy, August 4, 1951.

[29] *Cur. Dev.,* Vol. 5 (July–August, 1951), p. 42.

[30] BIS, *Iranian Oil: Britain's Approach to a New Agreement,* ID 1088, New York, October, 1951, pp. 6–7.

[31] Sir William Fraser, "Report to the Stockholders" [of AIOC], *The Economist,* Vol. 161 (December 1, 1951), p. 1366.

[32] The legal norm is discussed in greater detail in § 11, pp. 190–212, of the text.

[33] The text is not available, but the points that were made are discussed in two letters to Mr. Harriman from Finance Minister Varasteh and Prime Minister Mossadegh, dated August 19 and 24 respectively. These letters can be found in *Some Documents on the Nationalization . . . in Iran,* pp. 39–46.

[34] *Ibid.,* p. 40.

[35] *Ibid.,* p. 45.

[36] *Middle East Journal,* Vol. 6 (1952), p. 78.

[37] *Some Documents on the Nationalization . . . in Iran,* pp. 41, 45.

[38] *Ibid.,* p. 45.

[39] As quoted in *Cur. Dev.,* Vol. 5 (September, 1951), p. 34.

[40] The text of this letter is not available. This summary is taken from the same issue of *Cur. Dev.,* p. 35, as collated with Mossadegh's reply dated August 24, 1951, the text of which is reproduced in *Some Documents on the Nationalization . . . in Iran,* p. 44.

[41] As quoted in *Cur. Dev.,* Vol. 5 (September, 1951), p. 35.

[42] The vote was 33 to 0, with 3 abstentions, in the Senate, and 72 to 0, with 9 abstentions, in the Majlis. *Ibid.*

[43] Since the negotiations never proceeded far enough to include an exchange of views on important issues suggested by this paragraph, the discussion here is also postponed in accordance with the chronological pattern that has been adopted in the text. See § 11, pp. 211–212.

[44] U. N. Security Council, *Official Records,* 560th Meeting (October 15, 1951), pp. 24–25.

[45] Some of the details of that development are discussed in the text at p. 216.

[46] As quoted in *Cur. Dev.,* Vol. 5 (September, 1951), p. 35.

[47] *Ibid.*

[48] *Ibid.,* p. 36.

[49] *Some Documents on the Nationalization . . . in Iran,* pp. 44–46.

[50] *Cur. Dev.,* Vol. 5 (September, 1951), p. 37.

[51] This conclusion was explicitly set forth by Stokes in a statement to the press on August 17 in Tehran. *Ibid.,* p. 34.

[52] E.g., *Wall Street Journal* (Pacific Coast ed.), September 17, 1951, p. 4; *San Francisco Chronicle,* December 21, 1951, p. 24. The first action reported to have been taken by the AIOC against a purchaser from the Iranian government occurred almost one year later. The voyage of the tanker *Rose Mary* was reported by *The Economist* as "an attempt by merchant adventurers of the oil world to turn the Anglo-Persian dispute to account, by channeling oil on to the world market at cut prices . . ." The *Rose Mary,* owned by a naturalized Swiss named Rizzi, was chartered by an Italian firm called "EPIM." While en route from Abadan to an Italian port, the master of the *Rose Mary* received orders from its charterer, backed by a group of interested tanker owners ready to buy or charter more tankers if cheap oil

was to be had without litigation, to proceed directly to Italy. The master also received orders from Rizzi, at the instigation of AIOC, to put in at Aden. The order from Rizzi was obeyed. In the courts of Aden, the AIOC obtained a temporary injunction to prevent the removal of the oil from that port pending litigation. The injunction was later sustained and AIOC's title to the oil affirmed by the Supreme Court of the Colony of Aden. See "The *Rose Mary's* Test Run," *The Economist*, Vol. 163 (June 21, 1952), p. 800; and "International Law for the *Rose Mary*," *The Economist*, Vol. 166 (January 17, 1953), p. 134. The decision of the Supreme Court of the Colony of Aden is reported in *AJIL*, Vol. 47 (1953), pp. 325–328.

The departure of the tanker S.S. *Miriella* loaded with Iranian oil caused excited celebrations in the port of Abadan. This tanker, chartered by an Italian firm called "Supor," was bound for Genoa, but it actually put into port at Venice, where the AIOC sued the charterer in the local courts to establish its ownership of the cargo. The Civil Tribunal of Venice held for the defendant, saying that Iranian laws could not be called into question in Italian courts, and that the defendant-charterer had good title to the oil under Iranian law. See "Mossadegh's Dangerous Deal," *The Economist*, Vol. 166 (January 24, 1953), pp. 191–192. The decision of the Civil Tribunal of Venice is reported in *AJIL*, Vol. 47 (1953), pp. 509–510.

The only other European company known to have purchased Iranian oil after the expulsion of AIOC was the owner of the cargo vessel *Issa Vigo*, which ran out of bunker fuel in the Persian Gulf and purchased 32 tons to enable it to return to Europe. However, its owner paid the AIOC in sterling for the transaction. See "The *Rose Mary's* Test Run," p. 800.

[53] Fraser, *op. cit.*, p. 1366; *Cur. Dev.*, Vol. 5 (September, 1951), p. 37. Emphasis added.

[54] The dollars were used to pay for imports from the United States, which in 1949 amounted to $265.6 million (excluding those of AIOC) as compared with $43.7 million in exports to the United States. U. N. Secretariat, Department of Economic Affairs, *Review of Economic Conditions in the Middle East* (1951), pp. 68, 73.

[55] Especially goods urgently needed in the United Kingdom—steel, for example— and goods that could be readily sold for dollars.

[56] *Cur. Dev.*, Vol. 5 (September, 1951), pp. 38–39.

[57] *Ibid.*, p. 39.

[58] U. S. Department of State, Press Release No. 852, Washington, D.C., September 18, 1951, 6 pp. mimeo.

[59] *Ibid.*

[60] *Cur. Dev.*, Vol. 5 (September, 1951), p. 39.

[61] Most of Harriman's letter is quoted in BIS, *Iranian Oil: Britain's Approach to a New Agreement*, ID 1088, pp. 4–5.

[62] *Cur. Dev.*, Vol. 5 (September, 1951), pp. 40–41. See also U. N. Security Council, *Official Records*, 559th Meeting (October 1, 1951), p. 19 [Sir Gladwyn Jebb of the United Kingdom], and 560th Meeting (October 15, 1951), p. 26 [Mr. Saleh of Iran]. The text of the memorandum and Ambassador Shepherd's reply are quoted by Mr. Saleh in Security Council, *Official Records*, 563d Meeting (October 17, 1951), pp. 28–30.

[63] *Wall Street Journal* (Pacific Coast ed.), September 18, 1951, p. 4.

[64] *Middle East Journal*, Vol. 6 (1952), p. 75.

[65] *Cur. Dev.*, Vol. 5 (September, 1951), p. 39.

[66] *Ibid.*, p. 40.

[67] The *San Francisco Chronicle*, September 27, 1951, p. 5.
[68] *Ibid.*, September 28, 1951, p. 1.
[69] *Ibid.*, September 27, 1951, p. 5, and September 30, 1951, p. 1.
[70] *Ibid.*, September 29, 1951, p. 1; Sir Gladwyn Jebb, in U. N. Security Council, *Official Records*, 559th Meeting (October 1, 1951), p. 26. And see pp. 128 and 222 in the present work.
[71] "Middle East Munich," *The Economist*, Vol. 161 (October 6, 1951), pp. 779–780.

§ 8. THE DEBATE IN THE SECURITY COUNCIL

[1] As quoted in the *San Francisco Chronicle*, September 29, 1951, p. 1.
[2] U. N. Document S/2357; quoted in *New York Times*, September 30, 1951, p. 6.
[3] U. N. Document S/2358.
[4] The *San Francisco Chronicle*, September 30, 1951, p. 1.
[5] U. N. Security Council, *Official Records*, 559th Meeting (October 1, 1951), pp. 1–2. This position is reported to have been previewed by an editorial in *Pravda* on September 30, 1951. See the *San Francisco Chronicle*, October 1, 1951, p. 6.
[6] U. N. Security Council, *Official Records*, 559th Meeting (October 1, 1951), pp. 2–3.
[7] *Ibid.*, at pp. 2, 3, 5, 7, and 8 respectively.
[8] *Ibid.*, pp. 3–4.
[9] *Ibid.*, p. 5.
[10] *Ibid.*, pp. 5–7.
[11] *Ibid.*, p. 10. *In favor:* Brazil, China, Ecuador, France, India, the Netherlands, Turkey, the United Kingdom, and the United States. *Against:* The USSR and Yugoslavia.
[12] *Ibid.*, pp. 11–26.
[13] *Ibid.*, p. 21.
[14] *Ibid.*, p. 26.
[15] Because Iran was not a member of the Council, its representative was invited to sit with the Council and to participate in the discussion, in accordance with Article 32 of the United Nations Charter and Rule 37 of the Provisional Rules of Procedure of the Council.
[16] U. N. Security Council, *Official Records*, 559th Meeting (October 1, 1951), p. 26.
[17] U. N. Document S/2358/Rev.1, October 12, 1951; BIS, *Iranian Oil: Britain's Approach to a New Agreement*, ID 1088, New York, October, 1951, p. 1.
[18] *Cur. Dev.*, Vol. 5 (October, 1951), p. 33; and see note 90 below.
[19] U. N. Security Council, *Official Records*, 561st Meeting (October 16, 1951), pp. 7–8; and see n. 90 below and p. 224 of the text.
[20] U. N. Security Council, *Official Records*, 561st Meeting (October 16, 1951), p. 24; and see the discussion in n. 47 below.
[21] U. N. Security Council, *Official Records*, 560th Meeting (October 15, 1951), p. 10. See also p. 224 of the text.
[22] U. N. Security Council, *Official Records*, 560th Meeting (October 15, 1951), p. 2.
[23] *Ibid.*
[24] *Ibid.*, p. 3.
[25] *Ibid.*, pp. 3–6.
[26] *Ibid.*, p. 3.
[27] *Ibid.*, pp. 3–4, 5.
[28] *Ibid.*, p. 5.

[29] *Ibid.*

[30] *Ibid.*, pp. 5–6.

[31] *Ibid.*, p. 6.

[32] See Appendix IV, Law Regulating Nationalization of the Oil Industry, Section 2.

[33] *Ibid.*, Section 3.

[34] U. N. Security Council, *Official Records*, 560th Meeting (October 15, 1951), p. 7.

[35] *Ibid.*

[36] In the course of his statement Mr. Saleh intimated that Iran was not contesting the validity of the 1933 concession, at least for the purpose of the proceedings in the Security Council: "Notwithstanding the fact that Iran was coerced into concluding the 1933 Agreement, which according to universally established legal principles would be null and void, yet, in order to avoid futile debate and prevent any confusion, I must state that the Iranian Government does not wish to enter into any discussion regarding the nullity of the agreement imposed upon us." *Ibid.*, p. 18. Compare Part I, § 4, pp. 17–19 and the accompanying notes, esp. n. 8. See also Dr. Mossadegh's speech to the foreign press representatives, quoted in part on pp. 59–60.

[37] From the point of view of the doctrine of international law, it is interesting to note that the Iranian representative injected the so-called "equality doctrine" into his argument. In discussing Iran's exercise of the "prerogatives of national sovereignty" in nationalizing the oil industry, he said: "The fact that the imposed agreement was made with a foreign national does not alter the case. No evidence can be deduced to show that international law puts aliens in a favored position over the nationals of a country, which nationals are unquestionably subject to its general legislation. If governments have sovereignty in internal affairs only in respect of their nationals but not in respect of foreigners who have the support of powerful governments, the latter would enjoy special rights and privileges incompatible with the equality of rights. Such a doctrine would subvert the law and could only ensue in a modern revival of the system of capitulatory privileges. No independent state would willingly subject itself to such degradation and slavery." U. N. Security Council, *Official Records*, 560th Meeting (October 15, 1951), p. 8. However, some evidence can be adduced to show that, under certain conditions, international law does put aliens in a favored position as compared with that of the nationals of a country. There is also authority to show that Mr. Saleh's exposition is not a good statement of present international law. The "equality doctrine," as Mr. Saleh states it, would, if carried to its logical conclusion, amount to a denial of the international minimum standard, and thus a denial of the (international law) institution of diplomatic protection. See Green H. Hackworth, *Digest of International Law*, Vol. III (1942), pp. 656, 659–660; Alfred Verdross, "Les Règles internationales concernant le traitement des étrangers," *Recueil des cours*, Vol. 37 (1931), p. 352; Alwyn V. Freeman, *The International Responsibility of States for Denial of Justice* (1938), pp. 504–507 and the many references there cited; Josef L. Kunz, "The Mexican Expropriations," *New York University Law Quarterly Review*, Vol. 17 (1940), pp. 355, 358–359; PCIJ, *Certain German Interests in Polish Upper Silesia* (*Judgment—Merits, 1926*), Ser. A.7.32–33. Compare Sir John Fischer-Williams, "International Law and the Property of Aliens," in *The British Year Book of International Law, 1928*, pp. 1–30. (*The British Year Book of International Law* is cited hereafter as *BYBIL, 19—* [the particular year].)

A statement similar to that by Mr. Saleh was made several days later by the representative of Ecuador; see U. N. Security Council, *Official Records*, 562d Meeting (October 17, 1951), p. 3.

[38] U. N. Security Council, *Official Records*, 560th Meeting (October 15, 1951), pp. 8–9.

[39] *Ibid.*, p. 10.

[40] *Ibid.*

[41] *Ibid.*, pp. 10–11.

[42] U. N. Security Council, *Official Records*, 559th Meeting (October 1, 1951), p. 21.

[43] U. N. Security Council, *Official Records*, 560th Meeting (October 15, 1951), p. 12.

[44] On this point it is interesting to compare Mr. Saleh's statement with the language of Article 92 of the Charter: "The International Court of Justice shall be the principal judicial organ of the United Nations. It shall function in accordance with *the annexed Statute, which ... forms an integral part of the present Charter.*" Emphasis added.

[45] It has been discussed in some detail; see pp. 92–94.

[46] U. N. Security Council, *Official Records*, 560th Meeting (October 15, 1951), p. 13.

[47] *Ibid.*, p. 28. Compare this with the statement made by Prime Minister Mossadegh to the Council on the following day: "I appeal to you to take pity on the Iranian people in their utter poverty, misery and destitution. It will be extremely dangerous if present conditions continue. I call upon the President and members of the Council and I say: *Beware of taking a decision which may endanger international peace.*" U. N. Security Council, *Official Records*, 561st Meeting (October 16, 1951), p. 24. Emphasis added.

At the meeting of the Council on October 17 the American delegate built a convincing case on excerpts from Iranian statements at previous Council meetings on the Anglo-Iranian dispute to the effect that there was a dispute which involved a threat to international peace and security. U. N. Security Council, *Official Records*, 563d Meeting (October 17, 1951), pp. 2–8.

[48] U. N. Security Council, *Official Records*, 565th Meeting (October 19, 1951), pp. 4–5. And see *Official Records*, 559th Meeting (October 1, 1951), pp. 1–2; and 561st Meeting (October 16, 1951), pp. 21–22.

[49] U. N. Security Council, *Official Records*, 561st Meeting (October 16, 1951), pp. 17–19; 565th Meeting (October 19, 1951), pp. 1–2. See also *Official Records*, 559th Meeting (October 1, 1951), pp. 2–3.

[50] U. N. Security Council, *Official Records*, 562d Meeting (October 17, 1951), pp. 6–7.

[51] U. N. Security Council, *Official Records*, 559th Meeting (October 1, 1951), p. 2.

[52] U. N. Security Council, *Official Records*, 562d Meeting (October 17, 1951), p. 8.

[53] *Ibid.*, pp. 9–10.

[54] U. N. Security Council, *Official Records*, 563d Meeting (October 17, 1951), p. 5.

[55] *Ibid.*, pp. 8–9.

[56] *Ibid.*, p. 41.

[57] *Ibid.*, p. 40.

[58] U. N. Security Council, *Official Records*, 561st Meeting (October 16, 1951), pp. 19–21. See also *Official Records*, 559th Meeting (October 1, 1951), pp. 8–9.

[59] Mr. Tsiang's statement of this problem is worth repeating: "It is clear to me that the nationalization of the oil industry in Iran is entirely a matter within the domestic jurisdiction of Iran; but I am not ready to accept the extremist, absolutist thesis that all the consequences of and developments following that nationalization

are all beyond the jurisdiction of the Security Council and that no matter what international complications may develop out of the situation, they are entirely beyond the jurisdiction of the Council." U. N. Security Council, *Official Records*, 563d Meeting (October 17, 1951), p. 35.

[60] *Ibid.*, p. 34; and see p. 141 herein.

[61] U. N. Security Council, *Official Records*, 561st Meeting (October 16, 1951), pp. 15–16; U. N. Document S/2379.

[62] Compare the argument of Sir Gladwyn Jebb for the inclusion of a reference to the provisional measures, pp. 131–132 herein.

[63] U. N. Security Council, *Official Records*, 561st Meeting (October 16, 1951), p. 17.

[64] U. N. Security Council, *Official Records*, 562d Meeting (October 17, 1951), p. 3.

[65] *Ibid.*, pp. 5–6.

[66] *Ibid.*, p. 6. The representative of Ecuador also said that it was the view of his government that the provisions of Article 94, paragraph 2, of the Charter referred only to *final* judgments, and that the Security Council could not properly act under that article to enforce an indication of interim measures by the ICJ. But, he added, his delegation would be prepared to support a resolution by the Council asking for an advisory opinion by the Court on the question of enforceability, under Article 94, paragraph 2, of indications of interim measures. U. N. Security Council, *Official Records*, 562d Meeting (October 17, 1952), p. 8. Compare pp. 92–94 herein.

[67] U. N. Security Council, *Official Records*, 562d Meeting (October 17, 1951), p. 10; U. N. Document S/2380. This resolution was never put to a vote, but the representative of Ecuador quite readily voted in favor of the French resolution for adjournment.

[68] U. N. Security Council, *Official Records*, 565th Meeting (October 19, 1951), pp. 2–3.

[69] *Ibid.*, pp. 3–4.

[70] *Ibid.*, p. 5.

[71] *Ibid.*, pp. 5–6.

[72] *Ibid.*, pp. 9–12, and especially p. 10.

[73] *Ibid.*, p. 12. *In favor:* Brazil, China, Ecuador, France, India, the Netherlands, Turkey, and the United States. *Against:* The USSR. *Abstaining:* The United Kingdom and Yugoslavia.

[74] *Ibid.*, p. 13.

[75] This interpretation is reasonable, whether enforcement action by the Council under chapter vii of the Charter is considered as a legal sanction or as a political measure. Hans Kelsen, *The Law of the United Nations* (1951), pp. 786–791. That the Security Council is not barred from intervening in a dispute which it considers a threat to the maintenance of international peace and security, despite a claim of domestic jurisdiction, is affirmed by the Council's action in the Indonesian case. See *ibid.*, pp. 440–443, 785, 789.

[76] The ICJ is specifically given this right by Article 36, paragraph 6, of its Statute. The Council must be considered as coming within the general rule expressed by the PCIJ in the following terms: "... as a general rule, any body possessing jurisdictional powers has the right in the first place to determine the extent of its jurisdiction ..." *Interpretation of the Greco-Turkish Agreement of 1926*, Ser. B.16.20. See also, to the same effect, Kelsen, *op. cit.*, pp. 154, 279 ff., 483 ff., and esp. pp. 783–784; Georg Schwarzenberger, *International Law as Applied by International Courts and Tribunals* (2d ed., 1949), p. 386.

[77] For example, compare the concept implicit in the Council's action in the Indonesian case, mentioned in n. 75 above, with that expressed by the PCIJ in the case of the *Nationality Decrees Issued in Tunis and Morocco:* "The words 'solely within the domestic jurisdiction' [the formula of Article 15, paragraph 8, of the League Covenant] seem rather to contemplate certain matters which, though they may very closely concern the interests of more than one state, are not, in principle, regulated by international law. As regards such matters, each state is sole judge. [But] . . . the right of a state to use its discretion [in matters normally within its domestic jurisdiction] is nevertheless restricted by obligations which it may have undertaken towards other states. In such a case, jurisdiction which, in principle, belongs solely to the state, is limited by rules of international law." PCIJ, Ser. B.4.23, 26–28.

[78] "Matters" (Article 2, paragraph 7) includes both "disputes" and "situations." See Kelsen, *op. cit.*, p. 775, n. 8.

[79] Kelsen, *op. cit.*, pp. 781–783, 788.

[80] *Ibid.*, pp. 772–773.

[81] See *ibid.*, pp. 770 ff.

[82] Other changes, such as the elimination of the word "dispute" and the substitution of "matters," the difference between the functions of the League Council and those of the United Nations Security Council, are discussed in detail by Kelsen, *op. cit.*, pp. 770 ff.

[83] UNCIO Document 1019, I/1/42, p. 1.

[84] UNCIO Document 976, I/1/40, p. 1.

[85] Dr. Liang Yuen-li, "The Question of Domestic Jurisdiction in the Anglo-Iranian Oil Dispute Before the Security Council," *AJIL*, Vol. 46 (1952), p. 282.

[86] Kelsen, *op. cit.*, p. 778.

[87] *Ibid.*, p. 779.

[88] *Ibid.*, p. 776.

[89] U. N. Security Council, *Official Records*, 565th Meeting (October 19, 1951), p. 9.

[90] Deputy Prime Minister Hossein Fatemi said at a press conference on October 16 that Iran would reject the United Kingdom's draft resolution if adopted by the Security Council, and would refuse to participate in any further discussions in the Council if that body adopted any measure affirming its jurisdiction over the dispute. *Oakland Tribune*, October 16, 1951, p. 2. In the Council on the same day, Prime Minister Mossadegh said that if the United Kingdom once more refused the Iranian government's offer to negotiate (that is, not under the aegis of the Security Council) on the questions of compensation and sale of oil to the United Kingdom, "we shall have no alternative but to go home, and we think that others [that is, members of the Security Council] may well follow our example." U. N. Security Council, *Official Records*, 561st Meeting (October 16, 1951), pp. 7–8.

[91] For a penetrating discussion of the problems mentioned in this last paragraph, see Georg Schwarzenberger, *Power Politics* (2d ed., New York, Praeger, 1951), chap. xxxii: "The Phenomenon of Power Politics in Disguise."

§ 9. FURTHER DEVELOPMENTS

[1] U. N. Security Council, *Official Records*, 565th Meeting (October 19, 1951), pp. 8–9.

[2] The Iranian government still wished to discuss the questions of compensation and sale of oil to the United Kingdom (see pp. 113 and 133 of the present work). Mr. Eden, describing the policy of the new Conservative government, said that a

satisfactory solution of the dispute must be based on three essential principles, none of which, he said, was inconsistent with the principle of nationalization. The three principles were: (1) practicability, that is, the solution must provide a means to ensure that the oil fields, the refinery, and the world-wide marketing organization are run efficiently; (2) the price of Iranian oil must be competitive and the profits fairly shared between Iran and those who develop its oil resources and provide the refining and marketing facilities; (3) fair compensation, to be settled by negotiation, must be paid for the act of nationalization. BIS, *The Iranian Oil Dispute; Statement by Mr. Eden* [in the House of Commons on November 19], T. 73, Washington, D.C., British Embassy, November 20, 1951.

[3] "Anglo-Iranian Dispute Remains Unsettled," *DSB*, Vol. 25 (November 26, 1951), p. 864.

[4] *San Francisco Chronicle*, November 15, 1951, p. 5.

[5] *Ibid.*, November 23, 1951, p. 6.

[6] *Ibid.*, November 27, 1951, p. 4.

[7] See Appendix II, table 4.

[8] *Cur. Dev.*, Vol. 5 (December, 1951), p. 37.

[9] *San Francisco Chronicle*, December 6, 1951, p. 7.

[10] *Ibid.*, December 7, 1951, p. 6.

[11] *Cur. Dev.*, Vol. 5 (December, 1951), p. 37.

[12] *San Francisco Chronicle*, December 13, 1951, p. 5.

[13] *Ibid.*, December 23, 1951, p. 6; *Cur. Dev.*, Vol. 5 (December, 1951), p. 38.

[14] "Persia's Economic Position," *The Economist*, Vol. 161 (December 8, 1951), pp. 1412–1414. See also "Persia Seeks a Master," *The Economist*, Vol. 164 (July 19, 1952), pp. 171–172, and the discussion in § 11, n. 120, below.

[15] *San Francisco Chronicle*, December 23, 1951, p. 6.

[16] *Ibid.*, December 19, 1951, p. 5.

[17] *Cur. Dev.*, Vol. 5 (January, 1952), pp. 38–39.

[18] *Ibid.*; and see *San Francisco Chronicle*, January 13, 1952, p. 5. The Iranian note, in addition to making the charge of interference in internal affairs, alleged that since Britain no longer represented India and Pakistan in commercial affairs it did not need as many consulates, and that, since Iran maintained no consulates in the United Kingdom, on the basis of reciprocity Britain should have no consulates in Iran. However, as the British ambassador pointed out in his reply, the Paris Treaty of 1857 and the Commercial Convention of 1903 between Britain and Iran both recognized the mutual establishment of consulates on a most-favored-nation basis. The fact that Iran had not taken advantage of this provision was no ground for denial of it to the British. To deny Britain the right to maintain consulates in Iran was, the ambassador said, a breach of treaty obligation. See "Commercial Convention Between Great Britain and Persia, Signed at Tehran, February 9th, 1903," *British and Foreign State Papers*, Vol. 96 (1903), pp. 51–84, affirmed, in the main, by the "Agreement Between the United Kingdom and Persia, Modifying the Commercial Convention of February 9, 1903. Tehran, March 21, 1920," *LNTS*, Vol. 4 (1921), pp. 48–92, Reg. No. 102. For the text of the British ambassador's note, see BIS, *Iranian Threat to Close British Consulates*, T. 6, Washington, D.C., British Embassy, January 21, 1952.

[19] *San Francisco Chronicle*, January 21, 1952, p. 4.

[20] *Cur. Dev.*, Vol. 5 (January, 1952), p. 39.

[21] *San Francisco Chronicle*, December 30, 1951, p. 4.

[22] *Ibid.*, January 21, 1952, p. 4; "Persia Stays Neutral," *The Economist*, Vol. 162 (January 12, 1952), p. 74; *Point 4 Program in Iran to be Expanded*, U. S. Department of State, Press Release No. 53, Washington, D.C., January 21, 1952, 2 pp. mimeo.

[23] A fact reflected in the following statement of Majlis Deputy Moatamed Damavandi on the floor of the Majlis, August 3, 1952: "They [the Americans] have said they are going to give Iran 20 million dollars [in Point Four aid]. We have seen nothing of this." *San Francisco Chronicle*, August 4, 1952, p. 4.

[24] See "Persia Stays Neutral," p. 74.

[25] *San Francisco Chronicle*, January 4, 1952, p. 4; *Cur. Dev.*, Vol. 5 (January, 1952), p. 38.

[26] In effect, the Bank's proposal gave the bulk buyer a wholesale price, but made the amount of the discount dependent on net profits.

[27] *Cur. Dev.*, Vol. 5 (January, 1952), p. 38.

[28] *Ibid.*

[29] Rules of Court of the ICJ (1946), Article 62, paragraph 3.

[30] *San Francisco Chronicle*, February 14, 1952, p. 4.

[31] That is, Prime Minister Mossadegh did not want to give the distributor a wholesale price. He apparently thought that the distributor should buy f.o.b. Abadan at a retail price and rely on freight charges for his profit.

[32] *Cur. Dev.*, Vol. 5 (January, 1952), p. 38; "World Bank and Persian Oil," *The Economist*, Vol. 162 (February 9, 1952), p. 328.

[33] *Cur. Dev.*, Vol. 5 (February, 1952), p. 35.

[34] *Ibid.* (March, 1952), p. 33.

[35] See IBRD, *Review of the International Bank's Negotiations Concerning the Iranian Oil Problem*, Press Release No. 285, Washington, D.C., April 3, 1952, 9 pp. mimeo.

Commenting on the Bank's report that its efforts at mediation had been recessed, British Foreign Secretary Eden said, in the House of Commons, "while I should be the first to welcome any sign from Tehran which would further efforts to find an acceptable basis of agreement, I am bound to say that at the moment I agree with the Bank." BIS, *Questions of the Day*, P. 104/2, Washington, D.C., British Embassy, April 22, 1952, p. 4.

Prime Minister Mossadegh said in Tehran on April 7 that the two conditions for reopening the discussions of the Bank's proposals were: (1) technicians must come from "neutral" countries (that is, not Britain [or the United States?]); (2) the IBRD must manage the oil industry as the agent of the Iranian government. *Cur. Dev.*, Vol. 5 (April, 1952), p. 35. In its press release the IBRD made it clear that it could not accept a position as agent, since that would commit it to favoring the legal position of Iran against that of the United Kingdom.

[36] World crude-oil production in 1950 was 523.6 million metric tons. Production in 1951, representing an increase of 13.4 per cent, amounted to 593.7 million metric tons. Production in the Middle East in 1951 (97.5 million metric tons) represented an increase of 11.1 per cent over production in 1950, slightly less than the rate of increase in the world as a whole. This increase in the Middle East, remarkable in view of the Iranian shutdown, was due primarily to the great increases in production in Saudi Arabia (from 26 million tons to 38 million tons) and Kuwait (from 17 million tons to 28½ million tons). See "Oil Output Record," *The Economist*, Vol. 162 (January 19, 1952), p. 173; and "Anglo-Iranian Without Abadan," *The Economist*, Vol. 163 (May 11, 1952), p. 611.

[37] U. S. Department of State, Press Release No. 207, March 20, 1952.
[38] *Cur. Dev.*, Vol. 5 (April, 1952), p. 36.

§ 10. PRELIMINARY OBJECTION TO THE JURISDICTION OF THE INTERNATIONAL COURT OF JUSTICE

[1] The United Kingdom's application is quoted by the Court in its judgment of July 22, 1952, on Iran's preliminary objection. See ICJ, *Anglo-Iranian Oil Company Case (Preliminary Objection)*, 1952 ICJ Reports 95–96.

[2] Rules of Court of the ICJ (1946), Article 62.

[3] ICJ, *op. cit.* (in n. 1 above), pp. 114–115.

[4] The full text of the declaration is reproduced in Appendix V.

[5] Subject, of course, to the exceptions spelled out in the second paragraph of the Iranian declaration. However, these were not in point in the proceeding being discussed and therefore are not mentioned in the text.

[6] ICJ, *op. cit.* (in n. 1 above), p. 104.

[7] The Court, at one point, did state that from a "purely grammatical point of view" either construction could be regarded as compatible with the text. But this statement of the alternative is immediately qualified by the statement that the "Court cannot base itself on a purely grammatical interpretation" but must seek an interpretation "which is in harmony with a natural and easy way of reading the text." Thus, the Court did not believe that it was faced with a real alternative. *Ibid.*

[8] See pp. 226–227 in the present work; "Persia and the Court," *The Economist*, Vol. 163 (June 7, 1952), pp. 662, 665; and "Persia Seeks a Master," *The Economist*, Vol. 164 (July 19, 1952), p. 171.

[9] ICJ, *op. cit.* (in n. 1 above), p. 105.

[10] *Ibid.*

[11] *Ibid.*

[12] *Ibid.*, p. 106.

[13] *Ibid.*, p. 107.

[14] *Ibid.*

[15] *Ibid.*, p. 121.

[16] *Ibid.*, pp. 136, 137.

[17] Article IX of the British-Persian Treaty of 1857, as quoted by the Court, *Anglo-Iranian Oil Company Case (Preliminary Objection)*, p. 108. See also Article II of the "Commercial Convention Between Great Britain and Persia, Signed at Tehran, February 9th, 1903," *British Foreign and State Papers*, Vol. 96 (1903), p. 51, affirmed in the "Agreement Between the United Kingdom and Persia, Modifying the Commercial Convention of February 9, 1903. Tehran, March 21, 1920," *LNTS*, Vol. 4 (1921), pp. 48–92, Reg. No. 102.

[18] "Treaty of Friendship, Establishment and Commerce Between Denmark and Persia. Signed at Teheran, February 20th, 1934," *LNTS*, Vol. 158 (1935–1936), p. 300, Reg. No. 3640.

[19] This issue was not discussed by the Court. In keeping with the chronological pattern adopted in the text, discussion of this issue is postponed. See § 11, pp. 180–190.

[20] ICJ, *op. cit.* (in n. 1 above), p. 110.

[21] *Ibid.*

[22] *Ibid.*, pp. 122–123.

[23] *Ibid.*, pp. 137–141.

[24] *Ibid.*, pp. 157–158.

[25] In the exchange of notes between the United Kingdom and Persia, dated May 10, 1928, the two nations pledged treatment of each other's nationals in accordance with the principles of international law. "Note Respecting the Position of British Nationals in Persia, May 10, 1928," in Arthur B. Keith, ed., *Speeches and Documents on International Affairs*, Vol. I (1938), pp. 148–153.

[26] ICJ, *op. cit.* (in n. 1 above), pp. 146–147.

[27] *Ibid.*, pp. 111–113.

[28] *Ibid.*, pp. 121–122, 137, and 153 respectively.

[29] *Ibid.*, pp. 148–150.

[30] None of the dissenting judges mentioned the problem of jurisdiction based on the principle *forum prorogatum.* The Court indicated that this contention was not pressed very hard. *Ibid.*, p. 114.

[31] The conclusions reached in the text can be compared with those of Professor Pitman Potter, who is of the opinion that the Court's judgment was "from a juridical point of view ... a rather commonplace and technical decision and a sound one," and that the Court's reasoning was "rather orthodox." Professor Potter concludes his comment by stating that the Court's decision "encourages a belief in its growing stability and authority." Pitman Potter, "Anglo-Iranian Oil Co. Case (Jurisdiction)," *AJIL*, Vol. 47 (1953), pp. 114–115.

[32] "Persia and the Court," p. 662; and "The Hague Court Verdict," *The Economist*, Vol. 164 (July 26, 1952), p. 213.

[33] See Georg Schwarzenberger, *International Law as Applied by International Courts and Tribunals* (2d ed., 1949), pp. 24–26; and Manley O. Hudson, *The Permanent Court of International Justice, 1920–1942* (1943), pp. 628–631.

§ 11. SOME LEGAL ISSUES ON THE MERITS OF THE DISPUTE

[1] Article IX of the British-Persian Treaty of 1857 has been quoted in the text at p. 172. See also, to the same effect, Article II of the "Commercial Convention Between Great Britain and Persia, Signed at Tehran, February 9th, 1903," *British and Foreign State Papers*, Vol. 96 (1903), p. 51, affirmed in the "Agreement Between the United Kingdom and Persia, Modifying the Commercial Convention of February 9, 1903. Tehran, March 21, 1920," *LNTS*, Vol. 4 (1921), pp. 48–92, Reg. No. 102.

[2] Article IV in the "Treaty of Friendship, Establishment and Commerce Between Denmark and Persia. Signed at Teheran, February 20th, 1934," *LNTS*, Vol. 158 (1935–1936), p. 301, Reg. No. 3640. See also Article I of the "Convention of Establishment Between the Empire of Persia and the Swiss Confederation. Signed at Berne, April 25th, 1934," *LNTS*, Vol. 160 (1935), p. 174, Reg. No. 3691. And see the Iranian note quoted in n. 3 below.

[3] The Persian government, in its "Note Respecting the Position of British Nationals in Persia, May 10, 1928," pledged: "1. On the basis of perfect reciprocity, [British nationals] will be admitted and treated on Persian territory in conformity with the rules and practice of international law ..." The full text of the note is given in Arthur B. Keith, ed., *Speeches and Documents on International Affairs, 1918–1937*, Vol. I (1938), pp. 248–253.

[4] The principle was stated by the PCIJ in the following terms: "It is an elementary principle of international law that a state is entitled to protect its subjects, when injured by acts contrary to international law committed by another state, from

whom they have been unable to obtain satisfaction through the ordinary channels. By taking up the case of one of its subjects and by resorting to diplomatic action or international judicial proceedings on his behalf, a state is in reality asserting its own rights—its right to ensure, in the person of its subjects, respect for the rules of international law.

"The question ... whether the ... dispute originates in an injury to a private interest ... is irrelevant from this standpoint. Once a state has taken up a case on behalf of one of its subjects before an international tribunal, in the eyes of the latter the state is the sole claimant." *Mavrommatis Palestine Concessions (Jurisdiction)*, PCIJ, Ser. A.2.12.

[5] Originally as the Anglo-Persian Oil Company, Ltd. The change to its present name was made June 7, 1935.

[6] It should perhaps be noted that the United Kingdom's argument before the ICJ that the 1933 concession should be regarded as a "treaty or convention" within the meaning of the Iranian declaration accepting the compulsory jurisdiction of the ICJ was not based upon the theory that AIOC was merely an alter ego of the British government. Instead, the argument was developed on the basis that the concession had been negotiated under the auspices of the League of Nations. The argument before the Court is discussed at pp. 175–176 of the text.

[7] The texts of these laws are reproduced in Appendix IV.

[8] Article 1. See Appendix I.

[9] See Appendix IV, especially Articles 2 and 4.

[10] The word "appropriate" is used here to describe a mere taking to one's own use, without any of the imputations of lawfulness or unlawfulness usually accompanying the words "expropriate" and "confiscate."

[11] A concept developed from the municipal institutions of "eminent domain" and "police power." See John W. Cutler, "The Treatment of Foreigners," *AJIL*, Vol. 27 (1933), pp. 236–237; the decision of the PCIJ in the case of *Certain German Interests in Polish Upper Silesia*, Ser. A.7.22; and the *Norwegian Shipowners' Claims* (Norway / U. S., 1921), in *UNRIAA*, p. 332.

[12] Charles C. Hyde, *International Law, Chiefly as Interpreted and Applied by the United States* (2d rev. ed., 1945), pp. 710–717, "Confiscatory Expropriation," *AJIL*, Vol. 32 (1938), pp. 759–766, and "Compensation for Expropriations," *ibid.*, Vol. 33 (1939), pp. 108–112; Josef L. Kunz, "The Mexican Expropriations," *New York University Law Quarterly Review*, Vol. 17 (1940), pp. 347, 349–359; the letters of Secretary of State Cordell Hull to the Mexican ambassador, July 21 and August 22, 1938, in Green H. Hackworth, *Digest of International Law*, Vol. III (1942), pp. 655–665; A. P. Fachiri, "Expropriation and International Law," in *BYBIL, 1925*, pp. 151–171, and "International Law and the Property of Aliens," in *BYBIL, 1929*, pp. 32–55; Georges Kaeckenbeeck, "La Protection internationale des droits acquis," *Recueil des cours*, Vol. 59 (1937), pp. 321–418, and "The Protection of Vested Rights in International Law," in *BYBIL, 1936*, pp. 1–18; and the *de Sabla Claim* decided by the Panama–United States Claims Commission (1933), reported in Hackworth, *op. cit.*, Vol. III, pp. 653–654, and in *AJIL*, Vol. 28 (1934), p. 602.

[13] Alwyn V. Freeman, *The International Responsibility of States for Denial of Justice* (1938), pp. 467 ff.; the *Norwegian Shipowners' Claims* (Norway / U. S., 1921), in *UNRIAA*, pp. 331, 338; *Neer Claim* (Mexico / U. S.), in *AJIL*, Vol. 21 (1927), pp. 555–557; and *Certain German Interests in Polish Upper Silesia*, PCIJ, Ser. A.7.21.

[14] Freeman, *op. cit.*, pp. 461–463 and references cited there; *Shufeldt Claim* (U. S. / Guatemala), in *UNRIAA*, p. 1098.

[15] See Georg Schwarzenberger, *International Law as Applied by International Courts and Tribunals* (2d ed., 1949), pp. 98–103, and cases cited there; Freeman, *op. cit.*, pp. 461–463.

[16] See, in addition to the materials cited in nn. 12 and 13 above, International Law Association, *Report of the Thirty-fourth Conference, Held at the Imperial Palace and at the Chamber of Commerce, Vienna, August 5th to August 11th, 1926* (1927), pp. 228–233; and the indicated provisions of the following treaties: Treaty of Versailles, Articles 297 and 298; Treaty of St. Germain, Articles 249, 250, and 272; Treaty of Neuilly, Articles 177 and 178; and the Treaty of Trianon, Articles 232, 233, and 255.

[17] See "The International Standard of Substantive Justice," chap. x in Freeman, *op. cit.*, pp. 497–531.

[18] The work by Freeman, cited in n. 13 above, is the best attempt that has yet been made to set forth the meaning of this term with precision.

[19] See Appendix IV, Article 3.

[20] Freeman, *op. cit.*, pp. 264–308, 531–571; the decisions of the United States–Mexican General Claims Commission (1923–1934) in the *Janes Claim* (1926), reported in *AJIL*, Vol. 21 (1927), pp. 362 ff., the *Chattin Claim*, in *AJIL*, Vol. 22 (1928), pp. 667 ff., and the *Mallén Claim*, in *AJIL*, Vol. 21 (1927), pp. 803 ff. See also Article 9, and the comment following it, of the draft convention on the responsibility of states in Research in International Law, Harvard Law School, *Nationality; Responsibility of States; Territorial Waters* (1929), pp. 173–174.

[21] Freeman, *op. cit.*, pp. 403–417; Edwin M. Borchard, *The Diplomatic Protection of Citizens Abroad* (1928), pp. 332 ff.; and Hackworth, *op. cit.*, Vol. V (1943), pp. 501–519. Extensive collections of authorities appear in these three works, and because the rules are so well settled it is unnecessary to review those authorities here.

[22] In addition to the works cited in the preceding note, see the decision in the *de Sabla Claim*, in Hackworth, *op. cit.*, Vol. III, pp. 653–654; the *El Triunfo Case* (U. S. / Salvador), in *Foreign Relations of the United States, 1902* (Washington D.C., Government Printing Office, 1903), at pp. 870–871; John B. Moore, *A Digest of International Law*, Vol. VI (1906), §§ 987–992; the *Finnish Ships Arbitration* (U. K. / Finland, 1934), in *UNRIAA*, pp. 1479 ff. The opinion of the arbitrator, Dr. Bagge, in the *Finnish Ships Arbitration* is a detailed and scholarly exposition of the law of the so-called "local remedy rule."

[23] It is interesting to compare this apparent attempt to apply a legal remedy through a parliamentary board with the language of the Persian government in its "Note Respecting the Position of British Nationals in Persia, May 10, 1928": "3. To the exclusion of all other jurisdiction, only the courts and tribunals subordinate to the Ministry of Justice will be competent to deal with cases in which one of the parties is a foreigner." Keith, ed., *op. cit.* (in n. 3 above), Vol. I, p. 149.

[24] It has been suggested by Borchard and others that in cases in which the delinquent sovereign itself has intentionally inflicted the injury on an alien by appropriation of his property (as in the Anglo-Iranian case) much less is required in the way of exhaustion of local remedies. This situation is different from that present in many international reclamations, and it is questionable whether the sovereign that has inflicted the injury and benefited by the appropriation should be the proper party to pass on the facts and the law relevant to the claim of the injured alien. Borchard suggests that the delinquent sovereign should be allowed only a very limited time to

make an adequate redress before the claimant state has the right to interpose. Edwin M. Borchard, "The Local Remedy Rule," *AJIL*, Vol. 28 (1934), pp. 729–733; Freeman, *op. cit.*, pp. 422, 433–434; L. H. Woolsey, "The Expropriation of Oil Properties in Mexico," *AJIL*, Vol. 32 (1938), pp. 522–523.

[25] See Appendix II, table 5. See also n. 120 below.

[26] See Appendix II, table 4.

[27] "Another 'No' to Premier Petrol," *The Economist*, Vol. 164 (July 12, 1952), p. 116.

[28] In the discussion in the text the writer is assuming that compensation must be paid on the basis of some formula such as "replacement value" or "fair market value."

[29] See "Dr. Mossadegh and the Facts," *The Economist*, Vol. 163 (April 19, 1952), p. 149, and press reports issued in the spring and summer of 1952; and see n. 120 below.

[30] *The Economist* has estimated that three-fourths of AIOC's profits in 1951 (a bad year for purposes of comparison) were derived from Iranian sources. "Anglo-Iranian Without Abadan," *The Economist*, Vol. 163 (May 31, 1952), p. 611.

[31] The subject has been treated under several widely differing categories, for example, "denial of justice," "protection of nationals," and "international responsibility of states." The theoretical basis of the law regarding expropriation is the subject of discussion in the article by John H. Herz, "Expropriation of Foreign Property," *AJIL*, Vol. 35 (1941), pp. 243–262. See also, Freeman, *op. cit.*, especially Part I and the bibliography on pp. 731–739; Fred K. Nielsen, *International Law Applied to Reclamations* (1933), chap. ix of Part I; Suzanne Basdevant, "Théorie générale de la condition de l'étranger," *in* Albert de Lapradelle and J. P. Niboyet, eds., *Répertoire de droit international*, Vol. VIII (1930), pp. 1–61; Kaeckenbeeck, "La Protection internationale des droits acquis," pp. 321–418, and "The Protection of Vested Rights in International Law," pp. 1–18; Fachiri, "Expropriation and International Law," pp. 151–171, and "International Law and the Property of Aliens," pp. 32–55. Compare the treatment of the problem in Moore, *op. cit.*, Vol. IV (1906), §§ 534–537, and Vol. VI (1906), §§ 986–997, and in Hackworth, *op. cit.*, Vol. V (1943), chap. xviii.

[32] This body of rules was crystallized during the modern world's era of free trade. However, it was also an era in which "alien" investments seldom approached the magnitude of many of those which exist in the mid-twentieth century, especially in the oil and mining industries.

[33] This so-called "equality doctrine," which has been discussed in § 8, n. 37, above, has been the focal point of much argument and discussion. However, since it is not an issue in the Anglo-Iranian oil dispute it is not elaborated in these pages. It is sufficient to observe that if the equality doctrine is accepted (that is, that international law obligates a state to give aliens the same treatment that it gives its own nationals and no better), it will completely negate the principle that a state is obligated to provide a *minimum* of protection to aliens lawfully within its borders. Regardless of how infamous its treatment of aliens, the equality doctrine would prevent the state of which the alien is a national from interposing if the delinquent state treated its own nationals in the same infamous fashion. This, it is submitted, is not the law. Both sides of the argument are developed in the correspondence between United States Secretary of State Cordell Hull and the Mexican ambassador to the United States during the summer of 1938. This correspondence is reproduced

in Hackworth, *op. cit.*, Vol. III, pp. 655–665. Most of the doctrinal literature is referred to by Freeman, *op. cit.*, at pp. 504–507.

[34] See, for general discussions, Borchard, *The Diplomatic Protection of Citizens Abroad;* Frederick S. Dunn, *The Protection of Nationals* (1932) and *The Diplomatic Protection of Americans in Mexico* (1933) ; and Freeman, *op. cit.*, pp. 96–116.

[35] So much so that there was practically no monographic writing on this subject before World War I—a state of affairs that changed radically during the interwar period.

[36] The decisions of the international arbitral tribunals can be approached through Hackworth, *op. cit.*, Vol. V, pp. 471–851; John B. Moore, *History and Digest of the International Arbitrations to Which the United States Has Been a Party*, Vol. VI (1898), pp. 605–1037; Marjorie M. Whiteman, *Damages in International Law*, Vol. II (1937), pp. 1386 ff.; and Nielsen, *op. cit.*, Part II. See also Schwarzenberger, *op. cit.*, whose discussion is not limited to the arbitral tribunals but includes the work of the PCIJ and ICJ as well.

[37] For example, the Mexican (1910) and the Bolshevik (1917) revolutions, two of the most violent of this era, were widely separated both geographically and ideologically, yet both expressed a changing philosophic concept of private property and its social function. Cf. Nikolai Lenin, *State and Revolution* (New York, International Publishers, [1932]) ; John Reed, *Ten Days That Shook the World* (New York, Boni & Liveright, 1919) ; and F. S. C. Northrop, *The Meeting of East and West* (New York, Macmillan, 1946), esp. pp. 42–48 on the Mexican Revolution. For further references on the philosophic background of the Mexican Revolution see the works cited in Kunz, *op. cit.*, pp. 327, 342; and on the revolution in Russia, see E. H. Carr, *The Bolshevik Revolution, 1917–1923* (New York, Macmillan, 1950).

[38] See Karl R. Popper, *The Open Society and Its Enemies* (Princeton, Princeton University Press, 1950), Part II; Joseph Schumpeter, *Capitalism, Socialism, and Democracy* (New York, Harper & Bros., 1942) ; and John B. Condliffe, *The Commerce of Nations* (1950), Part II.

[39] See Roscoe Pound, *Introduction to the Philosophy of Law* (1922), pp. 191–235.

[40] Déclaration des droits de l'homme et du citoyen (1791), Article 17.

[41] Code Napoléon, Articles 544 and 545.

[42] For example, see Introductory Act to the German Civil Code (1896), Article 109.

[43] In the common law institution of "eminent domain" which has been incorporated in the Fifth and Fourteenth Amendments to the United States Constitution. *Kohl v. United States*, 91 U. S. 367 (1875) ; *Jacobs v. United States*, 290 U. S. 13 (1933) ; *Chicago, C. & Q. R. Co. v. Chicago*, 166 U. S. 226 (1896) ; *Clark v. Nash*, 198 U. S. 361 (1905) ; *Strickley v. Highland Boy G. M. Co.*, 200 U. S. 527 (1905). And see Pound, *op. cit.*, p. 194, where he develops the idea that the individualist conception of private property grew "out of the facts of time and place as explanation thereof and then [was] given universal application...."

The individualist conception (or something closely approaching it) was formulated and guaranteed by the law of the land very early in the history of the English common law (much earlier than in most of the rest of Europe, where feudalism persisted longer) : Magna Charta (1215), chap. xxxix: "no man shall be deprived of his freehold"; Petition of Right (1628) : "the ancient and undoubted right of every Freeman is that he hath a full and absolute property in his goods and estate"; Bill of Rights (1689) : "whereas by the common law and statutes every freeman hath a proprietie in his goods and estate..."

[44] Condliffe, *op. cit.*, chapters xiv and xv, and the bibliography given at pp. 857–860.

[45] E.g., Giorgio del Vecchio, *The Formal Bases of Law*, Modern Legal Philosophy Series, Vol. X (1914), and *Justice, an Historical and Philosophical Essay* (ed. by A. H. Campbell, trans. by Lady Guthrie, 1952).

[46] Gustav Radbruch, "Legal Philosophy," Part II in *Legal Philosophies of Lask, Radbruch, and Dabin*, Twentieth Century Legal Philosophy Series, Vol. IV (trans. by Kurt Wilk, 1950), esp. pp. 160–168.

[47] R. C. Renard, *Le Droit, l'ordre et la raison* (1927), and *La Philosophie de l'institution* (1939); Jacques Maritain, *Les Droits de l'homme et la loi naturelle* (1942).

[48] Léon Duguit, *Les Transformations générales du droit privé depuis le Code Napoléon* (1920), esp. pp. 147–148.

[49] Pound, *op. cit.*, pp. 191–235, and *Social Control Through Law* (1942); Eugen Ehrlich, *Fundamental Principles of the Sociology of Law* (trans. by W. L. Moll, 1936).

[50] In addition to the standard Marxist and Stalinist literature, see Rudolph Schlesinger, *Soviet Legal Theory* (New York, Oxford University Press, 1945); Vladimir Gsovski, *Soviet Civil Law* (Ann Arbor, University of Michigan Law School, 1948–1949, 2 vols.); and Andrei I. Vyshynski, *The Law of the Soviet State* (trans. by Hugh W. Babb, New York, Macmillan, 1949).

[51] Wolfgang Friedmann, *Legal Theory* (2d ed., 1949), p. 431. Professor Friedmann concludes his survey of the conflict between individualism and collectivism by stating that there is no irreconcilable antagonism between the two, and that the claims of the community can be met without at the same time sacrificing the "essential individual freedoms." This position has some similarities to that of Radbruch, *op. cit.*, §§ 17–19, although there are important differences. Whether or not the conflict is bound to be a perpetual one—and it has existed at least since the time of Plato—is not, in the opinion of Professor Friedmann, as well as in that of Radbruch, a matter of political or legal theory, but of human morality. See Friedmann, *op. cit.*, pp. 429–433.

[52] In the United States the trend seems to be toward greater governmental regulation of business, in contrast, for example, to the nationalization programs of postwar Britain. Yet the *raison de validité* of the programs in both countries is essentially the same.

[53] The USSR, which has gone as far as any other nation in abolishing private ownership of the means of production and distribution, has not completely abolished the institution of private property. Constitution of the Union of Soviet Socialist Republics (1936), Articles 9 and 10. See also the Yugoslav Constitution (1946), Articles 14, 18; Constitution of the Ukrainian Soviet Socialist Republic (1937), Articles 9, 11.

[54] E.g., German (Weimar) Constitution (1919), Article 153; Czechoslovak Constitution (1920), Article 109; Estonian Constitution (1920), Article 24; Mexican Constitution (1917), Articles 22, 27.

[55] See the Mexican Constitution (1917), Article 27; and the Civil Code of the Russian Soviet Federated Socialist Republic (1927), Articles 69 and 70. See also the Czechoslovak Constitution (1948), Section 9, paragraph 2; and the Yugoslav Constitution (1946), Article 18.

[56] In the "Report of the Committee on the Protection of Private Property" of the 1926 Conference of the International Law Association, five members (Brunet, Bewes, Bellot, Pollock, and Radcliffe) made the following interesting reservation to the statement that a state's treatment of its own nationals was a matter within its

domestic jurisdiction: "Although, in the absence of constitutional limitation, the power of a sovereign state to expropriate the property of its own nationals may not be disputed by process of *law* within its own jurisdiction, nevertheless such expropriation is contrary to *law* (droit)." International Law Association, *op. cit.*, pp. 247–248. Compare this with Articles 55 and 62 of the United Nations Charter, and Hans Kelsen, *The Law of the United Nations* (1951), pp. 25 ff., 565 ff.

[57] *Tinoco Claims* (G. B. / Costa Rica, 1923), in *UNRIAA*, p. 386; PCIJ, *Treatment of Polish Nationals in Danzig*, Ser. A/B.44.24; Hackworth, *op. cit.*, Vol. V, pp. 485 ff. and references cited there. See also the *Shufeldt Claim* (U. S. / Guatemala, 1930), in *UNRIAA*, at p. 1098.

[58] Cf. Kelsen, *op. cit.*, pp. 431–434; Schwarzenberger, *op. cit.*, pp. 8–18.

[59] E.g., *Sazanow v. District Land (Reform) Board of Bialystok* (Supreme Court of Poland, October 2, 1922), in *Annual Digest of Public International Law Cases, 1919–1922* (ed. by Sir John Fischer-Williams and Hersch Lauterpacht, 1932), pp. 247–248; the decision of the Supreme Court of Czechoslovakia, April 28, 1925, reported in *Annual Digest of Public International Law Cases, 1925–1926* (ed. by Arnold D. McNair and Hersch Lauterpacht, 1929), pp. 133 ff.

[60] E.g., *Pallavicini v. Czechoslovak State* (Hungaro-Czechoslovak Mixed Arbitral Tribunal, 1929), in *Annual Digest of Public International Law Cases, 1929–1930* (ed. by Hersch Lauterpacht, 1935), pp. 440–443. And see Albert G. de Lapradelle, *La Réforme agraire tchécoslovaquie devant la justice internationale* (1929).

[61] PCIJ, *Pazmany University v. Czechoslovakia*, Ser. A/B.61; *Pajzs, Czaky, Esterhazy Case (Judgment)*, Ser. A/B.68.

[62] "My Government maintains . . . that there is in international law no rule universally accepted in theory nor carried out in practice, which makes obligatory the payment of immediate compensation nor even of deferred compensation, for expropriations of a general and impersonal character . . ." Mexican minister of foreign affairs to United States secretary of state, August 3, 1938. Hackworth, *op. cit.*, Vol. III, p. 657. Almost a month later President Cárdenas of Mexico used identical words in addressing the Mexican Congress. *El Universal*, Mexico City, September 2, 1938, pp. 1, 4, quoted by Kunz, *op. cit.*, p. 352. A similar position was maintained by Rumania. Much of the important diplomatic correspondence relating to the "Optants' Dispute" is reproduced in Francis Déak, *The Hungarian-Rumanian Land Dispute* (1928), pp. 159 ff.

[63] See the discussion in § 8, n. 37, above, and in n. 33 of this section.

[64] In a note of August 3, 1938, to the United States secretary of state, the Mexican minister of foreign affairs expressed this argument in the following terms: "I wish to draw your attention very specially to the fact that the agrarian reform is not only one of the aspects of a program of social betterment attempted by a government or a political group for the purposes of trying out new doctrines, but also constitutes the fulfilling of the most important of the demands of the Mexican people, who, in revolutionary struggle, for the purpose of obtaining it, sacrificed the very lives of their sons. The political, social, and economic stability and the peace of Mexico depend on the land being placed anew in the hands of the country people who work it; a transformation of the country, that is to say, the future of the nation, could not be halted by the impossibility of paying immediately the value of the properties belonging to a small number of foreigners who seek only a lucrative end." Hackworth, *op. cit.*, Vol. III, p. 658.

On the Rumanian expropriations, see: Déak, *op. cit.*; Edwin M. Borchard, *Opin-*

ion on the Rumanian-Hungarian Dispute Before the Council of the League of Nations (1927), esp. pp. 23–30, and "Confiscations: Extraterritorial and Domestic," *AJIL*, Vol. 31 (1937), pp. 675–681; Valeriu Bercaru, *La Réforme agraire en Roumanie* (Paris, Librairie universitaire J. Gamber, 1928) ; and *Some Opinions, Articles, and Reports Bearing upon the Treaty of Trianon and the Claims of the Hungarian Nationals with Regard to Their Lands in Transylvania* (London, W. P. Griffith & Sons, Ltd. [1929?], 2 vols.).

On the Mexican expropriations, see: Hyde, "Confiscatory Expropriation," pp. 759–766, "Compensation for Expropriations," pp. 108–112, and *International Law . . .* (2d rev. ed.), pp. 710–717; Kunz, *op. cit.*, pp. 327–384; Woolsey, *op. cit.*, pp. 519–526; Frederic R. Coudert, "The Mexican Situation and the Protection of American Property Abroad," *American Bar Association Journal*, Vol. 24 (1938), 813–822, 848; Arthur K. Kuhn, "The Mexican Supreme Court Decision in the Oil Companies Expropriation Cases," *AJIL*, Vol. 34 (1940), pp. 297–300, an analysis of the decision of the Mexican Supreme Court upholding the constitutionality of the expropriatory statutes and decrees; Frederick S. Dunn, *The Diplomatic Protection of Americans in Mexico*, and "International Law and Private Property Rights," *Columbia Law Review*, Vol. 28 (1928), pp. 166–180, especially the conclusion on p. 180, in which he expresses a view remarkably similar to that expressed by the Mexican government ten years later in its correspondence with the United States secretary of state.

[65] These included Alvarez, Duguit, Le Fur, Picard, and Strupp, all of whose opinions appear in Bercaru, *op. cit.*

[66] This was particularly the argument of Strupp and Marburg, as related by Kunz, *op. cit.*, pp. 337–338. See also the citation by Basdevant, *op. cit.*, pp. 13–14; and the remarks of the Rumanian delegate (Sipsom) at the Hague Codification Conference of 1930, reproduced in Freeman, *op. cit.*, pp. 672–677.

[67] Sir John Fischer-Williams, "International Law and the Property of Aliens," in *BYBIL, 1928*, pp. 1–30. An article bearing the same title but reaching the opposite conclusion appeared a year later: A. P. Fachiri, in *BYBIL, 1929*, pp. 32–55.

[68] J. L. Brierly, *The Law of Nations* (2d ed., 1936), p. 177, and *ibid.* (4th ed., 1949), p. 211. The statement that the precedents are indecisive seems to be inaccurate. A reading of the remainder of Brierly's discussion indicates that he is apparently trying to appraise the virtues of competing economic policies rather than to perform the lawyer's job of determining which rule is confirmed by positive law. He concludes his discussion with the following: "The sanctity of private property may be in general a sound maximum of legislative policy, but it is difficult in these days to hold that it may in no circumstances be required to yield to some higher public interest. 'It is surely impossible, whatever may be our views as to the relative merits of socialist and individualist doctrines, to assert that modern civilization requires all states to accept unreservedly the theories of one side in the great economic conflict.' " *Ibid.* (2d ed.), pp. 177–178, and *ibid.* (4th ed.), p. 211, quoting Sir John Fischer-Williams, *op. cit.*, p. 20. It should be noted that Brierly did not take this position in the first edition of his *The Law of Nations* (1928), nor in the "Report of the Committee on the Protection of Private Property" at the 1926 Conference of the International Law Association. See International Law Association, *op. cit.*, pp. 227–279. Further, Brierly gives no indication of the ways in which the precedents changed between 1928 and 1936, other than his reference to the paper by Sir John Fischer-Williams, which does not support his argument on grounds of precedent.

Another eminent jurist, Lauterpacht, also seems to have changed his views at approximately the same time, and similarly without explanation. In L. F. L. Oppenheim, *International Law*, Vol. I (5th ed., edited by Hersch Lauterpacht, 1937), p. 284, a new paragraph was added: the pre-1914 rule is qualified, not abolished, "in cases in which fundamental changes in the political system and economic structure of the State of far-reaching social reforms entail interference, on a large scale, with private property. In such cases neither the principle of absolute respect for alien private property nor rigid equality with the dispossessed nationals offers a satisfactory solution. It is probable that, consistently with legal principle, such solution must be sought in the granting of partial compensation." With the last sentence may be compared the words of the arbitrator in *L'Affaire Goldenberg* (Germany / Rumania, 1928): "Dans les deux cas, en effet, l'allocation formelle d'une indemnité notoirement insuffisante ne peut satisfaire aux exigences du droit." *UNRIAA*, p. 909.

[69] Many of the states and writers that indicated their support of the pre-1914 rule are mentioned in the materials cited in nn. 70 and 91–93 below.

[70] See League of Nations, *Conference for the Codification of International Law*, Vol. III: *Bases of Discussion for the Conference, Drawn up by the Preparatory Committee. Responsibility of States for Damage Caused in Their Territory to the Person or Property of Foreigners*, 1929 (League of Nations Document C.75. M.69. 1929.V.3), and Vol. IV: *Acts of the Conference ... Minutes of the Third Committee. Responsibility of States for Damage Caused in Their Territory to the Person or Property of Foreigners*, 1930 (League of Nations Document C.351[c]. M.145[c]. 1930.V.17).

[71] The failure of the delegates to this conference to reach an agreement has been cited by some writers as evidence that there are no generally accepted rules on this question; however, see Freeman, *op. cit.*, p. 516, n. 1, in which he rightly points out that "the unsatisfactory character of the replies [to questions about the applicable rules of law] may well have proceeded more from the faulty manner in which the question was put than from the non-existence of ascertainable international rules on the subject."

[72] The agreement was embodied in an exchange of notes dated November 9 and 12, 1938. It was agreed that the value of the properties expropriated by Mexico would be fixed by a three-member commission, and that Mexico would pay to the United States, as compensation, on or before May 31, 1939, the sum of $1 million as first payment. Another $1 million was to be paid annually thereafter, on June 30, until the amount equaled that determined by the commission. The notes are quoted in Hackworth, *op. cit.*, Vol. III, pp. 660–661.

[73] Even the welcomeness is somewhat questionable. See the discussion in n. 110 below.

[74] The Mexican agrarian expropriations must be distinguished from the oil expropriations of March 18, 1938. As Kunz has pointed out (*op. cit.*, p. 349), the legal disputes between Mexico and the United States in the two cases were very different. The disagreement of the two governments on the agrarian expropriations was much more fundamental, since it turned on principles, rather than details; that is, the dispute was not centered on the question how to carry out a recognized norm of international law, but involved a denial of the very existence of that norm. See the discussion in the second paragraph of n. 91 below.

[75] Much of this correspondence is quoted in Hackworth, *op. cit.*, Vol. III, pp.

655–666; and in William W. Bishop, Jr., *International Law, Cases and Materials* (preliminary ed., 1951), chap. vi, pp. 9–19.

[76] Secretary of State Cordell Hull to the Mexican ambassador in Washington, July 21, 1938. Hackworth, *op. cit.*, Vol. III, p. 657.

[77] The American government seems, however, to have had some reservations on the question whether the agrarian expropriations had in fact been carried out in accordance with the municipal law of Mexico. In the note of August 22, 1938, Secretary of State Hull charged that "the very provisions of the Mexican Constitution and of the Mexican laws have already been negatived in practice and would seem now to have been abrogated in practical effect." "Mexico: Expropriation of American Properties," U. S. Department of State, *Press Releases*, Vol. 19, No. 465 (August 27, 1938), pp. 142–143.

[78] Secretary of State Hull to the Mexican ambassador, August 22, 1938. Hackworth, *op. cit.*, Vol. III, pp. 658–659.

[79] Secretary of State Hull to the Mexican ambassador, July 21, 1938. *Ibid.*, p. 656.

[80] See Hyde, "Compensation for Expropriations," pp. 108–112, and "Confiscatory Expropriation," pp. 759–766. See also Alfred Verdross, "Les Règles internationales concernant le traitement des étrangers," *Recueil des cours*, Vol. 37 (1931), pp. 359–360: "Le droit international ne veut nullement empêcher les réformes qu'exige le développement social ... Toutefois, même pour ces motifs, si l'État exproprie directement un étranger d'un droit acquis, il doit l'indemniser."

[81] Mexican minister of foreign affairs to United States secretary of state, August 3, 1938. Hackworth, *op. cit.*, Vol. III, p. 358, quoted in part in n. 64 above.

[82] The Iranian government has taken a position similar to that of Mexico. See pp. 135–136 of the present work.

[83] See Dunn, *The Diplomatic Protection of Americans in Mexico*, for an historical survey of this question; the exchange of notes quoted in Hackworth, *op. cit.*, Vol. III, pp. 655–665; and the copious citation of historical materials by Kunz, *op. cit.*, pp. 327, 342–343.

[84] The arguments of the Iranian delegate in the Security Council (see pp. 132–136 of the present work) show a remarkable similarity to those of Mexico, except that the Iranian government has never admitted financial impossibility. However, there can be no question that Iran is just as financially embarrassed as was Mexico. See pp. 187–189 of the text.

[85] Mexican minister of foreign affairs to United States secretary of state, August 3, 1938. Hackworth, *op. cit.*, Vol. III, p. 657. Emphasis added.

[86] The constant use of the phrase "universally accepted" by the Mexican government should be noted. The orthodox positivist view holds, of course, that a rule acquires its legal validity by the consent of the "overwhelming majority" of states, or variously the "majority" of states. The Mexican government never seems to have elaborated on the significance of its use of the term, although it is hardly to be supposed that it would deny the validity of all international law norms in the absence of universal acceptance. Yet that would appear to be the plain meaning of Mexico's use of the phrase. Compare the slightly different implications of the similar language quoted in n. 88 below.

[87] Compare the argument of Sir John Fischer-Williams, *op. cit.*, pp. 15–30, and Fachiri's criticism (Fachiri, "International Law and the Property of Aliens," pp. 32–34, 48–55).

[88] In a note of August 22, 1938, Secretary of State Hull said: "The universal

acceptance of this rule of the law of nations, which, in truth, is merely a statement of common justice and fair-dealing, does not in the view of this government admit of any divergence of opinion." Hackworth, *op. cit.*, Vol. III, p. 659.

[89] *Ibid.*, p. 657.

[90] Mexican minister of foreign affairs to United States secretary of state, August 3, 1938: "Nevertheless Mexico admits, in obedience to her own laws, that she is indeed under obligation to indemnify in an adequate manner; but the doctrine which she maintains on the subject . . . is that the time and manner of such payment must be determined by her own laws." *Ibid.*, p. 658.

[91] See the materials cited in n. 70 above; the review of the municipal laws of England, the United States, France, Belgium, Italy, Spain, Argentina, Peru, Chile, Uruguay, Holland, Denmark, Sweden, Norway, Germany, and Switzerland in International Law Association, *op. cit.*, pp. 228–233; Treaty of Versailles, Articles 297 and 298; Treaty of St. Germain, Articles 249, 250, and 272; Treaty of Neuilly, Articles 177–178; Treaty of Trianon, Articles 232, 233, and 255. See also the note from the Spanish minister of state to the United States ambassador in Madrid, August, 1936: ". . . the Government of the Republic holds as unalterable principle not to take possession of any property, movable or immovable, belonging to Spanish citizens or foreigners, except . . . in cases [in which] public interests so require. In such a case it will pay the value after a just and equitable appraisement . . ." Quoted in Hackworth, *op. cit.*, Vol. III, p. 654. See also the German-Russian Treaty of August 27, 1918, Article 18.

The expropriation of oil properties belonging to British and American nationals by the Mexican government on March 18, 1938, led to a series of notes in which all three governments consistently affirmed the general validity of the pre-1914 rule requiring, in cases of expropriation in the public interest, the payment of prompt, adequate, and effective compensation. The real dispute turned on the problems involved in the application of the general rule: What was expropriated (merely the surface land or the oil in the subsoil) ? What is the amount and measure of compensation? What is prompt payment? What is a deferred payment? Were the expropriations in good faith and for reasons of public utility? Does a government have a right of diplomatic intervention on behalf of shareholders in foreign corporations? (The British companies were registered in Mexico.) What is the nature and effect of a "Calvo Clause"? Some of the diplomatic correspondence is reproduced in Hackworth, *op. cit.*, Vol. III, pp. 661–665. See also, Hyde, *International Law* . . . (2d rev. ed.), pp. 710–717, and "Compensation for Expropriations," pp. 108–112; Woolsey, *op. cit.*, pp. 519–526; Coudert, *op. cit.*, pp. 813–822, 848; Kuhn, *op. cit.*, pp. 297–300; and Kunz, *op. cit.*, *passim*.

For an extensive collection of treaties, to which the United States has been a party, which recognize the general validity of the pre-1914 rule, see Robert R. Wilson, "Property Protection Provisions in United States Commercial Treaties," *AJIL*, Vol. 45 (1951), pp. 90–104.

In the course of the Security Council's consideration of the complaint of the United Kingdom against the Iranian government's nationalization of AIOC's property in Iran, the delegate of Ecuador expressed the view that "expropriation must be accompanied by prompt, adequate, and effective compensation." U. N. Security Council, *Official Records*, 562d Meeting (October 17, 1951), p. 4.

[92] *Norwegian Shipowners' Claims* (Norway / U. S.), in *UNRIAA*, pp. 330–339; the *de Sabla Claim* (U. S. / Panama), in Hackworth, *op. cit.*, Vol. III, pp. 653–654; the

Shufeldt Claim (U. S. / Guatemala), in *UNRIAA*, pp. 1097–1098; *Certain German Interests in Polish Upper Silesia*, PCIJ, Ser. A.7; *L'Affaire Goldenberg* (Germany / Rumania, 1928), in *UNRIAA*, p. 909; *Pazmany University v. Czechoslovakia*, PCIJ, Ser. A/B.61; *Pajzs, Czaky, Esterhazy Case (Judgment)*, PCIJ, Ser. A/B.68; Fred K. Nielsen, ed., *American-Turkish Claims Settlement* (1937), especially: *U. S. ex rel. MacAndrews & Forbes Co. v. The Republic of Turkey*, pp. 87–128, *U. S. ex rel. Mrs. Spiros Raissis v. The Republic of Turkey*, pp. 342–344, and *U. S. ex rel. Singer Sewing Machine Co. v. The Republic of Turkey*, pp. 490–498; Basdevant, *op. cit.*, pp. 50–54; International Law Association, *op. cit.*, pp. 233–234; *British Reclamations in the Spanish Zone of Morocco* (U. K. / Spain, 1925), in *UNRIAA*, pp. 639–642; *French Claims Against Peru* (1920), in *ibid.*, pp. 216–221; and Nielsen, *International Law Applied to Reclamations*, pp. 33–42. Cf. *Pallavicini v. Czechoslovak State* (Hungaro-Czechoslovak Mixed Arbitral Tribunal, 1929), in *Annual Digest . . . 1929–1930*, pp. 440–443. See also, Schwarzenberger, *op. cit.* (2d ed.), pp. 98–103.

[93] Freeman, *op. cit.*, pp. 515–522; Hyde, *International Law . . .* (2d rev. ed.), pp. 710–717, "Confiscatory Expropriation," pp. 759–766, and "Compensation for Expropriations," pp. 108–112; Basdevant, *op. cit.*, pp. 1–61; Borchard, "Confiscations: Extraterritorial and Domestic," pp. 675–681; Fachiri, "Expropriation and International Law," pp. 151–171, and "International Law and the Property of Aliens," pp. 32–55; Kaeckenbeeck, "La Protection internationale des droits acquis," pp. 321–418, and "The Protection of Vested Rights in International Law," pp. 1–18; Nielsen, *International Law Applied to Reclamations*, pp. 33–42; Erich Kauffmann, "Règles générales du droit de la paix," *Recueil des cours*, Vol. 54 (1935), p. 429; Chandler P. Anderson, "Basis of the Law Against Confiscating Foreign-owned Property," *AJIL*, Vol. 21 (1927), pp. 525–526; International Law Association, *op. cit.*, pp. 227–279 ("Report of the Committee on the Protection of Private Property," of which committee the members were Frank Russell, Sir Frederick Pollock, R. V. Williams, Sir Charles Radcliffe, René Brunet, J. L. Brierly [for Brierly's changing views, see the remarks in n. 68 above], Wyndham Bewes, Arnold D. McNair, Alfred P. Fachiri, Tompkins McIlvaine, and H. H. L. Bellot), and see also the remarks in n. 56 above; "Report on Expropriations of Immovable Property" (1938), by a subcommittee of the American Bar Association (members: J. W. Ryan, G. Auchinloss, M. B. Carroll, R. M. Carson, J. R. Clark, H. B. Crawford, John Foster Dulles, S. H. E. Freund, Arthur K. Kuhn, Garrett McEnerney, H. M. O'Melveny, T. W. Palmer, R. T. Swaine, and Charles Cheney Hyde, who drafted the report), quoted in Hyde, *International Law . . .* (2d rev. ed.), pp. 716–717; Edwin M. Borchard, "The Citizen Abroad," *Proceedings of the American Society of International Law*, 1927, pp. 23–27, and, in the same volume, Philip C. Jessup, "Confiscation," pp. 38–40. Cf. Dunn, "International Law and Private Property Rights," pp. 166–180; and, in Hans Kelsen, "Théorie générale du droit international public, problèmes choisis," *Recueil des cours*, Vol. 42 (1932), pp. 253–254: "Il se pourrait sérieuses limitations apportées à l'idée de la propriété privée . . . ne fussent en tout cas pas très favorable à la formation d'une règle de droit international aboutissant à faire aux étrangers une situation privilégiée dans la question de la propriété."

[94] See Condliffe, *op. cit.*, chaps. xvi and xvii, and, in the same work, the bibliography on pp. 860–862.

[95] See especially Hyde, "Compensation for Expropriations," p. 112.

[96] For a general treatment of the subject, see: Samuel Herman, "War Damage and Nationalization in Eastern Europe," *Law and Contemporary Problems*, Vol. 16

(1951), pp. 498–518; Samuel L. Sharp, *Nationalization of Key Industries in Eastern Europe* (1946); Seymour J. Rubin, "Nationalization and Compensation—A Comparative Approach," *University of Chicago Law Review*, Vol. 17 (1950), pp. 458–477; Nicholas R. Doman, "Compensation for Nationalized Property in Eastern Europe," *International Law Quarterly*, Vol. 3 (1950), pp. 323–342, and "Postwar Nationalization of Foreign Property in Europe," *Columbia Law Review*, Vol. 48 (1948), pp. 1125–1161; G. Hornsey, "Foreign Investment and International Law," *International Law Quarterly*, Vol. 3 (1950), pp. 552–561; Joyce Gutteridge, "Expropriation and Nationalization in Hungary, Bulgaria and Roumania," *International and Comparative Law Quarterly*, Vol. 1 (1952), pp. 14–28; J. E. S. Fawcett, "Some Foreign Effects of Nationalization of Property," in *BYBIL, 1950*, pp. 355–375; Alan R. Rado, "Czechoslovakian Nationalization Decrees," *AJIL*, Vol. 41 (1947), pp. 795–806; and B. A. Wortley, "Expropriation in International Law," *Transactions of the Grotius Society* (for 1947), Vol. 33 (1948), pp. 25–48.

[97] The connection between foreign investments and expansionist state policies is described in Herbert Feis, *Europe, the World's Banker, 1870–1914* (1930). See also his *Diplomacy of the Dollar* (1951); Parker T. Moon, *Imperialism and World Politics* (1939), chap. iv; and Condliffe, *op. cit.*, chaps. viii and xi.

[98] Kelsen, *The Law of the United Nations*, pp. 99 ff.; Philip C. Jessup, *A Modern Law of Nations* (1949), p. 97.

[99] See especially Article 8 of the Articles of Agreement of the International Monetary Fund. See also, Condliffe, *op. cit.*, pp. 623–629; Donald B. Marsh, *World Trade and Investment* (New York, Harcourt Brace, 1951), chap. xxvi.

[100] Brierly, *op. cit.* (4th ed.), pp. 75–76; Jessup, *A Modern Law of Nations*, chap. v.

[101] Although there has been no serious formal challenge to the pre-1914 rule, its once clear meaning has been indirectly questioned in international discussions concerned with specific aspects of the rule. For example, in the discussion of the investment provisions of the proposed charter for an International Trade Organization, the representative of Canada, having in mind American investors and American dollars, said that the right to appropriate the property of an alien could not be conditioned on a state's ability to make compensation to him in his own currency. However, most delegates agreed that payment in local currency would not at all times be "effective" compensation. In the final draft the problem was stated in a vague and equivocal fashion, but the views which were expressed during the negotiations were sufficient to indicate that there was little unanimity on what constituted "effective" compensation. See Rubin, *op. cit.*, pp. 461–462 and nn. 12–14; and the discussion in "The Restoration of World Trade," *International Conciliation*, No. 434 (New York, Carnegie Endowment for International Peace, October, 1947), pp. 548–551.

[102] Mr. Herman, formerly Legal Adviser for International Claims to the Department of State, has indicated (Herman, *op. cit.*, pp. 504, 518) that in his opinion the lack of capacity of the eastern European countries to pay prompt, adequate, and effective compensation for their postwar nationalizations was primarily the result of the destruction caused by World War II. For the reasons given in the text, and even when due allowance is made for the importance of war damage, it would appear that this was not the major cause.

[103] It could be asked: If the United States, the richest country in the world, suddenly nationalized all of its industries, would it be able to pay prompt, adequate, and effective compensation?

[104] Rubin, *op. cit.*, pp. 461–463; Herman, *op. cit.*, pp. 504–505; Gutteridge, *op. cit.*,

pp. 23–28. Cf. Doman, "Postwar Nationalization of Foreign Property in Europe," p. 1159.

[105] That the difficulties of settlement between the creditor nations of western Europe and the United States and the nationalizing countries of eastern Europe have been immeasurably increased by the "Iron Curtain" and the "cold war" is of sufficiently common knowledge that it need not be labored in the text. The reader may take judicial notice.

[106] This is especially true of the nationalizations in eastern Europe, where many of the nationalization laws provide local remedies for compensation in local currency or in long-term government bonds redeemable in local currency. All these currencies are "blocked," and this fact, when coupled with the legal prohibitions on new foreign-owned investments, makes the local remedy valueless to the foreign investor whose property has been expropriated. See Herman, *op. cit.*, pp. 503–508; Gutteridge, *op. cit.*, pp. 16–26; and Doman, "Compensation for Nationalization in Eastern Europe," pp. 333–342. AIOC would be faced with a similar lack of investment opportunity in Iran should the Iranian government offer to pay compensation in Iranian rials.

[107] It may be observed, without elaboration, that the greatest industrialized nation to undertake an extensive nationalization program, the United Kingdom, did not have international reclamations problems—despite a severe shortage of foreign exchange—primarily because of the confidence of investors, who were willing to take government securities in lieu of their expropriated property interests.

[108] Brierly, *op. cit.* (4th ed.), pp. 43, 74. See also Georg Schwarzenberger, *Power Politics* (2d ed., New York, Praeger, 1951), pp. 12–15, 254–257.

[109] See Herman, *op. cit.*, pp. 502–503.

[110] Compensation claims for American-owned oil properties which had been appropriated by Mexico in 1938 were settled in 1943 for a lump sum of $29 million, including $5 million interest. It has been estimated that this settlement represented a loss of approximately 75 per cent to the American investors. Cleona Lewis, *The United States and Foreign Investment Problems* (1948), pp. 152–153.

[111] The more important agreements are listed by Herman, *op. cit.*, p. 504, n. 21.

[112] These two agreements are analyzed and discussed in some detail by Rubin, *op. cit.*

[113] Announced September 28, 1949. "Agreement . . . Relating to the Settlement of Certain Inter-governmental Debts," *British Treaty Series*, No. 60, Cmd. 7797 (H. M. Stationery Office, 1949). Mr. Rubin reports (Rubin, *op. cit.*, p. 458) that an agreement has also been concluded by the United Kingdom and Yugoslavia.

[114] *British Treaty Series*, No. 62, Cmd. 7799 (H. M. Stationery Office, 1949).

[115] See "U. S.–Yugoslav Claims Settlement," *DSB*, Vol. 19 (August 1, 1948), pp. 137–140, for the text of the agreement, which was announced July 19, 1948.

[116] The agreement required payment of the $17 million in dollars within forty-five days after the date of the agreement. It was also provided that the United States would unblock the Yugoslav gold deposit within five days after the date of the agreement. Yugoslavia could, therefore, dispose of the gold on the free market at a price considerably higher than the United States Treasury's official price of $35 per ounce.

[117] *Census of American-owned Assets in Foreign Countries* (Washington, D.C., U. S. Department of the Treasury, 1947), p. 68.

[118] The terms of the American-Mexican settlement and one estimate of the loss it entailed for American investors are given in n. 110 above.

[119] The International Claims Commission was established by Congress to administer

the American-Yugoslav settlement. It was directed to decide claims according to the "applicable principles of international law, justice, and equity." Public Law No. 453, 81st Cong., 2d sess. (March 10, 1950), Sec. 4, paragraph *a. 64 Stat.* 14.

[120] See pp. 187–189 in the present work. *The Economist* reports, on the basis of figures available from the Bank Melli and the Iranian finance ministry, that the budgetary deficit of Iran for the period March, 1951–March, 1952, amounted to 4,000 million rials and was met by using a special sterling reserve of £14 million (see p. 157 herein), special pension and sugar-monopoly funds, a national bond issue (which obtained only 450 million rials instead of the anticipated 2,000 million rials—see text on p. 157), and profits from the sale of foreign exchange. By that means, wages and salaries were paid, although debts to contractors grew considerably. Most of the devices used to meet the deficit of the fiscal year 1951–52 cannot be repeated, and since March, 1952, the deficit has increased at the rate of 250–300 million rials monthly. As a result, *The Economist* estimates, only half the wages and salaries due at the end of July, 1952, could be met. The Iranian civil servants are accustomed to delays, but the army and oil-field workers are not. Those responsible for Iranian financial policy will, therefore, have to face the menacing problems created by a mass of unpaid workers and especially an unpaid army, or those created by a rapidly accelerating inflation that would result from an increased note issue or from fresh advances to the government from the Bank Melli reserve. But whatever direction the Iranian financial crisis takes, its solution will undoubtedly depend on Iran's securing help from the outside (see the discussion at pp. 215–219 herein). "Persia Seeks a Master," *The Economist,* Vol. 164 (July 19, 1952), pp. 171–172.

[121] See pp. 114 and 133 herein; and see the *San Francisco Chronicle,* August 3, 1952, pp. 1, 13.

[122] See, for example, the monumental three-volume work by Marjorie M. Whiteman (*op. cit.,* see n. 36 above), especially Volume II; and Freeman, *op. cit.,* chap. xix.

[123] The general principles of law relating to the measure of damages were eloquently stated by the Guatemalan agent in reference to his government's counterclaim to the *Claim of Robert H. May v. Guatemala:* "The law of Guatemala ... establishes, like those of all civilized nations of the earth, that contracts produce reciprocal rights and obligations between the contracting parties; that whoever concludes a contract is bound not only to fulfill it but also to recoup or compensate the other party for damages and prejudice which result directly or indirectly from the nonfulfillment or infringement by default or fraud of the party concerned and that such compensation includes both damage suffered and profits lost: *damnum emergens et lucrum cessans.*" *Claim of Robert H. May v. Guatemala,* in *Foreign Relations of the United States, 1900* (Washington, D.C., Government Printing Office, 1902), at p. 673. See also the PCIJ's statement of the principle in the case of the *Factory at Chorzów* (*Claims for Indemnity—Judgment, 1928*), Ser. A.17.31.

[124] PCIJ, *Factory at Chorzów* (*Claims for Indemnity—Judgment, 1928*), Ser. A.17.53; *Shufeldt Claim* (U. S. / Guatemala, 1930), in *UNRIAA,* p. 1099; *Norwegian Shipowners' Claims* (Norway / U. S., 1922), in *ibid.,* p. 338; Schwarzenberger, *International Law ...* (2d ed.), p. 206; *British Reclamations in the Spanish Zone of Morocco* (U. K. / Spain, 1925), in *UNRIAA,* pp. 657–658; and Nielsen, *International Law Applied to Reclamations,* pp. 61–62.

[125] U. N. Security Council, *Official Records,* 560th Meeting (October 15, 1951), p. 25.

[126] The figure $1,400 million was stated in a Reuters dispatch from London on August 3, 1952. *San Francisco Chronicle,* August 3, 1952, p. 1. See text on p. 188 herein.

[127] "Security Prices and Yields," *The Economist,* Vol. 161 (December 1, 1951), p. 1360.

[128] See Herman, *op. cit.,* pp. 502–503.

[129] See Lewis, *op. cit.,* pp. 152–153; and see the brief summary of the settlement in n. 110 above.

[130] See pp. 204–205 of the text in the present work. It should be noted that even if not inadequate (and this is not known), the Czech compensation payments will certainly not be prompt.

[131] See pp. 205–206. As has been pointed out (p. 206), it is probable that the Yugoslav payment of $17 million will prove inadequate to fully compensate the Americans whose property was expropriated by the Yugoslav government.

[132] Lewis, *op. cit.,* pp. 155, 255.

§ 12. ENVOY

[1] The history of AIOC's efforts in this regard has been discussed in § 7, n. 52. On July 23, 1952, Prime Minister Churchill announced that the British government would take all "practicable steps" to block sales of Iranian oil, stating the rather obvious fact that the ICJ's decision that it is not competent does not affect the validity of AIOC's claims. *San Francisco Chronicle,* July 24, 1952, p. 7. The announcement is important in that it apparently indicates that it has become the policy of the British government to lend its weight to what was formerly only a threat of legal action by a private corporation in municipal courts.

[2] The nonbarter imports have been primarily cereals and cereal products, sugar, tea, coffee, cocoa, cotton piece goods, rayon and woolen cloth, chemical and pharmaceutical products, rubber and rubber products, metal manufactures, machinery, and transport equipment.

The barter imports are primarily cereals, cereal products, and sugar from the Soviet Union; and metal, metal manufactures, and machinery from Germany. There is also a small barter trade in the products of the region with other Middle Eastern countries.

[3] A statement from the revised edition of one of Winston Churchill's early works (first published in 1905), in reference to the anti-British ("Home Rule") disturbances in Ireland during the "potato famine" of the 1880's, is interesting in this regard: "Economic well-being often takes the heart out of racial animosities. The cause of nationality may excite the educated revolutionist [as it has Dr. Mossadegh and his fellow leaders of the National Front party?]; but the pinch of famine is required before the humble tiller of the soil can be enlisted in his thousands. A political movement to be dangerous must find its substance in social evil." Winston Churchill, *Lord Randolph Churchill* (2d rev. ed., 1951), p. 144. These observations indicate the political wisdom of one of Mossadegh's first economic reforms, which was proclaimed by a decree ordering the landowners to give the share-cropping peasants a larger portion of their produce. Reported in the *San Francisco Chronicle,* August 14, 1952, p. 5.

[4] The following is a statement by Edwin M. Wright, Intelligence Adviser on Near Eastern Affairs in the Department of State: "If the Russians did attack Iran, an international, full scale war could not be avoided. It would come in twenty four hours.

If an internal take-over by the communists should occur, war might take somewhat longer, but the free world certainly could not remain inactive." *San Francisco Chronicle*, December 7, 1951, p. 5.

[5] For example, see the use of the British navy in the settlement of the dispute with the Kingdom of the Two Sicilies regarding the "Sicilian Sulphur Monopoly" (1839–1842), *British and Foreign State Papers*, Vol. 28 (1839–1840), pp. 1163–1242; Vol. 29 (1840–1841), pp. 175–204; and Vol. 30 (1841–1842), pp. 11–120. The British navy was also used without hesitation in the dispute over "Mr. Finlay's claims" ten years later (1849–1850), on the subject of which Richard Cobden made one of his most eloquent speeches. See John Bright and James E. Thorold Rogers, eds., *Speeches on Questions of Public Policy by Richard Cobden, M. P.* (London, Macmillan, 1870, 2 vols.), Vol. II, pp. 211–229.

[6] The Soviet-Persian Treaty of 1921 was not a mutual defense arrangement. See Part I, § 1, p. 8.

[7] The statements by Mossadegh and Fatemi have been quoted in part in § 8, n. 90.

[8] U. N. Security Council, *Official Records*, 560th Meeting (October 15, 1951), p. 10.

[9] *Mavrommatis Palestine Concessions (Jurisdiction)*, PCIJ, Ser. A.2.16.

[10] For example, "Persia and the Court," *The Economist*, Vol. 163 (June 7, 1952), pp. 662, 665; and "Persia Seeks a Master," *The Economist*, Vol. 164 (July 19, 1952), pp. 171–172.

[11] However, as has been noted above (n. 1), Prime Minister Churchill announced on July 23, 1952, that the British government would thenceforth take all "practicable steps" to prevent sales of oil by the NIOC.

Selected
Bibliography

BOOKS AND ARTICLES

Anderson, Chandler P. "Basis of the Law Against Confiscating Foreign-owned Property," *American Journal of International Law,* Vol. 21 (1927), pp. 525–526.

"Anglo-Iranian Without Abadan," *The Economist,* Vol. 163 (May 31, 1952), p. 611.

Annual Digest of Public International Law Cases, 1919–1922. Edited by Sir John Fischer-Williams and Hersch Lauterpacht. London, Longmans, Green & Co., 1932.

Annual Digest of Public International Law Cases, 1925–1926. Edited by Arnold D. McNair and Hersch Lauterpacht. London, Longmans, Green & Co., 1929.

Annual Digest of Public International Law Cases, 1929–1930. Edited by Hersch Lauterpacht. London, Longmans, Green & Co., 1935.

"Another 'No' to Premier Petrol," *The Economist,* Vol. 164 (July 12, 1952), p. 116.

Austin, Ambassador Warren R. "Right of U.N. to Consider Anglo-Iranian Dispute," *The Department of State Bulletin,* Vol. 25 (October 15, 1951), p. 615.

Basdevant, Suzanne. "Théorie générale de la condition de l'étranger," *in* Albert de Lapradelle and J. P. Niboyet, eds., *Répertoire de droit international.* Vol. VIII. Paris, Librairie du Recueil Sirey, 1930. Pp. 1–61.

Bishop, William W., Jr. *International Law, Cases and Materials.* Preliminary ed. New York, Prentice-Hall, 1951.

Borchard, Edwin M. "The Citizen Abroad," *Proceedings of the American Society of International Law,* 1927, pp. 23–27.

—— "Confiscations: Extraterritorial and Domestic," *American Journal of International Law*, Vol. 31 (1937), pp. 675–681.

—— *The Diplomatic Protection of Citizens Abroad*. New York, The Banks Law Publishing Co., 1928.

—— "The Local Remedy Rule," *American Journal of International Law*, Vol. 28 (1934), pp. 729–733.

—— *Opinion on the Rumanian-Hungarian Dispute Before the Council of the League of Nations*. [New Haven, The Tuttle, Morehouse & Taylor Co., 1927.]

"Breakdown in Persia," *The Economist*, Vol. 160 (June 23, 1951), pp. 1487–1488.

Brierly, J. L. *The Law of Nations*. London, Oxford University Press, 1928.

—— *Ibid*. 2d ed. London, Oxford University Press, 1936.

—— *Ibid*. 4th ed. London, Oxford University Press, 1949.

"Britain and Persia," *The Economist*, Vol. 115 (December 17, 1932), pp. 1125–1126.

Brown, Edward G. *The Persian Revolution of 1905–1909*. Cambridge, England, The [Cambridge] University Press, 1910.

Bullard, Sir Reader. *Britain and the Middle East from the Earliest Times to 1950*. London, Hutchinson's University Library, 1951.

"Can Persia Refine?" *The Economist*, Vol. 160 (June 30, 1951), pp. 1567–1568.

Caroe, Olaf. *Wells of Power. The Oilfields of South-Western Asia*. London, Macmillan, 1951.

Cheng, B. "The Anglo-Iranian Dispute," *World Affairs*, Vol. 5 (1951), pp. 387–405.

Churchill, Winston S. *The Grand Alliance*. New York, Houghton Mifflin Co., 1950.

—— *Lord Randolph Churchill*. 2d rev. ed. London, Odhams, [1951].

Condliffe, John B. *The Commerce of Nations*. New York, W. W. Norton & Co., 1950.

Conolly, Violet. *Soviet Economic Policy in the East*. London, Oxford University Press, 1933.

Coudert, Frederic R. "The Mexican Situation and Protection of American Property Abroad," *American Bar Association Journal*, Vol. 24 (1938), pp. 813–822, 848.

"A Cruiser for Abadan," *The Economist*, Vol. 160 (June 30, 1951), pp. 1547–1548.

Cutler, John W. "The Treatment of Foreigners," *American Journal of International Law*, Vol. 27 (1933), pp. 225–246.

Déak, Francis. *The Hungarian-Rumanian Land Dispute*. New York, Columbia University Press, 1928.

Doman, Nicholas R. "Compensation for Nationalized Property in Eastern Europe," *International Law Quarterly*, Vol. 3 (1950), pp. 323–342.

—— "Postwar Nationalization of Foreign Property in Europe," *Columbia Law Review*, Vol. 48 (1948), pp. 1125–1161.

"Dr. Mossadegh and the Facts," *The Economist*, Vol. 163 (April 19, 1952), p. 149.

Duguit, Léon. *Les Transformations générales du droit privé depuis le Code Napoléon*. Paris, F. Alcan, 1920.

Dumbauld, Edward. *Interim Measures of Protection*. New York, Van Riemsdyck Book Service, 1932.

Dunn, Frederick S. *The Diplomatic Protection of Americans in Mexico*. New York, Columbia University Press, 1933.

—— "International Law and Private Property Rights," *Columbia Law Review*, Vol. 28 (1928), pp. 166–180.

—— *The Protection of Nationals*. Baltimore, Johns Hopkins University Press, 1932.

Ehrlich, Eugen. *Fundamental Principles of the Sociology of Law*. Trans. by W. L. Moll. Cambridge, Mass., Harvard University Press, 1936.

Ellwell-Sutton, L. P. *Modern Iran*. London, G. Routledge, 1941.

Fachiri, A. P. "Expropriation and International Law," in *The British Year Book of International Law, 1925*. London, Oxford University Press, [n.d.]. Pp. 151–171.

—— "International Law and the Property of Aliens," in *The British Year Book of International Law, 1929*. London, Oxford University Press, [n.d.]. Pp. 32–55.

Fawcett, J. E. S. "Some Foreign Effects of Nationalization of Property," in *The British Year Book of International Law, 1950*. London, Oxford University Press, [n.d.]. Pp. 355–375.

Feis, Herbert. *The Diplomacy of the Dollar*. Baltimore, Johns Hopkins University Press, 1951.

—— *Europe, the World's Banker, 1870–1914*. New Haven, Yale University Press, 1930.

Fischer-Williams, Sir John. "International Law and the Property of Aliens," in *The British Year Book of International Law, 1928*. London, Oxford University Press, [n.d.]. Pp. 1–30.

Fraser, Sir William. "Report to the Stockholders" [of Anglo-Iranian Oil

Company, Ltd.], *The Economist*, Vol. 161 (December 1, 1951), pp. 1363–1369.

—— "Report to the Stockholders" [of Anglo-Iranian Oil Company, Ltd.], *ibid.*, Vol. 163 (June 7, 1952), pp. 707–709.

Freeman, Alwyn V. *The International Responsibility of States for Denial of Justice.* London, Longmans, Green & Co., 1938.

Friedmann, Wolfgang. *Legal Theory.* 2d ed. London, Stevens & Sons, Ltd., 1949.

Grady, Henry. "What Went Wrong in Iran?" *Saturday Evening Post*, January 5, 1952, pp. 30–32, 56–58.

Groseclose, Elgin. *Introduction to Iran.* London, Oxford University Press, 1947.

Gupta, R. N. *Iran, an Economic Study.* New Delhi, Indian Institute of International Affairs, [1947].

Gutteridge, Joyce. "Expropriation and Nationalization in Hungary, Bulgaria and Roumania," *International and Comparative Law Quarterly*, Vol. 1 (1952), pp. 14–28.

Haas, W. S. *Iran.* London, Oxford University Press, 1946.

Hackworth, Green H. *Digest of International Law.* Washington, D.C., Government Printing Office, 1940–1944. 8 vols.

Hammarskjöld, Ake. "Quelques questions des mesures conservatoires," *Zeitschrift für ausländisches öffentliches Recht und Völkerrecht*, Vol. 5 (1935), pp. 5–33. Reprinted in his *Juridiction internationale.* Leiden, Société d'Éditions A. W. Sitjhoff, 1938. Pp. 299–328.

Herman, Samuel. "War Damage and Nationalization in Eastern Europe," *Law and Contemporary Problems*, Vol. 16 (1951), pp. 498–518.

Herz, John H. "Expropriation of Foreign Property," *American Journal of International Law*, Vol. 35 (1941), pp. 243–262.

Hornsey, G. "Foreign Investment and International Law," *International Law Quarterly*, Vol. 3 (1950), pp. 552–561.

Hudson, Manley O. *The Permanent Court of International Justice.* New York, Macmillan, 1934.

—— *The Permanent Court of International Justice, 1920–1942.* New York, Macmillan, 1943.

—— "The Thirtieth Year of the World Court," *American Journal of International Law*, Vol. 46 (1952), pp. 1–39.

Hyde, Charles Cheney. "Compensation for Expropriations," *American Journal of International Law*, Vol. 33 (1939), pp. 108–112.

—— "Confiscatory Expropriation," *ibid.*, Vol. 32 (1938), pp. 759–766.

—— *International Law, Chiefly as Interpreted and Applied by the United States.* 2d rev. ed. Boston, Little, Brown & Co., 1945.

International Law Association. *Report of the Thirty-fourth Conference, Held at the Imperial Palace and at the Chamber of Commerce, Vienna, August 5th to August 11th, 1926.* London, Sweet & Maxwell, Ltd., 1927.

"International Law for the *Rose Mary*," *The Economist*, Vol. 166 (January 17, 1953), p. 134.

Iran: Point of World Interest. United States Department of State Publication 4262. General Foreign Policy Series 54. Washington, D.C., June, 1951. 8 pp.

Jessup, Philip C. "Confiscation," *Proceedings of the American Society of International Law*, 1927, pp. 38–40.

—— *A Modern Law of Nations.* New York, Macmillan, 1949.

—— "The Reality of International Law," *Foreign Affairs*, Vol. 18 (1940), pp. 244–253.

Kaeckenbeeck, Georges. "La Protection internationale des droits acquis," *Recueil des cours*, Vol. 59 (1937), pp. 321–418.

—— "The Protection of Vested Rights in International Law," in *The British Year Book of International Law, 1936.* London, Oxford University Press, [n.d.]. Pp. 1–18.

Kauffmann, Erich. "Règles générales du droit de la paix," *Recueil des cours*, Vol. 54 (1935), pp. 311–620.

Kelsen, Hans. *The Law of the United Nations.* New York, Praeger, 1951.

—— "Théorie générale du droit international public, problèmes choisis," *Recueil des cours*, Vol. 42 (1932), pp. 121–351.

Kertesz, Étienne. "Le Droit international et l'affaire des mitrailleuses de Szent Gotthard," *Revue générale de droit international public*, Vol. 35 (1928), pp. 466–498.

Khadduri. Majid. "Iran's Claim to the Sovereignty of Bahrayn," *American Journal of International Law*, Vol. 45 (1951), pp. 631–647.

Kuhn, Arthur K. "The Mexican Supreme Court Decision in the Oil Companies Expropriation Cases," *American Journal of International Law*, Vol. 34 (1940), pp. 297–300.

Kunz, Josef L. "The Mexican Expropriations," *New York University Law Quarterly Review*, Vol. 17 (1940), pp. 327–384.

Labour Conditions in the Oil Industry in Iran. Geneva, International Labor Organization, 1950.

Lapradelle, Albert G. de. *La Réforme agraire tchécoslovaquie devant la justice internationale.* Paris, Librairie du Recueil Sirey, 1929.

Lenczowski, George. "Iran: Nationalism Erupts," *Current History*, Vol. 21 (July, 1951), pp. 12–18.

―――― *Russia and the West in Iran, 1918–1948*. Ithaca, Cornell University Press, 1949.

Lesueur, Émile. *Les Anglais en Perse*. Paris, La Renaissance du Livre, [1922?].

Lewis, Cleona. *The United States and Foreign Investment Problems*. Washington, D.C., The Brookings Institution, 1948.

Liang Yuen-li. "The Question of Domestic Jurisdiction in the Anglo-Iranian Oil Dispute Before the Security Council," *American Journal of International Law*, Vol. 46 (1952), pp. 272–282.

Maritain, Jacques. *Les Droits de l'homme et la loi naturelle*. New York, Éditions de la Maison française, 1942.

―――― *Man and the State*. Chicago, University of Chicago Press, [1951].

McGhee, George. "The Oil Problem in the Middle East," *The Department of State Bulletin*, Vol. 25 (October 15, 1951), pp. 612–615.

Mesbah Zadeh, Mostafa. *La Politique de l'Iran dans la Société des Nations. La Conception iranienne de l'organisation de la paix*. Paris, Éditions A. Pédone, 1936.

"Middle East," *The Lamp* (New York, Standard Oil Co. [N. J.]), Vol. 33, No. 2 (June, 1951), pp. 1, 22–23.

The Middle East, a Political and Economic Survey. London, Royal Institute of International Affairs, 1950.

"Middle East Munich," *The Economist*, Vol. 161 (October 6, 1951), pp. 779–780.

Millspaugh, Arthur C. *Americans in Persia*. Washington, D.C., The Brookings Institution, 1946.

"Mobs Without Masters," *The Economist*, Vol. 161 (December 15, 1951), pp. 1443–1444.

Moon, Parker T. *Imperialism and World Politics*. New York, Macmillan, 1939.

Moore, John Bassett. *A Digest of International Law*. Washington, D.C., Government Printing Office, 1906. 8 vols.

―――― *History and Digest of the International Arbitrations to Which the United States Has Been a Party*. Washington, D.C., Government Printing Office, 1898. 6 vols.

Morgenthau, Hans. "Diplomacy," *Yale Law Journal*, Vol. 55 (1946), pp. 1067–1080.

―――― *Politics Among Nations*. New York, Knopf, 1949.

Nielsen, Fred K. *International Law Applied to Reclamations.* Washington, D.C., John Byrne & Co., 1933.

Nielsen, Fred K., ed. *American-Turkish Claims Settlement.* Washington, D.C., Government Printing Office, 1937.

"Oil Output Record," *The Economist,* Vol. 162 (January 19, 1952), p. 173.

Oliver, Covey T. "Reflections on Two Recent Developments Affecting the Function of Law in the International Community," *Texas Law Review,* Vol. 30 (1952), pp. 815–842.

Oppenheim, L. F. L. *International Law.* Vol. I. 5th ed., edited by Hersch Lauterpacht. London, Longmans, Green, 1937.

Overseas Consultants, Inc. *Report on the Seven Year Development Plan for the Plan Organization of the Imperial Government of Iran.* New York, Overseas Consultants, Inc., 1949. 5 vols.

"Persia and the Court," *The Economist,* Vol. 163 (June 7, 1952), pp. 662, 665.

"Persia Seeks a Master," *The Economist,* Vol. 164 (July 19, 1952), pp. 171–172.

"Persia Stays Neutral," *The Economist,* Vol. 162 (January 12, 1952), p. 74.

"Persian Oil," *The Economist,* Vol. 115 (December 3, 1932), pp. 1019–1020.

"Persia's Economic Position," *The Economist,* Vol. 161 (December 8, 1951), pp. 1412–1414.

Pound, Roscoe. *Introduction to the Philosophy of Law.* New Haven, Yale University Press, 1922.

—— *Social Control Through Law.* New Haven, Yale University Press, 1942.

Radbruch, Gustav. "Legal Philosophy," Part II in *Legal Philosphies of Lask, Radbruch, and Dabin.* Twentieth Century Legal Philosophy Series, Vol. IV. Trans. by Kirt Wilk. Cambridge, Mass., Harvard University Press, 1950. Pp. 47–224.

Rado, Alan R. "Czechoslovakian Nationalization Decrees," *American Journal of International Law,* Vol. 41 (1947), pp. 795–806.

Renard, R. C. *Le Droit, l'order et la raison.* Paris, Librairie du Recueil Sirey, 1927.

—— *La Philosophie de l'institution.* Paris, Librairie du Recueil Sirey, 1939.

Research in International Law, Harvard Law School. *Nationality; Responsibility of States; Territorial Waters.* Cambridge, Mass., Harvard Law School, 1929.

Ronaldshay, The Earl of. *The Life of Lord Curzon.* Vol. III. London, Ernest Benn, Ltd., [1928].

"The *Rose Mary's* Test Run," *The Economist,* Vol. 163 (June 21, 1952), p. 800.

Rubin, Seymour J. "Nationalization and Compensation—A Comparative Approach," *University of Chicago Law Review,* Vol. 17 (1950), pp. 458–477.

Schwarzenberger, Georg. *International Law as Applied by International Courts and Tribunals.* 2d ed. London, Stevens & Sons, Ltd., 1949.

"Security Prices and Yields," *The Economist,* Vol. 161 (December 1, 1951), p. 1360.

Sharp, Samuel L. *Nationalization of Key Industries in Eastern Europe.* Washington, D.C., Foundation for Foreign Affairs, 1946.

Shuster, Morgan. *The Strangling of Persia.* New York, The Century Co., 1912.

Stevens, G. G. "Reform and Power Politics in Iran," *Foreign Policy Reports,* Vol. 26 (February 15, 1951), pp. 214–223.

Sykes, Sir Percy M. *A History of Persia.* 3d ed. London, Macmillan, 1930. 2 vols.

Tarbell, Ida. *The History of the Standard Oil Company.* New York, Macmillan, 1904. 2 vols.

Thomas, L. V., and R. N. Frye. *The United States and Turkey and Iran.* Cambridge, Mass., Harvard University Press, 1951.

Toynbee, P. "Behind Iran's Seething Nationalism," *New York Times Magazine,* October 7, 1951, p. 13.

United Nations. *Reports of International Arbitral Awards.* [Leiden, A. W. Sitjhoff's Publishing Co., 1948.] 4 vols.

―――― Secretariat. Department of Economic Affairs. *Public Finance Information Papers: Iran.* ST/ECA/SER. A/4. New York, United Nations, 1951.

―――― *Review of Economic Conditions in the Middle East.* New York, United Nations, March, 1951.

United States. Congress. Senate. Select Committee on Small Business. *The International Petroleum Cartel.* 82d Cong., 2d sess. Washington, D.C., Government Printing Office, 1952. 377 pp.

Vecchio, Giorgio del. *The Formal Bases of Law.* Modern Legal Philosophy Series, Vol. X. Boston, The Boston Book Co., 1914.

―――― *Justice, an Historical and Philosophical Essay.* Ed. by A. H. Campbell, trans. by Lady Guthrie. Edinburgh, [Edinburgh] University Press, 1952.

Verdross, Alfred. "Les Règles internationales concernant le traitement des étrangers," *Recueil des cours*, Vol. 37 (1931), pp. 327–412.

Visscher, Ch. de. "Le Déni de justice en droit international," *Recueil des cours*, Vol. 52 (1935), pp. 365–442.

Whiteman, Marjorie M. *Damages in International Law*. Washington, D.C., Government Printing Office, 1937–1943. 3 vols.

Wilbur, Donald N. *Iran, Past and Present*. Princeton, Princeton University Press, 1948.

Wilson, Robert R. "Property Protection Provisions in United States Commercial Treaties," *American Journal of International Law*, Vol. 45 (1951), pp. 83–107.

Woolsey, L. H. "The Expropriation of Oil Properties by Mexico," *American Journal of International Law*, Vol. 32 (1938), pp. 519–526.

"World Bank and Persian Oil," *The Economist*, Vol. 162 (February 9, 1952), p. 328.

Wortley, B. A. "Expropriation in International Law," *Transactions of the Grotius Society* (for 1947), Vol. 33 (1948), pp. 25–48.

NEWS PERIODICALS

Current Developments in United States Foreign Policy (Washington, D.C., The Brookings Institution), Vol. 5, Nos. 1–9, July–August, 1951—April, 1952.

"Developments of the Quarter," *Middle East Journal*, Vol. 5 (1951), pp. 341–344, 486–489; Vol. 6 (1952), pp. 74–76, 78.

New York Times, October 25, 1944–October 21, 1951.

San Francisco Chronicle, September 27, 1951–August 14, 1952.

Wall Street Journal, September 17–November 30, 1951.

GOVERNMENT DOCUMENTS

"Agreement Between the United Kingdom and Persia, Modifying the Commercial Convention of February 9, 1903. Tehran, March 21, 1920," *League of Nations Treaty Series*, Vol. 4 (1921), pp. 48–92, Reg. No. 102.

British Information Services. *The Anglo-Iranian Oil Company*. E. 104/3. Washington, D.C., British Embassy, April 26, 1951. 3 pp. mimeo.

——— *Anglo-Iranian Oil Company*. P. 105/1. Washington, D.C., British Embassy, May 4, 1951. 6 pp. mimeo.

——— *Anglo-Iranian Oil Company, Some Background Notes*. ID 1059. New York, May, 1951. 16 pp. mimeo.

——— *Anglo-Iranian Oil Negotiations*. ID 1062. New York, June, 1951. 15 pp. mimeo.

——— *Britain and Iranian Oil: A Summary.* ID 1064. New York, July, 1951. 4 pp. mimeo.

——— "Britain and Iranian Oil: Case Laid Before the Security Council of the U. N.," 1951 (2–6), *British Record*, New York, October 3, 1951. 4 pp.

——— *Developments in Persia.* P. 107/1. Washington, D.C., British Embassy, July 10, 1951. 2 pp. mimeo.

——— *Iranian Oil.* [Statement issued in Tehran by Ambassador Sir Francis Shepherd.] P. 104/1. Washington, D.C., British Embassy, April 28, 1951. 2 pp. mimeo.

———*Iranian Oil: Britain's Approach to a New Agreement.* ID 1088. New York, October, 1951. 5 pp. mimeo.

——— *The Iranian Oil Dispute; Statement by Mr. Eden* [in the House of Commons on November 19]. T. 73. Washington, D.C., British Embassy, November 20, 1951. 2 pp. mimeo.

——— *Legal Aspects of the Anglo-Iranian Oil Question.* ID 1063. New York, June, 1951. 10 pp. mimeo.

——— *Middle East, Speech by Mr. Morrison* [in the House of Commons on July 30]. T. 52. Washington, D.C., August 8, 1951. 11 pp. mimeo.

———*Persia.* [Statement made in the House of Commons by Mr. Morrison on July 5.] T. 40. Washington, D.C., July 6, 1951. 2 pp. mimeo.

——— *Persia: Negotiations to Open.* 108/1. Washington, D.C., British Embassy, August 4. 1951. 2 pp. mimeo.

——— *Persian Oil.* [Statement made in the House of Commons by Mr. Morrison on June 20.] T. 34. Washington, D.C., June 21, 1951. 3 pp. mimeo.

——— *Persian Oil.* [Statement made in the House of Commons by Mr. Morrison on June 26.] T. 37. Washington, D.C., June 26, 1951. 2 pp. mimeo.

——— *Persian Oil: The Company's Aide-Memoire.* T. 35. Washington, D.C., June 22, 1951. 2 pp. mimeo.

——— *Persian Oil: World Court Meets. Essence of the British Case.* P. 106/2. Washington, D.C., British Embassy, June 27, 1951. 1 p. mimeo.

——— *Questions of the Day.* P. 104/2. Washington, D.C., British Embassy, April 22, 1952. 11 pp. mimeo.

"Commercial Convention Between Great Britain and Persia, Signed at Tehran, February 9th, 1903," *British and Foreign State Papers*, Vol. 96 (1903), pp. 51–84.

"Consultations with Iran on Anglo-Iranian Oil Dispute," *The Department of State Bulletin*, Vol. 25 (July 23, 1951), pp. 129–131.

"Convention of Establishment Between the Empire of Persia and the Swiss Confederation. Signed at Berne, April 25th, 1934," *League of Nations Treaty Series,* Vol. 160 (1935), pp. 174–183, Reg. No. 3691.

In Quest of Peace and Security. Selected Documents on American Foreign Policy, 1941–1951. United States Department of State Publication 4245. Washington, D.C., Government Printing Office, 1951.

International Bank for Reconstruction and Development. *Review of the International Bank's Negotiations Concerning the Iranian Oil Problem.* Press Release No. 285. Washington, D.C., April 3, 1952. 9 pp. mimeo.

International Court of Justice. *Anglo-Iranian Oil Company Case (Preliminary Objection),* 1952 International Court of Justice Reports 92–171.

———— *Anglo-Iranian Oil Company Case: Request for the Indication of Interim Measures of Protection. Order, 5th July, 1951,* 1951 International Court of Justice Reports 89–98.

The Nationalization of the Oil Industry in Iran. Washington, D.C., Iranian Embassy, [June, 1951?]. 12 pp.

Nazi-Soviet Relations. United States Department of State Publication 3023. Washington, D.C., Government Printing Office, 1948.

"Note Respecting the Position of British Nationals in Persia, May 10, 1928," *in* Arthur B. Keith, ed., *Speeches and Documents on International Affairs, 1918–1937,* Vol. I. London, Oxford University Press, 1938. Pp. 248–253.

Some Documents on the Nationalization of the Oil Industry in Iran. Washington, D.C., Iranian Embassy, [1951]. 46 pp.

Soskice, Sir Frank. *Attorney-General's* [of the United Kingdom] *Speech at International Court of Justice, The Hague, June 30, 1951.* Verbatim report. 20 pp.

Text of Speech of Dr. Mohammad Mossadegh, Prime Minister of Iran, to the Foreign Press Representatives on May 28th, 1951. [Washington, D.C., Iranian Embassy, June, 1951.] 10 pp.

Treaties, Conventions, International Acts, Protocols, and Agreements, Between the United States of America and Other Powers. Washington, D.C., Government Printing Office, 1910–1938. 4 vols.

"Treaty of Friendship, Establishment and Commerce Between Denmark and Persia. Signed at Teheran, February 20th, 1934," *League of Nations Treaty Series,* Vol. 158 (1935–1936), pp. 300–313, Reg. No. 3640.

340

United Nations. Security Council. *Official Records. Sixth Year.* 559th Meeting–565th Meeting, October 1–19, 1951.

"U. S. Position in the Anglo-Iranian Dispute," *The Department of State Bulletin,* Vol. 24 (May 8, 1951, and June 4, 1951), pp. 851, 891–892.

"U. S.–Yugoslav Claims Settlement," *The Department of State Bulletin,* Vol. 19 (August 1, 1948), pp. 137–140.

Index

Abadan refinery, seized by Iranian troops, 123

Amiranian Oil Company, concession in Khorasan, 22

Anglo-Iranian Oil Company: contract to furnish oil to British navy, 16; British government's interest in, 16, 181; royalty dispute with Iran submitted to arbitration, 17; concession annulled in 1932, 17; efforts to gain oil concession in northern Iran, 20–21; strike in Khuzistan, 44, 52; pressures for new royalty agreement with Iran, 49; errors in handling Supplementary Agreement, 49–50; properties in Iran nationalized, 51; arbitration of oil dispute requested by, 56; application to ICJ for appointment of an arbitrator, 60; negotiations with Iran, 62–69; property damage by riots in Iran, 70, 71; dispute with Iran over tanker receipts, 71–72, 73; oil shipments from Abadan stopped, 73; British staff in Iran refuse offers of employment from NIOC, 96; cutback in Iranian production, 95, 96; shutdown of installations at Gach Seran, 96; entire production in Iran shut down, 103; British staff evacuate outlying oil fields, 116; legal action threatened against purchasers of oil from Iran or NIOC, 118; declares Iran's attempts to sell oil are illegal and in violation of ICJ's order, 118, 156; British staff leave Iran, 124; development of non-

Iranian supplies and facilities, 163, 216

Anglo-Iranian Oil Company's concession (1933): terms of, 18–19; a victory for Reza Shah, 19; a treaty or convention, 175

Anglo-Iranian oil dispute of 1932–1933, 17–18

Anglo-Iranian oil dispute of 1951–1952, 51 ff.; problems of settlement, 209–210, 215–218

Anglo-Persian Oil Company, name changed to Anglo-Iranian Oil Company, 15

Anglo-Russian Agreement of 1907, 6

Arabian-American Oil Company, royalty arrangements in Saudi Arabia, 51

Attlee, Clement, 120, 123

Azerbaijan: Soviet activity in, 41; People's Republic of, 42; Tudeh party in, 43; Soviet interference charged by Iranian government in United Nations Security Council, 43; collapse of People's Republic of, 44

Badawi Pasha, Abdel Hamid, Judge, 82, 94

Bahrein: Iranian claims to, 13; British protectorate of, 13

Bakhtiari tribe of southern Iran, 16

Bank Melli: created by Reza Shah, 11; prohibits conversion of sterling into rials, 122; restrictions on import credits, 155

Bank of Iran and the Middle East, 122

341

346

Negotiations between the IBRD and Iran—*Continued*
Mossadegh to negotiate further with the IBRD, 162; second IBRD mission leaves Iran, 162; third round of discussions, 162; talks suspended, 162; Bank's representative says oil dispute is a political problem, 162

Negotiations between the United Kingdom and Iran, 106–119; British delegation submits "Outline of Suggestions," 106; subcommittee appointed to study tanker receipts dispute, 106; Stokes says "Outline" is consistent with the principle of nationalization, 106–107; discussion of British proposals, 109–112; Iranian reply to British proposals, 110; proposals withdrawn by Stokes, 112; further Iranian reply, 114–115; Iran offers to sell oil to United Kingdom, 115; Britain charges Iran refused to negotiate within the terms agreed upon, 116; Stokes announces that the negotiations are suspended, 116; Britain announces that negotiations are broken off, 119

Oil: discovery of, in Kermanshah, 15; and social revolution in the Middle East, 53–54; world production of, 163

Pahlevi, Mohammed Reza: takes throne, 30; assents to nationalization laws, 51; flees Iran, then reinstated, 231

Pahlevi, Reza Kahn: leader of coup d'état, 8; becomes Prime Minister, 9; succeeds Ahmed Qajar as Shah, 9; policy of his government, 9, 10; differences with Zia ed-din, 9–10; economic policy of, 11; builds Transiranian Railroad, 11, 12; and Persian nationalism, 12–14; anti-British, 12–14; attitude toward USSR, 20; Soviet attitude toward, 23; attitude toward Germany, 27, 29, 30; abdication, 30

Permanent Court of International Justice: *Polish Agrarian Reform* case, 80, 84; case of the *Administration of the Prince von Pless*, 80; case of the *De-*nunciation of the Sino-Belgian Treaty, 81, 84; case of the *Factory at Chorzów*, (*Indemnities*), 83; *Electricity Company of Sofia and Bulgaria* case, 85; *Free Zones* case, 91, 92. *See also* International Court of Justice

Persia: financial difficulties, 5; Reuter concession of 1872 and Russian protests to, 5; revolution of 1906, 5; and Morgan Shuster, 6; financial reorganization and creation of Bank Melli, 11; and Arthur Millspaugh, 12; Reuter concession of 1889, 14. *See also* Iran

Peshavari, Ja'afar, 33, 42, 43, 44

Point Four. *See* Iran; United States

Pound, Roscoe, 192

Private property, changing concept of, 191–192

Qavam, Ahmed, 43, 44, 213–214, 228

Qashqai tribes, Tudeh activity among, 45

Radbruch, Gustav, 192

Razmara, Ali: puts down Azerbaijan revolt, 44; and Supplementary Agreement, 50–51; assassinated, 51

Read, John M., Judge, 174

Reuter, Baron Julius de: and concessions, 5, 14; founds Imperial Bank of Iran, 14

Reza Kahn. *See* Pahlevi, Reza Kahn

Riots. *See* Iran

Russia: wars with Persia, 3; Treaty of Gulistan, 3; Treaty of Turkmanchai, 3–4; threat to British India, 4; expansionist policy toward Persia, 6–7; occupation of Tabriz, 6, 8. *See also* Union of Soviet Socialist Republics

Sa'ed, Mohammed, 34; Communist criticism of his oil policy, 35; resigns prime-ministership, 36

Saleh, Allahyar, 114, 134–136

Schacht, Hjalmar, 28

Schwarzenberger, Georg, 91

Security Council. *See* United Nations

Seddon, Richard, AIOC's representative in Tehran, 58, 60, 62, 95; indicted for